Applications of Undergraduate Mathematics in Engineering

Based on 45 contributions selected from a total of 200 submitted by engineers in universities and industries in the United States to the Commission on Engineering Education and the Committee on the Undergraduate Program in Mathematics. The selection was made by an Advisory Editorial Committee consisting of:

RUTHERFORD ARIS, *University of Minnesota*
R. CREIGHTON BUCK, *University of Wisconsin*
PRESTON R. CLEMENT, *Stevens Institute of Technology*
E. T. KORNHAUSER, *Brown University*
H. O. POLLAK, *Bell Telephone Laboratories*

Applications of Undergraduate Mathematics in Engineering

written and edited by
BEN NOBLE

Mathematics Research Center, United States Army,
The University of Wisconsin

The Mathematical Association of America

The Macmillan Company, New York
Collier-Macmillan Limited, London

Second Printing, 1967

Library of Congress catalog card number: 66–27577

The Macmillan Company, New York
Collier-Macmillan Canada, Ltd., Toronto, Ontario

Printed in the United States of America

Acknowledgments

The Committee on the Undergraduate Program in Mathematics wishes to take this opportunity to thank the Commission on Engineering Education for its participation in this venture, and for the confidence the Commission expressed in leaving publication in the hands of The Mathematical Association of America. As a result of the Commission's vigorous help, hundreds of problems or suggestions for problems were submitted. We are very grateful to the many contributors, who must perforce remain unnamed, whose problems we were finally unable to use. Our indebtedness for the contributions which form the basis of this book is acknowledged individually in each section.

It is perhaps most difficult to convey in full our gratitude to Ben Noble. Without his knowledge of mathematics and its applications, his sense of style and sense of humor, and his apparently boundless energy, this volume would not have been possible.

H. O. POLLAK
For the Editorial Committee

Preface

As recorded in some detail in Chapter 1, this book is based on examples of applications of undergraduate mathematics in engineering, submitted for the most part by members of engineering and mathematics departments of universities, with some contributions from industrial companies. These were requested by the Commission on Engineering Education and the Committee on the Undergraduate Program in Mathematics.

The original intention was to organize the submitted examples as an "engineering-mathematics problem book." After a few attempts to write problems on a strict "statement-answer-conclusion" basis, I found that it was difficult to do this in a way that would be informative to undergraduate and graduate mathematicians and engineers, for all of whom this book is intended. It seemed best to adopt the looser format outlined in Section 1.4. Perhaps the main reason for adopting this method of exposition is simply that it fits my own natural style.

It is possible to use most of the examples given here as "problems." In many cases the reader can close the book at an appropriate point in the argument and try to complete the solution for himself. It should be emphasized, however, that the technical details of the way in which the mathematical problems are solved provide only one aspect of the solution. It is important to evaluate the relevance of purely mathematical results to the ultimate objective, which is to provide insight into an engineering problem. The reader should also be reminded that the academic "problem-answer" format is not too suitable for many engineering problems. A major part of the work may be to decide what the problem is in the first place, and one of the major difficulties may be to decide what kind of answer we should try to obtain. The "problem-answer" format tends to conceal these aspects of the work.

A superficial examination may leave the impression that, in some of the chapters, there is little material suitable for direct use as problems in mathematics classes. Thus Chapter 3 provides applications of three-dimensional geometry, Taylor series in two variables, and the reduction of conics to their principal axes (among other things), but these applications are so bound up with the engineering context that it is difficult to extract tidy packages that can be used to illustrate topics in a mathematics class. The difficulty is partly that the time available in class is limited. A reasonable compromise may be to indicate that these applications are available, and refer the student to the text as supplementary reading.

One of the principal aims has been to write a book for a reader who has no specialized knowledge of any branch of mathematics, the physical sciences, or engineering.

With reference to the mathematical knowledge required, it so happened that most of the examples chosen by the selection committee could be solved using little more than the following tools: simple algebra, including the elimination method for the solution of simultaneous equations and the general idea of an algebraic or transcendental equation; elementary trigonometry; simple two- and three-dimensional analytical geometry, including the conic sections; basic differentiation and integration, including the idea of a derivative as a rate of change; partial differentiation, Taylor's theorem in one and two variables, and maxima-minima; and elementary differential equations.

In addition to these topics we assume general knowledge of how a computer works, of what a flow chart is, and of the power of computing (for example, that we can always solve a differential equation numerically if our computer is adequate, even though an analytical solution is impossible). In linear algebra we assume knowledge of matrix notation, the idea of linear dependence of vectors, and some properties of eigenvectors and eigenvalues. In probability theory we assume knowledge of the basic ideas, in particular the Poisson, binomial, and normal distributions. Although some of these topics are not at present part of the undergraduate mathematics program for all engineers, it should be emphasized that the mathematics required for understanding most of this book is an absolute minimum for any mathematically literate engineer. We are not talking about the research engineer or the engineer who could actually do the original work required for the material included in this book. We are talking about the engineer who wishes to read the current literature and keep himself abreast of developments in his subject.

We can indicate what we mean by "undergraduate mathematics" from another point of view by saying that we specifically exclude topics such as partial differential equations and contour integration, which are regarded as advanced. These topics are already present in the undergraduate curriculum for engineers who wish to go on to graduate school and into research, and in a few years they should become part of the course work for nearly all engineers. However, the level of this book is intended for all present-day undergraduate engineering students, who should have a sufficient mathematical background to understand most of the problems treated here.

We have tried to describe physical and engineering situations from first principles, by which we mean basic physical laws such as Newton's laws of motion, the decomposition of forces, Hooke's law in elasticity (extension proportional to force), the basic laws governing electrical networks, and some simple ideas in connection with chemical reactions.

If the reader thinks from these remarks that the problems treated here are mainly trivial, he need only dip into the book to have this impression rapidly dispelled. Perhaps the situation is best expressed by saying (echoing a remark the origin of which I cannot now remember), "The problems require only elementary mathematics and physics, but the reader must know his elementary groundwork *really well*." In some ways this should be one of the mottoes of any mathematician teaching engineers. The lecturer seeking mottoes might also bear in mind the following (echoing R. W. Hamming, who used a similar remark with reference to computing in the front of his book on numerical methods): "The object of mathematics in engineering is to provide insight." The function of mathematics in providing answers is often less important than its function in providing understanding. These two functions can be different.

The reader will find that the background required and also the difficulty of the material vary from chapter to chapter and section to section. However, it is hoped that the point of an example will be clear even though some of the technical details (physical or mathematical) may be unfamiliar. It has been found impracticable to arrange sections in order of difficulty. I have tried not to conceal difficulties or to solve them by "unfair" methods. In keeping with the purpose and character of the book, I have sometimes used an awkward method involving only elementary mathematics in preference to an elegant method requiring advanced mathematics. Of course, the most satisfying solutions are usually both simple and elegant, but occasionally it is necessary to use a blunderbuss.

The next point that should be emphasized is that there has been no attempt to provide systematic coverage of topics in either engineering or mathematics. I have merely taken the random sample of examples chosen by the selection committee and added a number of related examples suggested by other sources. It is purely accidental, for example, that the flow charts for computer programs given in the text involve only examples in probability, and that so much attention has been devoted to probability as opposed to statistics.

This book has been edited quite independently of the CUPM recommendations on the mathematics curriculum for engineers,* and I have not even had a copy of the recommendations by me while doing the writing. One can

---

* *Recommendations on the Undergraduate Mathematics Program for Engineers and Physicists*. Copies may be obtained by writing CUPM, P.O. Box 1024, Berkeley, California 94701.

visualize a series of textbooks, each of which systematically covers one of the CUPM syllabuses. When each mathematical topic is treated, one or more engineering examples would be included. However, nothing like this is attempted here. At best it might be claimed that we provide a few "specimen chapters" giving samples of how this might be done in special cases.

A few notes concerning the "writing and editing" may be of interest. I am most grateful to the Advisory Editorial Committee, whose names are listed on the title page. They produced a fascinating selection of examples which fired my interest in the project. These examples were a heterogeneous assortment. Many of them were either one-page contributions which needed expanding, or long articles which required shortening. It was clear that if the aim was to instruct the mathematician who knew no engineering, or the engineer who wished to see applications of mathematics, or the student who had little background in either engineering or mathematics, it would be necessary to do considerable rewriting. This I have done without consulting either the original contributors or the Advisory Editorial Committee, so the final responsibility for the correctness of the material is mine alone. The name of each contributor has been mentioned at the beginning of the section (or the series of sections) in which his contribution has been used. If I say, for example, "This section consists of material submitted by...," this means that the submitted material was included virtually unchanged. If I say, for example, "This section is based on...," this means that considerable rewriting was done. In any case, the credit lies with the contributors who submitted the ideas. A reader who wishes to see the amount of rewriting that has been done can compare the published articles (where they exist) with the versions here. If I ever have a nightmare associated with this book it will probably consist of an infuriated contributor, waving the book, open at the page containing his name, and shouting (with truth) that I have ruined his contribution by rewriting it.

My interest in editing this book is probably a delayed reaction from dissatisfaction with the way in which mathematics is taught to engineers. Because of human limitations inherent in the learning process it seems inevitable that mathematics must be taught as a separate "package," but this is no reason why theory should be taught in a way that is completely divorced from applications. The difficulty is that in an engineering problem there are many factors to be considered in addition to the mathematics. If we try to give realistic examples of applications in mathematics classes, we shall be teaching engineering and not mathematics. This book may focus attention on the fact that the problem exists. In any case, a positive contribution will have been made if the book conveys the feeling that engineering mathematics can be both interesting and useful, even on an elementary level.

I am indebted to R. Creighton Buck, who suggested that I edit the selection of examples made by the Advisory Editorial Committee and brought to my attention several relevant articles and books. I am also indebted to J. Barkley

Rosser, Director of the Mathematics Research Center, who encouraged me to work on this project, as part of the Center's program to encourage all aspects of applied mathematics.

Corrections and clarifications have been suggested by R. Aris, D. Bacon, R. Boas, P. R. Clement, T. E. Hull, A. L. Mullikin, J. B. Rosser, and M. Wing. I am particularly indebted to C. A. Desoer for a long list of detailed suggestions, and to P. R. Clement for a list of section summaries. Assistance on particular points of difficulty has been given by W. B. Brown, E. N. Gilbert, J. A. Lewis, W. P. Slichter, and E. E. Zajac.

A special word of thanks should go to H. O. Pollak, who has always been very clear about the motivation for this book. The exposition was enormously improved by his ruthless rejection of any explanation that might not be intelligible to the nonspecialist reader.

Above all, I am indebted to Dick and Dorothy Houden, our neighbors in Madison, who loaned us their summer cottage on Lake McKinley in northern Wisconsin, where the major part of the writing was carried out, without mail delivery or telephone, but with a lake at the bottom of the garden which helped keep my wife and children happy during a period of neglect.

BEN NOBLE

Madison, Wisconsin

Contents

Applications of
Undergraduate Mathematics
in Engineering

Chapter 1

Introduction

1.1 The Purpose of This Book

The problems presented in this book are intended to illustrate some applications of undergraduate mathematics in engineering and the applied sciences. However, the objective is much more than the provision of a set of academic examples. The motivation can be explained by quoting at length from the letter which was sent to engineering and other departments of universities in the United States and to some industrial companies, asking for contributions to an "engineering-mathematics problem book":

> The Commission on Engineering Education and the Committee on the Undergraduate Program in Mathematics are jointly looking for exciting engineering problems, from many different fields of engineering, whose study and solutions naturally lead to interesting mathematical questions connected with one or more fields in the undergraduate mathematics curriculum.
>
> We propose to collect such problems into a source book (or some similar format) to be used
>
> 1. by mathematics faculty to provide motivation and illustrations for various topics and concepts in mathematics courses. Here it is worth noting that the CUPM Recommendations on the mathematics curriculum for engineers stress a requirement for calculus, of linear algebra, and of probability and statistics;
>
> 2. by engineering faculty to see the current relevance and applications of various mathematical disciplines; and
>
> 3. by students of many different interests to appreciate the essential unity of their curriculum, and to challenge them to begin their own explorations.
>
> The multiplicity of these purposes shows that there can be no single pattern into which such problems should fall. Please send us, therefore,

your favorite engineering problems which you see as fulfilling at least one of these needs. Include something of the engineering motivation, the process of mathematical abstraction, the mathematical (and/or computational) treatment of the abstracted problem, and the relevance of the resulting insight to the original engineering situation. If you can supply references to the literature, so much the better.

About 200 problems were submitted in response to this letter. Of these, 45 were selected by a subcommittee of the Commission on Engineering Education and the Committee on the Undergraduate Program in Mathematics. Nearly all of the 45 examples have been incorporated into this book, in one form or another. Some have been included unchanged, others have been completely rewritten, some have been little more than mentioned in passing, and a few have provided ideas that have been elaborated into whole chapters. (The references to published articles supplied by contributors were particularly useful in the last connection.)

The editor was given a free hand to edit the 45 examples in any way he chose. It was obviously impossible to attempt complete or systematic coverage. All that the editor has done is provide a series of "specimen chapters" giving more or less typical engineering examples of undergraduate mathematics, based partly on the submitted examples and partly on supplementary material. There has been no attempt to give a strict interpretation of what constitutes an "engineering" problem, as opposed to a problem in, say, physics or chemistry. The line between engineering and the sciences is indistinct, and the fact that an example was submitted has been taken as sufficient evidence that it could be considered a problem in engineering.

The subject matter and treatment in the different chapters is so varied that it is difficult to generalize about the reasons for including (or the morals to be drawn from) any of the individual chapters. Without attempting to be exhaustive, we make the following comments.

1. Some chapters deal with a single engineering problem, with particular reference to a single mathematical tool. For example, the chapter on the structure of a linear chemical reaction system (Chapter 12) deals with the matrix analysis of linear differential equations. The analysis of a conveyor system in Chapter 14 is an application of repeated Bernoulli trials.

2. Other chapters deal with a single type of engineering problem but try various methods of approach. For example, Chapter 2, on optimum-location problems, discusses various analytical and graphical methods of approach, together with the use of digital computers and the mention of an application of an analog computer.

3. Some chapters illustrate that the same mathematical problem can arise in various apparently different engineering situations. A good example of this occurs in the optimization problems of Sections 3.1 to 3.3.

4. Some chapters are devoted to a collection of examples involving related physical ideas, for example, Chapters 7 and 9, on field problems.

5. Some chapters illustrate the use of a single mathematical tool in various engineering contexts, for example, Chapter 11, on applications of the idea of linear dependence of the rows of a matrix.

6. Some chapters show how mathematics can give insight into unusual engineering situations, for example, Chapters 4 and 16.

7. Some chapters illustrate the fact that unexpected insights can be obtained into engineering situations by means of simple mathematics, for example, the analysis of overthrust faulting in Chapter 8, the heat-transfer problems in Chapter 9, and the waiting-line problems in Chapter 15.

8. Some chapters are devoted primarily to technical problems of how best to perform certain more or less purely mathematical manipulations, for example, the matrix analysis of frameworks and electrical networks in Chapter 10 and the treatment of electrical transients in Sections 5.4 and 5.5.

9. Some chapters illustrate the fact that common mathematical ideas can be used in quite an unexpected way in engineering, for example, the use of conic sections and Taylor's theorem in two variables in Chapter 3.

The chapters have been grouped into five parts, I to V, but this is of no particular significance, except that it determined the order in which chapters have been included. Part I (Chapters 2 to 4) deals with some applications of elementary mathematics. It seemed appropriate to start with two chapters on optimization which illustrate many general points concerning the application of mathematics in engineering. These chapters show that similar mathematical problems turn up in widely different engineering situations, that one can make some progress with elementary methods but more difficult problems require more sophisticated methods of approach, and that automatic computers are indispensable. Part II on ordinary differential equations (Chapters 5 and 6) is an obvious topic for a subdivision of the subject matter. It is natural also to collect together (in a separate Part III) Chapters 7 to 9 which deal with field problems such as the flow of fluids or heat, the diffusion of gases, stresses and strains in solids, and so on. The emphasis is on the ingenious use of physical reasoning to formulate and solve approximately, by means of elementary mathematics, problems that require partial differential equations for a rigorous treatment. Finally, Part IV on linear algebra (Chapters 10 to 12) and Part V on probability (Chapters 13 to 16) correspond to CUPM proposals for engineering courses on these subjects. It was interesting and illuminating to the editor that so many interesting problems were submitted in these areas.

On the other hand, one of the disappointing features of the submitted examples was that so few of them involved computing directly. In fact, most of the applications of computers in this book have been added by the editor, who has tried to integrate relevant numerical and computer methods of attack into the discussion of the appropriate engineering problem. There is no separate part on the use of computers in engineering problems, although it is essential that all engineering students have some kind of introduction to computer science.

It has already been mentioned that no attempt was made at systematic coverage of topics. The editor can visualize that eventually complete books of applications of the present type could be produced to supplement each of the detailed courses proposed by CUPM. These books would systematically cover applications of each of the topics in the corresponding curricula, but the treatment would not have to be tied to the specific way in which the mathematical topics were taught. However, fulfillment of this dream lies in the future.

1.2   Mathematicians and Engineers

In view of the multiplicity of purposes this book is to serve, and the varied audience of mathematicians, engineers, and students for whom it is intended, it is obviously dangerous to embark on a philosophical discussion of the relationship between mathematics and engineering. In this section and the next, we have adopted the point of view that, although neither the professional mathematician nor the professional engineer might find these ideas either agreeable or necessary, they are very important for the engineering student to consider. The professional to whom this is old stuff, or unnecessary, may skip to Chapter 2.

It is appropriate at this point to quote some remarks made by Thornton C. Fry,[1] contrasting the habits of thought of mathematicians and engineers:

> Some men would be called mathematicians in any man's language; others physicists or engineers. These typical men are differentiated in certain essential respects:
>
> The typical mathematician feels great confidence in a conclusion reached by careful reasoning. He is not convinced to the same degree by experimental evidence. For the typical engineer these statements may be reversed. Confronted by a carefully thought-out theory which predicts a certain result, and a carefully performed experiment which fails to produce it, the typical mathematician asks first "What is wrong with the experiment?" and the engineer "What is wrong with the argument?" Because of this confidence in thought processes the mathematician turns naturally to paper and pencil in many situations in which the engineer or physicist would

[1] T. C. Fry, Industrial Mathematics, *Am. Math. Monthly*, **48**, 1–38 (1941), (Part II of the June–July supplement). See also comments in Brockway McMillan, Mathematicians and Their Uses, *Soc. Ind. Appl. Math. Review*, **4**, 79–90 (1962), and a later article by T. C. Fry, Mathematicians in Industry—The First 75 Years, *Science*, **143**, 934–938 (1964). Fry's original article is remarkably up to date, apart from two things that would have been difficult to predict in 1941. One is the revolution produced by the advent of computers. The other is the increasing function of mathematics in providing absolute standards of performance.

resort to the laboratory. For the same reason the mathematician in his "pure" form delights in building logical structures, such as topology or abstract algebra, which have no apparent connection with the world of physical reality and which would not interest the typical engineer; while conversely the engineer or physicist in his "pure" form takes great interest in such useful information as a table of hardness data which may, so far as he is aware, be totally unrelated to any theory, and which the typical mathematician would find quite boring.

A second characteristic of the typical mathematician is his highly critical attitude towards the details of a demonstration. For almost any other class of men an argument may be good enough, even though some minor question remains open. For the mathematician an argument is either perfect in every detail, in form as well as in substance, or else it is wrong. There are no intermediate classes. He calls this "rigorous thinking," and says it is necessary if his conclusions are to have permanent value. The typical engineer calls it "hair splitting," and says that if he indulged in it he would never get anything done.

The mathematician also tends to idealize any situation with which he is confronted. His gases are "ideal," his conductors "perfect," his surfaces "smooth." He admires this process and calls it "getting down to essentials"; the engineer or physicist is likely to dub it somewhat contemptuously "ignoring the facts."

A fourth and closely related characteristic is the desire for generality. Confronted with the problem of solving the simple equation $x^3 - 1 = 0$, he solves $x^n - 1 = 0$ instead. Or asked about the torsional vibration of a galvanometer suspension, he studies a fiber loaded with any number of mirrors at arbitrary points along its length. He calls this "conserving his energy"; he is solving a whole class of problems at once, instead of dealing with them piecemeal. The engineer calls it "wasting his time"; of what use is a galvanometer with more than one mirror?

In the vast army of scientific workers who cannot be tagged so easily with the badge of some one profession, those may properly be called "mathematicians" whose work is dominated by these four characteristics of greater confidence in logical than experimental proof, severe criticism of details, idealization, and generalization. The boundaries of the profession are perhaps not made sharper by this definition, but it has the merit of being based upon type of mind, which is an attribute of the man himself, and not upon such superficial and frequently accidental matters as the courses he took in college or the sort of job he holds.

It is, moreover, a more fundamental distinction than can be drawn between, say, physicist, chemist, and astronomer.

One might add that these remarks make a sharp distinction between engineers and mathematicians for the sake of effect. In many cases the engineer acts as his own mathematician, and then we are differentiating the occasions on which he acts as an engineer from those on which he uses his mathematical talents, but the two sets of occasions are not always very distinct. Also one is not superior to the other. They are different and complementary.

1.3   Some Comments on Mathematics in Engineering

The reason we have contrasted the habits of thought of mathematicians and engineers is simply that the services the mathematician can perform in engineering problems are closely connected with his habit of thought. The mathematician reasons, criticizes, idealizes, generalizes. Moreover, he does this in a precise and quantitative way. A problem cannot be formulated mathematically unless the underlying assumptions are made explicit. This insistence on clear thinking is perhaps the most important contribution of the mathematician.

The process of abstraction and idealization, or the setting up of a model, is the crucial part of the mathematical analysis of an engineering problem. The mathematics required to deduce the consequences of the model may require ability of a very high order, but no matter how much good mathematics goes into the analysis of a problem, the results are useless if the original model is wrong.

The advent of the computer is having a great liberating effect on industrial mathematics. There is no longer the overriding necessity to formulate problems in such a way that they can be handled by the limited tools of classical analysis. On the other hand, when using a computer we still must abstract and idealize a given engineering problem. We still must break the original problem into its elements, decide what is significant, specify the data we must start from, what the steps of the analysis are, and what end results are required. These steps require the habit of thought of the mathematician.

These comments have been summarized in Fry's paper by saying that mathematics "simplifies the process of thinking and makes it more reliable, and this is its principal service to industry." Apart from this general claim, it is perhaps instructive to distinguish certain specific categories of usefulness.[2] There is no attempt to be exhaustive, and some of these categories overlap:

1. *If data can be interpreted in terms of a preconceived theory, it is possible to draw deductions from the data regarding things that could not be observed conveniently, if at all, without a great deal of additional experimental work.*

A simple example occurs in Section 13.3 in connection with the breakdown voltage of a long transmission line, which can be deduced from data on short lengths of line. Further examples occur in Chapter 15 in connection with waiting-line problems, where information regarding the lengths of waiting lines under various conditions can be deduced from basic data on the rate of arrival and the service time.

2. *Mathematics often provides a quantitative check on a preconceived theory. If the data are incompatible with the theory, further mathematical study frequently aids in perfecting the theory.*

---

[2] The following comments were suggested by pages 17–27 of T. C. Fry's essay in *Am. Math. Monthly*, **48**, 1–38 (1941), although we do not follow his exposition in detail because we wish to refer to the problems in this book as examples of the categories.

All of Chapter 8, on the mechanism of overthrust faulting in geology, is an illustration of this point.

3. *It is frequently necessary in practice to extrapolate experimental data from one set of dimensions to a widely different set, and in such cases some sort of mathematical background is almost essential.*

The classic example of this is found in dimensional analysis. In Sections 9.4 to 9.6 we discuss problems of film condensation, film boiling, natural convection, and film melting by means of a simple unified method of approach that provides a basis for correlating experimental data obtained under widely different conditions.

4. *Mathematics frequently aids in promoting economy, either by reducing the amount of experimentation involved or by replacing it entirely.*

Examples of this function of mathematics are found everywhere in engineering, not only in research activities but also in design and production. Much of the point of Chapter 3 is that we wish to reduce the number of trials required to achieve optimum operating conditions.

5. *Sometimes experiments are virtually impossible, and mathematics must fill the breach.*

This is true of many waiting-line problems (Chapter 15), for which experiments would be very costly and time-consuming. It is also true when designing any complicated or large-scale engineering system, for example, the hydroelectric surge tank discussed in Sections 6.2 to 6.4.

6. *Mathematics is frequently useful in devising experiments to check whether a theory is correct.*

Thus the theory in Section 7.2 makes quantitative predictions that can be tested by experiment, thus checking whether the proposed mechanism for permeation of water through cable sheaths is likely to be correct.

7. *Mathematics also frequently performs a negative service but one that is sometimes of very great importance—that of forestalling the search for the impossible; for many objectives in industry are as unattainable as perpetual-motion machines, and frequently the only way to recognize the fact is by means of a mathematical argument.*

An instructive example of this type is given in Section 10.5, where we show that it is impossible to construct an electrical network with a certain kind of property.

8. *In a more positive sense, mathematics can often say what the best level of achievement is, thereby providing a target for the engineer to aim at.*

In Section 4.7 we show that theoretically it should be possible to recover, exactly, an original electrical signal from the form received at the end of a certain kind of transmission system.

9. *Mathematics frequently plays an important part in reducing complicated methods of calculation to readily available working form. In particular, the computer can free the engineer from the drudgery of routine calculations.*

Examples of this point are the problem of optical-lens design in Section 3.3 and the problem of the calculation of strains and stresses in mechanical structures, Sections 10.1 to 10.3.

   10. *Mathematics can help in the interpretation of experimental data.*

An example is given in Section 13.2, in connection with the analysis of speech dynamics. This point is also the theme of Chapter 12.

We conclude this section by making an additional remark about points 7 and 8 which stated that the mathematician can often predict the "best possible" level of performance. Today many engineers are competent mathematicians and can carry out, for themselves, many of the functions of mathematicians. In particular, engineers are often expert at finding ingenious special methods for using mathematics to solve specific problems. The efforts of the specialist in mathematics are now being directed, more and more, toward the provision of "absolute standards" against which the actual performance of a device or system can be measured. This helps the engineer in two ways. It enables him to avoid attempting to do things it is absurd to do. It tells the engineer how far he has to go before he reaches the best possible level of performance.[3] These functions of mathematics are well known. (The engineer computes the strength of an ideal structure and adds a "safety factor"; theoretical analysis shows that perpetual-motion machines are impossible; and so on.) However, the professional applied mathematician is becoming more and more involved in this kind of activity.

We could go on enumerating ways in which mathematics is useful in engineering, but we have mentioned some of the main points and others will become clear when we discuss the examples in detail.

1.4   The Method of Exposition

Because a varied selection of problems will be treated in this book, no uniform pattern of exposition is possible. In some chapters we have simply taken a single mathematical technique and given several examples of the way it can be used in connection with problems that arise in engineering. However, in other chapters we have been able to follow a problem through from the original engineering motivation to a discussion of the relevance of the final results to the initial problem.

It may help the reader to appreciate the object of this book if he bears the following "ideal" pattern of exposition in mind, even though we have not always followed it in detail.

---

[3] The point that mathematicians can often provide "absolute standards" has been stressed by H. O. Pollak in an article in *New Directions in Mathematics* (J. G. Kemeny, R. Robinson, and R. W. Ritchie, eds.), Prentice-Hall, Englewood Cliffs, N.J., 1963.

1. *Explanation of the engineering motivation of the problem.* We have interpreted the word "engineering" in a broad sense to include a wide variety of problems that can turn up in industry. In all cases the motivation is the wish to analyze a physical situation, using mathematics as a tool.

2. *Abstraction, idealization, and formulation.* Abstraction and idealization of the original problem lead to a simplified situation that can be formulated mathematically. This involves explicit recognition of the factors thought to be essential, and neglect of nonessentials. The result is usually a set of mathematical equations. We have placed abstraction, idealization, and formulation under one heading, because they are not distinct steps but a single process.

3. *Solution of the mathematical problem.* This is quite distinct from step 2. The infuriating thing about mathematics from the point of view of applications is that it is often possible to write down, in a few lines, the equations governing the behavior of a system, but the extraction of the solution of these equations may involve long and laborious investigations. Often this reduces to a computational rather than a purely mathematical problem.

4. *The relevance of the results to the original problem.* The object of the mathematics is to provide understanding and answers. It is important to relate the final results to the original problem to see whether we have obtained insight or answers from the analysis. These are the ultimate objects of using mathematics.

Although all the examples in this book do not illustrate all these points, it is hoped that at least they satisfy two criteria. First, mathematics plays an essential part in the solution of each problem. (This is quite different from saying that the mathematics used is highly significant in its own right!) Second, each problem has a certain physical or engineering importance, if possible outside the run of ordinary "textbook examples." Problems that are essentially games or puzzles have been excluded. On the other hand, there has been no attempt to distinguish engineering problems from problems in the basic sciences, because no clear distinction can (or should) be drawn.

An attempt has been made to explain enough of the background so that a reader who is not an expert in a given field can understand the significance of the problem. Sometimes, for this reason, the mathematics has tended to become submerged in a mass of descriptive detail, but this seems inevitable.

To conclude this chapter we return to a comparison of the roles played by the mathematician and the engineer, in the light of the above pattern of exposition. The engineer decides what the physical problem is, what factors are important, what factors can be ignored, and what answers he would like to have. The engineer and mathematician are jointly involved in setting up the idealized mathematical formulation of the problem. The mathematician then employs his technical skills to solve the purely mathematical questions.

Finally, the engineer must study the results of the mathematics and decide whether they are adequate for his purposes.

Occasionally we meet exceptional individuals who are able to combine both roles, but our educational system does not seem to encourage this combination of talents. On the whole, the mathematician seems to be trained to work in the realm of abstract theory and the engineer in the realm of concrete detail.

The mathematician's role is to advise the engineer concerning the mathematical tools available—the limitations of mathematics, on the one hand, and the power of mathematics, on the other. Although the mathematician can be very helpful in connection with setting up abstract models, his role is not, and cannot be, to formulate engineering problems mathematically in any absolute sense. Otherwise (echoing a comment of G. E. P. Box made in a slightly different connection) there would be no point in training engineers because we would need only mathematicians.

At the beginning of certain sections and chapters, short statements appear concerning the material that follows. The *engineering context* is usually indicated in the section heading, but may be stated separately. The *mathematics used* may be stated briefly. A short *comment* may be inserted to draw attention to one or more of the points illustrated in the text.

It should be emphasized that the purpose and value of the sections are in no way summarized in these statements, since the points of view, the approaches to the problem, and the details leading to a solution are necessarily not included. These statements serve merely as rapid reference for those who have read the book in its entirety and wish to refer quickly to a section illustrating a particular point or a particular mathematical technique. Such statements are omitted in some of the later chapters which deal with specific subjects, where the development is judged self-explanatory from the section headings or from the introduction to the chapter.

Part I

ILLUSTRATIVE APPLICATIONS OF ELEMENTARY MATHEMATICS

Chapter 2

Optimum-Location Problems

2.1 Optimum Location of a Power Plant

Comment: This section is concerned with the formulation of the two-dimensional problem of locating the point that minimizes the sum of the distances to *n* arbitrary points.

The following problem is part of the course work for engineering students at the Technological Institute of Northwestern University:[1]

> Located at random in a great level area devoted to large-scale wheat ranching are 10 towns. You are an engineer employed to determine the best possible location for a new cooperative power plant from which separate electric cables are to be run to serve each town which votes to join the proposed cooperative. The sole criterion in locating the power plant will be to minimize the total required length of electrical cable.

The first point to be made is that, from the point of view of producing a method for solving this problem, there is no significance in the number (10) of the towns, except that this number is so large that trial-and-error methods may not be very efficient. In any case, if all the towns do not join the cooperative, fewer than 10 towns may have to be considered. We therefore consider the general case of *n* towns, where *n* is an arbitrary number. It is an important principle that the structure of a problem is often clearer if we consider the general case rather than particular cases.

The mathematical problem is now clear-cut. We are given a set of *n* points (x_i, y_i), $i = 1, \ldots, n$, located at random in a plane. It is required to find a point (x, y) such that the sum of the lengths of independent curves joining

---

[1] This problem was drawn to our attention (without a solution!) by H. T. Fisher, Department of Civil Engineering, Northwestern University, Evanston, Ill.

(x, y) to each of the (x_i, y_i) is a minimum. The curve of minimum length joining two points in a plane is a straight line and the curves in the problem are independent, so we must minimize the sum of the straight-line distances from (x, y) to (x_i, y_i); that is,

$$D = \sum_{i=1}^{n} [(x - x_i)^2 + (y - y_i)^2]^{1/2}. \qquad (2.1)$$

The conditions for a stationary value are $\partial D/\partial x = 0$ and $\partial D/\partial y = 0$. (This is the only way in which we use calculus in connection with this problem. The remainder of the discussion will involve only simple algebra.) This gives

$$\sum_{i=1}^{n} \frac{x - x_i}{d_i} = 0, \quad \sum_{i=1}^{n} \frac{y - y_i}{d_i} = 0, \qquad (2.2)$$

where $d_i = [(x - x_i)^2 + (y - y_i)^2]^{1/2}$. Since the d_i are functions of the unknowns x and y, these are two simultaneous nonlinear algebraic equations for x and y. Special cases of (2.2) are considered in Section 2.3.

It would be misleading to claim that the problem had been "solved" at this point, for several reasons.

1. Although we have defined a quantity D in (2.1) which has to be minimized, and derived a pair of equations (2.2) which (presumably) contain the solution, this is only the preliminary part of the work. The next step is to produce a practical numerical method for finding x and y from the nonlinear equations. We shall see in Section 2.3 that difficulties can arise in this connection. In particular, the equations may not have a unique solution, or any solution.

2. Merely writing down the equations (2.2) and then obtaining a solution by means of a computer gives no insight into the original engineering problem. After all, the object of using mathematics in engineering problems is to provide insight and understanding. The problem was perhaps posed in too narrow a fashion in the first place. The engineer will probably wish to know how much he will be penalized if he adopts a location other than the optimum one. That is, how much does the value of D differ from the optimum value if for other reasons it is necessary to place the power station at a point that is not optimum according to the above criterion?

In addition to these objections to the proposed solution of the problem, it must be borne in mind that the original problem is highly idealized. The location of any power plant will depend on many factors other than the total length of cable connecting it to various towns. It may be necessary to locate the power station near a source of water or a railway. It may not be practicable or economical to acquire the land necessary to enable the cable to be laid along the theoretically best paths determined by the above equations (although the original problem did specify that the area was devoted to "wheat ranching," presumably to indicate that the cost of acquiring land and the nature of the terrain are independent of the location). Rather than run separate cables to each town, one can visualize situations in which a common cable should be run part of the way, before being split into cables for separate towns. In any case it would seem certain that in practice some cables would need to be heavier, and therefore more expensive, than others, which would introduce weighting factors, although this complication is easily taken into account (see Section 2.2).

This argument leads us to make the following point: The original idealization can be extended to cover much more complicated situations, for instance, by introducing weighting factors or by using a more sophisticated criterion than simply minimizing the sum of the cable lengths. However, the simple situation will provide a test problem, and we hope to develop a method to deal with the simple case which will also cope with the much more complicated factors visualized in the last paragraph.

2.2   A Machine-Location Problem[2]

Comment: A generalization of the problem considered in Section 2.1 appears here in a somewhat different context.

In this section we show that the mathematical problem of Section 2.1 can appear in a quite different engineering context. This is one of the fascinating things about mathematics—that the same mathematical tools can be applied to a wide variety of apparently unrelated problems.

We wish to consider the optimal location for a new machine in an established and fixed layout consisting of n machines located at n given points (x_i, y_i) in a plane. Suppose the new machine is placed at the point (x, y). It is assumed that there is some kind of interaction between the new machine and each of the other machines. For simplicity and concreteness, we suppose that this is some kind of material interchange. Products have to be transferred from each of the locations (x_i, y_i) to (x, y), or from (x, y) to (x_i, y_i), or both. Suppose we wish to locate the new machine so as to minimize the handling costs involved in these transfers. A rough measure of the handling costs can be obtained by considering two factors. First, there is a *distance factor*, where "distance" is understood in a general sense which can include physical distance, time, cost, or some other measure of difficulty of transfer of one unit of material from one position to the other. The second factor is a *volume factor*, which can be number of trips, total volume, total weight, or some other measure of the amount of material transported

---

[2] Much of the rest of this chapter was suggested by an article by A. E. Bindschedler and J. M. Moore, Optimal Location of New Machines in Existing Plant Layouts, *J. Ind. Eng.*, **12**, 41–48 (1961). Figures 2.1, 2.2, 2.7, 2.8, and 2.9 were suggested by figures in that article. The editor was led to this reference by the contribution of R. L. Francis, on which Section 2.4 is based.

between (x, y) and any other location. If d_i denotes the value of the distance factor associated with (x_i, y_i) and w_i denotes the corresponding volume factor, we might take the product $w_i d_i$ as a measure of the *merit factor* or *cost factor* involved in locating the additional machine at (x, y), relative to the machine at (x_i, y_i). A criterion for the optimum location might be the minimization of the sum of the individual cost factors:

$$M = \sum_{i=1}^{n} w_i \, d_i. \tag{2.3}$$

If the d_i are the straight-line distances between (x, y) and (x_i, y_i), then M reduces to

$$M = \sum_{i=1}^{n} w_i[(x - x_i)^2 + (y - y_i)^2]^{1/2}. \tag{2.4}$$

If, in addition, all the weighting factors w_i are unity, then M reduces to precisely the quantity D defined in (2.1) that had to be minimized in the power-plant problem.

The use of a simple weighted sum of distances involves severely restrictive assumptions.

1. The material flow between the new machine and the existing machines follows the straight-line paths joining the machines.
2. The material handling costs are simply proportional to the first power of the distance.
3. Variations in handling costs per unit distance between the existing machines and the new machine can be taken into account by means of the weighting factors w_i in (2.4).
4. Realistic estimates for the weighting factors w_i can be made.

In writing these in detail we are merely re-emphasizing that it is important (a) to state explicitly the assumptions that have been made, and (b) to decide whether they are valid to a sufficient degree of approximation.

It might be suggested that (2.4) would be improved by adding constants k_i to each of the distances, because, even if two machines are very close together, there may still be an irreducible amount of time or cost involved in transferring units from one machine to another. This would give a merit function

$$M = \sum_{i=1}^{n} w_i\{[(x - x_i)^2 + (y - y_i)^2]^{1/2} + k_i\}.$$

We see immediately that the k_i will not affect the optimum location, because, for instance, when all the w_i are unity, the conditions $\partial M/\partial x = \partial M/\partial y = 0$ give precisely equations (2.2) for x and y, independent of the k_i.

The general distance function d_i in (2.3) is related to the distance moved when transferring material between (x, y) and (x_i, y_i). It is appropriate to take this as $[(x - x_i)^2 + (y - y_i)^2]^{1/2}$ only if material moves along the direct

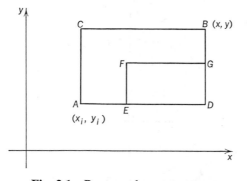

Fig. 2.1 Rectangular movement.

straight line joining the two locations, for example, on overhead conveyors. In many cases, however, the material must be transferred along fixed paths, for example, aisles arranged in a rectangular pattern parallel to the walls of the building. Thus to go from A to B in Fig. 2.1 it may be necessary to go along ACB, or ADB, or $AEFGB$. In each of these cases, the value of the distance d_i is the same,

$$d_i = |x - x_i| + |y - y_i|.$$

Instead of minimizing (2.4), we must minimize

$$M = \sum_{i=1}^{n} w_i[|x - x_i| + |y - y_i|]. \tag{2.5}$$

As we shall see, it may be easier to minimize this expression than (2.4). In many cases the optimum locations determined from (2.4) and (2.5) are not very different.

2.3 Special Cases of the Straight-Movement Model

Mathematics Used: Simple algebra and geometry; partial differentiation to find a minimum.

Comment: The solution of the straight-line distance problem is given for $n = 2, 3, 4$. The existence and uniqueness of solutions is considered.

In this section we consider, from an elementary point of view, the purely mathematical problem of minimizing expressions of the form

$$M = \sum_{i=1}^{n} w_i[(x - x_i)^2 + (y - y_i)^2]^{1/2}, \tag{2.6}$$

where the w_i are constant weighting factors. As often happens, although we wish eventually to deal with an arbitrary number of terms n, it is instructive

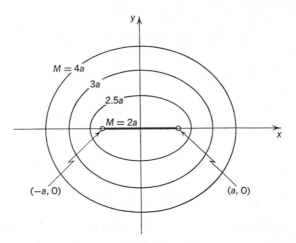

Fig. 2.2   Level curves for the case $n = 2$.

to start by considering special cases. In particular, we suppose that all the w_i are unity, and consider $n = 2, 3, 4$ in succession. For brevity we shall use the notation

$$d_i = [(x - x_i)^2 + (y - y_i)^2]^{1/2}. \tag{2.7}$$

For $n = 2$ there is no loss of generality in taking the two points to be $(-a, 0)$ and $(a, 0)$, so that (2.6) becomes

$$M = [(x + a)^2 + y^2]^{1/2} + [(x - a)^2 + y^2]^{1/2}. \tag{2.8}$$

It is left to the reader to show that the locus of points such that $M =$ constant $(M \geq 2a)$ is given by the ellipse with the points $(-a, 0)$ and $(a, 0)$ as foci. The resulting confocal ellipses for $M = 2a, 2.5a, 3a, 4a$, are shown in Fig. 2.2. The optimum location for the new machine in this case is any point on the straight line joining the two existing machines. For an algebraic point of view, the optimum position (x, y) is given by the conditions $\partial M/\partial x = 0$ and $\partial M/\partial y = 0$. From (2.8) this gives

$$\frac{x + a}{[(x + a)^2 + y^2]^{1/2}} + \frac{x - a}{[(x - a)^2 + y^2]^{1/2}} = 0, \tag{2.9}$$

$$y = 0. \tag{2.10}$$

Insertion of (2.10) in (2.9) gives

$$\frac{x + a}{|x + a|} + \frac{x - a}{|x - a|} = 0. \tag{2.11}$$

There are now three possibilities. If $x > a$ or $x < -a$, then (2.11) gives $2 = 0$, which is impossible. If $-a < x < a$, then (2.11) reduces to $1 - 1 = 0$, which is identically true. Hence any point $(x, 0)$, where $-a < x < a$, satisfies the condition for an extremum. The algebraic approach has led to the same conclusion as the geometric approach.

Consider next $n = 3$, in which case $M = d_1 + d_2 + d_3$, where the d_i are as defined in (2.7). The conditions $\partial M/\partial x = \partial M/\partial y = 0$ lead to

$$\frac{x - x_1}{d_1} + \frac{x - x_2}{d_2} + \frac{x - x_3}{d_3} = 0, \tag{2.12}$$

$$\frac{y - y_1}{d_1} + \frac{y - y_2}{d_2} + \frac{y - y_3}{d_3} = 0. \tag{2.13}$$

Recalling the definition of d_3,

$$d_3^2 = (x - x_3)^2 + (y - y_3)^2,$$

and substituting in this expression for $(x - x_3)$ and $(y - y_3)$ from (2.12) and (2.13), we obtain

$$\left(\frac{x - x_1}{d_1} + \frac{x - x_2}{d_2}\right)^2 + \left(\frac{y - y_1}{d_1} + \frac{y - y_2}{d_2}\right)^2 = 1.$$

Multiplying out and using the definitions of d_1 and d_2, we find

$$\frac{(x - x_1)(x - x_2) + (y - y_1)(y - y_2)}{d_1 d_2} = -\frac{1}{2}. \tag{2.14}$$

If the lines joining (x, y) to (x_1, y_1) and (x_2, y_2) make angles θ_1 and θ_2, respectively, with the x axis, it is easy to show that (2.14) is equivalent to

$$\cos (\theta_1 - \theta_2) = -\tfrac{1}{2} = \cos 120°.$$

Hence if (2.12) and (2.13) give a solution, it must be such that the lines joining (x, y) to (x_1, y_1) and (x_2, y_2) make an angle of 120° with each other. From symmetry, the third line joining (x, y) to (x_3, y_3) must also make angles of 120° with the other two, as illustrated in Fig. 2.3a. However, we must be

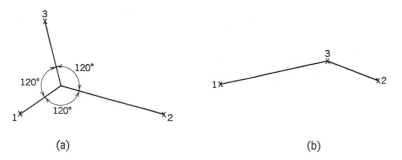

(a)   (b)

Fig. 2.3   Optimum location for the case of three existing machines: (a) solution given by (2.12) and (2.13); (b) solution not given by (2.12) and (2.13).

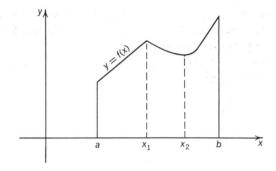

Fig. 2.4   Extrema in $a \leq x \leq b$ occur at $x = a$, x_1, x_2, and b.

careful, because there may be no such point; that is, (2.12) and (2.13) may not provide a solution of the problem. This occurs when one point subtends an angle greater than 120° at the remaining two, and the solution is then that the optimum location coincides with this point. The reason this is not given by (2.12) and (2.13), that is, by the conditions $\partial M/\partial x = \partial M/\partial y = 0$, is that setting first derivatives equal to zero does not reveal extrema either at points where a first derivative is discontinuous (illustrated for a one-dimensional case by the point $x = x_1$ in Fig. 2.4), or at the boundaries of a given region (the points $x = a$, b in Fig. 2.4).

Finally consider the case $n = 4$. If the four points can be arranged in pairs AB and CD so that the straight lines AB and CD intersect at a point P which lies between A and B and between C and D, as shown in Fig. 2.5a, it is clear that P is the optimum location, for if we move away from P we always increase either $PA + PB$ or $PC + PD$, or both. (The shortest distance between two points is a straight line.) However, if one point, say B, lies inside the triangle ACD formed by the remaining points as in Fig. 2.5b, then the optimum location is certainly not given by the intersection of AB and CD. We shall not deal further with such special cases.

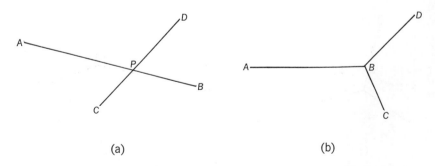

(a)   (b)

Fig. 2.5   Arrangements of four points: (a) optimum location at the intersection of AB and CD; (b) optimum location not given by the intersection of AB and CD.

Since the above was written the editor has realized that the problem of the shortest sum of distances between one moveable point and n fixed points in a plane is well known as *Steiner's problem*, having been considered by Steiner at the beginning of the nineteenth century. The case $n = 3$ has been examined in detail, using a geometric argument, by Courant and Robbins.[3] They make the following instructive comment concerning the problem of n fixed points:

> This ... does not lead to interesting results. It is one of the superficial generalizations not infrequently found in mathematical literature. To find the really significant extension of Steiner's problem we must abandon the search for a single point. Instead we look for the network of shortest total length.

This last problem is, in fact, the one suggested in Section 2.6 on physical grounds (see Fig. 2.10). The remark quoted about "superficial generalizations" prompts the comment (directed to students of mathematics reading this book) that, when faced with an engineering problem in three dimensions, one should not think that there is automatically some virtue in generalizing to n dimensions instead of three; in fact, the most fruitful approach *may* be to consider the problem in two dimensions instead of three.

We now make some comments about the general problem in which n locations are given. The problem becomes almost trivial if, instead of the cost function (2.6), which is a weighted sum of distances, we are willing to use a weighted sum of squares of distances:

$$M = \sum_{i=1}^{n} w_i \, d_i^2 = \sum_{i=1}^{n} w_i[(x - x_i)^2 + (y - y_i)^2]. \tag{2.15}$$

Then $\partial M/\partial x = \partial M/\partial y = 0$ gives simply

$$x = \left(\sum_{i=1}^{n} w_i x_i\right)\bigg/ \sum_{i=1}^{n} w_i, \qquad y = \left(\sum_{i=1}^{n} w_i y_i\right)\bigg/ \sum_{i=1}^{n} w_i. \tag{2.16}$$

It might seem that we are cheating by using (2.15) instead of (2.6), but the definition of cost function is to a large extent arbitrary, and in many cases the optimum location is not very sensitive to the precise definition of cost function that is used. The definition (2.15) may in some circumstances be adequate or even preferable for practical purposes. If we wish to give more weight to the effect of machines at large distances from (x, y), the definition (2.15) will be preferable to (2.6).

We return to the problem of minimizing the weighted sum of distances, equation (2.6). The equations obtained from (2.6) by setting $\partial M/\partial x = \partial M/\partial y = 0$ [(2.2), with the inclusion of weight factors w_i] can be rewritten

$$x = \left(\sum_{i=1}^{n} \frac{w_i x_i}{d_i}\right)\bigg/ \sum_{i=1}^{n} \frac{w_i}{d_i}, \qquad y = \left(\sum_{i=1}^{n} \frac{w_i y_i}{d_i}\right)\bigg/ \sum_{i=1}^{n} \frac{w_i}{d_i}, \tag{2.17}$$

[3] R. Courant and H. Robbins, *What Is Mathematics?*, Oxford Univ. Press, New York, 1941, pp. 354–361.

The quantities d_i depend on x and y. For the reader interested in the technical problem of solving these equations, we note that various iterative procedures can be suggested. Perhaps the most obvious is to start with an initial guess $(x^{(1)}, y^{(1)})$, which could be the values given by (2.16). If these are substituted for x and y in the d_i on the right of (2.17), this gives second estimates of x and y, and so on. This procedure is repeated until successive estimates agree. These very brief remarks about the iterative solution of equations (2.17) arising from (2.6) could be expanded considerably. The general technique is considered in most of the standard texts on numerical analysis. With reference to the particular problem of Steiner, considerable progress has been made recently.[4]

We have investigated special cases in perhaps excessive detail, in order to emphasize that if we merely write (2.17) by applying straightforward minimization and then assume that the problem has been solved, we have ignored many of the real difficulties. If we wish to program the solution of the original problem on a computer, we should ideally take account of all possibilities, including the nonexistence and nonuniqueness of solutions, and this promises to be a difficult task.

2.4 The Rectangular-Movement Case[5]

Mathematics Used: Simple algebra.

Comment: The rectangular-movement model is much simpler than the straight-line model with regard to the discussion of existence and uniqueness, as well as the practical determination of the solution.

In this section we consider briefly some analytical aspects of the case mentioned at the end of Section 2.2, in which only movements parallel to rectangular axes were permitted. The problem is then to minimize equation (2.5),

$$M = \sum_{i=1}^{n} w_i[|x - x_i| + |y - y_i|] = M_1 + M_2,$$

where $$M_1 = \sum_{i=1}^{n} w_i \, |x - x_i|, \qquad M_2 = \sum_{i=1}^{n} w_i \, |y - y_i|.$$

---

[4] See H. W. Kuhn, Locational Problems and Mathematical Programming, in *Colloquium on Applications of Mathematics to Economics*, Budapest, 1963, Hungarian Academy of Sciences, Budapest, 1965, pp. 235–242, where additional references may be found.

[5] This section is based on a submitted contribution: R. L. Francis, A Note on the Optimum Location of New Machines in Existing Plant Layouts, *J. Ind. Eng.*, **14**, 57–59 (1963). The article was originally drawn to our attention by J. C. Merriam, Western Electric Co.

We see immediately that because M_1 is a function of x only and M_2 is a function of y only, we can find the minimum of M by minimizing M_1 with respect to x and M_2 with respect to y, quite independent of each other. This is a very great simplification.

We need, therefore, to study the expression

$$M_1(x) = \sum_{i=1}^{n} w_i |x - x_i|,$$

where $w_i > 0$ for all i, and the x_i are arbitrary given numbers,

$$x_1 \le x_2 \le \cdots \le x_n.$$

For any given x between x_s and x_{s+1} we might write M_1 in the form

$$M_1(x) = \sum_{i=1}^{s} w_i(x - x_i) + \sum_{i=s+1}^{n} w_i(x_i - x)$$

$$= \left(\sum_{i=1}^{s} w_i - \sum_{i=s+1}^{n} w_i \right) x + \left(-\sum_{i=1}^{s} w_i x_i + \sum_{i=s+1}^{n} w_i x_i \right)$$

$$= A_s x + B_s, \tag{2.18}$$

where
$$A_s = \sum_{i=1}^{s} w_i - \sum_{i=s+1}^{n} w_i. \tag{2.19}$$

We note that

(a) $A_s - A_{s-1} = 2w_s > 0$.
(b) If $x > x_n$, then $M_1(x) = A_n x + B_n$, where

$$A_n = \sum_{i=1}^{n} w_i > 0.$$

(c) If $x < x_1$, then $M_1(x) = A_0 x + B_0$, where

$$A_0 = -\sum_{i=1}^{n} w_i < 0.$$

From these results we see that the graph of A_s against x (which is a step function) must look like the top half of Fig. 2.6, and, from the form of A_s, together with (2.18) and the fact that $M_1(x)$ is continuous, the graph of $M_1(x)$ against x must look like the bottom half of Fig. 2.6.

From (a), (b), and (c), since A_s is a step function that increases with s, and $A_0 < 0$, $A_n > 0$, we see that for some value of s we must have one of two cases.

1. $A_{s-1} < 0$, $A_s > 0$.
2. $A_{s-1} < 0$, $A_s = 0$, $A_{s+1} > 0$.

From the definition of B_r derived from (2.18) we see that

$$B_r - B_{r-1} = -2w_r x_r.$$

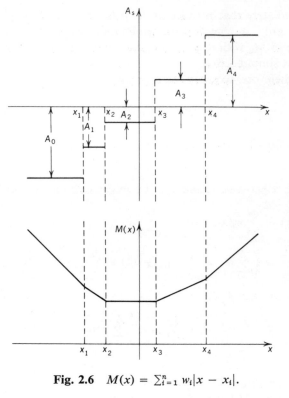

Fig. 2.6 $M(x) = \sum_{i=1}^{n} w_i |x - x_i|$.

Then

$$
\begin{aligned}
M_1(x_r) - M_1(x_{r-1}) &= A_r x_r + B_r - A_{r-1} x_{r-1} - B_{r-1} \\
&= x_r(A_r - A_{r-1}) + A_{r-1}(x_r - x_{r-1}) + (B_r - B_{r-1}) \\
&= A_{r-1}(x_r - x_{r-1}).
\end{aligned}
$$

Hence, in case 1,

$$
\begin{aligned}
M_1(x_s) - M_1(x_{s-1}) &= A_{s-1}(x_s - x_{s-1}) < 0, \\
M_1(x_{s+1}) - M_1(x_s) &= A_s(x_{s+1} - x_s) > 0,
\end{aligned}
$$

and $M_1(x)$ is a minimum at $x = x_s$. In case 2 we have

$$
\begin{aligned}
M_1(x_s) - M_1(x_{s-1}) &< 0, \\
M_1(x_{s+1}) - M_1(x_s) &= 0, \\
M_1(x_{s+2}) - M_1(x_{s+1}) &> 0,
\end{aligned}
$$

and $M_1(x)$ is a constant and a minimum for $x_s \le x \le x_{s+1}$. We note in passing that, from (2.19), case 1 is equivalent to

$$
\sum_{i=1}^{s-1} w_i < \sum_{i=s}^{n} w_i, \qquad \sum_{i=1}^{s} w_i > \sum_{i=s+1}^{n} w_i;
$$

that is,

$$\sum_{i=1}^{s-1} w_i < \frac{1}{2} \sum_{i=1}^{n} w_i, \qquad \sum_{i=1}^{s} w_i > \frac{1}{2} \sum_{i=1}^{n} w_i. \qquad (2.20)$$

Similarly, case 2 is equivalent to

$$\sum_{i=1}^{s} w_i = \frac{1}{2} \sum_{i=1}^{n} w_i. \qquad (2.21)$$

Formulas (2.20) and (2.21) are convenient for the practical determination of s. For the special situation in which all the w_i have the same value and n is an odd, positive integer, case 1 holds, and $s = \frac{1}{2}(n + 1)$; if n is an even integer, case 2 holds and $s = \frac{1}{2}n$.

Returning to the problem posed at the beginning of the section, the minimization of

$$M = \sum_{i=1}^{n} w_i[|x - x_i| + |y - y_i|] = M_1(x) + M_2(y),$$

we see that there are four possibilities.

1. $M_1(x)$ and $M_2(y)$ both fall under case 1. Then M has a minimum at exactly one point.
2. $M_1(x)$ and $M_2(y)$ both fall under case 2. Then M has a minimum constant value over a rectangular area in the xy plane.
3. $M_1(x)$ falls under case 1 and $M_2(y)$ under case 2. Then M has a minimum constant value along a line in the xy plane parallel to the y axis.
4. $M_1(x)$ is case 2, $M_2(y)$ is case 1; then M has a minimum constant value along a line parallel to the x axis.

These possibilities will be illustrated in Section 2.5, where we consider the graphical representation of M as a function of the variables x and y.

2.5   Level Curves

Comment: The object of this section is to compare the straight-line and rectangular-movement solutions by using a simple graphical method, the drawing of contour maps.

Although the analytical considerations in the last two sections are instructive, probably the most useful method when investigating optimum-location problems when only two variables are involved is the use of level surfaces, already mentioned in connection with Fig. 2.2. We shall talk in terms of "machines," but our remarks are equally applicable to "towns." Consider first a single machine located at the origin of coordinates. For a straight-line movement we define the cost function of any point (x, y) relative to the origin to be

$$M_s = (x^2 + y^2)^{1/2},$$

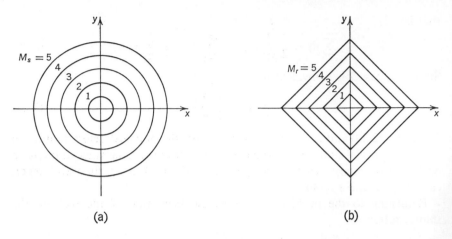

Fig. 2.7 Level curves for a single machine: (*a*) straight-line movement; (*b*) rectangular movement.

and for rectangular movement we define

$$M_r = |x| + |y|.$$

The level curves are obtained by plotting M_s = constant, and M_r = constant for various values of the constants. Some of the level curves for a single machine are shown in Fig. 2.7. The best location for a new machine at (x, y) is clearly the one already taken by the present machine (although it does not require level curves to tell us this). The level curves give curves on which the cost function of points x and y is the same, relative to the existing machine at the origin.

When two machines are present at points (x_1, y_1) and (x_2, y_2), the cost functions for straight-line and rectangular movement are, respectively, for the location (x, y), assuming equal weighting for the two machines,

$$M_s = [(x - x_1)^2 + (y - y_1)^2]^{1/2} + [(x - x_2)^2 + (y - y_2)^2]^{1/2}, \quad (2.22)$$

$$M_r = |x - x_1| + |y - y_1| + |x - x_2| + |y - y_2|. \quad (2.23)$$

The corresponding level surfaces are shown when (x_1, y_1) and (x_2, y_2) both lie on the x axis in Fig. 2.8, and for arbitrary (x_1, y_1) and (x_2, y_2) in Fig. 2.9. In the rectangular-movement case in Fig. 2.9*b*, the cost function M_r is a constant in the shaded area.

The reader is referred to the article by Bindschedler and Moore[6] for a discussion of more complicated cases, including a more detailed comparison

---

[6] A. E. Bindschedler and J. M. Moore, *J. Ind. Eng.*, **12**, 41–48 (1961).

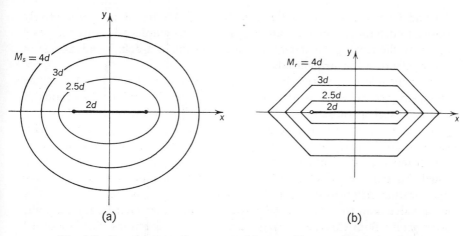

Fig. 2.8 Level curves for two machines on line parallel to x-axis.

of the straight-line and rectangular-movement cases, and level curves for various examples involving three and four machines. The diagrams we have given indicate one of the main points—that as far as applications of the above type are concerned, the differences between straight-line and rectangular-movement models are relatively unimportant. The optimal location of new machines is not very sensitive to the path pattern selected. Thus, even if the straight-line path would be a more appropriate assumption to make in a given problem, a rectangular movement may be substituted without a major shift in either the optimal location or in the relative preference of various available locations. As one can see from the discussion in Section

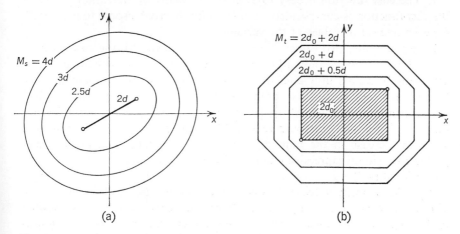

Fig. 2.9 Level curves for two machines on line not parallel to either the x or y axis.

2.4 and from the article by Bindschedler and Moore, it is comparatively simple to determine the optimum location and to graphically construct level curves in the rectangular-movement case, and this is a definite advantage of this model over the straight-line case.

We conclude this section by making two additional points. One of the main advantages of level-curve methods over purely analytical methods of approach such as those in Sections 2.3 and 2.4 is that level curves tell us at a glance how much we lose if we use a location other than the optimum. This is important in practice because we cannot usually include in the optimization criterion all the factors that ought to be taken into account. In a complicated situation we would usually include the most important factors in the optimization criterion to locate candidate areas of equal or approximately equal value, and then base the final decision on other factors, for example, accessibility, floor carrying capacity, and service connections. Because of the inadequacy of any conceivable optimization factor, it is usually necessary to use a certain amount of judgment based on intuition or experience or common sense before making a final decision, to be sure all factors have been taken into account.

The second point we wish to make is that although the analytical considerations presented earlier are useful in providing insight, it is not necessary to do any analytical work to apply the method of level surfaces. We can merely get a computer (human or automatic) to evaluate the cost function over, say, a rectangular grid of points covering the ranges of (x, y) values that are of interest. The level surfaces can then be drawn by interpolation between grid points. However, the reader should be warned that this blunderbuss approach via computer is useful only because of two special simplifying factors present in the problems discussed in this chapter.

1. The cost function is easy to evaluate. In many optimization problems the cost function is complicated, so it is relatively troublesome to evaluate it for even one set of values of the variable.

2. Because only two values of the variable are involved, the cost function has to be evaluated at only a limited number of points. Thus if we choose a grid with 10 points in x and 10 points in y we have to evaluate the cost function for only $10 \times 10 = 100$ pairs of values (x, y). However if we had six independent variables, which can easily happen in optimization problems, then the above method would require 10^6 evaluations of the cost function. With an increase in the number of variables, the labor quickly becomes prohibitive. (In an expressive phrase, R. Bellman has called this the "curse of dimensionality.")

It would be a pity to leave the question of optimization at this stage in the discussion, because the impression left on the reader would be somewhat misleading. For this reason we discuss in Chapter 3 another type of optimization problem, in which one of the main considerations is to minimize as much as possible the number of evaluations of the cost function.

2.6   Summary and Concluding Remarks

Comment : An experimental solution to the power-plant problem, with common transmission lines ; linear programming situations.

In Sections 2.1 and 2.2 we considered two optimum-location problems, one involving the location of a power station relative to existing towns, the other the location of a machine relative to existing machines. These problems can be formulated mathematically by making certain assumptions. We draw particular attention to two points.

1. The resulting equations turn out to be similar in the two cases. It often happens that the underlying mathematical problems turn out to be identical in widely different engineering situations.

2. The idealization of the problems in order to formulate them mathematically has involved considerable simplification and the neglect of many factors. The important thing in this procedure is that we should make the underlying assumptions explicit.

In connection with this second point, we quote the following[7]:

> It may be necessary to neglect a certain feature to reach equations that are sufficiently simple to solve, but this neglect, however unfortunate, must be intentional and not an oversight. It frequently happens that to get a set of manageable equations the final model is idealized to a much greater degree than one would wish. However, provided the dominant features are present, the resulting analysis is not valueless, for it is very often true that a qualitative understanding of the real problem can be obtained from the quantitative solution of the idealized one.

The discussion in Sections 2.3 to 2.5 of simple cases from an analytical and graphical point of view gives some qualitative insight into the kinds of results that can be obtained. It is clear from the discussion in Section 2.5 that much more complicated cases, including many factors that have been neglected here, can be tackled with the aid of a high-speed computer. The role of the computer is interesting, because the type of problem discussed in this chapter is such that a formal analytical solution, or set of equations containing the solution, is of little value in itself. However, the mathematical background is important, in fact, essential, in formulating the problem and in clarifying the kinds of results that can occur, for example, nonuniqueness in both the straight-line and rectangular-movement models and the line polygons that occur in the rectangular-movement case.

We have already met, in the difference between the straight-line and rectangular-movement cases, the fact that what might seem a comparatively small change in basic assumptions can cause a complete change in the mathematical character of the problem. Another example occurs in connection with the power-plant problem of Section 2.1. Suppose that instead of

[7] Reprinted by permission of the publisher from Rutherford Aris, *Discrete Dynamic Programming* (Waltham, Massachusetts: Blaisdell Publishing Company, 1964), p. 2.

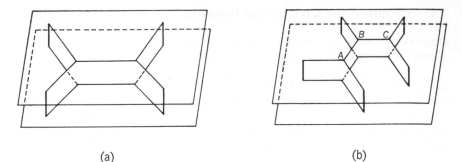

(a)   (b)

Fig. 2.10   Soap-bubble model: (*a*) the shortest connection between four points; (*b*) the shortest connection between five points.

insisting that we run separate lines from the power plant to each town, we allow common lines; that is, the power for two different towns can be carried on the same line for part of the way.

The solution of this problem can be obtained by a soap-bubble experiment,[8] which will make the situation clear. Owing to the action of surface tension, a film of liquid is in stable equilibrium only if its area is a minimum. If two parallel glass or transparent plastic plates are joined by three or more perpendicular bars, and we immerse this object in a soap solution and withdraw it, the film forms a system of vertical planes between the plates and joining the fixed bars. The projection appearing on the glass plates is the solution of the problem of finding the shortest straight-line connection between a set of fixed points. This is illustrated for four and five points in Fig. 2.10. It is clear that the problem of finding the total length of line by a digital-computer method, in this case, is much more difficult than the problem in which separate lines are run to each town, because we do not know before-hand the location of points such as *A*, *B*, and *C*, in Fig. 2.10. A solution of this problem in a finite (although impracticable) number of steps was given recently by Melzak.[9]

In this chapter we have confined our attention to the problem of the optimum location of a single additional machine. This immediately suggests generalizations connected with locating additional machines which interact with each other as well as with the original machines. It is possible to make some progress in solving this problem when $m = 2$ or even 3 by extending the methods discussed in this chapter. For example, a problem involving the location of two additional machines, using the rectangular-movement model, has been discussed in an elementary way by Francis.[10] However, the brute-force procedure of evaluating cost functions systematically

---

[8] R. Courant and H. Robbins, *What Is Mathematics?*, Oxford Univ. Press, New York, 1941.

[9] Z. A. Melzak, On the Problem of Steiner, *Can. Math. Bull.*, **4**, 143–148 (1961).

[10] R. L. Francis, *J. Ind. Eng.*, **14**, 57–59 (1963).

for a set of points covering the relevant area is not in general the best method for multiple-assignment problems, in which straightforward evaluation of all the possibilities can be prohibitively laborious. It is in this kind of situation that more advanced mathematics can be indispensable.

In the general assignment problem we are given N different facilities (machines, departments, factories, etc.) and M different locations, each of which can accommodate given numbers of facilities. The problem is to assign facilities to locations. We can again idealize the situation by assigning distance factors and volume factors, so that the mathematical problem is to minimize an expression such as (2.3), where now, however, this expression can be formed in different ways, depending on the allocation of facilities. This leads to mathematical problems that are much more complicated than those considered in this chapter.[11] In fact, these problems have not yet been investigated exhaustively, so the reader has been brought to the frontier of current research.

In conclusion, we mention two other optimization procedures, dynamic programming and linear programming. Dynamic programming[12] applies primarily to a situation in which many decisions have to be made to maximize the overall performance of a system, but the system is one in which distinct stages may be recognized, and decisions at later stages do not effect the performance of earlier ones. A typical example is a multistage chemical reaction, in which a raw material passes in sequence through a series of tanks in each of which chemical reactions take place, and it is required to optimize certain properties of the final product.

Linear programming[13] deals with a somewhat different type of situation. We state an example submitted for this book[14]: Draft quotas for the month

[11] An introduction to some aspects of this type of problem, with references, can be found in J. M. Moore, Optimal Locations for Multiple Machines, *J. Ind. Eng.*, **12**, 307–313 (1961).

[12] A most interesting elementary introduction to dynamic programming, using only undergraduate mathematics, is R. Aris, *Discrete Dynamic Programming*, Blaisdell (Ginn), Boston, 1964. The basic work can be found in books and papers by Richard Bellman, of which the most suitable for an elementary introduction is *Applied Dynamic Programming* (written with S. E. Dreyfus), Princeton Univ. Press, Princeton, N.J., 1962.

[13] An elementary introduction is given in A. M. Glicksman, *An Introduction to Linear Programming and the Theory of Games*, Wiley, New York, 1963. See also A. S. Barsov, *What Is Linear Programming?*, Heath, Boston, 1964. More advanced references are S. I. Gass, *Linear Programming*, 2nd ed., McGraw-Hill, New York, 1964; G. Hadley, *Linear Programming*, Addison-Wesley, Reading, Mass., 1962, and D. Gale, *The Theory of Linear Economic Models*, McGraw-Hill, New York, 1960.

[14] By Col. C. P. Nicholas, Head, Department of Mathematics, U.S. Military Academy, West Point. In his covering letter he states, "The problems in linear programming are somewhat elaborate, and we allow teams of cadets two or three days, with the help of the electronic computer. So far these linear programming problems constitute our best type of practical application of linear algebra. The cadets find them quite interesting, and in our opinion these problems are authentic forms of motivation. It may be a matter of special interest that some of the cadets who solve these problems are freshmen with no prior knowledge of linear algebra."

of December have been set as follows:

Boston	2000	Pittsburgh	1500
New York	2000	Dallas	500
Baltimore	1500	San Francisco	500
Chicago	2000		

Vacancies in training cycles exist at various basic training centers as follows:

Fort Jackson	1000	Fort Riley	2500
Fort Knox	1500	Fort Ord	3000
Fort Dix	1000	Fort Carson	1000

Contractual arrangements have established transportation rates per man (in dollars) as given in Table 2.1. The problem is to determine the allocation of the draftees to each of the training camps so as to minimize the cost to the government.

TABLE 2.1

From \ To	Jackson	Knox	Dix	Riley	Ord	Carson
Boston	40	30	10	45	90	60
New York	35	25	5	40	80	55
Baltimore	20	15	5	35	80	50
Chicago	45	10	25	10	50	40
Pittsburgh	30	20	15	35	70	50
Dallas	60	40	50	20	40	20
San Francisco	80	70	80	60	5	20

This problem is stated mathematically as follows. Let c_{ij} denote the cost of sending 1 man from city i to fort j. If we send x_{ij} men from city i to fort j, the total cost C is

$$C = \sum_{i=1}^{7} \sum_{j=1}^{6} x_{ij} c_{ij}.$$

We wish to find the x_{ij} that will minimize C subject to the following conditions. The total numbers of men sent to each fort and the total numbers taken from each town are given by

$$\sum_{i=1}^{7} x_{ij} = n_j \quad (j = 1, \dots, 6), \qquad \sum_{j=1}^{6} x_{ij} = m_i \quad (i = 1, \dots, 7),$$

where n_j is the number of vacancies at fort j and m_i is the draft call from city i. The n_j, m_i, and cost matrix c_{ij} are given. The above equations give only $7 + 6 - 1$ independent relations since the total number of men taken from the cities equals the total number of men sent to the forts. In addition, since the numbers of men cannot be negative, we must have $x_{ij} \geq 0$ for all i and j. The mathematical problem is to minimize a linear function, subject to linear constraints and inequalities, and this is a typical problem in linear programming.

In Chapter 3 we consider still another kind of optimization procedure.

Chapter 3

The Exploration of
Functional Relationships—
An Aspect of Optimization[1]

3.1   Introduction: An Underground-Exploration Problem

Mathematics Used: Elementary Taylor series in two variables; planes in three dimensions.

Comment: Introduction to the method of steepest descent for locating stationary points of a function of two variables.

In Chapter 2 we considered a special kind of optimization problem, one involving the finding of optimum locations. This was deliberately treated from a very elementary point of view, which was possible because the function to be optimized (the optimization criterion or cost function) was of known simple analytical form, and could be evaluated readily for any given set of independent variables. In this chapter we consider more difficult optimization problems in a more general setting. In practice it often happens that we do not know beforehand the form of the function to be optimized even qualitatively, let alone analytically, and this has to be found by laborious and costly experiments or calculations. This will, of course, change our whole outlook.

In this section we consider a simple example connected with underground geological or geophysical exploration. In Sections 3.2 and 3.3 we indicate

---

[1] This chapter was written partly because R. C. Buck, Department of Mathematics, University of Wisconsin, Madison, Wis., drew the editor's attention to an interesting book by D. J. Wilde, *Optimum Seeking Methods*, Prentice-Hall, Englewood Cliffs, N.J., 1964, and partly because of a conversation with G. E. P. Box, Department of Statistics, University of Wisconsin, on which most of Section 3.7 is based. Wilde gives such a delightful account of some theoretical aspects of finding an optimum empirically that there is some danger the mathematician will get the wrong end of the stick from reading this book. Mathematics provides essential tools, but in many ways it is the easiest part of the overall problem of finding optimum conditions. Section 3.1 is based on Wilde's book, pp. 109–112.

that similar but more difficult problems arise in completely different situations, the examples quoted being from chemical engineering and optical-lens design. The title of this chapter is somewhat ponderous but should convey the basic idea. We are trying to find out how certain unknown functions behave when given independent variables are altered. One important technique, the method of steepest descent (or ascent), is explained in this section. This depends on little more than the first terms in a Taylor-series expansion in several variables, and simple properties of linear functions. When we are near an optimum it is usually better to fit quadratic expressions, and the results depend on the properties of the conic sections, as discussed in Section 3.4. Later sections discuss specific examples; a relatively straight-forward example is discussed in Section 3.5, and an example in which a common difficulty occurs is discussed in Section 3.6.

As pointed out by Wilde,[2] the basis for a search technique known as the *method of steepest ascent* can be visualized by imagining an explorer searching for the top of a thickly wooded hill. Even if the density of the forest prevents him from seeing the summit, or even the general shape of the hill, he could eventually reach a local summit simply by continuing to gain elevation as he walks. In the case of an explorer, he could probably check whether he has reached the true top of the hill by climbing a tree, or looking through breaks in the trees. Unfortunately when we are trying to find the maximum of a mathematical function it is not so easy to check whether we have found an overall, or only a local, maximum. Another way in which the analogy breaks down is the following. If the explorer is in a hurry he would probably move in directions where the slope of the hill is greatest, provided, of course, that he does not run into obstacles he cannot surmount. In the case of the explorer this direction of steepest ascent is uniquely defined at every point. In the mathematical problem that turns up in engineering applications of the method, the path of steepest ascent may vary depending on the choice of scales for the independent variables. This is explained in Section 3.4. Some authors even omit the adjective "steepest" and talk merely of "ascent methods," because of the difficulty that the direction of steepest ascent depends on the scales used, and these are arbitrary.

We now consider a hypothetical geophysical-exploration problem. Suppose that geologists have discovered, by sinking a borehole, an underground deposit of mineral, and they wish to find the point at which the deposit is nearest the surface. We assume that no information is available concerning the slopes of the strata at the depth at which the mineral has been located, and that the only way of obtaining additional information is to sink additional boreholes.

We make the basic assumption that, in the vicinity of the first borehole, the top surface of the mineral deposit can be approximated by a plane. This

[2] D. J. Wilde, *Optimum Seeking Methods*, Prentice-Hall, Englewood Cliffs, N.J., 1964, p. 107.

will in general be true locally even if over a large area the surface is in the form of a dome, which is often the case, for example, for salt or oil deposits— in fact, the ultimate problem may be to find the top and the extent of the dome. Mathematically the assumption that the strata are locally plane is equivalent to the assumption that if the surface of the deposit is represented by a function $f(x, y)$, and the first borehole is located at the point (x_0, y_0), then near this point the surface can be approximated by retaining only the linear terms in a Taylor-series expansion of $f(x, y)$ about the point (x_0, y_0), neglecting higher-order terms:

$$f(x, y) \approx f(x_0, y_0) + (x - x_0)\left(\frac{\partial f}{\partial x}\right)_0 + (y - y_0)\left(\frac{\partial f}{\partial y}\right)_0$$

$$= \alpha + \beta(x - x_0) + \gamma(y - y_0), \tag{3.1}$$

where $(\cdots)_0$ means that the quantity in parentheses is calculated at the point (x_0, y_0). From the first borehole we know the quantity $\alpha = f(x_0, y_0)$. To specify the plane that approximates the surface of the mineral locally we need to determine β and γ in (3.1), which means that we need two more pieces of information, that is, two more boreholes. Suppose the mineral at the original borehole is at a depth of 1000 ft, and when we sink further boreholes 100 ft north and 100 ft east of the first borehole, we find that the mineral is at 950 ft and 1025 ft, respectively. (In a practical case we should, of course, use all the available information to make an intelligent guess at the most profitable directions in which we should move to sink the second and third holes, and how far these should be from the original holes.) Substituting these figures in (3.1), we obtain

$$-1025 = -1000 + 100\beta + 0\gamma, \qquad -950 = -1000 + 0\beta + 100\gamma.$$

Hence $\beta = -0.25$ and $\gamma = 0.5$, and the plane is given by

$$Z = -0.25X + 0.50Y, \tag{3.2}$$

where X and Y are the horizontal distances from (x_0, y_0) and Z is the difference in height, measured positive upward from the surface of the mineral at the first borehole as reference level.

If we wish to find the point at which the mineral is nearest the surface we naturally wish to explore in the direction of steepest ascent on the plane defined by (3.2). Consider a circle 100 ft in radius, centered at (x_0, y_0). We wish to locate the point on this circle where Z is greatest. The XY coordinates of any point on the circle are given by $X = 100 \cos \theta$ and $Y = 100 \sin \theta$. Substitution in (3.2) gives

$$Z = 100(-0.25 \cos \theta + 0.5 \sin \theta).$$

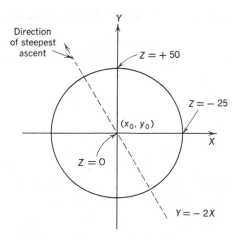

Fig. 3.1   Direction of steepest ascent.

The stationary values of Z are given by $dZ/d\theta = 0$, or

$$0.25 \sin \theta + 0.5 \cos \theta = 0, \qquad \tan \theta = -2. \qquad (3.3)$$

Hence the stationary values of Z occur at points where the line $Y = -2X$ cuts the circle with radius 100. There are two points of intersection, as in Fig. 3.1. The maximum occurs in the second quadrant and a minimum in the fourth, so the direction of steepest ascent is as shown.

Although we now know the direction of steepest ascent, we have no idea how far from the original hole it is advisable to go for the location in which to bore the next hole, and the method of steepest ascent alone cannot help us. It is necessary to weigh the risk of wasting money by boring the next hole unnecessarily close to the original holes, against the danger of overshooting the maximum of the mineral surface, which would lead to serious trouble if the level of the mineral surface, found by this new hole, were higher than any of the previous levels, since we might not realize that we had overshot the maximum.

We mention another feature, not present in the problems in Chapter 2, which enters into the geological problem introduced above—the presence of experimental error. The location of the depths of the mineral surfaces will not be measured exactly because of various kinds of experimental error, so the coefficients in (3.2) will be inaccurate. It is important in practice to obtain an estimate of the uncertainties introduced by random errors of this type, and we return to this point later.

This is a convenient stage in the discussion to digress to consider two other examples of optimization problems, occurring in quite different engineering circumstances. We shall then return, in Section 3.4, to a more detailed discussion of some of the mathematical problems involved.

3.2   An Optimization Problem in Chemical Engineering[3]

Comment: The objective of this section is to formulate the engineering problem in terms of minimization of a function of n variables, subject to certain inequalities.

We shall consider a manufacturing process that is converting certain raw materials into more valuable products. In such processes in chemical engineering there are usually a number of *responses*, such as rate of production, yield, and purity of the various products, which are influenced by the level of controllable *variables* such as temperature, pressure, concentration, and so on. If we denote the various responses $\eta_1, \eta_2, \ldots, \eta_n$, and the variables $x_1, x_2, \ldots, x_m$, the responses will be functions of the variables:

$$\eta_i = f_i(x_1, \ldots, x_m), \qquad i = 1, 2, \ldots, n, \tag{3.4}$$

although the exact forms of the functions f_i may not be known.

The aim of the chemical engineer is to operate the manufacturing process as efficiently as possible, where the crux of the matter lies in the way in which we define the word "efficiently." The difficulty is that we cannot simply say that we wish to minimize a single quantity such as the cost of manufacturing a unit quantity of the product, since various other factors are involved. Thus we usually wish to keep the purity at the best level possible, and the process should not take too long. Also it may be necessary to restrict the variables directly; for example, certain pressures and temperatures may be unobtainable or dangerous.

It can be argued that it should be possible to obtain a single function of the responses, for example, a criterion of profitability, which alone measures the desirability of a given setting of the variables. In practice it is not always easy to obtain such a function. In the case of the manufacture of a drug, for example, what monetary value could be placed on impurities which might make the drug dangerous? In practice the objective of the chemical engineer is often best expressed in terms of optimizing some *principle response*, usually related to cost, subject to certain restrictions on both the other responses (the dependent variables) and the controllable variables (the independent variables). The "principal response" here corresponds to the "cost function" that was optimized in Chapter 2. It should, of course, be emphasized that careful consideration is needed, in each case, to decide what quantity should be optimized, because if we are misled into optimizing the wrong criterion, our efforts may lead to losses rather than savings.

The situation is illustrated in Fig. 3.2, where the principal response is cost of product per unit weight η_1, and an auxiliary response is impurity of the product in some appropriate unit. Contours of cost η_1 and impurity η_2 are

[3] This section was adapted from the first section of G. E. P. Box, Some General Considerations in Process Optimization, *J. Basic Eng.* (Am. Soc. Mech. Engrs.), **82**, 113–119 (1960). Figures 3.2 and 3.4 are based on Figs. 1 and 3 of this reference.

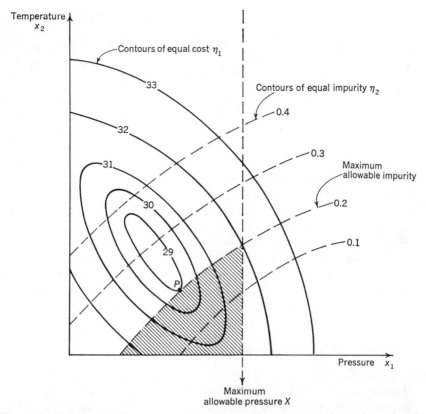

Fig. 3.2   Contours of response functions of cost and impurity, showing constraints.

shown in the space of the variables x_1 = pressure and x_2 = temperature. If the object is to minimize the cost η_1 subject to the restriction that the pressure should not be greater than a value $x_1 = X$ and impurity level not greater than $\eta_2 = 0.2$, the problem is to find that point of minimum cost within the restricted area denoted by the shading in Fig. 3.2. This is in fact point P.

In mathematical terms, the general problem can be posed as follows. We wish to minimize a principal response

$$\eta_1 = f_1(x_1, x_2, \ldots, x_m) \tag{3.5}$$

subject to restraints on auxiliary responses of the form

$$\alpha_i \le \eta_i = f_i(x_1, x_2, \ldots, x_m) \le \beta_i, \qquad i = 1, 2, \ldots, n \tag{3.6}$$

and to restraints on the independent variables

$$a_k \le g_k(x_1, \ldots, x_m) \le b_k, \qquad k = 1, 2, \ldots, n, \tag{3.7}$$

where the g_k are given functions of the x_j.

In this form the mathematical problem is obviously much more general than any of the problems considered in Chapter 2 or Section 3.1. In Chapter 2 we were given the forms of the functions f_i, whereas here they are not known beforehand. No constraints were present in Chapter 2, although constraints could have been introduced simply by saying that certain areas were not available for the location of power plants or machines. No constraints were present in the problem in Section 3.1, but again constraints could have been introduced by restricting the area in which we are allowed to sink boreholes.

At first sight it might seem remarkable that we can say anything at all about the very general problem represented by (3.5) to (3.7). The key to the treatment is that we investigate only the local behavior of the functions. In Section 3.1 we assumed that an unknown function could be represented locally by a plane. Later we shall consider quadratic expressions. This is made possible by assuming that the functions are sufficiently smooth that they can be expanded locally in a certain number of terms of a Taylor series in several variables. Before considering the quadratic case, we present another engineering situation, which gives rise to similar optimization problems.

3.3   Design of Optical Lenses[4]

Comment : In this section we wish to show, without going into excessive mathematical detail, that the problem of designing optical lenses can be reduced to an optimization problem which is, mathematically, almost identical to the formulation given in Section 3.2. This is one of the very remarkable things about the mathematical description of natural phenomena—the same mathematical problem appears in widely different contexts.

For concreteness suppose we wish to design what is known as a *Cooke triplet*, illustrated in Fig. 3.3. The surfaces of the lens are supposed to be spherical, and there is symmetry about the axis of the system. The geometry

---

[4] This section was suggested by an entertaining article by D. P. Feder, Automatic Lens Design with a High-Speed Computer, *J. Opt. Soc. Am.*, **52**, 177–183 (1962). The term "boundary conditions" in this paper will be replaced by "inequality conditions" here. Also the term "parameters" is replaced by "characteristics," because these are the independent variables of the problem and it would confuse the reader accustomed to mathematical terminology if we used the word "parameters" in connection with independent variables.

The following work was also consulted: D. P. Feder, *J. Opt. Soc. Am.*, **47**, 902–912, 913–925 (1957); W. Brouwer, *Matrix Methods in Optical Instrument Design*, Benjamin, New York, 1964, (an interesting application of elementary matrix methods); and O. N. Stavroudis, Automatic Optical Design, in *Advances in Computers*, Vol. 5 (F. L. Alt and M. Rubinoff, eds.), Academic, New York, 1964, pp. 227–255 (a useful source of references to recent work).

It is clear that the subject is in an active state of development.

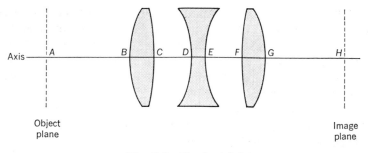

Axis

Object
plane

Image
plane

Fig. 3.3   Cooke triplet.

of the system can therefore be described by six radii of curvature and six separations. (There are eight points, A to H, but if the plane in which the object is assumed to lie is fixed, the paths of the rays are determined, so the position of the image plane cannot be chosen independent of A to G. There are only six independent separations involved.) The properties of the glass are usually specified by means of two parameters, the refractive index for light of a certain wavelength, and some measure of the dispersion or variation of the refractive index with wavelength.

We are now in a position to specify what we mean by the *characteristics* of the lens. These are the physical data the designer supplies to the optical shop so the lens can be made. In the case of the Cooke triplet they consist of 6 curvatures, 6 separations, and 3 refractive indexes and 3 measures of dispersion. For our purposes we lump these diverse quantities together and designate them by $x_1, x_2, \ldots, x_m$, or $\{x_k\}$ for short. These are the independent variables of the problem. In the design of the Cooke triplet there are 18 independent variables.

In order to recognize the dependent variables of the problem, let us consider an object point imaged by a lens at the focus. If the lens were perfect, all rays from the object would strike the image plane in a single point. Unfortunately the laws of optics do not work in this way. Even the light of a single wavelength does not possess a perfectly sharp image, but is subject to various errors, such as spherical aberration, coma, and astigmatism. If one traces from the object point a number of rays uniformly distributed in the entrance pupil, and plots their intersections with the image plane, one obtains an array of points known as a *spot diagram*, whose distribution is a measure of the monochromatic errors of the lens. These errors depend on the characteristics of the lens, and so constitute the dependent variables of our problem. They can be assigned numerical values in a variety of ways. In addition to the monochromatic errors, there may exist chromatic errors arising from the failure of the lens to bring all wavelengths equally to focus. Finally, even when all the points in the object plane are imaged sharply, the geometric properties of the object may be disturbed, owing to the presence of distortion in the lens.

If we are given a definite design, that is, a set of independent variables or characteristics, the errors in the resulting lens system can be analyzed by *ray tracing*. Conceptually this is very simple. We start at an object point which may be at a definite plane as in Fig. 3.3 or at infinity (in which case we imagine a bundle of rays coming in at a given angle with the axis). In either case the direction of the incoming ray is specified, and the point of intersection at the first lens surface can be calculated. Also the angle of incidence of the incoming ray (the angle it makes with the normal to the lens surface) can be calculated; call it i. Using Snell's law, the angle of refraction i' can be found. If the indices of refraction of the media on either side of the refracting surface are μ and μ', then i' is given by $\mu \sin i = \mu' \sin i'$. We can then calculate the point at which the ray hits the next refracting surface, and so on. Although the idea of ray tracing is exceedingly simple, the computational processes involved are annoyingly laborious. However, the process of ray tracing can be made completely routine, and automatic computers are ideally suited to this type of calculation. The reader interested in the details of the matters discussed in this paragraph and the next should consult the references given at the beginning of the section.

In the case of the Cooke triplet we might decide to trace four bundles of rays, one originating from the point at which the axis cuts the object plane, three originating from points in the object plane off the axis. Each bundle might be specified by tracing perhaps five rays in the same plane as the axis of the system and the point of origin, and two skew rays. To determine chromatic aberration, this must be done for two wavelengths of light. By analysis of individual rays we can produce numbers which measure the various image errors, monochromatic, chromatic, and distortion, associated with each bundle of rays and even, in some cases, associated with the individual rays. Even with the above relatively modest number of rays, the reader will appreciate that we quickly acquire a large collection of numbers representing errors. These are the dependent variables, because they depend on the characteristics of the system. We denote them by

$$\eta_i = f_i(x_1, x_2, \ldots, x_m), \qquad i = 1, 2, \ldots, n.$$

The $\{f_i\}$ are functions of the lens characteristics $\{x_k\}$. The problem is to choose the characteristics x_k so that the errors η_i are reduced to harmless magnitude.

Unfortunately there is somewhat more to the problem than this. It is not sufficient to merely make the η_i as small as possible. The components of the lens must not be allowed to become too thick, or too thin, or too close together. These conditions may be expressed in the form of inequalities. For example, suppose t is the thickness of one of the elements and t_{min} is the minimum allowable thickness. Defining $b = t - t_{min}$, it is clear that our condition is simply $b \geq 0$. It is also clear that b must be a function of the lens characteristics.

Another restriction is that the glass must be available from standard commercial catalogs. In practice the problem of selecting the glass is handled in the following way. We assume initially that the refractive index and dispersion properties of the available glasses can vary continuously within given limits. When the optimum design is obtained under this assumption, the nearest standard available glass is chosen, and the design is then reoptimized, using these fixed values of refractive index and dispersion.

The restrictions mentioned in the last two paragraphs are expressible as inequalities of the form

$$b_j(x_1, x_2, \ldots, x_m) \geq 0.$$

We are now in a position to state the problem of optical design in mathematical form. It is to select a set of independent variables $x_1, x_2, \ldots, x_m$ which reduces the aberrations

$$\eta_i = f_i(x_1, x_2, \ldots, x_m), \qquad i = 1, 2, \ldots, n \tag{3.8}$$

to as low values as possible, consistent with the conditions

$$b_j(x_1, x_2, \ldots, x_m) \geq 0. \tag{3.9}$$

There are usually more aberrations f_i than available design characteristics, so the best we can do is minimize some function of the aberrations. The phrase "as low values as possible" is too vague for quantitative work, and we have to give a more precise definition of what we mean by an optimum design. An obvious way of doing this is to define a merit function M by

$$M = w_1 f_1^2 + w_2 f_2^2 + \cdots + w_n f_n^2,$$

where $w_1, w_2, \ldots, w_n$ are a set of positive weighting factors which are at our disposal. The functions f_i are assumed to be real, so M is always positive. M will be zero if and only if all the f_i are zero. The smaller the aberrations f_i, the smaller M will be, and the greater the merit of the design. The weighting factors w_i can be adjusted so that greater importance is attached to the minimization of certain aberrations than others. In addition to the inequalities (3.9), it may be necessary to impose inequality conditions on the aberrations themselves (the η_i), so that, for example, the individual aberrations do not exceed certain amounts [compare the inequalities (3.6)].

In the present example the analytical forms of the functions f_i are assumed to be known. They depend on the equations for tracing rays through a lens, and they can be highly nonlinear. However, although the f_i are known analytically, it is often extremely laborious to evaluate the f_i and to obtain insight into their behavior, so in this sense the functions are unknown. The situation is the same as in Sections 3.1 and 3.2, except that whereas there the forms of the f_i had to be determined by laborious experimental work, here the forms have to be determined by laborious computation. The lens-design problem is also similar to the chemical engineering problem considered in

Section 3.2 by virtue of the inequalities (3.9) [compare (3.7)], which are awkward to handle.

In connection with lens design one may be tempted to ask: Why bother? Why not rely, in the future as in the past, on the skill and intuition of the lens designers?

Two answers of commercial interest are speed and cost. A large digital computer is roughly 10^6 times faster than a man with a desk computer and 10^4 times cheaper per operation. A factor of 10 often produces a revolution in human activities. Thus a motor car travels roughly 10 times faster than a man walking, and an aircraft travels roughly 10 times faster than a motor car. Small wonder that computers are revolutionizing lens design. It is possible to design on a computer, in a matter of hours, a lens that would formerly have taken months. Moreover, it is possible to do this using a much more sophisticated design method.

An answer of equal importance is that, by relieving the designer of the drudgery of numerical work, the computer allows him to concentrate his energy on design. In fact, the more aspects of the design problem that can be taken care of by a computer, the more efficient the use that can be made of the lens designers. The optimization approach via computer is a great stimulus to creative thinking.

The reader who wishes to pursue this topic further, and see some actual examples of lens design by computer, is referred to the article by Feder.[5]

3.4   Analysis of the General Second-Degree Surface

Mathematics Used: Conic sections; rotation of axes; second-degree surfaces. Mention of the reduction of quadratic forms to canonical form.

Comment: The importance of scaling in the method of steepest descent is noted.

Before considering other aspects of the basic optimization problem, as such, we deal with some technical mathematical problems that arise in connection with the general second-degree surface. We first indicate how this surface comes into the problem. In Section 3.1 we used a Taylor series to expand $f(x, y)$ around a point (x_0, y_0), including only the linear terms. If we include up to the quadratic terms, we obtain

$$f(x, y) \approx f_0 + (x - x_0)f_x + (y - y_0)f_y + \tfrac{1}{2}(x - x_0)^2 f_{xx}$$
$$+ (x - x_0)(y - y_0)f_{xy} + \tfrac{1}{2}(y - y_0)^2 f_{yy}, \qquad (3.10)$$

where the coefficients are all evaluated at the point (x_0, y_0). This leads us to examine the general surface in two variables:

$$z = ax^2 + 2hxy + by^2 + 2gx + 2fy + c, \qquad (3.11)$$

[5] D. P. Feder, *J. Opt. Soc. Am.*, **47**, 902–925 (1957).

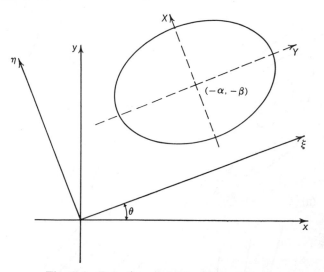

Fig. 3.4   Rotation and translation of axes.

where the surface is visualized geometrically by assuming that x and y are horizontal, and z is measured upward.

The clue to the analysis of this surface lies in transforming the equations to a new set of axes, ξ and η, rotated through an angle θ with respect to the x and y axes, and such that the resulting form of the equation has no cross term in $\xi\eta$. In order to do this (Fig. 3.4) we set

$$x = \xi \cos \theta - \eta \sin \theta, \qquad y = \xi \sin \theta + \eta \cos \theta.$$

If we substitute this in (3.11), we obtain a quadratic in ξ and η in which the coefficient of $\xi\eta$ is

$$(b - a) \sin 2\theta + 2h \cos 2\theta,$$

and this vanishes if we choose θ so that

$$\tan 2\theta = \frac{2h}{a - b}$$

We then have

$$z = a_1\xi^2 + b_1\eta^2 + 2g_1\xi + 2f_1\eta + c, \tag{3.12}$$

where the precise forms of a_1, b_1, g_1, and f_1 will not be important, because we shall be interested mainly in the qualitative properties of the results. We now distinguish two possibilities (we introduce new symbols as necessary).

1. If $a_1 \neq 0$ and $b_1 \neq 0$, we write (3.12) in the form

$$z = a_1(\xi + \alpha)^2 + b_1(\eta + \beta)^2 + c_1,$$

and the further substitutions $X = \xi + \alpha$, and $Y = \eta + \beta$ give a relation of the form

$$z = AX^2 + BY^2 + k. \tag{3.13}$$

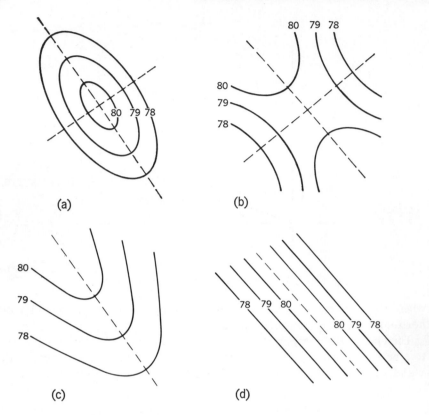

Fig. 3.5 Level surfaces generated by a second-degree equation in two variables. The numbers represent arbitrary levels.

2. If $a_1 = 0$ and $b_1 \neq 0$, we write (3.13) in the form

$$z = b_1(\eta + \beta)^2 + 2g_1(\xi + \alpha),$$

and on introducing X and Y, as before, this gives

$$z = p(Y^2 + 4\gamma X). \tag{3.14}$$

The case $a_1 \neq 0$ and $b_1 = 0$ is still another possibility, but it need not be considered separately.

These are the only possibilities, since if $a_1 = b_1 = 0$ this would imply that $a = h = b = 0$ in (3.11). We now set z equal to a given constant and consider the forms of the corresponding curves in the XY plane. We assume the reader is familiar with the following results.

1. If $A > 0$ and $B > 0$ in (3.13) and the constant value of z is greater than k, (3.13) represents an ellipse. [If $z < k$, there are no points (X, Y) that satisfy (3.13).]

2. If $A > 0$ and $B < 0$ in (3.13) or vice versa, and $z \neq k$, the curve represents a hyperbola. If $z = k$, the curve degenerates into a pair of straight lines.

3. If $\gamma \neq 0$ in (3.14), the curve is a parabola.

4. If $\gamma = 0$ in (3.14), the curve is a pair of parallel straight lines if $z/p > 0$.

If z is varied, we obtain a series of curves in the XY plane. On returning to xy coordinates (see Fig. 3.4), the four possibilities give families of curves such as those illustrated in Fig. 3.5. These are precisely analogous to the level surfaces discussed from a special point of view in Section 2.5, which were in fact an illustration of case a, Fig. 3.5. The importance of the present considerations is that we have shown that there are precisely four possibilities, and no more, for the effect of second-order terms on the local behavior of the function $z = f(x, y)$, provided the general function $f(x, y)$ is twice-differentiable in x and y.

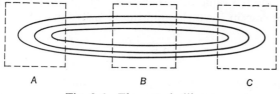

$$A \qquad\qquad B \qquad\qquad C$$

Fig. 3.6   Elongated ellipses.

In a sense, cases c and d in Fig. 3.5 are not distinct from a and b, but can be regarded as limiting forms. Thus if the ellipses in Fig. 3.5a are elongated as in Fig. 3.6, and we are working in the dashed area B, we are essentially in the case of Fig. 3.5d, and if we are working at some distance from the center of the ellipses, as in Fig. 3.6, areas A and C, then we are, in effect, working on the rising ridges of Fig. 3.5c.

We next discuss a point made in Section 3.1, that the method of steepest ascent (or descent) introduced in Section 3.1 depends on the scales used on the xy axes. It would not have been very illuminating to have discussed this in connection with the geophysical-exploration problem considered in Section 3.1, because a foot to the east is the same in distance as a foot to the north, and it would have seemed absurd to use, say, a unit of a foot to the east and a meter to the north. However, in the chemical engineering problem discussed in Section 3.2 (Fig. 3.2), the scales are for pressure and temperature, and it is quite natural that one person might use, say, psi and °F, and another dynes/cm² and °C. The reason the scales are important can be seen from the following analysis. Suppose we are investigating the surface $z = f(x, y)$ near the point (x_0, y_0). Then the local plane is given by

$$z \approx f_0 + (x - x_0)(f_x)_0 + (y - y_0)(f_y)_0.$$

We can find the direction of steepest descent by the same procedure as that of Section 3.1; we set $x - x_0 = a \cos \theta$ and $y - y_0 = a \sin \theta$, where a is a

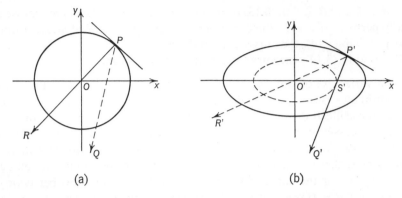

(a)   (b)

Fig. 3.7   Directions of steepest descent for different scales.

constant, and find the value of θ such that $\partial z/\partial\theta = 0$. The result is that the line of steepest descent has a slope in the xy plane given by

$$\tan\theta = \frac{(f_y)_0}{(f_x)_0}. \tag{3.15}$$

[This is simply a generalization of (3.3).] The slope in the xy plane of the tangent to the level surface $z =$ constant, passing through (x_0, y_0), is given by $dz/dx = 0$ at this point, or

$$\left(\frac{\partial f}{\partial x}\right)_0 + \left(\frac{\partial f}{\partial y}\right)_0\left(\frac{dy}{dx}\right)_0 = 0; \tag{3.16}$$

that is,

$$\left(\frac{dy}{dx}\right)_0 = -\frac{(f_x)_0}{(f_y)_0}.$$

We see that the product of the two slopes in (3.15) and (3.16) is -1; that is, the two lines are perpendicular. This means that the direction of steepest ascent (or descent) is perpendicular to the tangent to the level surface at any given point.

From this result it is easy to see by inspection of typical level-surface plots that the direction of steepest descent depends upon the scales. Thus if the level surfaces are given by the circles

$$z = x^2 + y^2, \tag{3.17}$$

the line of steepest descent must pass through the center of the circles, since a line perpendicular to a tangent of a circle is a radius of the circle. Suppose now that we decide to measure the scales in different units by introducing $X = (\sqrt{2})x$, $Y = y/\sqrt{2}$, so that the equation of the level surfaces in the XY plane is, from (3.17),

$$z = \tfrac{1}{2}X^2 + 2Y^2. \tag{3.18}$$

At a point like P' in Fig. 3.7b, the direction of steepest descent is perpendicular to the tangent at P', and this clearly goes nowhere near the center of the ellipse. In fact, the method of steepest descent would lead us to point S'. Quantitatively, consider the point $(1, 1)$ in the xy plane. The corresponding point in the XY plane is given by $X = \sqrt{2}$ and $Y = 1/\sqrt{2}$. From (3.18), using the notation of (3.15), and X, Y coordinates, $f_X = X$ and $f_Y = 4Y$, so the slope of the line of steepest descent in the XY plane is $4Y/X = 2$, and the equation of this line is

$$Y - \frac{1}{\sqrt{2}} = 2(X - \sqrt{2}).$$

In x, y coordinates this is the line

$$y = 4x - 3$$

shown by PQ in Fig. 3.7a.

In a practical case, the scales on the different axes are fixed by the judgment of the engineer. Thus in a chemical engineering example he might decide to change the temperature by 10°F and the pressure by 10 psi. In judging the amount by which the factors should be varied, the engineer is presumably attempting, subconsciously, to get as close as possible to circular level surfaces, for which the function is symmetric with respect to the variables. It is clear from this discussion that elongated ellipses, such as those in Fig. 3.6, will prove troublesome when applying the method of steepest descent if we are trying to find the center of the system. It is an important general principle that the information available at any stage should be used to adjust scales so that the level surfaces are approximately circular. Skillful choice of the amounts by which factors are varied can considerably reduce the work necessary to locate optima.

The reduction of the general second-degree equation (3.11) to the canonical forms (3.13) and (3.14) is, of course, a special case of the reduction of a quadratic form in n variables, instead of two:

$$z = \sum_{i=1}^{n} \sum_{j=1}^{n} a_{ij}x_i x_j + \sum_{i=1}^{n} b_i x_i + c. \tag{3.19}$$

We mention that this is reduced to canonical form by a standard procedure dealt with in undergraduate linear-algebra courses. The clue here is the remark made previously that the key to the analysis of the second-order equation (3.11) is to rotate the axes so that the coefficient of the cross term $\xi\eta$ in (3.11) is zero. In the general case (3.19), the quadratic terms can be represented, in matrix notation, by

$$\mathbf{x}^T\mathbf{A}\mathbf{x},$$

where $\mathbf{A}$ is the symmetrical $n \times n$ matrix whose (i, j)th element is a_{ij} and $\mathbf{x}$ is a column vector whose ith element is x_i. We wish to introduce a rotation of axes, which means, algebraically, a change of variable $\mathbf{x} = \mathbf{C}\boldsymbol{\xi}$, such that the resulting quadratic form

$$\boldsymbol{\xi}^T(\mathbf{C}^T\mathbf{A}\mathbf{C})\boldsymbol{\xi}$$

has no cross terms; that is, $\mathbf{C}^T\mathbf{A}\mathbf{C}$ is diagonal. This is accomplished by finding the eigenvalues and eigenvectors of $\mathbf{A}$. We shall not require the details of these results in subsequent developments.

3.5   A Straightforward Numerical Example

Mathematics Used: Method of steepest descent initially, followed by quadratic surface fitting in the neighborhood of the stationary point.

Comment: Determination from experimental data of the optimum values of two parameters in a prescribed function. The importance of statistical analysis is emphasized.

The general idea we now wish to illustrate by a numerical example is that if we are trying to determine the form of an unknown function, then, when we are far away from a hump or a saddle point or a ridge, we should use the method of steepest descent (or ascent). When we are in a region in which the behavior of the surface is like any of those shown in Fig. 3.5 (a problem we examine later is to decide if we are in this situation), we should fit a second-degree surface, to explore the nature of the surface in the neighborhood of the optimum. One of the objects of discussing a numerical example is to illustrate some of the technical points that arise in trying to apply this procedure.

The problem we shall consider is the following.[6] An experiment that depended on an integer r was repeated twice for each of $r = 1, 2, \ldots, 6$, with the results shown in Table 3.1. It is thought that these results can be predicted experimentally by an analytical expression of the form

$$(\eta_r)_{\text{theor}} = G(\theta_1, \theta_2; r), \tag{3.20}$$

[6] The numerical results in this section, including those in Fig. 3.9, are taken from G. E. P. Box and G. A. Coutie, Application of Digital Computers in the Exploration of Functional Relationships, *Proc. Inst. Elec. Engrs.* (*London*), **B103S**, 100–107 (1956). Three points should be mentioned: (1) We do not explain the precise origin of the numbers, which is not important from the present point of view. In fact, the original problem can be solved more conveniently by other methods. (2) There is no claim that the exact sequence of steps in the above paper is the best possible. Of course, in making this comment we are to some extent taking advantage of hindsight. It is always difficult to judge the best procedure before the answer is known. (3) We do not deal exhaustively with the statistical details, which form an important part of the analysis in practical situations. For this see the above paper and Chapter XI by G. E. P. Box in *The Design and Analysis of Industrial Experiments* (O. L. Davies, ed.), Oliver & Boyd, London, 1956.

TABLE 3.1

r	1	2	3	4	5	6
Experimental η_r	$\begin{cases}19.2 \\ 14.0\end{cases}$	$\begin{matrix}14.4 \\ 24.0\end{matrix}$	$\begin{matrix}42.3 \\ 30.8\end{matrix}$	$\begin{matrix}42.1 \\ 40.5\end{matrix}$	$\begin{matrix}40.7 \\ 46.4\end{matrix}$	$\begin{matrix}27.1 \\ 22.3\end{matrix}$
Mean $\eta_r = \bar{\eta}_r$	16.6	19.2	36.6	41.3	43.6	24.7

where θ_1 and θ_2 are unknown parameters we wish to determine and G is known but complicated.[7] The important thing about the function G from the present point of view is that if we are given θ_1, θ_2, and r, we can use a computer to find the numerical value of $G(\theta_1, \theta_2; r)$. In order to determine θ_1 and θ_2 we adopt the criterion that they should be chosen so as to minimize the sum of the squares of the deviations of the theoretical values of η_r given by (3.20) from the mean experimental values $\bar{\eta}_r$ given in Table 3.1; that is, we wish to minimize

$$M(\theta_1, \theta_2) = \sum_{r=1}^{6} [G(\theta_1, \theta_2; r) - \bar{\eta}_r]^2.$$

This quantity corresponds to the optimization criterion or cost function discussed earlier.

From an inspection of the particular form which seemed reasonable to the experimenter, together with the above experimental results, it was guessed that approximate values of the θ's were $\theta_1 = \theta_2 = 1.19$, and that it would be reasonable to use the method of steepest descent by varying θ_1 and θ_2 by ± 0.01. Accordingly, M was evaluated for the five combinations of θ_1 and θ_2 shown in Fig. 3.8, with the results shown at the appropriate points of the mesh. The advantage of using five points instead of three, as in the simple application of the method of steepest descent in Section 3.1, is that this provides a check on the assumptions, as we proceed to show. Although we

---

[7] In the specific case considered here, the original problem was concerned with the analysis of a chemical reaction $A \rightarrow B$, $B \rightarrow C$, governed by simultaneous linear differential equations

$$\frac{da}{dt} = -k_1 a, \qquad \frac{db}{dt} = k_1 a - k_2 b, \qquad \frac{dc}{dt} = k_2 b,$$

with $a = 100$, $b = c = 0$, at $t = 0$. The quantities η_r in the text are the experimental values of b for $t = 10, 20, 40, 80, 160$, and 320 minutes, for $r = 1, \ldots, 6$, respectively. On solving the preceding equations we see that

$$b = 100(k_1 - k_2)^{-1}[\exp(-k_2 t) - \exp(-k_1 t)], \qquad k_1 \neq k_2.$$

The k_i are related to the θ_i in the text by $\theta_i = 3 + \log k_i$, $i = 1, 2$, where the log is taken to the base 10. This information is given for the reader who is curious about the precise details of the original problem, but it is irrelevant for understanding the point we wish to illustrate—the way in which the θ_i can be determined by the particular method under consideration. It is, of course, also irrelevant to point out that this particular problem can be solved more efficiently or effectively by use of a different method.

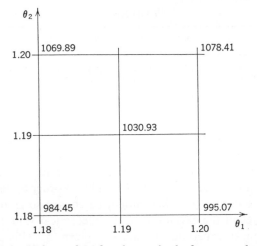

Fig. 3.8   Values of M for the method of steepest descent.

are ultimately interested in the plane that gives the local behavior of the data in Fig. 3.8, we try to fit a second-order surface

$$z = ax^2 + 2hxy + by^2 + 2gx + 2fy + c \qquad (3.21)$$

to these results. We see immediately that $c = 1030.93$ and, assuming we are working in terms of units of 0.01 in θ_1 and θ_2 (that is, $\theta_1 = 0.01x$ and $\theta_2 = 0.01y$),

$$a + 2h + b + 2g + 2f = 1078.41 - 1030.93 = 47.48,$$
$$a - 2h + b - 2g + 2f = 1069.89 - 1030.93 = 38.96,$$
$$a + 2h + b - 2g - 2f = 984.85 - 1030.93 = -46.08,$$
$$a - 2h + b + 2g - 2f = 995.07 - 1030.93 = -35.86.$$

These are four equations in the four unknowns $(a + b)$, h, g, and f, and the solution is found to be

$$a + b = 1.13, \qquad 2h = -0.43, \qquad 2g = 4.69, \qquad 2f = 42.10.$$

Since there are six unknowns in (3.21) and only five experimental results, it is not possible to determine all the constants $a, \ldots, c$, and this is reflected in the fact that we determine only $a + b$, not a and b separately. However, we assume that the merit function has a straightforward bowl-shaped behavior in the neighborhood of the minimum, which means that the contours of constant merit are ellipses and a and b are both positive. This means that if $a + b$ is small, both a and b are small. The above results then show that a, b, and h are much less than f and g, so that quadratic terms are not important in this region. Hence we consider the plane

$$z = 4.69x + 42.10y + 1030.93.$$

The line of steepest descent has a value given by (3.15), or

$$\tan \theta = 42.10/4.69 = 8.98.$$

The next question is how far we should move along the line of steepest descent. We note first that

$$z = a(x^2 + y^2) + 2gx + 2fy + c$$

represents a circle with center $(-g/a, -f/a)$. If we were to use the method of steepest descent, starting from the origin $(0, 0)$, we should reach the center by moving a distance equal to the radius of the circle, that is, $(g^2 + f^2)^{1/2}/a$. By a crude analogy, when working with elliptical level surfaces we might expect that the distance we should move in the direction of steepest descent would be something of the order of $2(|g| + |f|)/(a + b)$, where, for simplicity, we have used $|g| + |f|$ instead of $(g^2 + f^2)^{1/2}$ and $\frac{1}{2}(a + b)$ instead of a. (This estimate could obviously be refined, but there is little point in doing so here.) Since it is safer to underestimate the required distance, we try, in the above example,

$$\frac{g + f}{2(a + b)} = \frac{23.4}{2(1.13)} \approx 20$$

in the units of x and y, which means a step of 0.20 in the units of θ_1 and θ_2. We use a step of 0.20 in θ_2, and, because the slope of the line of steepest descent is given by $\tan \theta = 8.98$, this means $0.20/8.98 = 0.0223$ in θ_1. The results obtained are given in Table 3.2 and illustrated graphically in Fig. 3.9a.

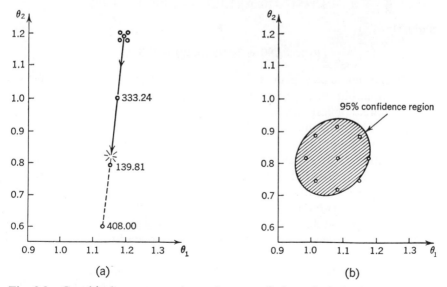

Fig. 3.9 Graphical representation of some of the calculations: (a) steepest descent; (b) local exploration.

TABLE 3.2

Step	Original	1	2	3
θ_1	1.1900	1.1677	1.1454	1.1231
θ_2	1.1900	0.9900	0.7900	0.5900
M	1030.93	333.24	139.81	408.00

We use interpolation to find the position of the minimum. On the line of steepest descent the cost function M can be considered a function of a single parameter λ, measuring distance along this line. The local behavior of M will be assumed to be quadratic in λ, $M = \alpha\lambda^2 + \beta\lambda + \gamma$. The unit in which λ is measured is immaterial. Since we consider values of M at three points equally spaced along the line of steepest descent, we can take $\lambda = +1, 0$, and -1 for the points corresponding to steps 1, 2, and 3 in Table 3.2. This gives $\gamma = 139.81$ and

$$\alpha + \beta = 333.24 - 139.81 = 193.43,$$
$$\alpha - \beta = 408.00 - 139.81 = 268.19.$$

Hence $\alpha = 230.8$, $\beta = -37.38$, and the minimum is given by $dM/d\lambda = 0$; that is, $\lambda = -\frac{1}{2}\beta/\alpha \approx 0.08$. The values of θ_1 and θ_2 corresponding to a given value of λ vary linearly with λ. Thus, from Table 3.2 we see that $\lambda = 0$ and 1 correspond to $\theta_1 = 1.1677$ and 1.1454, respectively, so that the value of θ_1 corresponding to $\lambda = 0.08$ is given by

$$\theta_1 = 1.1454 + (0.08)(1.1677 - 1.1454) = 1.147.$$

Similarly,

$$\theta_2 \approx 0.790 + (0.08)(0.20) = 0.806.$$

These results could be improved slightly by including the original point in the interpolation, but the improvement is probably not very significant.

Two more applications of steepest descent were made in the original paper, reaching a minimum of $M = 73.79$ at $\theta_1 = 1.0785$ and $\theta_2 = 0.8168$. At this point it was found, using the method discussed above in connection with equation (3.21), that the quadratic terms in (3.21) were becoming important, since the neighborhood of the minimum was being approached. It was necessary to abandon the one-dimensional method of steepest descent, and to make a two-dimensional exploration of the nature of the local extremum. This was done by using a nine-point design centered at the values of θ_1 and θ_2 just quoted, with eight points on a circle of radius 0.1 as shown in Fig. 3.10, which gives the results obtained. The reason for choosing a radius of 0.1 will be explained below. We now have nine results from which we wish to deduce the six constants in the second-degree equation (3.21). These constants were determined by least squares, and this led to the following

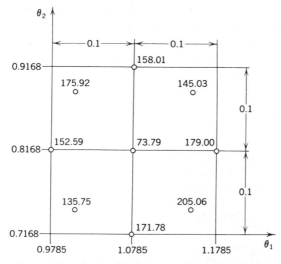

Fig. 3.10 Results for the second-degree surface.

equation, where a change of $\pm\sqrt{2}$ in x or y corresponds to a change of ± 0.1 in θ_1 or θ_2:

$$z = 45.87x^2 - 25.05xy + 45.42y^2 + 9.47x - 4.92y + 74.10. \quad (3.22)$$

The sum of squares of discrepancies between the values in Fig. 3.10 and the values given by this equation is 0.2, which means that the fit is very good. (This value may appear to be absurdly small, but it does seem to be correct. It is important to realize that this good fit simply means that the quadratic expression (3.22) is an excellent representation of M in the region involved in Fig. 3.10. Although M involves the experimental results, the good fit tells us nothing about whether the experimental results are consistent with the theory. This requires statistical analysis, as discussed later.) The minimum point is obtained by solving the equations found by setting $\partial z/\partial x = \partial z/\partial y = 0$. This gives

$$x = -0.096, \qquad y = 0.027.$$

Hence
$$\theta_1 = 1.0785 - (0.096)(0.0707) = 1.072,$$
$$\theta_2 = 0.8168 + (0.027)(0.0707) = 0.819. \qquad (3.23)$$

These are the final estimates of θ_1 and θ_2.

Finally we discuss an important aspect of the subject which has scarcely been mentioned so far. The original experimental results were subject to error. We have obtained θ_1 and θ_2 on the basis of an assumed theoretical representation for predicting the experimental results. The theoretical predictions do not, of course, give the experimental results exactly, since we are fitting only two parameters. This is why M cannot be reduced to zero. However, we can ask whether the discrepancies between the theoretical and experimental values are comparable to what we should expect in the light of the errors in the original experimental results. A detailed discussion requires fairly advanced knowledge of statistics and lies outside the scope of under-graduate mathematics. Thus in the remainder of this section we depart from the policy adopted in the rest of this book—that both the mathematical and engineering exposition should be reasonably self-explanatory. However, the fact that the reliability of the results can be established by statistical analysis (although outside the scope of this book) is so important that we quote some of the results.

If n is the number of points (six in this case) and p is the number of param-eters to be fitted (in this case the parameters are θ_1 and θ_2, so $p = 2$), it can be shown that the expected value of

$$s_1^2 = \frac{M(\theta_1, \theta_2)}{n - p} = \frac{1}{n - p} \sum_{r=1}^{6} [G(\theta_1, \theta_2; r) - \bar{\eta}_r]^2 \qquad (3.24)$$

is approximately equal to σ^2, the variance of the original experimental results. In this equation $M(\theta_1, \theta_2)$ is the minimum value of M, namely 74 in the above example, so that in this case $s_1^2 = 74/4 = 18.5$. The point of including repeated experiments in Table 3.1 is that it enables us to estimate σ^2. If we denote the estimated value of σ^2 by s_2^2, and the two values of η_r for any value of r by η_{1r} and η_{2r} [so that $\bar{\eta}_r = \frac{1}{2}(\eta_{1r} + \eta_{2r})$], then

$$s_2^2 = \frac{1}{12} \sum_{r=1}^{6} [(\eta_{1r} - \bar{\eta}_r)^2 + (\eta_{2r} - \bar{\eta}_r)^2]$$

$$= \frac{1}{24} \sum_{r=1}^{6} (\eta_{1r} - \eta_{2r})^2 = 12.9.$$

If we denote the number of degrees of freedom of this result by ν_2, then, since there are 12 results and 6 parameters $\bar{\eta}_r$ are estimated, we have $\nu_2 = 12 - 6 = 6$. We have said that s_1^2 is approximately σ^2, and σ^2 is estimated by s_2^2, so s_1^2 and s_2^2 should be approximately equal. This can be tested by referring s_1^2/s_2^2 to a table of the F distribution with $(n - p)$ and ν_2 degrees of freedom. In our case $s_1^2/s_2^2 = 18.5/12.9 = 1.43$, with 4 and 6 degrees of freedom. The corresponding 5% value of F is 9.15, so the actually observed difference between s_1^2 and s_2^2 is certainly not significant.

In this example, if we had been interested only in estimating θ_1 and θ_2, we need not have obtained the results in Fig. 3.10 and fitted a second-degree surface, since the argument in the last paragraph could have been used to show that the result $M = 73.79$ at $\theta_1 = 1.0785$ and $\theta_2 = 0.8168$, obtained by steepest descent alone, gave a fit consistent with the experi-mental data. However, the second-degree surface enables us to obtain a more detailed idea of the accuracy of the results, by the following argument.

1. The estimates s_1^2 and s_2^2 are of comparable magnitude, and they can be used to give an improved estimate of the experimental error:

$$s^2 = \frac{(n - p)s_1^2 + v_2 s_2^2}{n - p + v_2}$$

with $v = n - p + v_2$ degrees of freedom. In our case we find $s^2 = 15.1$, with 10 degrees of freedom.

2. It can be shown that the variances and covariances of the estimates of θ_1 and θ_2 are given approximately by the 2×2 matrix $V^{-1}s^2$, where V is the matrix whose (i, j)th element is given by

$$v_{ij} = \frac{\partial^2 M(\theta_1, \theta_2)}{2\partial\theta_i \, \partial\theta_j}, \qquad i, j = 1, 2.$$

Thus an estimate of the standard error of θ_i is given by $s\sqrt{V_{ii}}$, where V_{ii} is the ith diagonal element of V^{-1}. In our case M is represented accurately near its minimum by (3.22). Using this expression for M, it is found that

$$V = \begin{bmatrix} 9174 & -2505 \\ -2505 & 9084 \end{bmatrix}, \qquad V^{-1} = 10^{-6} \begin{bmatrix} 117.9 & 32.5 \\ 32.5 & 119.0 \end{bmatrix},$$

so for both θ_1 and θ_2 the standard error is approximately

$$[(15.1)(118)(10^{-6})]^{1/2} = 0.042.$$

3. It can be shown that the 95% confidence region in the $\theta_1\theta_2$ plane, which includes the true values 19 times out of 20, is given approximately by the inequality

$$\frac{1}{2} \sum_{i=1}^{p} \sum_{j=1}^{p} v_{ij}(\theta_i - \theta_i^*)(\theta_j - \theta_j^*) \leq ps^2 F(p, v), \qquad (3.25)$$

where p is the number of unknowns, two in our case, and θ_1^* and θ_2^* are the estimated values of θ_1 and θ_2 [given, in our case, by (3.23)]. Also, $F(p, v)$ is the 5% probability point in the F distribution with p and v degrees of freedom. In our case we require $F(2, 10)$, which is 4.10, and s^2 is 15.1 from step 1, so the corresponding value of $ps^2 F(p, v)$ is about 120. This means that in the 95% confidence region in the $\theta_1\theta_2$ plane, the value of M is less than about $74 + 120 \approx 190$. (This is a very rough estimate.) When fitting a second-degree surface, it is convenient to choose the points of the nine-point design shown in Fig. 3.10 so that eight of the points lie near the boundary of this region, the other being at the center of the region. Enough preliminary information is available from the steepest descent results (such as the data in Fig. 3.9a, for example) to fix some points where M has a value of 190. The radius of the appropriate octagon can be deduced and this is in fact the way in which the radius of 0.1 in Fig. 3.10 was determined. The actual figures confirm that this was indeed suitable, and further confirmation is provided by the 95% confidence region determined later from (3.25) and shown shaded in Fig. 3.9b.

3.6   A Stationary Plane Ridge in Three Variables[8]

Mathematics Used: Reduction of a quadratic form to a sum of squares.

Comment: Contrary to what one might expect, a single-humped optimum often does not exist in many engineering situations. An example is discussed in which the techniques already developed in this chapter are used to reduce the number of independent variables.

In this section we shall use the terminology of Section 3.2—that is, we phrase our descriptions in terms of an optimization problem in chemical engineering. We shall attempt to extremize some "response" such as the cost of a product per unit weight. The term *response* corresponds to the term *cost function* used in Chapter 2.

The reader may have gained the impression from the discussion so far that the nicely behaved single-hump set of level surfaces, as in Fig. 3.5a, is the one that usually occurs in practice. Intuition may suggest that the response can be expected to fall off in all directions going away from the optimum value. That such a generalization is entirely inadequate in practice is found as soon as we begin to plot actual level surfaces determined by calculation or experiment. It is then clear that ridge systems such as those in Fig. 3.5c and d occur frequently. The reason for the occurrence of such systems can be seen when it is remembered that, for instance, when we are considering a chemical reaction, factors such as temperature, time, pressure, and concentration are regarded as "natural" variables only because they happen to be conveniently measured separately. A more fundamental variable not directly measured, but in terms of which the behavior of the system could be described more economically (for example, frequency of a particular type of molecular collision), will often be a function of two or more natural variables. For this reason, many combinations of natural variables may correspond to the best level of a fundamental variable.

To give a simple (mathematical) example, suppose that in the region of interest the response can be described in terms of a fundamental variable w given by the product of two measured variables x and y, $w = xy$. Thus the response η is a function of w, say, $\eta = f(w)$, as in Fig. 3.11a. If the experimenter did not know that the system could be adequately described in terms of the compound variable $w = xy$, and carried out experiments in which he varied x and y separately, he would obtain the level surfaces for η shown in Fig. 3.11b, which was constructed from Fig. 3.11a in an obvious way.

---

[8] This section, including Figs. 3.11, 3.13, and 3.14, is based on G. E. P. Box, The Exploration and Exploitation of Response Surfaces: Some General Considerations and Examples, *Biometrics*, **10**, 16–60 (1954). This paper gives a clear exposition of several interesting and important general points. A much more detailed technical treatment of the main example is given by G. E. P. Box in Chapter XI of *The Design and Analysis of Industrial Experiments* (O. L. Davies, ed.), Oliver & Boyd, London, 1956.

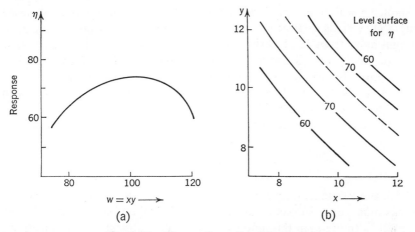

Fig. 3.11   Generation of a ridge system.

It should be emphasized that any method for exploring level surfaces that varies only one factor at a time will be almost valueless when the response surfaces are in the form of a rising or falling ridge (Fig. 3.5c), except possibly as a preliminary procedure. Thus if the experimenter starts at point A in Fig. 3.12 and performs a series of experiments in which x is varied, keeping y

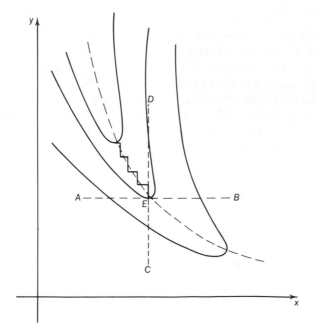

Fig. 3.12   Inadequacy of varying one factor at a time.

constant, he will be led to point E. Experiments in which y is now varied along CD, x being kept at the value for E, will lead to a point almost indistinguishable from E. The existence of the ridge will be concealed. If these two steps, first varying x and then y, are repeated a number of times, we find that we progress very slowly along the ridge, as illustrated by the zigzag line in Fig. 3.12. These difficulties can also, of course, occur in connection with the five-point design of Fig. 3.8.

We now consider a specific example, a chemical reaction of the type

$$A + B \rightarrow C \quad \text{followed by } A + C \rightarrow D,$$

in which two reactants form a mixture of C and D. The object was to obtain the maximum for C subject to the condition that the yield of D should not exceed 20% (more than this amount would cause difficulty in purification). The quantity of B used was kept constant throughout, the factors varied being the temperature T, the concentration c of A, and the time of reaction t. Preliminary experiments led to the levels $T = 167°C$, $c = 27.5\%$, and $t = 6.5$ hours, and indicated that T should be varied by $\pm 5°C$, c by $\pm 2.5\%$, and t by ± 1.5 hours. We introduce standardized variables:

$$x_1 = \frac{T - 167}{5}, \qquad x_2 = \frac{c - 27.5}{2.5}, \qquad x_3 = \frac{t - 6.5}{1.5}. \qquad (3.26)$$

The fact that there are now three variables instead of two, as in the examples discussed previously in this chapter, does not make any difference in principle, although the technical details (which will not be discussed here but can be found in the references) are of course more complicated.

Experimental results discussed in detail in the references give, in a way similar to that discussed above in connection with a two-variable example leading to (3.22), the following fitted second-degree surface relating the yield (or response) η and the independent variables

$$\eta = 57.71 + 1.94x_1 + 0.91x_2 + 1.07x_3 - 1.54x_1^2 - 0.26x_2^2$$
$$-0.68x_3^2 - 3.09x_1x_2 - 2.19x_1x_3 - 1.21x_2x_3. \qquad (3.27$$

This surface is next reduced to standard form. (Remarks were made about this problem at the end of Section 3.4.[9] Standard automatic computer routines are available for this procedure.) It is found that if we set

$$\mathbf{x} = \mathbf{AX} + \mathbf{b}, \qquad \mathbf{X} = \mathbf{A}^{-1}(\mathbf{x} - \mathbf{b}), \qquad (3.28)$$

---

[9] See also O. L. Davies (ed.), *The Design and Analysis of Industrial Experiments*, Oliver & Boyd, London, 1956.

where

$$\mathbf{x} = \begin{bmatrix} x_1 \\ x_2 \\ x_3 \end{bmatrix}, \quad \mathbf{X} = \begin{bmatrix} X_1 \\ X_2 \\ X_3 \end{bmatrix}, \quad \mathbf{b} = \begin{bmatrix} 0.061 \\ 0.215 \\ 0.499 \end{bmatrix},$$

$$\mathbf{A} = \begin{bmatrix} 0.7511 & 0.3066 & 0.5848 \\ 0.4884 & 0.3383 & -0.8044 \\ 0.4443 & -0.8897 & -0.1044 \end{bmatrix},$$

and, in fact, $\mathbf{A}^{-1} = \mathbf{A}^T$, then (3.27) becomes

$$\eta = 58.4 - 3.19X_1^2 - 0.07X_2^2 + 0.78X_3^2. \tag{3.29}$$

If X_1, X_2, and X_3 vary in the range ± 1, the response is given approximately by

$$\eta = 58.4 - 3.19X_1^2.$$

Clearly the maximum response is given by $X_1 = 0$. From (3.28) we see that

$$X_1 = 0.7511(x_1 - 0.061) + 0.4884(x_2 - 0.215) + 0.4443(x_3 - 0.499).$$

Expressing this in terms of the original variables by means of (3.26), we see that the relation $X_1 = 0$ is

$$0.1502T + 0.1954c + 0.2962t = 32.76. \tag{3.30}$$

The statement that from (3.29) the yield η is a maximum when $X_1 = 0$ is equivalent to the statement that any combination of T, c, and t lying on the plane (3.30) will maximize the yield.

The level surfaces are approximately planes, as illustrated graphically in Fig. 3.13. Over the range considered, the three variables T, c, and t are roughly "compensating." If we have a process working at one point on the maximum-yield plane and wish to change one or two of the factor levels without changing the maximum yield, this can be done by changing the remaining variable or variables so that (3.30) is satisfied. In Fig. 3.14 we have drawn the maximum plane of Fig. 3.13.

The existence of ridges of the type illustrated by this example may throw important light on the fundamental mechanism of the process. Also, they are extremely important, if they exist, since they provide the experimenter with a number of alternative processes he can use, some of which may be cheaper or more convenient than others. In addition, operating conditions can be chosen so that auxiliary responses such as purity can be brought to their most satisfactory levels. In the present example it is found that the proportion of the product D is less than 20% in the shaded region of Fig. 3.14. (This was mentioned as a condition when we first stated the problem.)

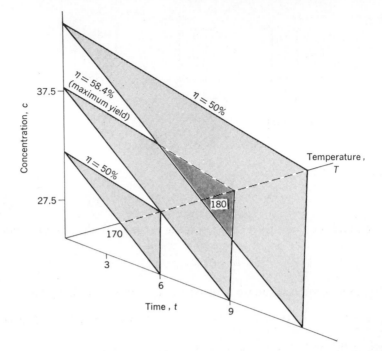

Fig. 3.13   Planes of constant yield.

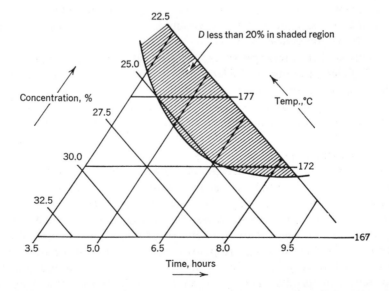

Fig. 3.14   Alternative processes giving the same maximum yield.

3.7   Some General Comments and Advice

This chapter has dealt with the problem of finding the optimum conditions in some engineering situations by maximizing or minimizing some merit factor such as cost, or yield, or height (in the case of a mineral dome), or aberrations (in the case of an optical lens). Mathematically the problem is to determine the behavior of a system of functions (responses)

$$\eta_i = f_i(x_1, x_2, \ldots, x_m), \qquad i = 1, 2, \ldots, n.$$

The f_i are of complicated analytical form, or are initially unknown, so the behavior of the f_i as functions of the x_j has to be determined by either laborious computation or laborious experimentation. The basic idea of the method of approach we have outlined is that if we are some distance away from the conditions giving an optimum result, we use the method of *steepest ascent* to approach the optimum conditions. However, this method becomes inefficient in the vicinity of an optimum and we then use *local exploration*, which enables the behavior in the neighborhood of the optimum to be investigated.

There are many other possible methods of attacking this kind of problem.[10] It should be emphasized that there is no "best" method, partly because there will be various definitions of what is meant by "best" depending on the context of the problem, and even if we agree on the meaning of "best," it will be found that different methods are "best" for different specific problems. In view of the difficulties that arise in connection with deciding what is meant by the optimum answer, and then deciding the best method for finding the optimum, it is understandable that in many cases one should be content with (quoting G. E. P. Box) "not the optimum but the preferable."

We single out four factors that are relevant when trying to decide whether one method is better than another.

1. The amount of effort involved in finding the optimum position. It is obviously of crucial importance that the number of experimental observations or numerical calculations of the response function for given values of the variables be kept to a minimum if each determination is expensive or laborious, as in the examples considered in this chapter.

2. The information the method gives about the behavior *near* the optimum position. It is usually essential to have some information about the local behavior, because this gives us insight into the situation, enables us to plan future work intelligently, tells us how much we shall be penalized if we work near, but not at, the optimum, and so on.

---

[10] Some of these are described in D. J. Wilde, *Optimum Seeking Methods*, Prentice-Hall, Englewood Cliffs, N.J., 1964. A more efficient method for the example in Section 3.5 (due to Gauss in 1809) is discussed briefly in G. E. P. Box, Use of Statistical Methods in the Elucidation of Basic Mechanisms, *Bull. Inst. Intern. Statist.*, 36 215–225 (1958).

3. The power of the method, which is usually connected with its complexity, is an important factor. There is a temptation when using an automatic computer to use a method that will guarantee results in even the most complicated cases. It is instructive to look at this from a probability point of view. A simple method will work in perhaps 90% of the examples and fail (or be unsatisfactory) in 10%. A more complicated method may work in 99% of the cases. However, this does not mean that we should prefer the complicated method. There are two other factors to be considered:

(a) If information is available concerning the geometry of the response surfaces, the method we use should be chosen to take advantage of this. "Strategy and surface-geometry are two sides of the same coin" (G. E. P. Box).

(b) In general we prefer a method that is adaptive. If we do not know what the response surface is like beforehand, the method will learn what the geometry is as the investigation proceeds, and change accordingly. In particular it may pay to start off with a simple method, and proceed to more complicated versions as a result of information given by the earlier stages. The method we have outlined, of first using steepest descent and then fitting second-degree surfaces, is of this type.

4. The effectiveness of a method in finding response surfaces from observations subject to experimental error is relevant. This will often be important in engineering situations. We have merely touched on the matter in this chapter because it lies somewhat outside the scope of this book.

The method of steepest descent followed by local exploration works well for symmetrically rounded surfaces with a single maximum, as in the example in Section 3.5. In the case of elongated ellipses, it indicates the scale changes required on the various axes, and it will also deal with ridge systems such as those in Section 3.6. Difficulties arise with almost any method when curved ridges are present. An example due to Rosenbrock,[11] also discussed by Wilde,[12] is

$$\eta = 100(x^2 - y)^2 + (1 - x)^2. \tag{3.31}$$

The minimum is in fact at $x = y = 1$, and if we set $x = 1 + X$ and $y = 1 + Y$, we see that the local behavior is given by

$$\eta = 100(2X - Y)^2 + X^2,$$

which is a series of elongated ellipses. However, inspection of (3.31) shows that for points some distance from $x = y = 1$, there will be a curved valley given by the parabola $x^2 = y$. If we start at the point, say, $(-1, -1)$, the method of steepest descent will progress only very slowly toward the maximum

[11] H. H. Rosenbrock, *Computer J.*, **3**, 175–184 (1960).

[12] D. J. Wilde, *Optimum Seeking Methods*, Prentice-Hall, Englewood Cliffs, N.J., 1964, p. 152.

at $x = y = 1$. It is very difficult to be authoritative about the best method to use in such a case, in the present state of the subject.

It should be stressed that, in the present context, the ultimate criterion for judging a method is its utility in the actual solution of practical problems. Although it may be beautiful mathematics to prove that a method always converges, this is not much comfort if it usually takes a million steps to give results of adequate accuracy.

It is obvious (and it has not been stressed because it *is* obvious) that the utility of the methods discussed in this chapter must depend on the use of automatic computers to perform the laborious calculations involved. In fact, the very existence of computers has changed the way we look at the methods proposed for solving these problems. Two comments of D. P. Feder[13] are relevant:

> It was fortunate for Cauchy's peace of mind that he did not have an electronic computer available to him in 1847 when he invented the method of steepest descent. If he had, he might have soon realized that in most practical problems the rate of convergence is so slow that the method is useless.

and

> Ask a computer a silly question and get a silly answer.

We conclude by emphasizing that the success of the effort to determine response surfaces must ultimately depend on the engineer, not the mathematician. The mathematician can advise on technique but it is the engineer who decides

1. The optimization criterion. (Perhaps we have not stressed sufficiently that this is often to a large extent arbitrary, for example, in the lens-design problems of Section 3.3.)
2. The available information regarding the geometry of the response surfaces.
3. What factors should be varied, and by how much they should be varied.

It is very often possible to achieve a satisfactory result by a poor mathematical method if the engineering assumptions are correct, but no matter how good the mathematics, the results will be useless if the optimization criterion is wrong or the wrong factors are changed. Both engineer and mathematician should bear in mind a remark of J. W. Tukey (made in another context), "If a thing is not worth doing, it is not worth doing well."

[13] D. P. Feder, *J. Opt. Soc. Am.*, **47**, 902–925 (1957).

Chapter 4

Miscellaneous Applications of
Elementary Mathematics

4.1 Summary

The contents of this chapter may be summarized as follows.

1. Section 4.2 is mainly an application of simple algebra to the problem of filling a bobbin with yarn, although we do make use of the fact that $v = dx/dt$ is the limiting form of $\Delta x = v\,\Delta t$.

2. In Section 4.3 simple algebra is used to examine an ingenious device for reducing the spin of a satellite to zero.

3. In Section 4.4 we discuss some straightforward applications of minimization in connection with the determination of ray paths in seismic prospecting.

4. Section 4.5 presents a maximization problem in chemical synthesis which can be solved by implicit differentiation, and leads to a discussion of the Lagrange multiplier and allied methods.

5. Results that facilitate the design of masks for a certain type of high-speed camera are considered in Section 4.6. The analysis depends on algebraic manipulation, a little geometry and trigonometry, elementary number theory, and the basic idea of a complex number for notational convenience.

6. In Section 4.7 we use a Fourier-series argument to make it plausible that it should be possible to recover a transmitted signal exactly, in circumstances where we might expect that some of the information is lost. A general proof requires use of the Fourier integral.

4.2 A Problem Arising in Yarn Spinning [1]

Mathematics Used: Simple algebra, geometry, and differentiation.

Comment: Note that, when discussing the shortening device, the model is indeterminate until an additional assumption is made.

[1] This problem was adapted from S. Kulik, A Problem in Yarn Spinning, *Am. Math. Monthly*, **65**, 680–684 (1958). Our treatment of the shortening device differs from that in this article. The paper was brought to the editor's attention by R. C. Buck.

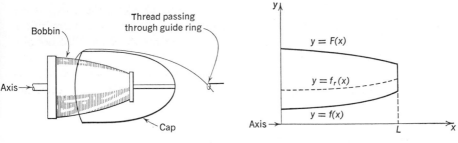

Fig. 4.1 Side view of bobbin.   **Fig. 4.2** Cross section of bobbin.

The problem discussed here arises in a yarn-spinning process in which thread passes through a small ring above the top of a cap, as in Fig. 4.1, slides over the edge of the cap, and winds on a bobbin that revolves on a spindle and moves horizontally (to the left and right) at the same time. Usually the axis of the bobbin and cap is vertical, but it has been placed horizontally in Fig. 4.1 because this is convenient for our analysis (compare Fig. 4.2). Sometimes the cap moves horizontally (vertically) instead of the bobbin, but the principle is unaffected.

By means of this arrangement, layers of thread are laid one over another. The manner in which the layers are arranged, and the final shape of the bobbin with yarn on it, are of importance in maintaining a stable shape when the bobbins are stored, and also during unwinding, particularly when this is done by pulling the thread over the edge of the cap. The results of winding depend upon the shape of the barrel of the empty bobbin, the velocity of revolution, the velocity and amplitude of the horizontal travel of the bobbin, and the rate of supply of yarn. The horizontal travel of the bobbin is controlled in such a way that its speed may differ at different positions but such that it passes each position with the same speed, regardless of which stroke it is making or whether it is a stroke moving to the left or right. Furthermore, the feed is arranged so that the rate of supply of yarn is constant.

The situation is therefore the following. We are given the initial shape of the empty bobbin and the desired final shape of the full bobbin. We wish to determine how the velocity of the bobbin should vary with the horizontal position of the bobbin to fill it in such a way that the full bobbin has the specified final shape.

When the yarn is being built up on the bobbin, the radius of the barrel of the bobbin increases, and therefore the speed of sliding of the thread along the edge of the cap increases. Consequently the twist of the yarn increases. There also may be a change of tension in the thread. We disregard the effect of these factors on the results of winding. Further, we assume that a unit of length of yarn occupies a fixed volume on the bobbin.

We first consider the case of constant-length strokes, in which the bobbin travels horizontally a constant distance at each stroke. Figure 4.2 represents schematically half of an axial section of the bobbin, where the x axis is the axis of the bobbin, $y = f(x)$ is the equation of the section of the barrel of the empty bobbin, and $y = F(x)$ is the equation of the profile of the filled bobbin, the bobbin extending from $x = 0$ to $x = L$.

Let the volume on the barrel filled with yarn in time t be $V = kt$, where k is a constant. Suppose the bobbin is filled by n strokes, where the rth layer lies between

$$y = f_{r-1}(x) \quad \text{and} \quad y = f_r(x),$$

so that
$$f_0(x) = f(x), \qquad f_n(x) = F(x).$$

Denote the velocity of the stroke at position x by $dx/dt = v(x)$. When the bobbin moves a distance Δx, the volume filled at the rth stroke is

$$\Delta V = \pi[f_r^2(x) - f_{r-1}^2(x)]\,\Delta x = \pi[f_r^2(x) - f_{r-1}^2(x)]v(x)\,\Delta t.$$

But $\Delta V = k\,\Delta t$, so that

$$f_r^2(x) - f_{r-1}^2(x) = \frac{k}{\pi v(x)}. \tag{4.1}$$

On summing from $r = 1$ to $r = n$, we see that

$$F^2(x) - f^2(x) = \frac{nk}{\pi v(x)}$$

or
$$v(x) = \frac{nk}{\pi}\,[F^2(x) - f^2(x)]^{-1}. \tag{4.2}$$

This equation tells us what the velocity v must be as a function of x to fill a bobbin with initial profile $f(x)$, by n strokes, to give a final profile $F(x)$. At the mth stroke the profile is given by summing (4.1) from $r = 1$ to m, substituting from (4.2) for $v(x)$:

$$f_m^2(x) = \frac{m}{n}\,F^2(x) + \left(1 - \frac{m}{n}\right)f^2(x). \tag{4.3}$$

We now discuss what is known as a *shortening device*. The bobbin still travels left and right with a velocity depending only on x, except that the motion to the right is reversed to the left before reaching the full length $x = L$. When the bobbin is empty, the stroke starts with a length $x = l < L$ and gradually increases to $x = L$ when the bobbin is full (see Fig. 4.3). A shortening device is useful when the final total thickness of the winding is to be made much less on the right end of the bobbin. If only strokes of full length were used, the velocity of the strokes would have to be very great toward the right end of the bobbin, and the curve $y = f_r(x)$ defining the shape of the rth layer would have a sharp change in slope around $x = l$.

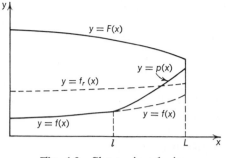

Fig. 4.3   Shortening device.

There is considerable indeterminancy in this problem as it stands, since we can vary

1. The velocity $v(x)$, $l \leq x \leq L$.
2. The rate at which the stroke is lengthened. If the rth stroke goes from $x = 0$ to $x = x_r$, then $x_r = X(r)$ is a function of r which is at our disposal.
3. The shape of the empty bobbin between $x = l$ and $x = L$, say, $y = p(x)$.

We shall make the problem definite by specifying the desired variation of the velocity $v(x)$ with x in terms of a bobbin given by a function $y = f(x)$ in $0 \leq x \leq L$, where $f(x)$ is the given shape of the empty bobbin for $0 \leq x \leq l$, and a fictitious shape from $x = l$ to L, chosen in such a way that (4.2) gives a conveniently smooth velocity $v(x)$. Having chosen $v(x)$, the problem is now to find the relation between a given shape of the empty bobbin in $l \leq x \leq L$, that is, $y = p(x)$ in (3) above, and the rate at which the stroke is lengthened, that is, the variation of x_r with r, where x_r was defined in **2** above.

We sum (4.1) from $r = m + 1$ to n, obtaining

$$F(x) - f_m^2(x) = \frac{(n - m)k}{\pi v(x)}$$

$$= \left(1 - \frac{m}{n}\right)[F^2(x) - f^2(x)], \tag{4.4}$$

where we have used (4.2). When $x = x_m$, then $f_m(x) = p(x_m)$, by definition of x_m. Setting $x = x_m$ in (4.4) and rearranging we see that

$$p^2(x_m) = \frac{(n - m)f^2(x_m) + mF^2(x_m)}{n}.$$

This equation is the desired result. It says that if we specify x_m as a function of m, we can find the corresponding values of $p(x_m)$. Conversely, if we are given $p(x)$ as a function of x, we can find the corresponding values of x_m by solving an algebraic equation. This last result is obvious graphically and x_m is merely the value of x corresponding to the intersection of $y = p(x)$ and $y = f_m(x)$.

4.3   A Yo-yo for De-spinning a Satellite[2]

Mathematics Used: Simple algebra.

Comment: The problem can be solved by simple algebra only because physical insight is used. A remarkable result is deduced—that the angular velocity of the satellite is reduced to zero by the device, regardless of the initial angular velocity.

When a satellite is placed in orbit, it usually spins around an axis. The direction of the axis of spin will be assumed to be known, but the angular velocity of spin is in general unknown and unpredictable. It is often desirable to reduce the rate of spin to zero, and this can be done by the following device.

Consider a disk-shaped satellite spinning about the axis of the disk. Assume that a wire is wrapped around the disk, friction preventing relative motion of the string and the edge of the disk when the two are in contact. The wire is wrapped around the disk in a direction opposite to the direction of rotation, and a weight is attached to the outer end of the wire and held against the circumference. At a given instant the weight is released. It swings out under centrifugal force and, through the wire, exerts a retarding moment on the satellite. Actually, two diametrically opposite weights and wires are released simultaneously, to avoid transverse forces on the axis of the disk. However, for simplicity, we shall consider the case of a single weight, and assume that the disk axis is fixed.

The geometry of the situation after release of the wire is shown in Fig. 4.4, where ϕ is the angle turned by the satellite after release of the weight, R the radius of the satellite, s the length of wire paid out, and $(r, \phi + \theta)$ the polar coordinates of the weight. If I is the moment of inertia of the satellite without the yo-yo weight and m the mass of the weight, then $I_0 = I + mR^2$ is the initial moment of inertia of the satellite before release of the weight.

If the initial angular velocity is w_0, then

$$\text{Initial angular momentum} = I_0 w_0,$$
$$\text{Initial kinetic energy} = \tfrac{1}{2} I_0 w_0^2.$$

Let the length of wire paid out when the angular velocity of the satellite is reduced to exactly zero be denoted by S, and suppose the wire has precisely this length, so that the wire then detaches from the satellite. At this instant,

---

[2] This device is explained on pages 214–216 of an article by R. B. Kershner and R. R. Newton, in *Space Astrophysics* (W. Liller, ed.), McGraw-Hill, New York, 1961, where the differential equations for the problem are written out in detail. J. P. Den Hartog of the Massachusetts Institute of Technology gave the analysis in the book to a class, and one of his students produced the method given in the text, with the comment that Lamé has said that if a simple answer comes out of a long analysis, then there is always a simple derivation. The difficulty is, of course, to find it. The problem was drawn to our attention by W. Bollay.

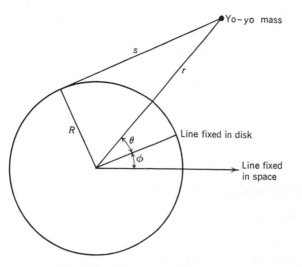

Fig. 4.4   Geometry of the yo-yo.

because the weight moves perpendicular to the wire and the satellite is assumed to have no angular velocity,

$$\text{Angular momentum of system} = mvS,$$
$$\text{Kinetic energy of system} = \tfrac{1}{2}mv^2.$$

From the conservation of momenta and kinetic energy we can equate the initial and final values of these quantities:

$$mvS = I_0w_0,$$
$$\tfrac{1}{2}mv^2 = \tfrac{1}{2}I_0w_0^2.$$

If the first equation is squared and divided by the second, we have

$$mS^2 = I_0 \quad \text{or} \quad S = (I_0/m)^{1/2}.$$

This gives the remarkable result that the length of wire required to reduce the angular velocity of the satellite to zero is *independent of the initial angular velocity*.

As an example, the initial moment of inertia of a satellite was 9.62 slug-ft², and the total yo-yo mass was 4.72 lb. Hence the theoretical length of wire was

$$S = (9.62 \times 32.2/4.72)^{1/2} = 8.1 \text{ ft} = 97.2 \text{ in.}$$

Actually, because of the specific details of the mechanical design, release was effected somewhat late, and the length determined experimentally by ground testing was $94\tfrac{5}{8}$ in. This device has been used successfully in several satellites.

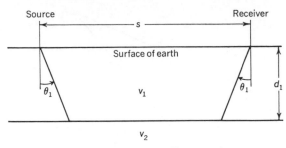

Fig. 4.5 Two-medium earth.

4.4 A Minimization Problem in Seismic Prospecting[3]

Mathematics Used: Minimization by differentiation.

It is possible to investigate earth and rock structures by means of waves artificially produced in the ground. Suppose there is a layer of soil of uniform thickness d_1, in which the wave velocity is a constant v_1, lying on top of soil in which the wave velocity is another constant, v_2, as in Fig. 4.5, where $v_2 > v_1$ (this is the usual situation in practice). We imagine that at the point marked "source" there is a device for producing a wave pulse at a given instant of time, such as a hammer or a small explosion. A receiving system is assumed to be available that will record the times taken for the wave pulse to travel from the source to other points on the surface of the earth. We consider two waves. The first is the surface wave, which goes directly from the source to the receiver with velocity v_1 along the surface of the earth. The time taken is given by

$$t_1 = \frac{s}{v_1}, \tag{4.5}$$

where s is the distance between the source and receiver. The second wave we consider is the wave that travels into the earth until it hits the interface between the two media, then travels in the lower medium along the interface (since this is faster than traveling in the upper medium), before coming back through the layer to the receiver. The total time taken by this wave in going from the source to the receiver is given by

$$t_2 = \frac{2d_1}{v_1} \sec \theta_1 + \frac{s - 2d_1 \tan \theta_1}{v_2}, \tag{4.6}$$

where θ_1 is the angle the path of the wave in the upper medium makes with the vertical, as shown in Fig. 4.5. The value of θ_1 can be determined by the condition that t_2 is a minimum for given s, d_1, v_1, and v_2. We require

$$\frac{dt_2}{d\theta_1} = \frac{2d_1}{v_1} \frac{\sin \theta_1}{\cos^2 \theta_1} - \frac{2d_1}{v_2 \cos^2 \theta_1}.$$

[3] This section was contributed by J. C. Spradling, Department of Mechanics, Wisconsin State College and Institute of Technology, Platteville, Wis.

Setting $dt_2/d\theta_1 = 0$ and solving for $\sin \theta_1$, we find that

$$\sin \theta_1 = \frac{v_1}{v_2}.$$

It is convenient to introduce the parameter

$$k = \frac{v_1}{v_2}.$$

Then (4.6) becomes

$$t_2 = \frac{2d_1}{v_1}(1 - k^2)^{1/2} + \frac{s}{v_2}. \tag{4.7}$$

Since we can measure t_1 and t_2 for various s, the velocity v_1 can be found from (4.5), but v_2 and d_1 are not known. Can we invent a practical method for finding v_2 and d_1 from these measurements? On dividing (4.7) by (4.5) we see that

$$\frac{t_2}{t_1} = [2d_1(1 - k^2)^{1/2}]\frac{1}{s} + k.$$

Hence if we plot $y = t_2/t_1$ against $x = 1/s$ in ordinary cartesian coordinates (both of these quantities being known experimentally), the results should lie on a straight line, as illustrated in Fig. 4.6. The point where the line cuts the y axis gives k, and hence v_2, and then d_1 can be determined from the slope m of the line:

$$d_1 = \frac{m}{2(1 - k^2)^{1/2}}.$$

From the geometry of the system, the experimental points for $1/s$ greater than the value given by $s = 2d_1 \tan \theta_1$ will *not* lie on the straight line in Fig. 4.6.

An important feature of the straight-line plot of Fig. 4.6 is that it provides a partial check on the validity of our assumptions. If the experimental points do not lie on a straight line, something is wrong; for example, the upper medium may not be a layer of constant thickness.

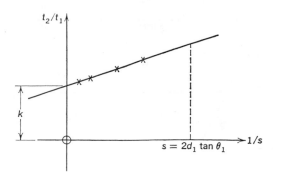

Fig. 4.6   Straight-line plot of t_2/t_1 vs. $1/s$.

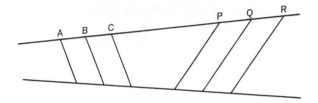

Fig. 4.7 Sloping interface.

This idea can be developed in various ways. The practical problem is often that the interface between the two media has an unknown form that we wish to elucidate. It will in general be necessary to work backward from assumed idealized structures to the effects they would produce experimentally. Then, by comparing the actual experimental results with predicted results, it may be possible to deduce the probable form of the structure. Thus to find out whether the interface is sloping as in Fig. 4.7, we may have to take readings of t_1, t_2, and s for various source positions A, B, and C as well as receiver positions P, Q, and R. If the buried structure is in the form of a dome (which may be important in oil-exploration problems), we shall have to work in two dimensions on the surface of the ground, and investigate the relation of t_1, t_2, and s to the positions of source and receiver, and the radius and position of the center of the sphere or ellipsoid representing the dome.

Another way in which this idea can be developed is in connection with multi-media problems. The case of three media is illustrated in Fig. 4.8, which should be self-explanatory. The time taken for a wave to go from the source to the receiver through both media is given by

$$t_2 = \frac{2d_1 \sec \theta_1}{v_1} + \frac{2d_2 \sec \theta_2}{v_2} + \frac{s - 2d_1 \tan \theta_1 - 2d_2 \tan \theta_2}{v_3}.$$

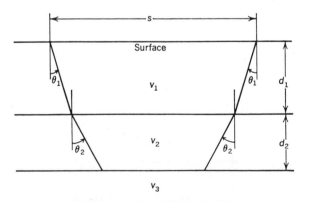

Fig. 4.8 Three-media problem.

The values of θ_1 and θ_2 are given by the condition that t_2 is a minimum with respect to both θ_1 and θ_2. This requires partial differentiation:

$$\frac{\partial t_2}{\partial \theta_1} = \frac{2d_1 \sin \theta_1}{v_1 \cos {}^2\theta_1} - \frac{2d_1}{v_3 \cos^2 \theta_1}, \qquad \frac{\partial t_2}{\partial \theta_2} = \frac{2d_2 \sin \theta_2}{v_2 \cos^2 \theta_2} - \frac{2d_2}{v_3 \cos^2 \theta_2}.$$

Hence
$$\sin \theta_1 = \frac{v_1}{v_3}, \qquad \sin \theta_2 = \frac{v_2}{v_3}.$$

We leave the problems of seismic waves at this point.

4.5   Maximum Yield in an Ammonia Reactor[4]

Mathematics Used: Minimization by implicit differentiation; use of Lagrange multipliers.

We shall state the problem briefly in chemical terminology, and then isolate the mathematical problem.

We wish to find the maximum concentration of ammonia in an ammonia-synthesis process

$$N_2 + 3H_2 \rightleftharpoons 2NH_3$$

We are considering a gaseous mixture of nitrogen, hydrogen, and ammonia in which the total pressure is the sum of partial pressures. The partial pressure associated with one of the components nitrogen, hydrogen, or ammonia is the pressure that this component would exert if it alone occupied the whole of the vessel in which the gases are contained. If the total pressure is denoted by P and the partial pressure of the nitrogen by p_{N_2}, etc., then, since it is verified experimentally that the total pressure is the sum of the partial pressures, we have

$$P = p_{NH_3} + p_{N_2} + p_{H_2}. \tag{4.8}$$

Each partial pressure is proportional to the number of molecules of the corresponding component in the vessel, and therefore the concentration of each component is proportional to its partial pressure. The composition of the mixture is given by the ratio of the partial pressures of nitrogen and hydrogen:

$$r = \frac{p_{N_2}}{p_{H_2}}. \tag{4.9}$$

We assume that, in the reaction, the temperature and total pressure are fixed. We then wish to find the ratio of nitrogen to hydrogen that we must

[4] This problem was suggested by G. A. Ratcliff, Department of Chemical Engineering, Oregon State University, Corvallis, Ore., while on leave from the Department of Chemical Engineering, Cambridge University, Cambridge, England.

start with, in the reaction vessel, to obtain maximum ammonia concentration when the system finally settles down to equilibrium.

The rate of the reaction is fixed by the probability of collisions between molecules of the reacting species. The probability of a collision between three molecules of H_2 and one molecule of N_2 to give one molecule of NH_3 is proportional to $[H_2]^3[N_2]$, where the brackets indicate concentration. The rate at which ammonia is being formed is therefore given by

$$K_1[H_2]^3[N_2],$$

where K_1 is a rate constant. Similarly, the probability of two molecules of NH_3 colliding to give $3H_2 + N_2$ is proportional to $[NH_3]^2$, so the rate of decomposition of the ammonia is given by

$$K_2[NH_3]^2,$$

where K_2 is a second rate constant. In equilibrium, the rate at which ammonia is being formed is equal to the rate at which ammonia is decomposing:

$$K_1[H_2]^3[N_2] = K_2[NH_3]^2.$$

Expressing concentrations in terms of partial pressures and setting $K_1/K_2 = K$, an equilibrium constant, we have, finally,

$$\frac{p_{NH_3}^2}{p_{N_2}p_{H_2}^3} = \text{constant} = K. \tag{4.10}$$

It is convenient to introduce the notation

$$z = p_{NH_3}, \qquad x = p_{N_2}, \qquad y = p_{H_2}.$$

Then in terms of these variables the mathematical problem is to find the ratio x/y that maximizes z, where

$$x + y + z = P = \text{constant}, \tag{4.11}$$

$$\frac{z^2}{xy^3} = K = \text{constant}. \tag{4.12}$$

The simplest procedure is probably to eliminate x between these equations, which yields

$$\frac{z^2}{Ky^3} + y + z = P. \tag{4.13}$$

This is an equation that expresses z in terms of y alone. Differentiate throughout with respect to y:

$$\frac{2z}{Ky^3}\frac{dz}{dy} - \frac{3z^2}{Ky^4} + 1 + \frac{dz}{dy} = 0.$$

The stationary values of z will be given by $dz/dy = 0$, or

$$\frac{3z^2}{Ky^4} = 1.$$

Introducing the value of K from (4.12), we see that this gives

$$\frac{3x}{y} = 1 \quad \text{or} \quad r = \frac{x}{y} = \frac{1}{3}, \tag{4.14}$$

which is the required answer.

Another way of solving the problem is to use the method of Lagrange multipliers. We remind the reader of the theory, because later we develop a different but related method. Suppose we wish to find the stationary values of z defined by

$$z = f(x, y) \tag{4.15}$$

subject to the condition

$$g(x, y) = 0. \tag{4.16}$$

We can imagine that (4.16) is solved for y in terms of x, and that this expression for y is substituted in (4.15) so that z can be regarded as a function of x alone. Then differentiation of (4.15) and (4.16) gives

$$\frac{dz}{dx} = \frac{\partial f}{\partial x} + \frac{\partial f}{\partial y}\frac{dy}{dx}, \quad 0 = \frac{\partial g}{\partial x} + \frac{\partial g}{\partial y}\frac{dy}{dx}.$$

For a stationary value, $dz/dx = 0$ so, denoting dy/dx by μ, we have

$$\frac{\partial f}{\partial x} + \mu\frac{\partial f}{\partial y} = 0, \tag{4.17a}$$

$$\frac{\partial g}{\partial x} + \mu\frac{\partial g}{\partial y} = 0. \tag{4.17b}$$

These two equations, together with

$$g(x, y) = 0, \tag{4.17c}$$

give three equations for x, y, and μ. The quantity μ is the value of dy/dx evaluated for the values x and y that give a stationary z.

The method of Lagrange multipliers is superficially different, and is stated as follows. We form the function

$$H(x, y) = f(x, y) + \lambda g(x, y), \tag{4.18}$$

where λ is a constant, known as the *Lagrange multiplier*, to be determined later. We find the stationary values of $H(x, y)$ by proceeding as if x and y were independent. This gives

$$\frac{\partial H}{\partial x} = \frac{\partial f}{\partial x} + \lambda\frac{\partial g}{\partial x} = 0, \tag{4.19a}$$

$$\frac{\partial H}{\partial y} = \frac{\partial f}{\partial y} + \lambda\frac{\partial g}{\partial y} = 0. \tag{4.19b}$$

These two equations, together with $g(x, y) = 0$, give three equations for the determination of x, y, and λ. It is easily shown that these three equations are equivalent to (4.17), which justifies the method.

The answer submitted for the problem stated earlier proceeds as follows. From (4.11),

$$z = P - x - y. \tag{4.20}$$

Using this to eliminate z from (4.12), we find

$$(P - x - y)^2 - Kxy^3 = 0. \tag{4.21}$$

As in (4.18), we form

$$H(x, y) = (P - x - y) + \lambda[(P - x - y)^2 - Kxy^3].$$

Equations (4.19) are

$$\frac{\partial H}{\partial x} = -1 - 2\lambda(P - x - y) - K\lambda y^3 = 0,$$

$$\frac{\partial H}{\partial y} = -1 - 2\lambda(P - x - y) - 3\lambda Kxy^2 = 0.$$

Subtraction immediately gives $y = 3x$, or $r = x/y = 1/3$, as before.

We can criticize the first method used, leading to (4.14), by implicit differentiation of a function of one variable, because we were obviously lucky to be able to eliminate x between (4.11) and (4.12) in a simple way to obtain (4.13). The method of Lagrange multipliers is not much better from this point of view, because we have to solve (4.11) for z and then substitute in (4.12), to obtain (4.20) and (4.21). We consider the whole problem from a more general point of view. Suppose we wish to find the stationary values of z, given that

$$f(x, y, z) = 0, \tag{4.22}$$

$$g(x, y, z) = 0, \tag{4.23}$$

where it is not easy to solve any of these equations for any of the variables. However, there is a functional relationship expressing x in terms of y and z implicit in (4.23):

$$x = G(y, z), \tag{4.24}$$

and this can be substituted in (4.22) to give

$$f(G(y, z), y, z) = 0,$$

which can then be used to express z as a function of y, say $z = F(y)$. If this is substituted in (4.24) we see that x can be regarded as a function of y. From this point of view, the variables x and z in (4.22) and (4.23) are both functions of y, say, $z = F(y)$ and $x = E(y)$. Differentiation of (4.22) and (4.23) with respect to y gives

$$\frac{\partial f}{\partial x}\frac{dE}{dy} + \frac{\partial f}{\partial y} + \frac{\partial f}{\partial z}\frac{dF}{dy} = 0, \tag{4.25a}$$

$$\frac{\partial g}{\partial x}\frac{dE}{dy} + \frac{\partial g}{\partial y} + \frac{\partial g}{\partial z}\frac{dF}{dy} = 0. \tag{4.25b}$$

We wish to find stationary values of z, that is, values where $dF/dy = 0$. Let $dE/dy = \eta$. Then equations (4.25) give

$$\eta \frac{\partial f}{\partial x} + \frac{\partial f}{\partial y} = 0, \qquad \eta \frac{\partial g}{\partial x} + \frac{\partial g}{\partial y} = 0. \qquad (4.26)$$

These two equations, together with

$$f(x, y, z) = 0, \qquad g(x, y, z) = 0$$

give four equations for x, y, z, and η. [Equations (4.26) are similar to (4.17). It would be possible to develop a Lagrange multiplier method, and replace (4.26) by (4.19), but we do not pursue the theory.]

In our example,

$$f(x, y, z) = x + y + z - P, \qquad g(x, y, z) = \frac{z^2}{xy^3} - K.$$

Equations (4.26) give

$$\eta + 1 = 0, \qquad -\frac{\eta z^2}{x^2 y^3} - \frac{3z^2}{xy^4} = 0.$$

These yield $3x = y$, as before. The algebra is somewhat easier than in the Lagrange multiplier method.

This is an example in which the structure of the method is much easier to see if we do the analysis in terms of the general equations (4.22) and (4.23) rather than deal directly with the special equations (4.11) and (4.12), where we are tempted to use special tricks because of simple but accidental properties of the original equations.

4.6   Masks to Pack Circles Densely[5]

Engineering Context: Design of a high-speed camera.

Mathematics Used: Elementary algebra, geometry, trigonometry; the idea of a vector and a complex number; simple properties of prime numbers.

When taking pictures at a very high rate of speed, say 500,000 pictures per second, a very difficult problem is the movement of the film between pictures. To minimize the necessary movement, one idea is to photograph each frame

[5] This section is based on a preliminary version of a paper by E. N. Gilbert, Bell Telephone Laboratories, Masks to Pack Circles Densely, *J. Soc. Motion Picture and Television Engrs.*, **72**, 606–608 (1963). The reader interested in number theory will find, in this paper, an application of properties of the field of "integers" $X + \omega Y$, where X and Y are real integers and $\omega = \exp(i\pi/3)$. The type of camera from which the problem arose is described in J. S. Courtney-Pratt, High-Speed X-ray Cinematography, *J. Soc. Motion Picture and Television Engrs.*, **70**, 637–642, 710–715 (1961).

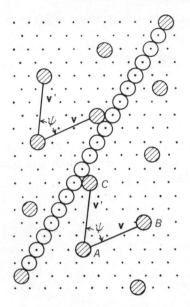

Fig. 4.9 Mask to achieve close packing. The points represent the centers of dots in the lattice L. The shaded circles give one position of the mask, that is, the lattice P.

through a mask containing an array of small holes spaced many diameters apart. On the film the picture appears as a corresponding array of small dots. Since one picture leaves most of the film unexposed, a similar pattern of dots for the next frame will fit between the dots of the first frame. After many frames have been photographed, the film contains many dot patterns jumbled together. A particular frame may be viewed alone by placing the mask in the appropriate position. As the film need move only one dot diameter between frames (instead of the length of the frame as in conventional movies), the film motion can be relatively slow. This technique is known as *image-dissection photography*.

Because dots belonging to different frames must not overlap, the number of frames to be photographed is limited. If the dots are circles, all of the same diameter, the largest number of dots per unit area will be achieved if the dots from all frames combined fall into the familiar close-packed pattern of circles in the plane. In this arrangement each dot touches six others, and, by comparing the area of a circle with the area of the circumscribing hexagon, it is seen that dots cover a fraction $\pi/\sqrt{12} = 0.907$ of the film area.

Only very special masks and film motions produce close-packed dots. Figure 4.9 shows a simple case in which dots from 19 different frames are close-packed. The shaded circles are dots of the first frame. The unshaded circles are the dots that one of the holes produces in the next 18 frames. The other dots in frames 2,..., 19 have centers at the points marked in Fig. 4.9.

In practice, masks for maximal film usage require very close tolerances and so may be less useful than more wasteful schemes. Still, such masks have at least a theoretical interest—for example, they provide bounds against which to judge practical systems. We consider masks in which the hole centers belong to a regular point lattice; that is, the hole centers are all points of the form $j\mathbf{v} + k\mathbf{v}'$, where $\mathbf{v}$ and $\mathbf{v}'$ are two vectors that generate the point lattice as j and k range over all integer values (see Fig. 4.9). The film is assumed to move a constant vector amount $\mathbf{t}$ between each pair of successive frames.

Let the dots be circles of unit diameter. It will be convenient to think of the film as the complex plane and to represent dot centers by complex numbers. The dot centers in the desired close-packed pattern form a lattice, denoted by L, of all points of the form $m - \omega n$, where m and n are integers and

$$\omega = e^{i\pi/3} = \frac{1 + i\sqrt{3}}{2}. \tag{4.27}$$

The centers of the holes in the mask form another point lattice P generated by two complex numbers, say V and V', corresponding to the vectors $\mathbf{v}$ and $\mathbf{v}'$ already introduced. Suppose

$$V = ae^{i\theta} = M + \omega N, \tag{4.28}$$

$$V' = be^{i(\theta + \psi)} = M' + \omega N', \tag{4.29}$$

where M, N, M', and N' must be integers because all the points of P belong to L.

We can immediately derive some relations that will be useful later. By taking the modulus of both sides of (4.28) and (4.29), we have

$$a^2 = M^2 + MN + N^2, \qquad b^2 = M'^2 + M'N' + N'^2. \tag{4.30}$$

From (4.28) and (4.29),

$$\begin{aligned} abe^{i\psi} &= (ae^{-i\theta})(be^{i\theta + i\psi}) \\ &= (M + \tfrac{1}{2}N - \tfrac{1}{2}i3^{1/2}N)(M' + \tfrac{1}{2}N' + \tfrac{1}{2}i3^{1/2}N'). \end{aligned}$$

Multiplying out and equating imaginary parts we see that

$$ab \sin \psi = \tfrac{1}{2}\sqrt{3}(MN' - M'N). \tag{4.31}$$

[We note in passing that an immediate result of this relation is that it is impossible to find a lattice P in which $\mathbf{v}$ and $\mathbf{v}'$ are at right angles, and $a = b$, for then (4.31) would give $\sqrt{3} = 2a^2/(MN' - M'N)$. However, from (4.30), a^2 is an integer, so this would show that $\sqrt{3}$ is rational.]

Suppose q different translates of the lattice P are possible, producing a pattern in which none of the circles overlap. The triangle ABC formed by $\mathbf{v}$ and $\mathbf{v}'$ in Fig. 4.9 contains altogether one-half of one of the shaded circles, with area $\tfrac{1}{8}\pi$. The area of the triangle ABC is $\tfrac{1}{2}ab\,|\sin \psi|$, so the fraction of the total area occupied by the q translates of P is

$$\frac{q(\tfrac{1}{8}\pi)}{\tfrac{1}{2}ab\,|\sin \psi|}.$$

This cannot exceed the fraction $\pi/\sqrt{12}$ which close-packed circles would occupy. Hence

$$q \le (2/\sqrt{3})ab \, |\sin \psi|. \tag{4.32}$$

If the q translates from a close-packed pattern, equality holds in this equation and, from (4.31) and (4.32) we see that

$$q = |MN' - M'N|. \tag{4.33}$$

Conversely, if this relation is true, the translates must be close-packed. As an example, in Fig. 4.9,

$$\mathbf{v} = 3 + 2\omega, \qquad \mathbf{v}' = -2 + 5\omega.$$

Hence $\qquad\qquad q = (3)(5) - (-2)(2) = 19,$

as already stated. The result (4.33) is useful because, for given $\mathbf{v}$ and $\mathbf{v}'$, it tells us immediately the number of translates we should look for.

Suppose now that the film is translated in constant steps described by a vector $\mathbf{t}$, and a corresponding complex number T. Since the mask P uncovers the dots at points $j\mathbf{v} + k\mathbf{v}'$, the dots uncovered after m steps are at points of the form

$$j\mathbf{v} + k\mathbf{v}' + m\mathbf{t}, \qquad j, k, m \text{ integers.} \tag{4.34}$$

For a given m, the set of points of the form (4.34) will be called P_m. The set of points obtained by all translations of P, that is, the union of $P_0, P_1, P_2, \ldots$, is a lattice which we denote by Q. The points of Q have the form (4.34) where j, k, and m are any integers. To obtain close-packed dots on the film we require $Q = L$.

Since $\mathbf{v}$ and $\mathbf{v}'$ belong to L, all the points in (4.34) will belong to L if and only if $\mathbf{t}$ belongs to L. Thus let

$$T = r + \omega s \tag{4.35}$$

for some integers r and s. If one must move the film only one dot diameter at a time (which is the common situation), then $T = \pm 1, \pm\omega,$ or $\pm\omega^2$. However, the general case (4.35) offers little extra difficulty.

Although the vectors $\mathbf{v}$ and $\mathbf{v}'$ of a point lattice P may have the required form (4.27), there may not exist a translation vector $\mathbf{t}$ such that $Q = L$, that is, such that the union of the translates is close-packed. For example, if $V = 2 + \omega 2$ and $V' = 4 - \omega 2$, equation (4.33) shows that 12 translates of P are required to cover all of L. However, for every choice of $\mathbf{t}$, one finds that the sequence $P_0, P_1, \ldots$ repeats with a period of 6 or less. We require rules that will enable us to decide easily whether, for given $\mathbf{v}$ and $\mathbf{v}'$, a suitable $\mathbf{t}$ exists such that $Q = L$. This is the problem we now investigate, together with the problem of deciding whether a given $\mathbf{t}$ is suitable.

We state the required results as follows: Let P_0 be the point lattice generated by vectors $V = M + \omega N$ and $V' = M' + \omega N'$, and let $P_0, P_1, P_2, \ldots$ be the sequence of point sets obtained by translating P_0 successively in steps of $T = r + \omega s$. Let

$$Ms \neq Nr, \qquad M's \neq N'r, \qquad MN' \neq M'N. \tag{4.36}$$

[This last set of conditions rules out only degenerate or trivial cases. Equality occurs in (4.36) only when two of the three vectors $\mathbf{v}$, $\mathbf{v}'$, and $\mathbf{t}$ are colinear. For example, if $\alpha\mathbf{v} = \beta\mathbf{t}$ with α and β relatively prime integers, then the sequence $P_0, P_1, P_2, \ldots$ contains only β distinct point lattices.] We now state

Theorem A.   *The translates $P_0, P_1, P_2, \ldots$ are close-packed if and only if the greatest common divisor of $Ms - Nr$, $M's - N'r$, and $MN' - M'N$ is unity (that is, these three numbers are relatively prime).*

Theorem B.   *A translation vector $\mathbf{t}$ exists such that the translates $P_0, P_1, P_2, \ldots$ are close-packed if and only if the greatest common divisor of M, N, M', and N' is unity (that is, M, N, M', and N' are relatively prime).*

We first prove Theorem A. Suppose P_m is the same set as P_0, and m is the smallest integer for which this is true. Then integers j and k must exist such that $j\mathbf{v} + k\mathbf{v}' = m\mathbf{t}$, so that

$$jM + kM' = mr, \qquad jN + kN' = ms. \tag{4.37}$$

We can solve these for j and k provided $MN' - M'N \neq 0$, as postulated in (4.36). This gives

$$j = \frac{m(M's - N'r)}{M'N - MN'}, \qquad k = \frac{m(Ms - Nr)}{MN' - M'N}. \tag{4.38}$$

If the greatest common divisor of $Ms - Nr$, $M's - N'r$, and $MN' - M'N$ is unity then j and k will be integers only if m is a multiple of $MN' - M'N$. Since we are looking for the smallest possible m for which P_m is the same set as P_0, we choose $m = MN' - M'N$, where we assume that this gives $m > 0$. [Otherwise we set $m = -(MN' - M'N)$.] Then, from (4.38),

$$j = -(M's - N'r), \qquad k = (Ms - Nr). \tag{4.39}$$

For the above value of m, the translates $P_0, P_1, \ldots, P_{m-1}$ must be distinct, since otherwise, if P_n coincides with P_0, $0 < n < m$, we could find integers j_1 and k_1 such that $j_1\mathbf{v} + k_1\mathbf{v}' = n\mathbf{t}$, which contradicts the result obtained above that m is the smallest integer for which the sum of integral multiples of $\mathbf{v}$ and $\mathbf{v}'$ is an integral multiple of $\mathbf{t}$. Also, since m is precisely the quantity q found in (4.33), we see that the translates must fill the whole plane. Hence we have shown that if $Ms - Nr$, $M's - N'r$, and $MN' - M'N$ are relatively prime, then the translates are close-packed.

Conversely, if $Ms - Nr$, $M's - N'r$, and $MN' - M'N$ have a common divisor d which is greater than unity, then, for the above values of j, k, and m, we have

$$\left(\frac{j}{d}\right)\mathbf{v} + \left(\frac{k}{d}\right)\mathbf{v}' = \left(\frac{m}{d}\right)\mathbf{t},$$

where j/d, k/d, and m/d are all integers. Hence P_n is the same as P_0, where $n = m/d < m$, and from (4.33) the translates cannot be close-packed.

Another proof of Theorem A is the following. On eliminating m between the two equations in (4.37) we find a single equation in j and k:

$$j(Ms - Nr) + k(M's - N'r) = 0.$$

If D is the greatest common divisor of $Ms - Nr$ and $M's - N'r$, this equation can be written

$$\frac{j(Ms - Nr)}{D} = -\frac{k(M's - N'r)}{D}.$$

By the definition of D, the coefficient of j on the left and the coefficient of k on the right have no common divisors. Hence j must be an integer multiple of the coefficient of k and vice versa:

$$j = \frac{C(M's - N'r)}{D}, \qquad k = -\frac{C(Ms - Nr)}{D}, \tag{4.40}$$

where C may be any integer. Substitution of (4.40) in (4.37) gives

$$m = \frac{C(MN' - M'N)}{D}. \tag{4.41}$$

Hence there must be some restriction on C to ensure that m is an integer. Let Δ denote the greatest common divisor of D and $MN' - M'N$; that is, Δ is the greatest common divisor mentioned in Theorem A. To make m an integer, C must be a multiple of D/Δ. Then (4.37) has integer solutions j and k if and only if m is a multiple of $(MN' - M'N)/\Delta$. We are looking for the smallest value of m, so we set

$$m = \frac{|MN' - M'N|}{\Delta}. \tag{4.42}$$

We can now prove the two parts of Theorem A.

1. If $P_0, P_1, \ldots, P_{m-1}$ are close-packed, then m must in fact agree with $q = |MN' - M'N|$, a result derived in (4.33). Hence from (4.42) we must have $\Delta = 1$; that is, the greatest common divisor, Δ, is 1.

2. If $\Delta = 1$, then $m = |MN' - M'N|$, and this shows that the translates are close-packed.

In the photography application, unit vectors $T = \pm 1$, $\pm \omega$, and $\pm \omega^2$ are the preferred translations. For a given mask V and V', Theorem A can quickly test each of these unit vectors as choices for $\mathbf{t}$. In some cases no unit vector is a suitable choice for $\mathbf{t}$, even though suitable longer vectors exist. One such case is the mask with $V = 2 + \omega 3$ and $V' = -4 + \omega 9$, for which a $\mathbf{t}$ satisfying Theorem A is given by $T = i\sqrt{3} = -1 + 2\omega$. It is perhaps worth noting that if $m = MN' - M'N$ is a prime number, Theorem A shows that any vector $\mathbf{t}$, other than the trivial cases ruled out by the inequalities (4.36), will produce close-packed translates.

Although Theorem A is sufficient for practical purposes if we wish to consider only specific vectors **t** such as the unit vectors, it is of some interest to know whether suitable vectors **t** exist for given **v** and **v'**. This question is covered in Theorem B, the answer being that suitable **t** exist if and only if M, N, M', and N' are relatively prime.

The necessity of this condition can be deduced immediately from Theorem A, since if M, N, M', and N' have a common divisor d greater than unity, then d also divides $Ms - Nr, M's - N'r$, and $MN' - M'N$, and Theorem A tells us that in this case the translates cannot be close-packed. An an example, the mask cited in the first paragraph of this section with $V = 2 + \omega2$, $V' = 4 - \omega2$, fails to produce close packing, because M, N, M', and N' are all divisible by 2.

It seems to be more difficult to prove the sufficiency of the condition, that is, that if M, N, M', and N' are relatively prime, at least one vector **t** exists such that the translations are close-packed. We shall show that if M, N, M', and N' are relatively prime, it is possible to find numbers r and s such that $Ms - Nr, M's - N'r$, and $MN' - M'N$ are relatively prime. The fact that the corresponding translates are close-packed will then follow from Theorem A. (The proof given below starts from first principles and follows that of Gilbert,[6] which depended on certain theorems in number theory.)

It suffices to construct r and s such that no prime less than or equal to $|MN' - M'N|$ divides both $Ms - Nr$ and $M's - N'r$. Let the primes less than or equal to $|MN' - M'N|$ be $p_1, p_2, \ldots, p_k$. Since M, N, M', and N' are relatively prime, no p_i divides all four of the M, N, M', and N'. Hence we can always find numbers r_i and s_i such that p_i does not divide both of

$$j_i = Ms_i - Nr_i, \qquad k_i = M's_i - N'r_i,$$

for if p_i does not divide one of M and M', for example, we can simply set $s_i = 1$ and $r_i = 0$. Let $p = p_1 p_2 \cdots p_k$, and define

$$q_i = \frac{p}{p_i} = \frac{p_1 p_2 \cdots p_k}{p_i}.$$

Then p_i does not divide q_i, but it divides all the other $q_n (n \neq i)$. Suppose now that we define

$$r = q_1 r_1 + q_2 r_2 + \cdots + q_k r_k, \qquad s = q_1 s_1 + q_2 s_2 + \cdots + q_k s_k,$$

so that

$$Ms - Nr = q_1 j_1 + q_2 j_2 + \cdots + q_k j_k,$$
$$M's - N'r = q_1 k_1 + q_2 k_2 + \cdots + q_k k_k.$$

The prime p_i divides $q_n j_n$ and $q_n k_n$ for all $n \neq i$. However, it does not divide both $q_i j_i$ and $q_i k_i$, because of the way in which these quantities were defined.

[6] E. N. Gilbert, *J. Soc. Motion Picture and Television Engrs.*, **72**, 606–608 (1963).

Hence it does not divide at least one of $Ms - Nr$ and $M's - N'r$, so these quantities have no common factor containing a prime less than or equal to $|MN' - M'N|$. Thus $Ms - Nr$, $M's - N'r$, and $MN' - M'N$ are relatively prime, and this is the required result.

Having stated and proved Theorems A and B, we now illustrate the application of these results in practice to construct masks that will produce close-packed dots. We remind the reader that (Fig. 4.9) the point lattice of holes is specified by two vectors $\mathbf{v}$ and $\mathbf{v}'$, corresponding to steps $M + \omega N'$ and $M' + \omega N'$, respectively, where M and M' are the number of steps in the direction of the x axis (to the right) in Fig. 4.9 and N and N' are the number of steps in a direction making $60°$ with the x axis $[\omega = \exp(i\pi/3) = \frac{1}{2}(1 + i\sqrt{3})]$. The frame is moved by a vector $\mathbf{t}$ given by $T = r + \omega s$ at each step. If the dots are close-packed after q translations, then, from (4.33),

$$q = |MN' - M'N|. \tag{4.43}$$

Suppose now that the generating vectors $\mathbf{v}$ and $\mathbf{v}'$ make an angle of $60°$ to each other, so that

$$M' + \omega N' = \omega(M + \omega N),$$

or, since $\omega^2 = -1 + \omega$,

$$M' = -N, \qquad N' = M + N. \tag{4.44}$$

Combining this result with (4.43), we see that if the dots are close-packed after q translations,

$$q = M^2 + MN + N^2. \tag{4.45}$$

Theorem B requires, for close packing to be possible, that M, N, M', and N' be relatively prime, that is, in the present case, from (4.44), that M and N be relatively prime. Theorem A requires that, for close packing, the numbers $Ms - Nr$, $M + N(r + s)$, and $q = M^2 + MN + N^2$ have no common factor greater than unity. Such a factor certainly exists if M and N are not relatively prime, or if $M = 0$, or $N = 0$, with $q > 1$. Conversely, if M and N are nonzero and relatively prime, then $r = 1$ (or $r = \pm 1$, $s = \pm 1$) satisfies the conditions of Theorem A. Hence only translations of one dot diameter need be considered. We enumerate in Table 4.1 the first eight possible values of q, the number of translates producing close packing of dots, corresponding to relatively prime M and N. The picture corresponding to the case $q = 19$ was given in Fig. 4.9.

TABLE 4.1

$q = M^2 + MN + N^2$	3	7	13	19	21	31	37	39
M	1	2	3	3	4	5	4	5
N	1	1	1	2	1	1	3	2

4.7   Recovery of a Band-Limited Signal[7]

Mathematics Used: Fourier series and (at the end of the section) Fourier integrals.

Comment: Mathematics is used to show that something which seems impossible is in fact possible, thus encouraging further work that may lead to improved methods for the transmission of information.

In this section we use mathematics to show that something which at first sight seems impossible is in fact possible. The proof will be nonconstructive; that is, although we shall show that something is possible, the proof will not indicate how the theoretically possible procedure can be carried out in practice. Nevertheless the existence of the proof is important, because it means that there is some point in persevering in the effort to invent a practicable procedure by some other method. (In Section 10.5 we shall give an example that, in a sense, illustrates the converse of the point made in the present example. We shall show that something which at first sight seems plausible is in fact impossible, namely, that it is not possible to design a resistor network with a certain property.)

When a signal $g(t)$ is transmitted over a communication channel, there is a tendency for the low-amplitude part of $g(t)$ to become masked by the presence of channel noise and for the high-amplitude part of $g(t)$ to become distorted by the nonlinearity of components in those ranges. It would be valuable, therefore, to find a way of assigning to $g(t)$ another signal, from which $g(t)$ could be recovered, but which would have the property that its amplitude lay more nearly in the middle ranges than that of $g(t)$. This second signal is then transmitted, instead of the original $g(t)$. One relatively simple way of obtaining such a signal is by what is known as *instantaneous companding*. Let $\phi(x)$ be a continuous, odd function of x, so that $\phi(-x) = -\phi(x)$ and $\phi(0) = 0$. Also let $\phi(x)$ be monotonic, that is,

$$\phi(x_1) > \phi(x_2) \qquad \text{if} \qquad x_1 > x_2,$$

and let $y = \phi(x)$ have a large slope at $x = 0$ and let it approach a constant value as x tends to infinity (see Fig. 4.10). Then the signal sent is $\phi\{g(t)\}$ instead of $g(t)$. The large slope of $y = \phi(x)$ around $x = 0$ magnifies signals of low amplitude, and the fact that ϕ approaches a constant value for large x means that high-amplitude signals are cut down.

---

[7] This section was suggested by a submitted contribution: H. J. Landau, On the Recovery of a Band-Limited Signal, after Instantaneous Companding and Subsequent Band Limiting, *Bell System Tech. J.*, **39**, 351–366 (1960). We shall be concerned mainly with a result due to A. Beurling in Appendix A of the paper. The original version will probably prove difficult for the average engineer-reader of this book. We hope that the version given here is an example of how mathematical arguments can often be made more palatable. However, the engineer should not therefore conclude that the original type of treatment is unnecessary. Results are often found initially by complicated mathematical reasoning which is then simplified. Also arguments often become "obvious" only after they have been proved rigorously. In the present case we cannot avoid ultimate use of the Fourier integral.

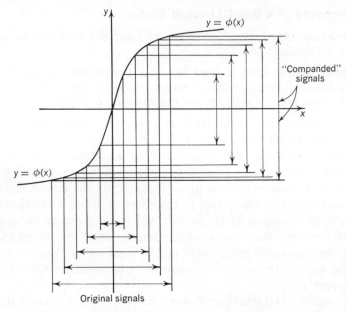

Fig. 4.10   Effect of the monotonic function $y = \phi(x)$.

A signal is said to be *band-limited* when it contains frequencies f which lie only in a restricted range, $|f| \le F$, say. The drawback of instantaneous companding is that it destroys the property of being band-limited. We usually start with a signal $g(t)$ that is band-limited. The signal $\phi\{g(t)\}$ will not in general be band-limited. In particular, it will usually contain harmonics of the frequencies in $g(t)$, so it will contain frequencies above f_2. Suppose the signal is to be sent over an idealized band-limited channel which transmits perfectly all frequencies in the range $|f| \le F$ but no frequencies outside this range. Then $\phi\{g(t)\}$ is distorted during transmission, even though the original $g(t)$ would not have been. In effect, part of $\phi\{g(t)\}$ is thrown away (the frequencies above f_2), and we might think that it would therefore be impossible to recover $g(t)$ precisely. Actually this is not true. To recover $g(t)$ band-limited in $|f| \le F$, we need only know $\phi\{g(t)\}$ for frequencies in the same range, $|f| \le F$. The object of the discussion below is to make this result plausible by elementary arguments, before outlining the proof using the Fourier integral.

We shall proceed in the following way. Suppose $g_1(t)$ and $g_2(t)$ are band-limited in $|f| \le F$, and suppose $\phi\{g_1(t)\}$ and $\phi\{g_2(t)\}$ have frequency spectra that are identical in amplitude and phase for frequencies in $|f| \le F$, only. Then we shall show that $g_1(t)$ and $g_2(t)$ must be identical. This may be interpreted as saying that "no information is lost" in transmitting $\phi\{g(t)\}$ over an idealized band-limiting channel since the transmitted signal is still sufficient to determine $g(t)$ uniquely, although there is no simple way of recovering $\phi\{g(t)\}$, and hence $g(t)$, from the transmitted signal.

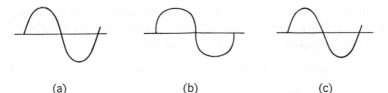

(a)   (b)   (c)

Fig. 4.11 Situation when $g(t)$ is a simple sine wave: (a) $g(t)$; (b) $\phi[g(t)]$; (c) fundamental of $\phi[g(t)]$.

The procedure is easily understood when $g(t)$ is a simple sine wave:

$$g(t) = A \sin(\omega t + \alpha), \tag{4.46}$$

where $\omega = 2\pi f > 0$, and we assume $f < F < 2f$; that is, harmonics lie outside the range. Then $\phi\{g(t)\}$ might have the form shown in Fig. 4.11b. (This is deduced from the effect of ϕ as shown in Fig. 4.10.) When $\phi\{g(t)\}$ is band-limited in the same range as $g(t)$, we again obtain a simple sine wave, because of the assumption $F < 2f$. We require the Fourier decomposition of $\phi\{g(t)\}$, and it is convenient to use the complex form of the Fourier series:

$$\phi\{g(t)\} = \sum_{r=-\infty}^{\infty} a_r e^{ir\omega t},$$

where

$$a_r = \frac{\omega}{2\pi} \int_0^{2\pi/\omega} \phi\{g(t)\} e^{-ir\omega t}\, dt.$$

We see that $a_0 = 0$ since $\phi(x)$ is an odd function of x. The function that is actually transmitted over the band-limited channel is, because $F < 2f$,

$$a_1 e^{-i\omega t} + a_{-1} e^{i\omega t}. \tag{4.47}$$

Suppose now that two functions

$$g_1(t) = A_1 \sin(\omega t + \alpha_1), \qquad g_2(t) = A_2 \sin(\omega t + \alpha_2)$$

are converted by the function ϕ into signals whose Fourier-series decompositions have coefficients a_r' and a_r'', respectively. Suppose the band-limited signals that are transmitted are identical, that is, from (4.47),

$$a_1' = a_1'', \qquad a_{-1}' = a_{-1}'', \tag{4.48}$$

but we know nothing about the other coefficients. We shall show that $g_1(t)$ and $g_2(t)$ must be identical. Consider

$$\int_0^{2\pi/\omega} [\phi\{g_1(t)\} - \phi\{g_2(t)\}][g_1(t) - g_2(t)]\, dt \tag{4.49}$$

$$= \int_0^{2\pi/\omega} \left[\sum_{r=-\infty}^{\infty} (a_r' - a_r'') e^{ir\omega t} \right] [A_1 \sin(\omega t + \alpha_1) - A_2 \sin(\omega t + \alpha_2)]\, dt$$

$$= \int_0^{2\pi/\omega} [(a_1' - a_1'') e^{i\omega t} + (a_{-1}' - a_{-1}'') e^{-i\omega t}]$$

$$\times [A_1 \sin(\omega t + \alpha_1) - A_2 \sin(\omega t + \alpha_2)]\, dt$$

$$= 0,$$

where all the terms that arise from the infinite series except the four in the second-to-last line are zero because of orthogonality, and the last line follows from (4.48). Because ϕ is monotonic, we always have

$$[\phi(x_1) - \phi(x_2)](x_1 - x_2) > 0 \qquad \text{if} \qquad x_1 \neq x_2. \tag{4.50}$$

The integral in (4.49) is zero, so it follows immediately that $g_1(t) \equiv g_2(t)$. This is the required result.

So far we have considered only a special single-frequency wave. To prove the result in general we need to use the Fourier integral. Let

$$g(t) = \frac{1}{2\pi} \int_{-\infty}^{\infty} G(\omega)e^{i\omega t}\, d\omega, \qquad G(\omega) = \int_{-\infty}^{\infty} g(t)e^{-i\omega t}\, dt,$$

and, similarly, introduce a function $\Phi(\omega)$ defined by

$$\phi\{g(t)\} = \frac{1}{2\pi} \int_{-\infty}^{\infty} \Phi(\omega)e^{i\omega t}\, d\omega.$$

Suppose $g_1(t)$ and $g_2(t)$ are two band-limited functions such that

$$G_1(\omega) = G_2(\omega) = 0, \qquad \text{for} \qquad |\omega| > 2\pi F; \tag{4.51}$$

that is, G_1 and G_2 are zero outside the range $|\omega| \leq 2\pi F$. Suppose g_1 and g_2 are converted by the function ϕ into signals such that the Fourier transforms of $\phi\{g_1(t)\}$ and $\phi\{g_2(t)\}$ are given by $\Phi_1(\omega)$ and $\Phi_2(\omega)$, respectively. Suppose the corresponding band-limited signals have identical frequency distributions,

$$\Phi_1(\omega) = \Phi_2(\omega), \qquad |\omega| \leq 2\pi F, \tag{4.52}$$

but we know nothing about the behavior of Φ_1 and Φ_2 outside this range. Then we assert that $g_1(t)$ and $g_2(t)$ must be identical. The argument is completely analogous to that for the single frequency:

$$\int_{-\infty}^{\infty} [\phi\{g_1(t)\} - \phi\{g_2(t)\}][g_1(t) - g_2(t)]\, dt \tag{4.53}$$

$$= \frac{1}{2\pi} \int_{-\infty}^{\infty} \int_{-\infty}^{\infty} [\Phi_1(\omega) - \Phi_2(\omega)]e^{i\omega t}\, d\omega [g_1(t) - g_2(t)]\, dt$$

$$= \frac{1}{2\pi} \int_{-\infty}^{\infty} [\Phi_1(\omega) - \Phi_2(\omega)] \int_{-\infty}^{\infty} [g_1(t) - g_2(t)]e^{i\omega t}\, dt\, d\omega.$$

$$= \frac{1}{2\pi} \int_{-\infty}^{\infty} [\Phi_1(\omega) - \Phi_2(\omega)][G_1(\omega) - G_2(\omega)]\, d\omega$$

$$= 0,$$

where the last line follows from the next-to-last line by using (4.51) and (4.52). The same argument that was applied to (4.49) shows, from (4.50) and (4.53), that $g_1(t)$ and $g_2(t)$ are identical.

Part II

APPLICATIONS OF ORDINARY DIFFERENTIAL EQUATIONS

Chapter 5

Differential Equations and Electrical Circuits

5.1 The Ignition System of an Internal Combustion Engine[1]

Mathematics Used: First- and second-order linear differential equations with constant coefficients, and matching of solutions.

Comment: Note the way in which a complicated situation is analyzed in a piecewise fashion.

In this and the following section we consider the ignition system of an automobile engine. This consists essentially of a direct-current source of electricity (battery or generator), and a transformer, the transformer being connected across the spark plug, as shown diagrammatically in Fig. 5.1. There is a switch (circuit breaker) in the primary circuit which is closed mechanically by the rotation of the engine for a certain period of time. The effect of the spark gap in the secondary of the transformer is that no current flows in the secondary unless the voltage exceeds a certain limit. When the voltage exceeds this limit, the effect of the spark can be represented by assuming that a switch is closed in the secondary of the transformer, and current flows through a resistance R_s until the voltage in the secondary drops to a certain amount, when the spark ceases (diagrammatically, the switch opens) in the secondary.

The process can be divided into four steps (see Fig. 5.1).

Step (a). Initially the currents in the primary and secondary circuits are zero and the switch (circuit breaker) in the primary is open. At the initial instant of time the switch is closed. (Mechanically, the points of the circuit breaker are closed by rotation of the engine.) The current in the primary circuit then builds up, while the secondary circuit is open (no spark in the spark plug).

---

[1] The first two sections of this chapter are based on course material used at the U.S. Military Academy, West Point, collected by Col. Billingsley, Head, Department of Ordnance.

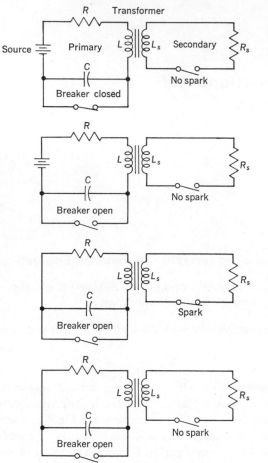

(a) Build-up of current in primary, secondary open-circuited.

(b) Collapse of magnetic field in primary when breaker opened, emf induced in secondary.

(c) Spark jumps spark-plug gap, current flows in secondary.

(d) Spark has taken place, no current in secondary, breaker still open.

Fig. 5.1   Ignition-system cycle.

Step (b). The breaker switch in the primary is opened. The inductance of the primary and the capacity form an oscillatory circuit. The collapse of the magnetic field in the inductance induces an electromotive force in the secondary. This is before the secondary has any current flow; that is, there is voltage build-up but no discharge of electricity across the spark-plug gap.

Step (c). When the voltage builds up sufficiently in the secondary, this causes a spark to jump the spark-plug gap, allowing current to flow in the secondary. The capacity in the primary reacts with the inductances to produce oscillatory currents.

Step (d). When the voltage across the spark gap falls below a certain amount, the spark will cease. There will be no current flow in the secondary and whatever (unimportant) oscillatory currents remain in the primary will decay to zero, owing to the resistance R_p.

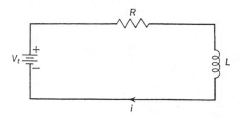

Fig. 5.2 Circuit diagram of the ignition system during step (a).

The first step in understanding the functioning of the ignition system is to consider the transient currents.

Step (a). The build-up of current in the primary. From Fig. 5.1a we see that the circuit diagram during step (a) is simply that shown in Fig. 5.2: the primary resistance R and the primary inductance L in series with a voltage V_t, which may be either the battery terminal voltage (during starting) or the generator terminal voltage (when the engine is running).

Applying Kirchhoff's law in the usual way we obtain the equation

$$L \frac{di}{dt} + Ri = V_t.$$

This is a standard first-order linear equation with constant coefficients, which can be solved by writing it in the form

$$\frac{d}{dt} (ie^{Rt/L}) = \frac{V_t}{L} e^{Rt/L}.$$

Integration of both sides gives

$$i = \frac{V_t}{R} + Ce^{-Rt/L},$$

where C is an arbitrary constant. This constant is determined by the initial condition that $i = 0$ at $t = 0$, which gives, finally,

$$i = \frac{V_t}{R} (1 - e^{-Rt/L}).$$

This means that during step (a) the current in the primary builds up exponentially from a value of zero to a value V_t/R.

Step (b). Collapse of the field in the primary, with no current flow in the secondary. When the breaker points open, the condenser is no longer short-circuited but is now in the primary circuit, as shown in Fig. 5.1b, redrawn in simplified form in Fig. 5.3. Again applying Kirchhoff's law, we can write the differential equation for the circuit:

$$L \frac{di}{dt} + Ri + \frac{1}{C} \int_0^t i \, dt = V_t.$$

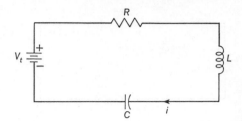

Fig. 5.3   Circuit diagram of the ignition system during step (b).

Setting $i = dq/dt$ in the usual way, where q is the electrical charge in the condenser, this can be written in the more familiar form

$$L\frac{d^2q}{dt^2} + R\frac{dq}{dt} + \frac{1}{C}q = V_t.$$

This is a second-order linear equation with constant coefficients which can be solved by standard methods. The general solution is

$$q = CV_t + e^{-Rt/2L}(A \sin \omega t + B \cos \omega t),$$

where A and B are arbitrary constants, and

$$\omega = \left(\frac{1}{LC} - \frac{R^2}{4L^2}\right)^{1/2}.$$

The initial conditions at $t = 0$ [now measuring time from the instant step (b) begins, that is, the circuit breaker opens] are [because initially there is no charge in the condenser and the beginning of step (b) follows the end of step (a)]

$$q = 0, \quad i = \frac{dq}{dt} = i_0 \qquad \text{at } t = 0,$$

where i_0 is the current in the primary circuit at the end of step (a), when the circuit breaker opens to initiate step (b), as determined by the analysis of step (a). On determining the arbitrary constants A and B by means of these initial conditions, we find, eventually,

$$i = i_0 e^{-Rt/2L}\left[\cos \omega t + \frac{1}{L\omega}\left(\frac{V_t}{i_0} - \frac{R}{2}\right) \sin \omega t\right].$$

The important feature of this solution is that ω is large, so this is a highly oscillatory solution, the amplitude of which is decaying exponentially.

The action of the transformer can be represented crudely by saying that a voltage appears across the secondary of the transformer which is proportional to N times the voltage across the primary, where N is (roughly) the ratio of the number of turns of the secondary to the number of turns in the primary. The ratio N is large. The voltage across the primary is $L(di/dt)$, so the voltage across the secondary is $NL(di/dt)$. Because di/dt is proportional to ω where ω

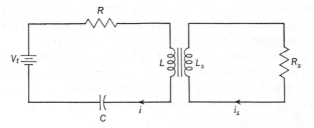

Fig. 5.4   Circuit diagram of the ignition system during step (c).

is large, and N is large, the voltage across the secondary (and hence also the voltage across the spark gap) is large, and this causes a spark in the spark gap. This initiates step (c) of the sequence.

Step (c). Current flowing in both primary and secondary.   The circuit in this case is shown in Fig. 5.4. Now the circuit equations are

$$\frac{1}{C} \int_0^t i\, dt + Ri + L\frac{di}{dt} + M\frac{di_s}{dt} = V_t, \qquad M\frac{di}{dt} + L_s\frac{di_s}{dt} + R_s i_s = 0,$$

where i is again the current in the primary circuit, i_s the current in the secondary, M the mutual inductance between the primary and secondary of the transformer, and the other symbols are as indicated in Fig. 5.4. We shall not solve the above equations in detail. We merely remark that, as in step (b), the solution is an exponentially decaying oscillation, the rate of decay being more rapid than in step (b), owing to the presence of the additional resistance R_s of the spark gap, causing dissipation of energy in the secondary.

Step (d). The aftermath of the spark.   When the amplitude of the voltage (or the current) across the spark gap in the secondary falls below a certain

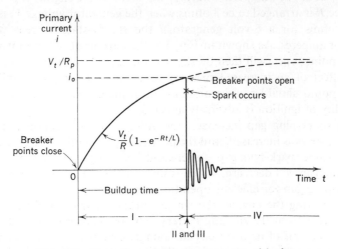

Fig. 5.5   Variation of primary current with time.

amount, the spark will cease. The circuit then reverts to the condition in step (b); that is, there is no current in the secondary and a decaying oscillatory solution (of unimportant amplitude) exists in the primary.

The variation of the primary current i with time is shown diagrammatically in Fig. 5.5. The duration of the spark is very short (of the order of 0.001 sec), and the interval between the opening of the breaker and the spark is also very small. Steps (b) and (c) are therefore shown in the figure as occurring simultaneously and instantaneously.

5.2   Deductions from the Analysis in Section 5.1

The object of the ignition system is to release sufficient energy at the spark gap to initiate combustion. This energy is supplied by the conversion of electrical energy to heat in the combustible mixture in the spark gap. For a given ignition system the electrical energy is proportional to the square of the current in the secondary circuit, which is proportional to the square of the primary current at the instant when the spark is formed, i_0^2. In addition, a spark is formed only if the voltage across the spark-plug gap is large enough during step (b). This voltage is proportional to i_0, which again indicates that for a given ignition system the value of i_0 must not be too small.

On the other hand, when the breaker points open, arcing occurs, with consequent release of heat energy and deterioration of the points. Experience indicates that the points can be expected to have a reasonable life if the value of i_0 when the engine is running at a constant speed is held to 4 amperes. The other factors mentioned in the last paragraph indicate that i_0 should be kept as large as possible. This means that we should try to keep the primary current i_0 at about 4 amperes whatever the speed of the engine. If the primary resistance R is arranged to be 3 ohms when the generator voltage V_t is 12 volts (or 1.5 ohms for a 6-volt generator), the steady-state current would be $V_t/R = 4$ amperes. As shown in Fig. 5.5, the current at the instant when the breaker points open will then be slightly less than 4 amperes.

The effect of an increased primary resistance due to pitted and burned breaker points should now be obvious. As R increases, i_0 decreases, and the probability of ignition is adversely affected.

If the spark-plug gap increases, the voltage in the secondary needed to produce a spark is increased, and the probability of ignition is again adversely affected. If the spark-plug gap is decreased, the energy released in the form of heat in the gap will decrease, which is undesirable. There is an optimum size of spark-plug gap for efficient operation.

When starting the engine, the starter motor is almost stalled and draws heavy current from the starting battery. The battery-terminal voltage drops to about one half of its open-circuit voltage, 6 volts in the case of a 12-volt battery. When starting, the voltage V_t for the ignition is provided by the battery, so the steady-state current at the instant of starting will be only $6/3 = 2$ amperes. This will, of course, gradually increase to 4 amperes as the starter motor and engine speed increase. However, this effect can result in poor starting performance of the engine. To overcome this difficulty, the resistance of 3 ohms in the primary is separated into two parts, a primary circuit resistor of 1.5 ohms in series with the remainder of the primary circuit, which also has a resistance of 1.5 ohms. Arrangements are made so that the primary circuit resistor is bypassed (short-circuited) when the starter switch is closed and inserted in the circuit when the starter switch is open. Thus the engine is started, the primary circuit resistance is 1.5 ohms, and when the engine is running, the primary resistance is 3 ohms. The starting performance of the engine is, therefore, improved.

The design of an efficient ignition system requires a careful balancing of the values of the primary resistance, the transformer inductances and the transformer ratio, the breakdown voltage of the spark gap, the resistance of the spark gap, and the build-up time between closing and opening the breaker points. We cannot hope to discuss this in any detail, but we indicate briefly some of the reasons why, although most electrical systems were 6-volt in the early days of the automobile, it was desirable from the point of view of the ignition system to change to 12 volts when high-speed, high-compression V-8 engines were introduced.

The interval between the closing and opening of the breaker (see Fig. 5.5) is known as the *build-up time* (or *dwell time*). This time is proportional to the ratio (cam angle)/rpm, where the term *cam angle* refers to the angle of a cam in the breaker system. For a given ignition system, the value of i_0 is solely dependent on the rpm, or the speed of the engine. The larger the engine speed, the smaller the current when the breaker points open, as illustrated in Fig. 5.6,

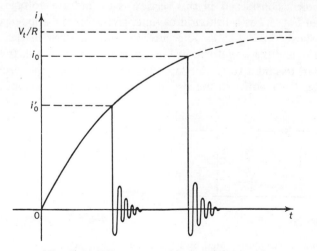

Fig. 5.6   Effect on i_0 of increasing speed.

where the rpm corresponding to the current i_0' is twice the rpm for i_0. When high-speed, high-compression V-8 engines were produced, it was found that increasing the number of cylinders resulted in smaller cam angles. High engine speeds reduced the time available for current to build up in the primary, and high compression ratios increased the value of the voltage required to produce a spark. The addition of these effects resulted in i_0 approaching values where misfiring occurred when 6-volt systems were used. If the voltage is changed to 12 volts and the primary resistance R is also doubled, the steady-state current V_t/R is unchanged, but the rate at which the current increases from zero to the steady state is governed by the term

$$1 - e^{-R_p t/L},$$

where R_p is the primary resistance. If R_p changes from R to $2R$, L remaining constant, the steady state is reached more quickly. Thus the value of i_0 will be greater in the 12-volt system than in the 6-volt system.

This concludes our discussion of ignition systems.

5.3 A Difference-Equation Example[2]

Engineering Context: Electrical network.

Mathematics Used: First-order linear differential equations with constant coefficients and simple first-order difference equations.

The examples in the remainder of this chapter analyze specific electrical circuits, and their interest lies primarily in the mathematical techniques used in their solution.

The problem considered in this section is to find the voltage across the capacitor in Fig. 5.7 as a function of time, given that the applied voltage has the form shown in Fig. 5.8. The currents and voltages in the circuit are initially zero, and the waveform in Fig. 5.8 is applied at $t = 0$. It is required, in particular, to find a time constant describing how fast the circuit reaches steady state. The rectifier in the circuit is assumed to pass current freely (that

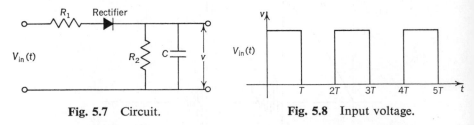

| Fig. 5.7 Circuit. | Fig. 5.8 Input voltage. |

[2] This example was contributed by F. J. Young, Electrical Engineering Department, Carnegie Institute of Technology, Pittsburgh, Pa.

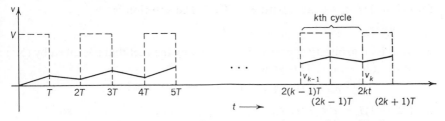

Fig. 5.9   Variation of the voltage v across the capacitor with time.

is, to present no resistance to current) in the forward direction, but to prevent current flow completely in the reverse direction.

The variation of the voltage v across the capacitor with time is shown diagrammatically in Fig. 5.9. In the kth cycle the voltage v starts at some undetermined value v_{k-1}. In the time interval $2(k-1)T \le t \le (2k-1)T$, a voltage V is applied to the system. The current through the capacitor is given by $C(dv/dt)$ and the current through the resistor R_2 by v/R_2, so that the current through R_1 is given by $C(dv/dt) + v/R_2$.

Hence

$$V = R_1\left(C\frac{dv}{dt} + \frac{v}{R_2}\right) + v.$$

On rearranging,

$$\tau\frac{dv}{dt} + v = \alpha V,$$

where

$$\tau = \frac{R_1 R_2}{R_1 + R_2}\,C, \qquad \alpha = \frac{R_2}{R_1 + R_2}.$$

The solution of this simple first-order linear equation with constant coefficients is

$$v = \alpha V + Ae^{-t/\tau},$$

where A is an arbitrary constant. The initial condition that $v = v_{k-1}$ at $t = 2(k-1)T$ gives

$$v = \alpha V + (v_{k-1} - \alpha V)e^{-[t - 2(k-1)T]/\tau}.$$

At time $(2k-1)T$ the voltage has therefore risen to

$$\alpha V + (v_{k-1} - \alpha V)e^{-T/\tau}. \tag{5.1}$$

At time $t = (2k-1)T$ the applied voltage goes to zero. There is a rectifier in the circuit, so no current flows back into the source but C discharges into R_2. The equation for v during this period is

$$\sigma\frac{dv}{dt} + v = 0$$

for $(2k - 1)T \le t \le 2kT$, with $\sigma = R_2C$. The solution is

$$v = Be^{-t/\sigma},$$

where B is an arbitrary constant determined by the fact that v is given by (5.1) when $t = (2k - 1)T$. This yields

$$v = [\alpha V + (v_{k-1} - \alpha V)e^{-T/\tau}]e^{-[t - 2(k-1)T]/\sigma}$$

for $(2k - 1)T \le t \le 2kT$. At $t = 2kT$, this voltage is in fact v_k, so

$$v_k = \{\alpha V + (v_{k-1} - \alpha V)e^{-T/\tau}\}e^{-T/\sigma}. \tag{5.2}$$

This is a simple difference equation in v_k.

Rearranging (5.2) we see that it is of the form

$$v_k - pv_{k-1} = q, \tag{5.3}$$

where p and q are independent of k,

$$p = e^{-T(\tau + \sigma)/\tau\sigma}, \qquad q = \alpha V(1 - e^{-T/\tau})e^{-T/\sigma}.$$

Perhaps the simplest way to solve (5.3) is to write this equation for $k = n$, $n - 1, n - 2, \ldots, 1$, in turn. Then by multiplying the first, second, third,$\ldots$, nth equations by $1, p, p^2, \ldots, p^{n-1}$, respectively, and adding, we find

$$v_n - p^n v_0 = q(1 + p + p^2 + \cdots + p^{n-1})$$

$$= q\frac{(1 - p^n)}{1 - p}.$$

In our case the initial voltage v_0 is zero, so that, on inserting the explicit expressions for p and q,

$$v_n = \alpha V(1 - e^{-T/\tau})e^{-T/\sigma}\frac{1 - e^{-nT(\tau + \sigma)/\tau\sigma}}{1 - e^{-T(\tau + \sigma)/\tau\sigma}}. \tag{5.4}$$

If a voltage varies as $\exp(-t/\eta)$, we say the system has a time constant η. In the above example the time t is represented by nT, so from (5.4) the overall time constant is $\tau\sigma/(\tau + \sigma)$.

5.4   A Linear-Algebra Treatment of Transients in an Electrical Circuit[3]

Mathematics Used: Solution of a system of simultaneous linear differential equations with constant coefficients by means of linear algebra, using matrix eigenvalues and eigenvectors.

Comment: The objective is to uncouple a set of coupled equations [see (5.15)]. Not only is the formal method extremely powerful, but it provides insight into the structure of a large class of problems of a similar type.

---

[3] This example was contributed by C. A. Desoer, Department of Electrical Engineering, University of California, Berkeley, Calif.

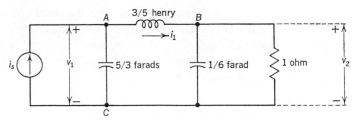

Fig. 5.10   Electrical circuit considered in Section 5.4.

In this section we discuss the electrical transients in the circuit shown in Fig. 5.10. The current source i_s is connected to nodes A and C. At time t the current source causes a current of $i_s(t)$ amp to leave node C and enter node A. The function i_s is a known function of time.

This is, of course, a standard problem. It could be tackled, for example, by means of the Laplace transform, although the fact that $i_s(t)$ is an arbitrary function of t means that we shall have to use the convolution theorem to obtain the final answer in a convenient form. The object of this section is to show that there is some advantage in solving the problem by means of linear algebra. We assume no more than a sophomore course in linear algebra and differential equations. The solution will illustrate the concepts of eigenvalue, eigenvector, basis, and change of basis, within the framework of linear electrical systems.

To set up the equations, we use as variables v_1, the voltage across the $\frac{5}{3}$-farad condenser; v_2, the voltage across the $\frac{1}{6}$-farad condenser; and i_1, the current through the $\frac{3}{5}$-henry inductance. The polarities are those indicated in Fig. 5.10. When v_1 is positive, the electrical potential of node A is larger than that of node C (both potentials being measured with respect to a common reference). Similarly, i_1 is positive when the current goes through the inductance from A to B.

We use the well-known formulas $i = C(dv/dt)$ and $v = L(di/dt)$, relating the "current through" to the "voltage across" condensers and inductances, respectively. Kirchhoff's current law, applied to node A, states that the sum of the currents entering node A is zero. Thus

$$\frac{5}{3}\frac{dv_1}{dt} = -i_1 + i_s.$$

Similarly, at node B,

$$\frac{1}{6}\frac{dv_2}{dt} = i_1 - v_2.$$

Expressing the voltage across the inductance in terms of the derivative of i_1, we get

$$\frac{3}{5}\frac{di_1}{dt} = v_1 - v_2.$$

These are a set of three ordinary differential equations in the three unknowns v_1, i_1, and v_2, and describe the behavior of the circuit. It is well known that if we are given the values of v_1, i_1, and v_2 at, say, time $t = 0$, and the function $i_s(t)$ for $t \geq 0$, then v_1, i_1, and v_2 are uniquely determined for any $t > 0$.

We rewrite the above equations in the form

$$
\begin{bmatrix} \dfrac{dv_1}{dt} \\[2mm] \dfrac{di_1}{dt} \\[2mm] \dfrac{dv_2}{dt} \end{bmatrix} = \begin{bmatrix} 0 & -\frac{3}{5} & 0 \\[1mm] \frac{5}{3} & 0 & -\frac{5}{3} \\[1mm] 0 & 6 & -6 \end{bmatrix} \begin{bmatrix} v_1 \\[1mm] i_1 \\[1mm] v_2 \end{bmatrix} + \begin{bmatrix} \frac{3}{5} \\[1mm] 0 \\[1mm] 0 \end{bmatrix} i_s
$$

or
$$
\dot{\mathbf{x}} = \frac{d\mathbf{x}}{dt} = \mathbf{A}\mathbf{x} + \mathbf{b}i_s, \tag{5.5}
$$

where

$$
\mathbf{x} = \begin{bmatrix} v_1 \\ i_1 \\ v_2 \end{bmatrix}, \qquad \mathbf{A} = \begin{bmatrix} 0 & -\frac{3}{5} & 0 \\[1mm] \frac{5}{3} & 0 & -\frac{5}{3} \\[1mm] 0 & 6 & -6 \end{bmatrix}, \qquad \mathbf{b} = \begin{bmatrix} \frac{3}{5} \\[1mm] 0 \\[1mm] 0 \end{bmatrix}.
$$

As a first step we calculate the eigenvalues and eigenvectors of $\mathbf{A}$. The eigenvalues are given by $\det (\mathbf{A} - \lambda\mathbf{I}) = 0$:

$$
\begin{vmatrix} -\lambda & -\frac{3}{5} & 0 \\[1mm] \frac{5}{3} & -\lambda & -\frac{5}{3} \\[1mm] 0 & 6 & -(\lambda + 6) \end{vmatrix} = -(\lambda^3 + 6\lambda^2 + 11\lambda + 6) = -(\lambda + 1)(\lambda + 2)(\lambda + 3).
$$

Hence the three eigenvalues of $\mathbf{A}$ are $\lambda_1 = -1$, $\lambda_2 = -2$, and $\lambda_3 = -3$. Standard procedures for solving algebraic equations of the form $(\mathbf{A} - \lambda_i\mathbf{I})\mathbf{u}_i = 0$ give the following eigenvectors:

$$
\mathbf{u}_1 = \begin{bmatrix} 0.6 \\ 1.0 \\ 1.2 \end{bmatrix}, \qquad \mathbf{u}_2 = \begin{bmatrix} 0.3 \\ 1.0 \\ 1.5 \end{bmatrix}, \qquad \mathbf{u}_3 = \begin{bmatrix} 0.1 \\ 0.5 \\ 1.0 \end{bmatrix}.
$$

For numerical convenience these eigenvectors have been scaled so that each has one component that is unity. The reader can verify that $\mathbf{A}\mathbf{u}_i = \lambda_i\mathbf{u}_i$ ($i = 1, 2, 3$), as should be the case according to the definition of eigenvectors.

Since $\mathbf{u}_1$, $\mathbf{u}_2$, and $\mathbf{u}_3$ are eigenvectors of $\mathbf{A}$ that correspond to distinct eigenvalues, they are *linearly independent vectors*, and they also contribute a *basis* for the space; that is, any vector $\mathbf{x}$ can be written in the form of a linear combination of the $\mathbf{u}_i$:

$$
\mathbf{x} = a_1\mathbf{u}_1 + a_2\mathbf{u}_2 + a_3\mathbf{u}_3. \tag{5.6}
$$

The scalar coefficients a_i can be found conveniently by using the eigenvectors of the transpose matrix $\mathbf{A}^T$ (that is, the matrix obtained by changing the rows and columns of A). The matrix A^T has the same eigenvalues as A, namely λ_1, λ_2, and λ_3. Denote the corresponding eigenvectors by v_1, v_2, and v_3, so that

$$A^T v_i = \lambda_i v_i \qquad i = 1, 2, 3.$$

Taking the transpose of both sides of this equation, we have

$$v_i^T A = \lambda_i v_i^T.$$

We also have

$$A u_j = \lambda_j u_j.$$

Postmultiplying the first equation by u_j, premultiplying the second by v_i^T and subtracting, we find that

$$(\lambda_i - \lambda_j) v_i^T u_j = 0.$$

Hence if $\lambda_i \neq \lambda_j$, we have (since the eigenvalues are distinct)

$$v_i^T u_j = 0 \qquad i \neq j. \tag{5.7}$$

We say that the sets of vectors v_i and u_j are *biorthogonal*. (This is a generalization of the idea that vectors w_i form an orthogonal set if $w_i^T w_j = 0$, for $i \neq j$). If we now multiply (5.6) by v_1^T, v_2^T, and v_3^T in turn, we see that

$$a_i = \frac{v_i^T x}{v_i^T u_i}. \tag{5.8}$$

This gives us an easy method for the determination of the a_i. In our concrete example we find

$$v_1 = \begin{bmatrix} 1.0 \\ -0.6 \\ 0.2 \end{bmatrix}, \qquad v_2 = \begin{bmatrix} 1.0 \\ -1.2 \\ 0.5 \end{bmatrix}, \qquad v_3 = \begin{bmatrix} 1.0 \\ -1.8 \\ 1.0 \end{bmatrix}, \tag{5.9}$$

where the magnitudes have been adjusted so that the first element is unity in each case.

5.5   A Linear-Algebra Treatment of Transients (continued)

The key to the simplification of the original equations (5.5) is the identity (5.11), which we proceed to derive. Let T be the matrix that has as elements of its ith column the components of u_i ($i = 1, 2, 3$), the eigenvectors of A:

$$T = [u_1 \quad u_2 \quad u_3] = \begin{bmatrix} 0.6 & 0.3 & 0.1 \\ 1.0 & 1.0 & 0.5 \\ 1.2 & 1.5 & 1.0 \end{bmatrix}.$$

Since

$$A u_i = \lambda_i u_i, \qquad i = 1, 2, 3,$$

we can readily verify that

$$\mathbf{AT} = \mathbf{T\Lambda},\tag{5.10}$$

where $\mathbf{\Lambda}$ is a diagonal matrix with diagonal elements λ_1, λ_2, and λ_3; that is,

$$\mathbf{\Lambda} = \begin{bmatrix} \lambda_1 & 0 & 0 \\ 0 & \lambda_2 & 0 \\ 0 & 0 & \lambda_3 \end{bmatrix}.$$

Since the eigenvectors $\mathbf{u}_i$ are linearly independent we know that $\mathbf{T}$ has an inverse, so (5.10) can be written

$$\mathbf{A} = \mathbf{T\Lambda T}^{-1} \quad \text{or} \quad \mathbf{T}^{-1}\mathbf{AT} = \mathbf{\Lambda}.\tag{5.11}$$

We say that $\mathbf{T}$ *diagonalizes* $\mathbf{A}$.

By straightforward calculation we can find $\mathbf{T}^{-1}$,

$$\mathbf{T}^{-1} = \begin{bmatrix} \frac{25}{6} & -2.5 & \frac{5}{6} \\ -\frac{20}{3} & 8 & -\frac{10}{3} \\ 5 & -9 & 5 \end{bmatrix}.\tag{5.12}$$

Alternatively, the inverse of $\mathbf{T}$ can be found in the following way. Consider the matrix $\mathbf{S}$ whose rows are the transposes of the eigenvectors $\mathbf{v}_i$ of $\mathbf{A}^T$:

$$\mathbf{S} = \begin{bmatrix} \mathbf{v}_1^T \\ \mathbf{v}_2^T \\ \mathbf{v}_3^T \end{bmatrix}.$$

Using (5.7) we see that, for example,

$$\mathbf{ST} = \begin{bmatrix} \mathbf{v}_1^T\mathbf{u}_1 & 0 & 0 \\ 0 & \mathbf{v}_2^T\mathbf{u}_2 & 0 \\ 0 & 0 & \mathbf{v}_3^T\mathbf{u}_3 \end{bmatrix} = \mathbf{D}.$$

Hence $\mathbf{D}^{-1}\mathbf{ST} = \mathbf{I}$, or

$$\mathbf{T}^{-1} = \mathbf{D}^{-1}\mathbf{S},$$

where the inverse $\mathbf{D}^{-1}$ of $\mathbf{D}$ is simply the diagonal matrix whose diagonal elements are the inverses of the elements of $\mathbf{D}$. In the above specific example we find

$$\mathbf{T}^{-1} = \begin{bmatrix} (0.24)^{-1} & 0 & 0 \\ 0 & (-0.15)^{-1} & 0 \\ 0 & 0 & (0.2)^{-1} \end{bmatrix}\begin{bmatrix} 1.0 & -0.6 & 0.2 \\ 1.0 & -1.2 & 0.5 \\ 1.0 & -1.8 & 1.0 \end{bmatrix},$$

and it is easily checked that this gives (5.12).

We now consider the system

$$\dot{z} = Az,$$ (5.13)

where A is a given 3×3 matrix and z is an unknown vector with components z_i. In the usual way $\dot{z}$ is the vector with components dz_i/dt. We change variable from z to y by setting

$$z = Ty, \qquad y = T^{-1}z,$$ (5.14)

where T is the 3×3 matrix whose columns are the eigenvectors of A, as introduced previously. Multiplying both sides of (5.13) by T^{-1}, since $T^{-1}\dot{z} = \dot{y}$, we see that, using (5.11),

$$\dot{y} = \Lambda y;$$

in longhand

$$\dot{y}_1 = \lambda_1 y_1, \qquad \dot{y}_2 = \lambda_2 y_2, \qquad \dot{y}_3 = \lambda_3 y_3$$ (5.15)

or

$$y_1 = ae^{\lambda_1 t}, \qquad y_2 = be^{\lambda_2 t}, \qquad y_3 = ce^{\lambda_3 t},$$ (5.16)

where a, b, and c are arbitrary constants. The values of z can then be recovered by using (5.14). In the specific case considered above,

$$z = \begin{bmatrix} 0.6 & 0.3 & 0.1 \\ 1.0 & 1.0 & 0.5 \\ 1.2 & 1.5 & 1.0 \end{bmatrix} \begin{bmatrix} ae^{-t} \\ be^{-2t} \\ ce^{-3t} \end{bmatrix};$$

that is,

$$\begin{aligned} z_1 &= 0.6ae^{-t} + 0.3be^{-2t} + 0.1ce^{-3t}, \\ z_2 &= ae^{-t} + be^{-2t} + 0.5ce^{-3t}, \\ z_3 &= 1.2ae^{-t} + 1.5be^{-2t} + 1.0ce^{-3t}. \end{aligned}$$ (5.17)

The point here is that the original equations (5.13) are complicated coupled equations in which each equation involves all three variables z_1, z_2, and z_3. The solutions (5.17) are also of complicated form, each involving all the unknown constants a, b, and c. On the other hand, equations (5.15) are *uncoupled*, since Λ is of diagonal form. Each of the solutions (5.16) of (5.15) is of simple form.

The solution of (5.13) is not quite complete since we still have to determine the arbitrary constants a, b, and c in terms of given conditions—the values of the components of z at $t = 0$, which we denote by the vector z_0. However, this is easy, since, from (5.14),

$$\begin{bmatrix} a \\ b \\ c \end{bmatrix} = (y)_{t=0} = T^{-1}z_0.$$

Combining all these results we see that

$$z = TDT^{-1}z_0,$$

where

$$D = \begin{bmatrix} e^{\lambda_1 t} & 0 & 0 \\ 0 & e^{\lambda_2 t} & 0 \\ 0 & 0 & e^{\lambda_3 t} \end{bmatrix} = \begin{bmatrix} e^{-t} & 0 & 0 \\ 0 & e^{-2t} & 0 \\ 0 & 0 & e^{-3t} \end{bmatrix}.$$

Talking in terms of the electrical circuit we have been considering, if $v_1(0) = 0.6$ volt, $i_1(0) = 1.0$ amp, and $v_2(0) = 1.2$ volts (that is, $z_0 = u_1$), then at time t we have

$$v_1(t) = 0.6e^{-t}, \qquad i_1(t) = 1.0e^{-t}, \qquad v_2(t) = 1.2e^{-t}.$$

If we consider these three functions as defining the trajectory of the point $[v_1(t), i_1(t), v_2(t)]$ in the three-dimensional picture in which v_1, i_1, and v_2 are plotted along the three coordinate axes, we see that the trajectory is a straight-line segment. In general, in the absence of any excitation ($i_s \equiv 0$), whenever the initial conditions are such that the point $[v_1(0), i_1(0), v_2(0)]$ has components which are proportional to one of the eigenvectors of A, the resulting trajectory is a straight-line segment. More generally, if we decompose the initial-conditions vector $x(0) = [v_1(0), i_1(0), v_2(0)]$ along the directions of the eigenvectors, that is, if we calculate three numbers α_1, α_2, and α_3 such that

$$x(0) = \alpha_1 u_1 + \alpha_2 u_2 + \alpha_3 u_3,$$

then the resulting trajectory, in the case $i_s \equiv 0$, is given by

$$x(t) = \alpha_1 u_1 e^{-t} + \alpha_2 u_2 e^{-2t} + \alpha_3 u_3 e^{-3t}.$$

We can now very quickly dispose of the general case $i_s \neq 0$. The original system (5.5) is

$$\dot{x} = Ax + bi_s.$$

Multiplying by T^{-1} and setting $x = Tw$, we find, using (5.11),

$$\dot{w} = \Lambda w + ci_s,$$

where

$$c = T^{-1}b;$$

that is,

$$\frac{dw_i}{dt} = \lambda_i w_i + c_i i_s, \qquad i = 1, 2, 3,$$

where c_i is the ith component of c. The solution of these equations for any set of initial conditions and input $i_s(t)$ is well known:

$$w_i(t) = w_i(0)e^{\lambda_i t} + c_i e^{\lambda_i t} \int_0^t e^{-\lambda_i \tau} i_s(\tau)\, d\tau, \qquad i = 1, 2, 3. \qquad (5.18)$$

The procedure is, therefore, as follows:

1. From the initial conditions $x(0)$ calculate $w(0)$ from $w(0) = T^{-1}x(0)$.
2. Use (5.18) to obtain $w(t)$.
3. Obtain $x(t)$ from $x(t) = Tw(t)$.

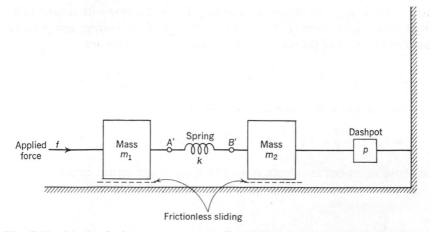

Fig. 5.11   Mechanical system corresponding to the electrical system of Fig. 5.10.

If one or more of the eigenvalues is complex (which is possible, since **A** is not in general symmetrical), the analysis is slightly more complicated, but it can still be carried through in much the same way. In this case the solutions have oscillatory as well as exponential components.[4] We have been careful to insist that the eigenvalues are distinct. The presence of equal eigenvalues complicates the analysis.

The diagonalization of **A** has the following interpretation. As long as **A** has distinct eigenvalues, any motion of the system (driven by any input and starting from any set of initial conditions) can be thought of as the super-position of the motions of uncoupled first-order systems. In the present case, from the relation **x** = **Tw**, we have

$$x_k(t) = t_{k1}w_1(t) + t_{k2}w_2(t) + t_{k3}w_3(t),$$

where t_{kj} is the (k, j)th element of **T**, and the time behavior of each $w_j(t)$ is independent of all the other w's. This decomposition of the motion of linear systems is well known in classical dynamics in the case of conservative systems, but the results presented here are more general because the systems considered are not necessarily conservative.

For readers who prefer mechanical systems to electrical circuits we give the idealized linear mechanical system shown in Fig. 5.11. Two masses m_1 and m_2 are connected by a spring and slide on frictionless supports. A force f is applied to m_2, and m_1 is connected to a rigid wall by a dashpot (resistance). All motions take place in a straight line. Positions x_1 and x_2 of m_1 and m_2 are measured from the equilibrium positions when f is zero and the system is at rest. The velocities of the masses are denoted by $v_i = dx_i/dt$ $(i = 1, 2)$. We

---

[4] For details see L. A. Zadeh and C. A. Desoer, *Linear System Theory*, McGraw-Hill, New York, 1963, Chap. 5, Sec. 4.

introduce $l = x_2 - x_1$, the increase in length of the spring with respect to its length under no tension. If k is the compliance of the spring, and p is the damping constant of the dashpot, the equations of motion are

$$f = m_1 \frac{dv_1}{dt} - \frac{1}{k}l, \qquad \frac{dl}{dt} = v_2 - v_1, \qquad 0 = m_2 \frac{dv_2}{dt} + pv_2 + \frac{1}{k}l.$$

It is obvious that if we make the identifications

$$f = i_s, \qquad -\frac{l}{k} = i_1, \qquad m_1 = \frac{5}{3}, \qquad m_2 = \frac{1}{6}, \qquad p = 1, \qquad k = \frac{3}{5},$$

the above equations are identical with (5.5) for the electrical circuit.

Chapter 6

Examples Involving Nonlinear Differential Equations

Comment : In this chapter certain engineering problems are formulated in mathematical terms. The resulting differential equations are nonlinear, but it is possible to develop approximate solutions from which physical conclusions can be drawn.

6.1   Introduction

It is a source of surprise and gratification to both the engineer and the mathematician when an explicit solution in closed form can be found for a nonlinear ordinary differential equation.[1]

When dealing with nonlinear differential equations it is usually necessary to resort either to a digital (or analog) computer or to approximate methods. By using a computer it is often possible to produce numerical solutions for specific problems, but to obtain insight it is often preferable to use analytical methods.

Physical insight can often be used to decide which terms are important in the equations, and this sometimes enables the equation to be approximated

---

[1] One example was contributed by William Squire, Department of Aerospace Engineering, West Virginia University, Morgantown, W. Va., who pointed out that the equation

$$m\frac{d^2x}{dt^2} = mg - c_D\rho_0 e^{-\alpha x}\left(\frac{dx}{dt}\right)^2,$$

which occurs in connection with the problem of a body with a drag proportional to its velocity squared falling in an atmosphere with an exponential density variation (for example, a diving airplane or a re-entry vehicle), can be reduced to a first-order equation, because

$$\frac{d^2x}{dt^2} = v\frac{dv}{dx}, \qquad v = \frac{dx}{dt}.$$

See the note by W. Squire in *Jet Propulsion*, **28**, 838–839 (1958). Another example will be found in Section 9.3.

by a form that can be integrated analytically. There are also various mathematical techniques that can be used to reduce the equations to another approximately equivalent set that can be integrated exactly, or to provide qualitative information, especially in connection with stability.

All these points will be illustrated by the examples in this chapter.

6.2   Surge Tanks in a Hydroelectric System[2]

Comment: This section is concerned with formulation of the problem in mathematical terms, leading to a set of nonlinear differential equations.

A simple hydroelectric generator system would consist merely of a water reservoir supplying water to a turbine through a pipe, as shown in Fig. 6.1*a*. To provide sufficient water pressure and velocity at the turbine, the pipe is

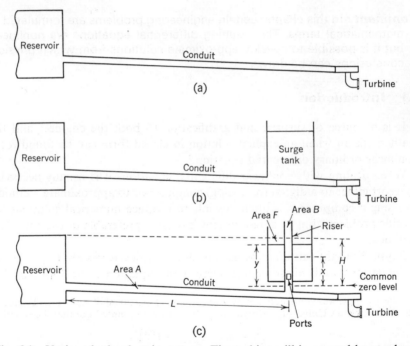

Fig. 6.1   Various hydroelectric systems. The turbine will in general be at a lower level than the surge tank.

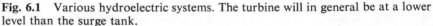

[2] This topic came to the editor's attention through a section in A. S. Jackson, *Analog Computation*, McGraw-Hill, New York, 1960, pp. 403–416, contributed by P. L. Monkmeyer, Department of Hydraulics, University of Wisconsin, Madison, Wis. Material has also been incorporated from the article on surge tanks by G. R. Rich in the *Handbook of Applied Hydraulics*, 2nd ed. (C. V. Davis, ed.), McGraw-Hill, New York, 1952, pp. 671–704.

often of considerable length, which causes two difficulties if there is a sudden increase or decrease in the demand for power (for example, a power failure).

The first difficulty of the simple system is that if there is a sudden demand for power the generator will require more water. This involves accelerating the entire mass of water in the conduit, which takes time. Until the water is accelerated, the generator voltage will drop, which is obviously unsatisfactory. A similar difficulty occurs when demand drops. Time is required to decelerate the water in the conduit.

One way (although not the only way) to overcome this difficulty is to install a *surge tank*, which is a large tank connected to the conduit near its downstream end as close as possible to the turbine (see Fig. 6.1*b*). In the case of load demand this temporarily supplies water directly to the turbine, and in the case of a drop in load, it stores water rejected by the turbine. In this way high conduit accelerations or decelerations are avoided.

The second difficulty is the phenomenon of *water hammer*, caused by the unsteady flow conditions that exist in the conduit when the flow is accelerated or decelerated. It is found that pressure waves travel along the conduit. The mass of water being accelerated can be large, and the resulting forces can also be large and can cause rapid and violent pressure variations traveling up and down the conduit; these (if not eliminated) can damage the system, partly by direct action and partly by causing instability in the associated turbine-generator equipment.

Because inertia causes water to overshoot its steady-state position in a surge tank, the characteristic physical action of the tank is an oscillation of the water surface level. (It is possible but usually not economical, or even desirable, to eliminate overshoot.) Mass acceleration (the first difficulty) usually takes a fairly long time, sometimes as much as 30 min, to settle down to a second steady state for long conduits, but water hammer has a much shorter time scale, 30 sec or less. Because of the different time scales, it is usually desirable to use a differential surge tank, illustrated in Fig. 6.1*c*. This consists of a vertical pipe (known as a *riser*) connected to the conduit, passing through the center of the main surge tank and connected to it by openings or ports. The differential surge tank is essentially two surge tanks connected together, one to deal with short-time water-hammer effects and the other to deal with longer time surges. The ports provide a damping effect which reduces the amplitudes of the oscillations.

The amount of water required by the turbine depends on the power output, the pressure of the water, and the position of a control valve or gate associated with the turbine. A typical performance chart for a large turbine is shown in Fig. 6.2. The percentages associated with the gate refer to the extent to which the gate valve is open. The pressures are expressed in terms of the equivalent "head" of water which would give the corresponding static pressure; a column of water l feet in height gives a pressure of $\rho g l$, where ρ is the density of water and g the acceleration due to gravity. The turbine may

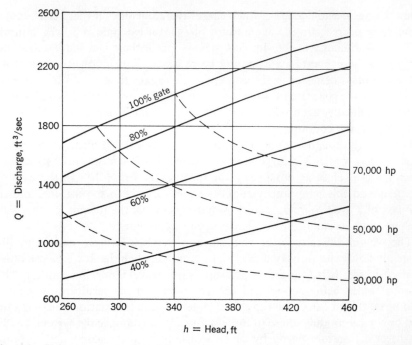

Fig. 6.2 Power output of turbine under various conditions. (The Appalachia system consists of two turbines of this type.)

be situated considerably below the surge tank, connected to it by a short but relatively steep length of conduit. It will be convenient to measure heads from the riser-conduit junction as in Fig. 6.1c, so that the head h, in terms of which we shall specify the turbine performance, will not be the head shown in Fig. 6.2 but will differ from it by a constant. If we denote flow into (discharge from) the turbine by Q, the relationship shown in Fig. 6.2 can then be represented by

$$Q = f(h, P), \tag{6.1}$$

where P is the power output of the turbine and we assume that the gate is adjusted by the governor in some way, depending on the values of Q, h, and P. The transient situation is quite complicated, because the gate will not respond instantaneously to changes in load, the time required to open the gate for the turbine of Fig. 6.2 from 0 to 100% being of the order of 5 seconds. This effect will be ignored here, although it can be included comparatively easily when numerical-integration procedures are used.

We now discuss the basic equations for the differential-surge-tank system shown in Fig. 6.1c. The water in the length of conduit from the riser-conduit junction to the turbine will be assumed to have negligible dynamic effects. This means that the head of water h for the turbine in (6.1) is assumed to be the same as the head at the riser-conduit junction (the pressure there being ρgh). We define the following (see Fig. 6.1c):

A = area of conduit,

B = area of riser,

F = net area of surge tank (total area less area of riser),

v = velocity of water in conduit from the reservoir to the riser-conduit junction,

V = velocity of water in conduit from riser-conduit junction to turbine (so that discharge $Q = AV$),

x = height of water in riser,

y = height of water in surge tank,

h = head of water corresponding to the pressure at the riser-conduit junction.

The condition of continuity at the riser-conduit junction gives

$$\begin{bmatrix} \text{Flow into} \\ \text{turbine} \end{bmatrix} = \begin{bmatrix} \text{Flow from} \\ \text{reservoir} \end{bmatrix} + \begin{bmatrix} \text{Flow from} \\ \text{riser} \end{bmatrix} + \begin{bmatrix} \text{Flow from tank} \\ \text{through ports} \end{bmatrix}$$

or
$$Q = AV = Av - B\frac{dx}{dt} - F\frac{dy}{dt}. \tag{6.2}$$

We next establish two differential equations.

(a) *Motion of water in the conduit.* The application of Newton's second law to the conduit flow yields, in words (RCJ denotes "riser-conduit junction"),

$$\left\{ \begin{bmatrix} \text{Pressure head at RCJ} \\ \text{if water were at rest} \end{bmatrix} - \begin{bmatrix} \text{Actual pressure} \\ \text{at RCJ} \end{bmatrix} - \begin{bmatrix} \text{Pressure drop due to} \\ \text{friction loss in pipe} \end{bmatrix} \right\}$$

$$\times \begin{bmatrix} \text{Area of} \\ \text{conduit} \end{bmatrix} = \begin{bmatrix} \text{Total mass of} \\ \text{water in conduit} \end{bmatrix} \times \begin{bmatrix} \text{Acceleration of} \\ \text{water in conduit} \end{bmatrix}$$

Let H denote the difference in elevation between the water in the reservoir and the riser-conduit junction. Then the pressure at the riser-conduit junction if the water were at rest would be ρgH. It is found experimentally that, for the range of conduit velocities in which we are interested, the pressure drop due to friction losses is approximately proportional to the square of the velocity. We define an empirical constant c as follows:

c = a coefficient such that the pressure drop in the conduit due to the frictional losses is given by ρgcv^2; that is, the equivalent loss of head is cv^2.

The equation stated above in words therefore becomes

$$(\rho gH - \rho gh - \rho gcv^2)A = \rho LA\frac{dv}{dt}$$

or
$$H - h = cv^2 + \frac{L}{g}\frac{dv}{dt}. \tag{6.3}$$

(b) *Motion of water through the ports, in and out of the main surge tank.* It is found experimentally that the flow of water through the ports is approximately proportional to the square root of the pressure differential across the ports. If the pressure in the riser at the ports corresponds to a head z, measured from the same zero as the height of the water in the main surge tank, the pressure differential across the ports can be taken to be $\rho g(y - z)$. The equation governing the flow of water through the ports is then

$$F\frac{dy}{dt} = \begin{cases} -a[2g(y - z)]^{1/2}, & y > z, \\ a[2g(z - y)]^{1/2}, & y < z, \end{cases} \tag{6.4}$$

where a is an experimentally determined parameter which, as mentioned earlier, is approximately constant but does vary to some extent with the velocity and direction of flow through the ports.

Strictly speaking, we should now study the motion of the water in the riser. This would yield two equations relating h, x, and z. These two equations, together with (6.4), (6.3), and (6.2) [with Q given by (6.1)], would provide five equations for the five unknowns h, v, x, y, and z. However, we shall avoid a detailed study of the water in the riser by assuming $h = x = z$, which amounts to neglecting the dynamic effects of the water in the riser. This would seem reasonable since the volume of water in the riser is much less than the volume in either the conduit or the main surge tank. The basic equations thus reduce to

$$f(x, P) = AV = Av - B\frac{dx}{dt} - F\frac{dy}{dt}, \tag{6.5}$$

$$H - x = cv^2 + \frac{L}{g}\frac{dv}{dt}, \tag{6.6}$$

$$F\frac{dy}{dt} = \begin{cases} -a[2g(y - x)]^{1/2}, & y > x, \\ a[2g(x - y)]^{1/2}, & y < x. \end{cases} \tag{6.7}$$

These are three equations for the three unknowns v, x, and y.

In general it will not be possible to solve these equations analytically, and it is necessary to resort to numerical methods. Qualitative information about the solution will be obtained in Section 6.3 by analytical methods. The results also provide a qualitative guide to the parameters required for design work, but it should be emphasized that these give only trial values for tank dimensions. Using these trial values, the resulting performances would be checked by direct numerical integration of (6.5) to (6.7).

Examples of such numerical integration (performed by hand) are given by Rich,[3] although it should be noted in passing that much more sophisticated numerical methods would be used nowadays.

---

[3] G. R. Rich in *Handbook of Applied Hydraulics*, 2nd ed. (C. V. Davis, ed.), McGraw-Hill, New York, 1952, pp. 671–704.

6.3   Approximate Solution of the Equations for the Differential Surge Tank

Mathematics Used: Simple nonlinear ordinary differential equations.

Comment: Simplifying assumptions and approximations lead to apparently inconsistent equations, but this difficulty is circumvented.

When the surge-tank system is in a steady state, we have $x = y =$ constant and $dx/dt = dy/dt = 0$. The velocity in the conduit between the reservoir and the riser-conduit junction must be equal to the velocity between the riser-conduit junction and the turbine, $v = V$. This is obvious either physically or from (6.5). From (6.6) we have

$$x = y = H - cv^2 = H - cV^2.$$

If the velocity into the turbine changes from V_1 to V_2, then x and y must change from an initial value of $H - cV_1^2$ to a final value of $H - cV_2^2$. The water level x in the riser changes much more rapidly than the level y in the main surge tank. As a reasonable approximation we shall assume that the riser level changes instantaneously from $x = x_1 = H - cV_1^2$ to $x = x_2 = H - cV_2^2$ at $t = 0$.

The other source of complexity in (6.1) to (6.7) is the water-throughput/power-output relationship (6.1) for the turbine. For simplicity we shall assume simply that the velocity of the water in the conduit between the riser-conduit junction and the turbine changes instantaneously from V_1 to V_2.

With these simplifications (6.5) to (6.7) become

$$AV_2 = Av - F\frac{dy}{dt}, \tag{6.8}$$

$$H - x_2 = cv^2 + \frac{L}{g}\frac{dv}{dt}, \tag{6.9}$$

$$F\frac{dy}{dt} = \begin{cases} -a[2g(y - x_2)]^{1/2}, & y > x_2, \\ a[2g(x_2 - y)]^{1/2}, & y < x_2, \end{cases} \tag{6.10}$$

with initial conditions

$$v = V_1, \quad y = x_1, \qquad \text{at } t = 0.$$

These equations are unfortunately inconsistent, since (6.9) can be solved for v and then (6.8) can be solved for y, or y can be found directly and independently from (6.10). However, this need not worry us if we interpret (6.8) to (6.10) in the following way. We are trying to design a system to give a certain idealized response. In the above equations the parameters F and a are at our disposal when designing the surge tank. We first find v from (6.9), then y from (6.8). In order that y found in this way should tend to the known value $y_2 = x_2$ as t tends to infinity, an algebraic equation needs to be satisfied, and this will give a value for F. Knowing dy/dt for all t we can deduce what the value of a should be from (6.10), for all y. If these values turn out to be reasonably constant over the whole range of y, this gives an estimate of what design value should be chosen for a. Numerical integration of (6.5) to (6.7) can then be used to discover how the design will actually behave.

As an illustration we consider a specific approximate set of figures for the surge tank of the Appalachia project of the Tennessee Valley Authority. (A detailed discussion of the design procedure is given by Rich.[4] The following is academic.) The length L is 43,000 ft, the area A is 250 ft^2. Consider the case of a sudden load demand with $v = V_1 = 0$ at $t = 0$, and $V_2 = 13.7$ ft-sec for $t > 0$, with $c = 0.58$. Then

$$x_1 = y_1 = H, \qquad x_2 = y_2 = H - cV_2^2 = H - 0.58(13.7)^2 = H - 109.$$

Equation (6.9) becomes

$$(0.58)(13.7)^2 = 0.58v^2 + \left(\frac{43,000}{32.2}\frac{dv}{dt}\right)$$

or
$$\frac{dv}{(13.7)^2 - v^2} = \frac{dt}{2300}.$$

Integration yields

$$\log\left(\frac{13.7 + v}{13.7 - v}\right) = 0.0119t$$

or
$$v = 13.7 \tanh 0.0060t.$$

Equation (6.8) now gives

$$-F\frac{dy}{dt} = 13.7A(1 - \tanh 0.0060t)$$

or, on integrating,

$$F(H - y) = 13.7A\left[t - \frac{\log(\cosh 0.0060t)}{0.0060}\right]. \tag{6.11}$$

For large t,

$$\log(\cosh pt) = \log[\tfrac{1}{2}(e^{pt} + e^{-pt})] \approx pt - \log 2.$$

If we let t tend to infinity in (6.11), we obtain (since $H - y$ then tends to 109)

$$F = \frac{13.7 \log 2}{(109)(0.0060)}A \approx 14.5A.$$

This suggests that F should be approximately $(14.5)(250) = 3,880$ ft^2. Of course, the design procedure is actually much more complicated than this, and the actual value adopted was 3220 ft^2.

---

[4] *Ibid.*

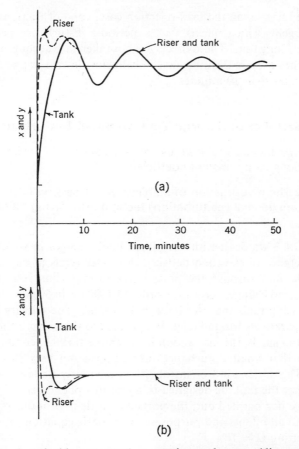

Fig. 6.3 Appalachia surge tank—experimental curves (diagrammatic).

Near $t = 0$, elimination of $F(dy/dt)$ between (6.8) and (6.10) suggests that a should have the value

$$\frac{AV_2}{[2g(y_1 - x_2)]^{1/2}} = \frac{(250)(13.7)}{[(64.4)(109)]^{1/2}} \approx 41.$$

This is nearly the same as the design value actually used, although various factors enter into the design of the ports to deliberately make a have different values for water flowing in each of the two directions through the port, and to vary in a definite way with velocity through the port.

An interesting verification of the theory by comparison with experimental results is given by Rich.[5] A diagrammatic reproduction of the experimental curves is given in Fig 6.3. The theory applies only to the behavior in the first few minutes. In the load-demand case, the load itself is a means of damping

[5] *Ibid.*, pp. 700–701.

the response, whereas in the load-rejection case, conduit friction is the main dissipative agent, which means that a periodic disturbance persists for a comparatively long time. These effects are not taken into account in the above theory, but they explain the difference in behaviors in cases *a* and *b* in Fig. 6.3 for times greater than 10 minutes.

6.4   The Stability of a Surge Tank to Small Disturbances

Mathematics Used: Taylor series ; ordinary second-order linear differential equations with constant coefficients.

Comment: The investigation of stability in this section is an example of an important general (perturbation) technique involving "local linearization."

In Section 6.3 we dealt with very large load changes in which there is a marked difference in elevation between the water levels in the riser and the tank, and the flow through the ports plays an important role. In contrast, during small load changes, say of the order of 1000 kw in 50,000, the difference between the main tank and riser levels is also small. The velocity through the ports is comparatively insignificant. We proceed to show that if the surge-tank diameter is too small, the interaction between the turbine, conduit, and tank can be such that small disturbances are damped out very slowly, or even magnified. This latter kind of instability is obviously undesirable, and it is important that the tank be designed to avoid this phenomenon.

As we have just pointed out, the ports play little part in this phenomenon, and $x = y$, to all intents and purposes, so the basic equations are, from (6.5) and (6.6), setting $G = B + F$,

$$f(x, P) = Av - G\frac{dx}{dt}, \tag{6.12}$$

$$H - x = cv^2 + \frac{L}{g}\frac{dx}{dt}. \tag{6.13}$$

Suppose the system is oscillating about a steady state,

$$v = V + u, \qquad x = X + z,$$

where V and X are the steady values of v and x, given by

$$f(X, P) = AV, \qquad H - X = cV^2.$$

The values of u and z are assumed to be small[6] compared with V and X, so

$$v^2 \approx V^2 + 2Vu, \qquad f(x, P) \approx f(X, P) + z\frac{\partial f}{\partial X}.$$

---

[6] This is an example of a perturbation method, which is a common technique in applied mathematics. The interested reader can find further information in, for example, R. Bellman, *Perturbation Techniques in Mathematics, Physics and Engineering,* Holt, New York, 1964.

The precise value for $\partial f/\partial X$ depends on the operating conditions assumed for the turbine. If the turbine is operated at constant power, the gate being adjusted automatically to ensure this, then from Fig. 6.2 we can see that $\partial f/\partial X$ is negative, $\partial f/\partial X = -\alpha AV$, say, where this defines the constant α which is greater than zero, and, since $f(X, P) = AV$,

$$f(x, P) = AV(1 - \alpha z). \tag{6.14}$$

An approximate argument is as follows. Let H_t be the total head on the turbine in the steady state (as measured on the horizontal scale in Fig. 6.2). The corresponding steady-state velocity through the turbine is V. Suppose that when the head changes from H_t to $H_t + z$, the velocity through the turbine changes to V'. For constant power output we have, approximately, $H_t V = (H_t + z)V'$. Hence

$$f(x, P) = AV' = AV\left(1 + \frac{z}{H_t}\right)^{-1} \approx AV\left(1 - \frac{z}{H_t}\right).$$

Comparing with (6.14) we see that this argument gives $\alpha = 1/H_t$. From Fig. 6.2 we see that a typical value of α is $1/300$ or less.

Inserting the above approximations in (6.12) and (6.13) and neglecting second-order terms, we find

$$-\alpha AVz = Au - G\frac{dz}{dt}, \qquad -z = 2cVu + \frac{L}{g}\frac{du}{dt}.$$

Elimination of u gives

$$\frac{d^2z}{dt^2} - \left(\frac{A\alpha}{G} - \frac{2cg}{L}\right)V\frac{dz}{dt} + \frac{gA}{LG}(1 - 2c\alpha V^2)z = 0. \tag{6.15}$$

To analyze the implications of this equation we study

$$\frac{d^2z}{dt^2} + 2a\frac{dz}{dt} + bz = 0, \tag{6.16}$$

where a and b are real constants. The solutions of this equation are of the form $z = Z\exp(\lambda t)$, where

$$\lambda^2 + 2a\lambda + b = 0;$$

that is, $$\lambda = -a \pm (a^2 - b)^{1/2}.$$

If Re $\lambda < 0$, the solutions tend to zero as t tends to infinity, and we say that the solutions are *stable*. There are two possibilities:

1. If $a^2 < b$, λ is complex, and the solutions are stable if and only if $a > 0$, $b > 0$.
2. If $a^2 > b$, the solutions are real, and they are stable if and only if $a > +(a^2 - b)^{1/2}$, that is, $a > 0$ and $a^2 > a^2 - b$, or $b > 0$.

In both cases the solutions are stable if and only if $a > 0$, $b > 0$.

Returning to (6.15) we see that the solutions of this equation are stable if and only if

$$-\frac{A\alpha}{G} + \frac{2cg}{L} > 0, \tag{6.17}$$

$$1 - 2c\alpha V^2 > 0. \tag{6.18}$$

In the case of the Appalachia surge tank, the maximum value of V is 14 ft-sec, c is about 0.6, and we have already quoted a value of 1/300 for α, so that the condition $1 - 2c\alpha V^2 > 0$ is satisfied. Condition (6.17) gives

$$G > \frac{A\alpha L}{2cg}; \tag{6.19}$$

that is, the area of the surge tank and riser must be greater than a certain minimum. As pointed out earlier, c is not an absolute constant, but varies with the rate of flow. To be conservative we should use the smallest value of c that is likely to occur in practice. For the Appalachia surge tank Rich[7] uses 0.3 and then (6.19) gives

$$G > \frac{(250)(43,000)}{(64.4)(0.3)(300)} \approx 1850 \text{ ft}^2.$$

Equation (6.19) gives only a lower limit; to obtain a satisfactory approach to the equilibrium level, the area given by this formula should be increased by at least 60%. The actual design area F was about 3200 ft^2.

6.5 Chemical-Tank-Reactor Stability[8]

Comment: Mathematical formulation of the problem leads to an ordinary-differential-equation model with an inherent stability problem, which is examined by physical arguments.

A continuous-flow stirred tank reactor is represented diagrammatically in Fig. 6.4. A stream of chemical C flows in, and products, mixed with a residue of C, flow out of a reaction vessel of volume V at a constant rate q. The reaction goes on continuously in the stirred vessel, so the composition and temperature of the contents of the tank are constant throughout, and these

[7] G. R. Rich in *Handbook of Applied Hydraulics*, 2nd ed. (C. V. Davis, ed.), McGraw-Hill, New York, 1952, pp. 671–704.

[8] This example was submitted by Rutherford Aris, Department of Chemical Engineering, University of Minnesota, Minneapolis, Minn. A much more detailed account (from which material has been taken) can be found in R. Aris and N. R. Amundson, An Analysis of Chemical Reactor Stability and Control, I to III, *Chem. Eng. Sci.*, **7**, 121–155 (1958). An elementary exposition is given in R. Aris, *An Introduction to the Analysis of Chemical Reactors*, Prentice-Hall, Englewood Cliffs, N.J., 1965.

Fig. 6.4   Continuous-flow stirred tank reactor.

are the composition and temperature of the output stream. The feed flows in with a high concentration c_{in} of C, and the output flow has a low concentration c of C and a high concentration of products. We wish to study the stability of the steady state in such a reactor.

The equations that represent the behavior of the reactor are derived from mass and heat balances on the flow. It is assumed that the reaction is first order and irreversible, the chemical C being changed into products at a rate proportional to the concentration c of C. It is assumed that the corresponding constant of proportionality $k(T)$ depends on the temperature T according to the Arrhenius law,

$$k = k(T) = Ae^{-B/T}. \tag{6.20}$$

The conservation law for the chemical C is

$$\begin{bmatrix} \text{Rate of change} \\ \text{of amount of C} \\ \text{in the reactor} \end{bmatrix} = \begin{bmatrix} \text{Rate at} \\ \text{which C} \\ \text{flows in} \end{bmatrix} - \begin{bmatrix} \text{Rate at} \\ \text{which C} \\ \text{flows out} \end{bmatrix} - \begin{bmatrix} \text{Rate at which} \\ \text{C disappears} \\ \text{by the reaction} \end{bmatrix} .$$

In symbols,

$$\frac{d}{dt} Vc = qc_{in} - qc - Vk(T)c,$$

where V is the volume of the reactor tank, and c_{in} and c are the concentrations of C in the input and in the tank, as illustrated in Fig. 6.4. Since V is constant, this can be written

$$\frac{dc}{dt} = \frac{q}{V}(c_{in} - c) - k(T)c. \tag{6.21}$$

The heat-balance equation is similar. If C_p is the specific heat, regarded as constant, the heat content of a unit volume of reaction mixture at temperature T is C_pT. The reaction gives out heat at a rate H times the rate of the reaction, where H is assumed to be a constant. In addition there may be a cooling system associated with the tank which removes heat at a rate depending on the temperature of the tank, which we denote by $VS(T)$. Thus

$$\begin{bmatrix} \text{Rate of} \\ \text{change of} \\ \text{heat content} \end{bmatrix} = \begin{bmatrix} \text{Heat} \\ \text{brought} \\ \text{in} \end{bmatrix} - \begin{bmatrix} \text{Heat} \\ \text{flowing} \\ \text{out} \end{bmatrix} - \begin{bmatrix} \text{Heat} \\ \text{removed by} \\ \text{cooling} \end{bmatrix} + \begin{bmatrix} \text{Heat} \\ \text{generated by} \\ \text{reaction} \end{bmatrix} .$$

In symbols,

$$VC_p \frac{dT}{dt} = qC_pT_{in} - qC_pT - VS(T) + HVk(T)c;$$

that is, $$\frac{dT}{dt} = \frac{q}{V}(T_{in} - T) - \frac{1}{C_p}S(T) + \frac{H}{C_p}k(T)c. \qquad (6.22)$$

Equations (6.21) and (6.22) are a pair of ordinary nonlinear differential equations in the dependent variables $c(t)$ and $T(t)$, which describe the behavior of the system.

We study the steady state of the above system, assuming first, for simplicity, that $S(T) = 0$; that is, no cooling system is used. In the steady state $dc/dt = dT/dt = 0$, so that (6.21) and (6.22) give

$$c_{in} - c = \alpha c k(T), \qquad \text{where } \alpha = \frac{V}{q}, \qquad (6.23)$$

$$T - T_{in} = \beta c k(T), \qquad \text{where } \beta = \frac{HV}{qC_p}. \qquad (6.24)$$

If we solve (6.23) for c and substitute in (6.24), we obtain

$$T - T_{in} = \frac{c_{in}\beta k(T)}{1 + \alpha k(T)}. \qquad (6.25)$$

We consider the special form of $k(T)$ given in (6.20), and in this case the curve

$$y = \frac{c_{in}\beta k(T)}{1 + \alpha k(T)} \qquad (6.26)$$

has a sigmoid shape, as shown in Fig. 6.5. This curve and the curve $y = T - T_{in}$ can intersect in one or three points, as shown in Fig. 6.5a and b, respectively, thus giving either one or three steady-state values of T for which (6.25) is satisfied. Physically the left side of (6.25) is proportional to the heat required to raise the temperature of the reactants from T_{in} to T, and the right side is proportional to the heat produced by the reaction. Hence the roots of (6.25) give the temperatures at which there is a heat balance. However, on

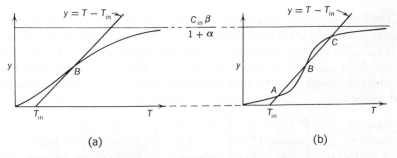

(a)   (b)

Fig. 6.5   The curves $y = c_{in}\beta k(T)/[1 + \alpha k(T)]$ and $y = T - T_{in}$.

pursuing this argument, we see that point B in Fig. 6.5b represents an unstable situation, because a slight temperature increase makes the rate of heat generation greater than the rate of heat absorption required to maintain balance, so the temperature will continue to increase until point C is reached. Similarly, if the temperature is initially at B and decreases, the rate of heat generation will be less than the rate of heat absorption required to maintain balance, so the temperature will continue to drop until point A is reached. In contrast, the situation at point B in Fig. 6.5a is stable since a slight temperature increase provides an increase in the rate of heat generation less than the rate of heat absorption required to maintain balance, and the temperature will therefore move back to point B, (similarly if the temperature at B decreases).

Mathematically it is clear that this argument is equivalent to saying that the reaction is stable (unstable) if dy/dT is less (greater) than unity, where y is given by (6.26). This gives stability if

$$c_{in}\beta k'(T) < [1 + \alpha k(T)]^2 \tag{6.27}$$

and instability if the inequality sign is reversed.

In the above argument we assumed that $S(T) = 0$ in (6.22), but the reasoning is not essentially altered if this term is nonzero. Instead of (6.24) we shall have

$$T - T_{in} = \beta\left[ck(T) - \frac{1}{H}S(T)\right].$$

Equations (6.25) and (6.26) become

$$T - T_{in} = \frac{c_{in}\beta k(T)}{1 + \alpha k(T)} - \frac{\beta}{H}S(T) = y,$$

and the condition $dy/dT < 1$ gives stability when

$$c_{in}\beta k'(T) < \left[1 + \frac{\beta}{H}S'(T)\right][1 + \alpha k(T)]^2 \tag{6.28}$$

and instability if the inequality sign is reversed.

Unfortunately these results, which we derived from a physical argument based on Fig. 6.5, are not quite complete. The steady-state condition is in fact unstable if (6.27) and (6.28) are true with the reverse inequality signs, but the converse is not true; that is, (6.27) and (6.28) do not guarantee stability. There is a second necessary condition that must also be satisfied, and this will be investigated in Section 6.6.

This argument has been included as an interesting example of the dangers of physical reasoning, unsupported by rigorous mathematical analysis. In this case, if we wish to argue about what happens if the temperature varies around point B in Fig. 6.5b, we must go back to the general differential equations (6.21) and (6.22). A dynamical situation can never be fully analyzed if only steady-state equations are employed.

6.6 Chemical-Tank-Reactor Stability (continued)

Mathematics Used: Taylor series in two variables; ordinary linear differential equations with constant coefficients.

Comment: This is another example of a perturbation method involving local linearization. The purely mathematical argument clarifies and extends the physical argument of Section 6.5.

We approach the problem of stability from a purely mathematical point of view. Consider the pair of equations

$$\frac{dx}{dt} = P(x, z), \tag{6.29}$$

$$\frac{dz}{dt} = Q(x, z). \tag{6.30}$$

The steady state of the system is given by setting $dx/dt = dz/dt = 0$. If we denote the corresponding values of x and z by x_0 and z_0, respectively, then x_0 and z_0 satisfy the equations

$$P(x_0, z_0) = 0, \qquad Q(x_0, z_0) = 0.$$

Suppose $x = x_0 + u$ and $z = z_0 + w$, where u and w are small compared with x_0 and z_0, respectively. Then

$$P(x, z) \approx P(x_0, z_0) + (x - x_0)\left(\frac{\partial P}{\partial x}\right)_0 + (z - z_0)\left(\frac{\partial P}{\partial z}\right)_0$$
$$= au + bw,$$

where

$$a = \left(\frac{\partial P}{\partial x}\right)_0, \qquad b = \left(\frac{\partial P}{\partial z}\right)_0.$$

Similarly,

$$Q(x, z) \approx du + fw,$$

where

$$d = \left(\frac{\partial Q}{\partial x}\right)_0, \qquad f = \left(\frac{\partial Q}{\partial z}\right)_0.$$

Substituting these approximations in (6.29) and (6.30), they reduce to

$$\frac{du}{dt} = au + bw, \qquad \frac{dw}{dt} = du + fw.$$

These are linear equations, and we can study the behavior of their solutions by setting

$$u = Ue^{\lambda t}, \qquad w = We^{\lambda t}.$$

The equations give

$$(\lambda - a)U = bW, \qquad dU = (\lambda - f)W;$$

that is, the permissible values of λ are given by $(\lambda - a)/b = d/(\lambda - f)$, or

$$\lambda^2 - (a + f)\lambda + (af - bd) = 0. \tag{6.31}$$

The solutions are stable if they tend to zero as t tends to infinity, that is, if the real part of λ is less than zero. We have already studied this problem. Applying the results following (6.16), we see that the real parts of the roots of (6.31) are less than zero if

$$-(a + f) > 0, \tag{6.32}$$

$$af - bd > 0. \tag{6.33}$$

In the problem studied in Section 6.5 we have, using c in place of x, and T in place of z,

$$P(c, T) = \frac{q}{V}(c_{\text{in}} - c) - k(T)c,$$

$$Q(c, T) = \frac{q}{V}(T_{\text{in}} - T) - \frac{1}{C_p}S(T) + \frac{H}{C_p}k(T)c,$$

so that

$$a = -\frac{q}{V} - k(T), \qquad b = -ck'(T),$$

$$d = \frac{H}{C_p}k(T), \qquad f = -\frac{q}{V} - \frac{1}{C_p}S'(T) + \frac{H}{C_p}ck'(T).$$

Condition (6.32) gives, for stability,

$$\frac{2q}{V} + k(T) - \frac{H}{C_p}ck'(T) + \frac{1}{C_p}S'(T) > 0. \tag{6.34}$$

Condition (6.33) gives, on rearranging slightly, a second condition for stability,

$$-\frac{VH}{qC_p}ck'(T) + \left[1 + \frac{VS'(T)}{qC_p}\right]\left[1 + \frac{V}{q}k(T)\right] > 0. \tag{6.35}$$

This is precisely the condition (6.28) found by physical reasoning in the last section. However, condition (6.34) is independent of (6.35), and this additional condition was missed in the argument given in Section 6.5. [Of course, if $S'(T) = 0$, then (6.34) is automatically implied by (6.35).]

There are many ramifications of this problem, explored in the series of papers by Aris and Amundson.[9]

1. In the case of unstable steady states it may be possible to stabilize the reaction by suitable choice of $S(T)$, which controls the cooling of the tank.

2. We have studied only local linearization in the vicinity of the steady state. Since dc/dt and dT/dt are functions of only c and T, and not t, by

[9] R. Aris and N. R. Amundson, *Chem. Eng. Sci.*, **7**, 121–155 (1958).

dividing the differential equations we obtain an equation of the form $dc/dT = F(c, T)$, which can be used to study the behavior of the system over the whole range of c and T by what is known as *phase-plane analysis*.

3. It is possible to consider several simultaneous reactions instead of only one.

4. The equations can always be integrated numerically, and the organization of this is discussed by Aris and Amundson. (The remark is made that the cost of using an automatic computer for their work is equivalent to using human beings at 10 cents per hour—undoubtedly this figure would be even less with the present generation of automatic computers.)

6.7   A Nonlinear Electrical Circuit [10]

Mathematics Used: Elementary calculus and differential equations.

Comment: A semiphysical argument is sustained by consideration of a more complex model.

A two-terminal electrical direct-current device is known to have the voltage-current characteristic shown by the solid line in Fig. 6.6. We suppose that the characteristic has the equation $v = f(i)$. The device is connected in series with a battery of 100 volts and a 1000-ohm resistor. The equation for the current i in the resulting circuit is

$$100 = 1000i + f(i). \tag{6.36}$$

If we rewrite this in the form $v = f(i) = 100 - 1000i$, the possible values of i are given by the intersections of the curves $v = f(i)$ and $v = 100 - 1000i$. The first curve is given by the solid line in Fig. 6.6 and the second curve by the dashed line ABC. The points of intersection A, B, and C of the curves correspond to the possible steady-state currents: 30, 54, and 78 ma, approximately.

It is found experimentally that it is possible to operate this circuit in equilibrium at only two of the predicted values of the current, 30 and 78 ma. It is found experimentally that circuit operation is not stable at 54 ma, and if an attempt is made to operate at this current, the circuit actually settles down to operate at either 30 or 78 ma.

One can argue that if the circuit is operating at 54 ma and we decrease the current slightly, we can see from Fig. 6.6 that the voltage across the nonlinear device increases by more than the decrease in voltage across the resistor; that is, the combined voltage increases above 100 volts. This means that the 100-volt battery will be able to push even less current through than before,

---

[10] This section is based on an example submitted by the School of Electrical Engineering, Georgia Institute of Technology, Atlanta, Ga.

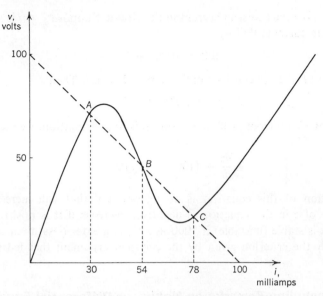

Fig. 6.6   Characteristic of nonlinear device.

and the current will continue to drop. Similarly, if the current increases to slightly above 54 ma, there will be a tendency for it to keep increasing. In contrast, at point A, if the current increases, the voltage across both the non-linear device and the resistance will increase and the total voltage will increase to above 100 volts. The 100-volt battery will not be able to provide the required current and the current in the circuit will decrease, bringing the operating point back to A.

In mathematical terms this argument means that if the current at an operating point is i, this is a stable operating point if

$$\frac{d}{di}[1000i + f(i)] > 0;$$

that is, $$1000 + f'(i) > 0. \qquad (6.37)$$

This condition is obviously satisfied at A and C since $f'(i)$ is greater than zero at both these points. The operating point is unstable if the inequality is reversed in (6.37). At point B we have $f'(i) \approx -2,500$; this implies that point B is unstable.

Such semiphysical arguments can be dangerous, as already pointed out, and it is more satisfactory to argue as follows. There is always some residual inductance in an electrical circuit, and, when currents are slowly changing, a better model than (6.36), assuming that the $v - i$ characteristic for the nonlinear device is still adequate, is

$$100 = L\frac{dx}{dt} + 1000x + f(x), \qquad (6.38)$$

where x is now the transient current in the circuit. Suppose $x = i$ is a possible steady-state current; that is,

$$100 = 1000i + f(i). \tag{6.39}$$

We set $x = i + z$, where z is small compared with i. Then

$$f(x) \approx f(i) + zf'(i).$$

Subtracting (6.39) from (6.38) and using this approximation, we see that, for small z,

$$L\frac{dz}{dt} + [1000 + f'(i)]z = 0.$$

The solution of this equation is an exponential that will increase if the coefficient of z in this equation is negative, decrease if it is positive. Hence the circuit is stable (unstable) if $1000 + f'(i)$ is greater (less) than zero. This is precisely the criterion given by the physical argument that led to (6.37).

6.8   Concluding Remarks on Nonlinear Differential Equations

Linear equations are comparatively easy for the mathematician to deal with. Nonlinear equations present difficulties of a completely different order of magnitude. Unfortunately, it is not always possible to formulate physical problems in terms of linear equations. Nature is often essentially nonlinear.

The example of the differential surge tank in Section 6.2 was included partly because comparatively crude approximations have to be made in both the formulation and the solution of the equations. The mathematician may be quite upset by the presentation in Section 6.2 and may have grave doubts about the validity of the reasoning—the editor admits that some of the arguments in the literature tended to make his hair stand on end—at least at first sight. The justification, after all, is that the Appalachia surge tank, costing a quarter of a million dollars, was designed using this kind of mathematics, and it worked. This is, of course, no reason why we should not try to improve the mathematical reasoning and techniques used, which would certainly be possible. But the mathematician tends to forget that experience and judgment are as important as rigorous reasoning in engineering design—as in real life.

We have mentioned several times that nonlinear ordinary differential equations can often be solved numerically, although we have not devoted much space to this aspect of the subject. The main emphasis in this chapter has been on the use of analytical tools as an aid to understanding the behavior of solutions of nonlinear differential equations. Once we understand how the solutions are behaving, it is possible to compute intelligently. It is often inevitable that one should use a computer to produce the final answers, but it may be difficult to obtain insight by using a computer.

Perhaps too much emphasis has been placed on the method of local linearization for determining stability conditions, but this is an accident of the examples included rather than deliberate policy. We are not attempting complete coverage in this book, and the reader must regard this chapter as merely a taste of what can be done.

Part III

APPLICATIONS TO FIELD PROBLEMS

Chapter 7

The Approximate Formulation and Solution of Field Problems

7.1 Introduction

One of the main distinctions between the problems considered in Chapters 5 and 6 and the problems considered in this chapter is the following. In Chapters 5 and 6 the problems could be formulated in terms of ordinary differential equations in a reasonably straightforward and definite way. In this chapter we deal with "field" problems, for example, the diffusion of water vapor or the flow of salt underground, where several independent variables are present, such as a space variable and time, or two space variables. Strictly speaking, these problems should be formulated as partial differential equations, but by making appropriate assumptions it is sometimes possible to formulate the problems in terms of ordinary differential equations. In this way insight can be obtained into phenomena that would otherwise require advanced mathematical treatment. In any case, a more exact treatment is usually obtained only at the expense of making it much more difficult to obtain insight into the results.

The point of this chapter is that judgment and ingenuity are used to set up models for problems that are difficult to handle with a satisfactory degree of exactitude and rigor.

7.2 The Permeation of Water Vapor Through Cable Sheaths [1]

Mathematics Used: Complex numbers; first-order ordinary differential equation; small approximations.

Comment: An approximate model is developed for a distributed system, using lumped analog elements.

[1] This section is based on a contribution by J. W. Lechleider, Bell Telephone Laboratories, Murray Hill, N.J., "Preliminary Report on the Possibility of Pumping of Water Vapor through Cable Sheaths."

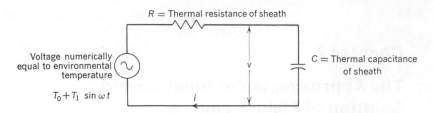

Fig. 7.1   Electrical analog of heat transfer.

Telephone companies have a large capital investment in buried cable. The soil surrounding these cables is often saturated with water, and the possibility arises that water may permeate the cables when they are not provided with metallic moisture barriers. This is not too serious under steady-state conditions. If a dry cable is placed in saturated surroundings, any air in the inside of the cable will also become saturated after sufficient time has elapsed. If the external temperature is constant, permeation ceases when saturation is achieved in the inside of the cable.

Unfortunately cables are often subject to a daily variation in temperature. Saturation pressure and permeability both depend on pressure, and this may lead to accumulation of liquid water in the core of the cable, even though the plastic sheath of the cable is perfectly intact. It is the purpose of the following analysis to explain how this may take place. Such a phenomenon would clearly be of great importance, because the presence of water in a cable produces serious degradation of its transmission characteristics.

As an approximation it will be sufficient to assume that the temperature outside the cable varies sinusoidally; for example,

$$T = T_0 + T_1 \sin \omega t.$$

If the temperature on the outside of the cable changes periodically, the temperature on the inside will also vary periodically. Since it takes time for heat to pass through the sheath of the cable to the core, the periodic changes of temperature inside the cable will tend to lag behind those of the environment. In a lumped circuit analog, the sheath of the cable represents a thermal impedance. Because of this impedance, the range of variation of the temperature inside the cable will be less than the range of variation of the environmental temperature. To formulate this in a semiquantitative form, we can draw the electrical analog of the heat transfer involved as in Fig. 7.1. We say that the formulation is "semiquantitative" because it would be difficult to assign numerical values to R and C, given only the dimensions of the cable and the thermal properties of the sheath and the core. Nevertheless, the theory predicts certain quantitative results that can be checked experimentally, as listed in the sentence following equation (7.8) below. If v is the voltage across the capacitor (that is, the temperature of the inside of the sheath), the current through the capacitor is $C(dv/dt)$, and the equation for the circuit is

$$CR\frac{dv}{dt} + v = T_0 + T_1 \sin \omega t = T_0 + \text{Im} (T_1 e^{i\omega t}).$$

The solution of this equation is of the form

$$v = T_0 + \text{Im} (V),$$

where V is the solution of

$$CR\frac{dV}{dt} + V = T_1 e^{i\omega t};$$

that is,

$$V = Ae^{-CRt} + \frac{T_1}{1 + i\omega CR} e^{i\omega t}.$$

We are interested only in the steady state as t tends to infinity and, since $CR > 0$, this gives

$$v = T_0 + \text{Im} \left(\frac{T_1 e^{i\omega t}}{1 + i\omega CR}\right)$$

$$= T_0 + \text{Im} \left(\frac{T_1 e^{i(\omega t - \theta)}}{(1 + \omega^2 C^2 R^2)^{1/2}}\right)$$

$$= T_0 + \frac{T_1 \sin (\omega t - \theta)}{(1 + \omega^2 C^2 R^2)^{1/2}} \tag{7.1}$$

where $\tan \theta = \omega CR$. This is plotted in Fig. 7.2, together with the outside temperature T.

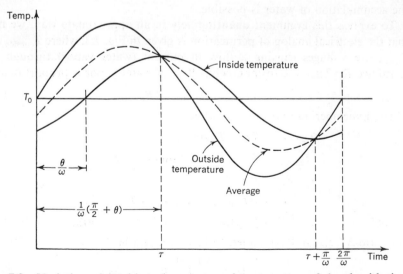

Fig. 7.2   Variation of outside temperature and temperature of sheath with time.

It is next necessary to consider the permeation process. The temperature dependence of the permeability of many gases and vapors through high polymers in the neighborhood of temperatures of interest here would make the resistance to permeation depend on temperature according to a relation of the form

$$R_p = R_0 e^{A/T}, \tag{7.2}$$

where R_0 and A are constants, R_p is the resistance to permeation, and T is the absolute temperature. The cable sheath cannot be at a uniform temperature throughout since heat is being conducted through it. However, as a rough approximation we can take T to be the average of the temperatures outside and inside the sheath. This average is indicated by the dashed line in Fig. 7.2.

The significance of these results is as follows. Vapor will permeate into (out of) the cable when the vapor pressure outside is greater (less) than the vapor pressure inside. Since the greater the temperature the greater the vapor pressure, vapor will permeate into (out of) the cable when the temperature outside is greater (less) than the temperature inside. If we now consider the time average of the curve marked "average" in Fig. 7.2, which gives a rough overall time and space average, it is clear that this overall average temperature of the sheath is greater when vapor is permeating into the cable than when vapor is permeating out of the cable. From (7.2) this means that the resistance to permeation is less when vapor is permeating into the cable, on the average. Since the time when vapor is entering the cable is equal to the time when vapor is leaving, the net diffusion current will be inward over a complete temperature cycle. This means that water is being pumped into the cable. As the temperature on the inside of the cable varies, some of the vapor will condense and form liquid water. Over an extended period it would seem that the accumulation of water is possible.

To express this argument quantitatively in an approximate way, we note that the electrical analog of permeation is given in Fig. 7.3, where T_{outside} and T_{inside} are voltages causing a flow of current (water vapor) through the resistance R_p. Then the instantaneous flow of water vapor is proportional to

$$(T_{\text{outside}} - T_{\text{inside}})/R_p, \tag{7.3}$$

where, remembering that $\tan \theta = \omega C R$,

$$T_{\text{outside}} = T_0 + T_1 \sin \omega t, \tag{7.4}$$

$$T_{\text{inside}} = T_0 + T_1 \cos \theta \sin (\omega t - \theta), \tag{7.5}$$

$$R_p = R_0 e^{A/T},$$

$$T = \tfrac{1}{2}(T_{\text{outside}} + T_{\text{inside}}) = T_0 + \Delta T,$$

where

$$\Delta T = \tfrac{1}{2}T_1[\sin \omega t + \cos \theta \sin (\omega t - \theta)]. \tag{7.6}$$

The ratio $\Delta T/T_0$ can be assumed to be small, and in this case

$$\frac{1}{T} = \frac{1}{T_0}\left(1 + \frac{\Delta T}{T_0}\right)^{-1} \approx \frac{1}{T_0} - \frac{\Delta T}{T_0^2}.$$

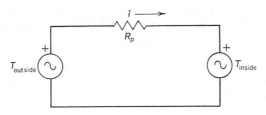

Fig. 7.3   Electrical analog of water permeation.

Then

$$\frac{1}{R_p} = \frac{1}{R_0} e^{-A/T} = \frac{1}{R_0} e^{-A/T_0} e^{A \Delta T/T_0^2} \approx \frac{1}{R_0} e^{-A/T_0} \left(1 + \frac{A \Delta T}{T_0^2}\right)$$

$$= a + b \Delta T, \tag{7.7}$$

where a and b are constants defined by this equation. From (7.3), the net accumulation of water per cycle will be given by

$$\int_\tau^{\tau + 2\pi/\omega} \left(\frac{T_{\text{outside}} - T_{\text{inside}}}{R_p}\right) dt.$$

For a fixed period of time, the number of cycles will be proportional to ω, so, using the approximation (7.7) for $1/R_p$, we find that the total accumulation of water will be proportional to

$$\omega \int_\tau^{\tau + 2\pi/\omega} (T_{\text{outside}} - T_{\text{inside}})(a + b \Delta T) \, dt.$$

Using (7.4) to (7.6) we see that the integral multiplying a is zero, and this expression becomes

$$\tfrac{1}{2}\omega b T_1^2 \int_\tau^{\tau + 2\pi/\omega} [\sin^2 \omega t - \cos^2 \theta \sin^2 (\omega t - \theta)] \, dt$$

$$= \tfrac{1}{2}\pi b T_1^2 (1 - \cos^2 \theta) = \tfrac{1}{2}\pi b T_1^2 \frac{\omega^2 C^2 R^2}{1 + \omega^2 C^2 R^2}. \tag{7.8}$$

This predicts that the rate of accumulation of water should be proportional to the square of the amplitude of the temperature oscillation T_1, and it predicts a specific form for the dependence on the angular frequency ω, containing only one arbitrary constant, CR. These predictions could be checked against experiment.

The following points are made in conclusion.

1. The above theory is not rigorous, but it is essentially clear and simple, and provides considerable insight into one possible mechanism by which water can accumulate in the core of a cable.

2. The theory gives a good idea of how experiments could be designed to test whether the proposed mechanism is really significant.

3. The proposed mechanism should be treated with considerable reserve until (a) rough calculations are performed to estimate the orders of magnitude of the factors involved, to see whether the effect is likely to be significant, and (b) experimental information is available against which the theory can be checked. The important thing is whether the theory applies to the practical situation. However, whether it applies or not, we have included this as an example of methodology, using elementary mathematics to elucidate the consequences of a theory.

7.3 The Flow of Fluids in Porous Media [2]

Mathematics Used: Simple nonlinear ordinary differential equations.

Comment: A distributed system is approximated by a nonlinear ordinary-differential-equation model.

We consider some simple problems connected with the flow of fluids in porous media such as sandstone. This subject is of course important in many branches of engineering, such as irrigation, the construction of dams, and the production of oil and gas from oil reservoirs.

The basic law governing the flow of fluids in porous media, at low velocities of flow, is known as *Darcy's law*, after its discoverer, who deduced it from experiments on "Les fontaines publique de la ville de Dijon."[3] Darcy's law is essentially an Ohm's law for fluids. It states that the velocity of flow is proportional to the difference between the actual pressure gradient and the static pressure gradient that would exist if the fluid in the system were at rest. The static pressure will vary with the height when the system is at rest due to gravity. If z denotes the height, the static pressure at any point is given by $p_0 - \rho g z$, where p_0 is a constant and ρ is the density of the fluid. Our statement of Darcy's law therefore gives

$$v = -a \frac{d}{ds}(p - p_0 + \rho g z) = -a \frac{d}{ds}(p + \rho g z), \qquad (7.9)$$

where s denotes distance measured in the direction of v and a is a constant. The minus sign is necessary because if $p + \rho g z$ decreases in the direction of s,

---

[2] The subject considered in this section was suggested by a contribution from Jan van Schilfgaarde, The Drainage Design Procedure for Falling Water Tables, *Proc. Am. Soc. Civil Engrs., J. Irrigation Drainage Div.*, **89**,(2), 1–11 (1963). This was brought to our attention by C. W. Suggs, Department of Agricultural Engineering, North Carolina State University at Raleigh. However, for the purpose of this book it was thought desirable to treat more elementary examples suggested by the author's experience in the Anglo-Iranian Oil Co. (as it was then). General references are M. E. Harr, *Groundwater and Seepage*, McGraw-Hill, New York, 1962, and M. Muskat, *The Flow of Homogeneous Fluids Through Porous Media*, McGraw-Hill, New York, 1937 (reprinted by Edwards, Ann Arbor, Mich., 1946).

[3] *Les fontaines publique de la ville de Dijon*, Paris, 1856.

then v is positive. The velocity v is defined as the quantity of fluid that passes through a unit area in the porous medium in a unit time. This is different from the mean velocity of the fluid, since the fluid occupies only a fraction of the volume. Instead of working in terms of the pressure, it is sometimes convenient to work in terms of the equivalent "head" of fluid, a term we met in Section 6.2. If h is the head corresponding to a pressure p, then $p = \rho g h$, where ρ is the density of the fluid; that is, the head is the height of the equivalent column of fluid that would produce a static pressure p at its base. We therefore set

$$h = z + \frac{p}{\rho g} \tag{7.10}$$

and write (7.9)

$$v = -k \frac{dh}{ds}, \tag{7.11}$$

where k is a constant of proportionality that depends on both the nature of the solid and the nature of the fluid. The dependence on the solid and on the fluid can be separated in a simple way, for it is found that

$$k = \frac{k_0 \rho g}{\mu},$$

where μ is the viscosity of the fluid; ρ the density of the fluid; and k_0 a constant characteristic of the porous solid alone, independent of the fluid, known as the *permeability* of the solid. All these results are essentially experimental. In addition, there are other effects that should be taken into account in a rigorous treatment, such as capillarity, which we shall ignore.

Suppose water is seeping through a bed of soil (or rock or concrete) lying in $0 \le x \le L$, with an impervious base, as shown in Fig. 7.4. The depth of water is assumed to be h_1 on the left and h_2 on the right, as shown. We represent the surface of the water by an equation $z = f(x)$, where $f(x)$ varies continuously from $f(0) = h_1$ at $x = 0$ to $f(L) = h_2$ at $x = L$. [A difficulty

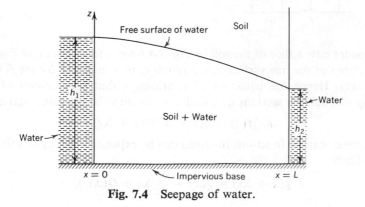

Fig. 7.4   Seepage of water.

that may arise in practice is that there may be a "surface of seepage" at $x = L$; that is, $f(L)$ may be greater than h_2. The water that arrives at $x = L$ at a height greater than h_2 simply trickles down the face $x = L$. However, we ignore this case here.]

The basic approximation we make is to assume that the pressure in the soil is equal to the static pressure. Since the pressure on the free surface is everywhere equal to atmospheric pressure, say p_0, this means that the pressure in the soil at the point (x, z) is given by

$$p(x, z) = p_0 + \rho g[f(x) - z].$$

Hence, from (7.10),

$$h = \frac{p_0}{\rho g} + f(x),$$

and, from (7.11), if we denote the horizontal velocity by u and the vertical velocity by w, we have

$$u = -k \frac{\partial h}{\partial x} = -k \frac{df(x)}{dx}, \qquad w = -k \frac{\partial h}{\partial z} = 0.$$

It is a consequence of our basic assumption that the vertical velocity is zero, and this obviously means that the subsequent analysis, known as the *Dupuit theory of flow*, will apply even approximately only if the length L is much larger than h_1 or h_2. There are many situations in which this is true.

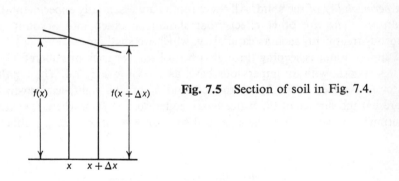

f(x)   f(x + Δx)   **Fig. 7.5**   Section of soil in Fig. 7.4.

x   x + Δx

Consider now a slice of the soil in Fig. 7.4 from x to $x + \Delta x$ (see Fig. 7.5). The heights of the free surface corresponding to x and $x + \Delta x$ are $f(x)$ and $f(x + \Delta x)$. Hence the equation of continuity—that the amount of fluid flowing through the sections at x and $x + \Delta x$ must be the same—gives

$$u(x)f(x) = u(x + \Delta x)f(x + \Delta x). \qquad (7.12)$$

We assume that the functions involved can be expanded by Taylor's theorem in the form

$$g(x + \Delta x) = g(x) + \frac{dg}{dx} \Delta x + O(\Delta x^2),$$

where the notation $k = O(\Delta x^2)$ means

$$|k| < C\,\Delta x^2$$

for some constant C, independent of Δx, for sufficiently small Δx. Equation (7.12) becomes

$$uf = \left[u + \Delta x\,\frac{du}{dx} + O(\Delta x^2)\right]\left[f + \Delta x\,\frac{df}{dx} + O(\Delta x^2)\right].$$

From the definition of the O-symbol it is easy to show that this reduces to

$$\Delta x\left(f\frac{du}{dx} + u\frac{df}{dx}\right) + O(\Delta x^2) = 0.$$

Dividing by Δx and then letting Δx tend to zero (remembering that a quantity that is $O(\Delta x^2)$ divided by Δx gives a quantity that is $O(\Delta x)$, and such a quantity tends to zero as Δx tends to zero), we see that

$$\frac{d}{dx}(uf) = 0 \qquad \text{or} \qquad \frac{d}{dx}\left(f\frac{df}{dx}\right) = 0;$$

that is,

$$\frac{d^2(f^2)}{dx^2} = 0. \tag{7.13}$$

Integration gives

$$f^2 = ax + b,$$

and, determining the constants a and b so that $f = h_1$ at $x = 0$ and $f = x_2$ at $x = L$, we find that

$$f = \left[h_1^2 - (h_1^2 - h_2^2)\frac{x}{L}\right]^{1/2}.$$

The rate of discharge Q at $x = L$ is given simply by $hu = -kf(df/dx) = -\tfrac{1}{2}k(df^2/dx)$, which in this case is a constant independent of x,

$$Q = \frac{k(h_1^2 - h_2^2)}{2L}.$$

In the book by Harr,[4] various direct extensions of this analysis are given, to cases where the lower boundary is sloping, or there is evaporation, or addition of water (due, for example, to rainfall).

We next consider the case of a circular well or borehole of radius b, Fig. 7.6. The equation of continuity in this case is obtained by considering the cylindrical region between the radii r and $r + \Delta r$. If the height of the free surface at radius r is denoted $f(r)$, then

$$2\pi r u(r)f(r) = 2\pi(r + \Delta r)u(r + \Delta r)f(r + \Delta r).$$

[4] M. E. Harr, *Groundwater and Seepage*, McGraw-Hill, New York, 1962.

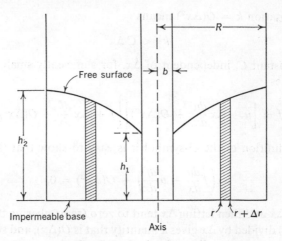

Fig. 7.6 A circular well.

Following the same steps as before we find, instead of (7.13), remembering that now $u = -\,k\,df/dr$,

$$\frac{d}{dr}\left(r\,\frac{df^2}{dr}\right) = 0. \tag{7.14}$$

Integration, using the boundary conditions $f = h_1$ at $r = b$ and $f = h_2$ at $r = R$, gives

$$f^2 = (h_2^2 - h_1^2)\frac{\log\,(r/b)}{\log\,(R/b)} + h_1^2. \tag{7.15}$$

The rate of discharge Q is given by

$$Q = \frac{\pi k(h_2^2 - h_1^2)}{\log\,(R/b)}. \tag{7.16}$$

Apparently this rate of discharge gives reasonably good agreement with experiment, as does the free surface (7.15) for sufficiently large values of the radius r. However, the shape of the free surface in the vicinity of the well apparently does not agree with that predicted by (7.15), although this is not unexpected since our assumptions break down near the well.[5]

Finally we consider briefly the phenomenon of water "coning" which can occur in oil wells.[6] Figure 7.7a represents a simplified and idealized oil field consisting of a porous medium between two layers of impervious rock. In the porous medium, owing to separation under gravity, a layer of oil lies on top of a layer of water, the two layers having constant thicknesses under static conditions. We assume that the reservoir is circular with a single

[5] *Ibid.*, pp. 58–59.

[6] See H. I. Meyer and A. O. Garder, Mechanics of Two Immiscible Fluids in Porous Media, *J. Appl. Phys.*, **25**, 1400–1406 (1954).

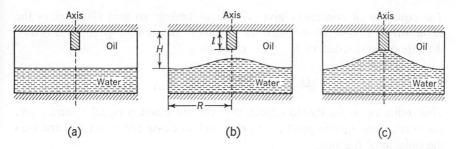

Fig. 7.7 Water coning: (*a*) no production; (*b*) intermediate production; (*c*) water breakthrough.

central well (borehole) which penetrates only partially into the oil layer if no oil is being produced; the interface between water and oil is then horizontal, as illustrated in Fig. 7.7*a*. If oil is produced, it is found that the water level tends to rise somewhat below the oil well, as shown in Fig. 7.7*b*. If the rate of oil production is sufficiently large, the oil-water level may rise so far that water does enter the well, as shown in Fig. 7.7*c*.

We assume that the radii of the reservoir and borehole are R and b, respectively. Let the thickness of the oil layer at $r = R$ be denoted H, and let the length of the well below the top impervious layer be denoted by l, as illustrated in Fig. 7.7*b*. We denote the oil-water interface (which is to be determined) by $z = F(r)$, where for convenience we arrange that $z = 0$ at $r = R$. Let ρ_w and ρ denote the densities of water and oil, respectively, where of course $\rho < \rho_w$. We consider the limiting case of Fig. 7.7*c*—the case where the water-oil interface just touches the bottom of the oil well.

Our fundamental assumption, as before, is that the pressure at any point is the same as the static pressure, justified on the basis that the velocities are small and R is much greater than H. This will be true in many practical cases, since thicknesses are usually of the order of tens of feet, and distances of the order of hundreds. In the oil,

$$
\begin{aligned}
p &= p_0 - \rho_w g F(r) - \rho g[z - F(r)] \\
  &= [p_0 - (\rho_w - \rho)gH] + (\rho_w - \rho)gf(r) - \rho gz,
\end{aligned}
$$

where for convenience we have introduced $f(r) = H - F(r)$. Corresponding to (7.10) we have

$$
h = \left(\frac{\rho_w}{\rho} - 1\right)f(r) + \frac{p_0'}{\rho g},
$$

where p_0' is a constant. Equation (7.11) shows that the horizontal velocity is given by

$$
u = -k\frac{dh}{dr} = -k\left(\frac{\rho_w}{\rho} - 1\right)\frac{df}{dr}. \tag{7.17}
$$

The equation of continuity gives (7.14), as before, so that (7.15) gives the variation of $F(r) = H - f$ with the radius r. In view of (7.16) and (7.17), the rate of production of oil, Q, is given by

$$Q = \pi k \left(\frac{\rho_w}{\rho} - 1 \right) \frac{(H^2 - l^2)}{\log (R/b)}.$$

This indicates, as we should expect, that the more nearly equal ρ_w and ρ are, the smaller the rate of production required to cause the water to cone into the bottom of the well.

We conclude this discussion of fluid flow in porous media by emphasizing that the results presented above are the consequence of many simplifying assumptions and approximations. From a purely mathematical point of view, we should solve Laplace's equation instead of reducing problems to the solution of ordinary differential equations. (In the case of the coning problem, the solution of Laplace's equation would involve a difficult free-boundary problem.) It is clear that our approximations break down for small radii when we are considering the circular well or the coning problem. From a physical point of view, the porous medium is often anisotropic or fissured, and frequently several fluids, such as oil, gas, and water, are flowing simultaneously in the porous medium instead of being separate, as in the coning problem. On the other hand, the above approximate methods are instructive even in situations where exact analytical solutions are known, and they often provide a valuable guide to more complicated situations, where exact analytical methods of solution are not available.

7.4   Closure of a Cavity in a Salt Dome[7]

Comment: By assuming spherical symmetry, the problem is formulated in terms of a simple partial differential equation that can be solved directly by an elementary method.

On the coast of the Gulf of Mexico there are buried mountains of salt several thousand feet below the surface of the earth. These are known as *salt domes*. In some places salt is obtained by pumping fresh water into a salt dome through the center part of an annular pipe and recovering the brine that comes up through the annulus. This process dissolves large cavities in the salt, as illustrated in Fig. 7.8.

A cavity in a salt dome closes gradually. The rate of closure has been investigated by several theories of creep. The simplest theory employs the assumption that salt flows as a very viscous liquid under the high pressures and temperatures that exist in a salt dome. The following analysis develops

[7] This is an expanded version of a problem contributed by H. L. Langhaar, College of Engineering, University of Illinois, Urbana, Ill.

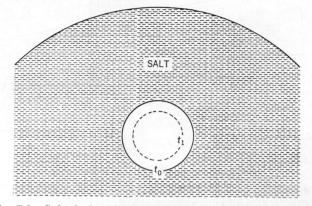

Fig. 7.8 Spherical cavity in salt dome at times t_0 and $t_1 > t_0$.

this idea, with the further approximation of spherical symmetry. Inertial forces are discarded, because a creeping type of motion is considered.

Denote the radial velocity (positive outward) by $u(r, t)$, where r is the distance from the center of the cavity to the point under consideration and t represents time. The condition of continuity (incompressibility) states that at any instant the rate at which salt is moving through the surface of a sphere of radius r is independent of r; that is,

$$4\pi r^2 u(r, t) = 4\pi (r + \Delta r)^2 u(r + \Delta r, t)$$

or, on using Taylor's theorem,

$$\left[2ru(r, t) + r^2 \frac{\partial u(r, t)}{\partial r} \right] \Delta r + O(\Delta r^2) = 0.$$

Dividing by Δr, and letting Δr tend to zero, gives

$$\frac{\partial}{\partial r} (r^2 u) = 0.$$

Integration gives

$$u = \frac{f(t)}{r^2}, \tag{7.18}$$

where $f(t)$ is an arbitrary function of time that is to be determined.

We now consider some properties of the stresses and distortions that must be established (or accepted) before we can make further progress. The equations we wish to establish are (7.23) and (7.26). The distortion of a small element of salt is illustrated diagrammatically in Fig. 7.9, where the solid line depicts a cross section of the element at t and the dashed line shows the shape of this element at time $t + \Delta t$. Because of spherical symmetry, there are no shearing stresses on the coordinate surfaces (that is, parallel to the surfaces of any sphere r = constant, or in a direction lying in a plane through the center of the sphere). The only stresses are the principal stresses σ_r and σ_t, where σ_r is the tensile stress in the radial direction and σ_t is the tangential

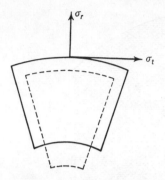

Fig. 7.9 Distortion in spherical geometry.

(tensile) stress in the circumferential direction. These stress components are functions of the radius and the time.

The forces resisting motion are viscous in nature. To obtain insight into these forces, suppose a fluid is moving along a straight line, with velocity $u(x)$ at position x. If $u(x + \Delta x)$, the velocity at $x + \Delta x$ is the same as $u(x)$, the fluid is simply moving as a whole, and no internal forces are produced. However, if

$$\lim_{\Delta x \to 0} \frac{u(x + \Delta x) - u(x)}{\Delta x} = \frac{du}{dx} = k \neq 0, \tag{7.19}$$

then the quantity k is a measure of the rate of distortion of the fluid, known as the *rate of strain*. We assume that the salt behaves as a Newtonian fluid, in which the viscous forces are linearly proportional to the rate of strain. To derive the precise form of the relationship we shall rely heavily on a symmetry argument. To do this we work temporarily in rectangular coordinates x, y, and z. As indicated in the last paragraph, we need consider only the case where no shearing stresses are present. Suppose σ_x, σ_y, and σ_z are the three components of normal stress, u_x, u_y, and u_z are the corresponding velocities, and

$$d_x = \frac{\partial u_x}{\partial x}, \qquad d_y = \frac{\partial u_y}{\partial y}, \qquad d_z = \frac{\partial u_z}{\partial z}$$

are the space derivatives of the velocities. When the material is at rest, it must be in a state of hydrostatic pressure. Denoting this pressure by p, we have

$$\sigma_x = \sigma_y = \sigma_z = -p$$

when the salt is at rest, where a negative sign is necessary since tensile stresses are taken to be positive, whereas positive pressure is compressive. We are considering a situation in which shearing stresses are absent (Fig. 7.10a). When the salt is in motion, we have

$$\sigma_x = -p + f(d_x, d_y, d_z), \qquad \sigma_y = -p + g(d_x, d_y, d_z),$$
$$\sigma_z = -p + h(d_x, d_y, d_z),$$

where f, g, and h, the *viscous stresses*, vanish when d_x, d_y, and d_z vanish. The Newtonian assumption (which is the simplest possible assumption, confirmed

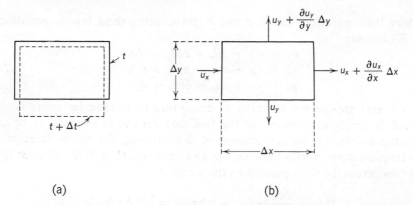

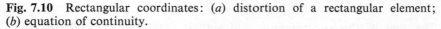

(a)   (b)

Fig. 7.10 Rectangular coordinates: (*a*) distortion of a rectangular element; (*b*) equation of continuity.

experimentally for many fluids) is that the difference between σ_x and $-p$ is a linear function of d_x, d_y, and d_z, and similarly for σ_y and σ_z:

$$\begin{aligned}
\sigma_x &= -p + a_{11}\, d_x + a_{12}\, d_y + a_{13}\, d_z, \\
\sigma_y &= -p + a_{21}\, d_x + a_{22}\, d_y + a_{23}\, d_z, \\
\sigma_z &= -p + a_{31}\, d_x + a_{32}\, d_y + a_{33}\, d_z.
\end{aligned} \tag{7.20}$$

We now assume that the medium is isotropic, which means that the properties of the medium do not depend on the direction we are considering. If we consider a distortion in the x direction, say, $d_x = 1$ and $d_y = d_z = 0$, then the stresses in the y and z directions are the same; that is, from (7.20),

$$\sigma_y = -p + a_{21} = \sigma_z = -p + a_{31} \qquad \text{or} \qquad a_{21} = a_{31};$$

similarly,

$$a_{12} = a_{32}, \qquad a_{13} = a_{23}.$$

The assumption that the properties of the medium do not depend on the direction considered in the medium also implies that two states of deformation, differing only by a rotation, will produce two states of stress differing only by a rotation. Thus if $d'_x = 1$ and $d'_y = d'_z = 0$ produce stresses $\sigma'_x = \alpha$ and $\sigma'_y = \sigma'_z = \beta$, then $d''_y = 1$ and $d''_x = d''_z = 0$ will produce stresses $\sigma''_y = \alpha$ and $\sigma''_x = \sigma''_z = \beta$. Hence, from (7.20),

$$\begin{aligned}
\alpha &= -p + a_{11} = -p + a_{22}, \\
\beta &= a_{21} = a_{31} = a_{12} = a_{32}.
\end{aligned}$$

Applying a similar argument for a deformation in the z direction we see that all the diagonal coefficients a_{ii} are equal, and all the off-diagonal a_{ij} are equal:

$$\begin{aligned}
a_{11} &= a_{22} = a_{33} = a, \\
a_{12} = a_{13} = a_{21} &= a_{23} = a_{31} = a_{32} = b,
\end{aligned}$$

where these equations define a and b. Introducing these results, equations (7.20) become

$$\sigma_x = -p + ad_x + b(d_y + d_z),$$
$$\sigma_y = -p + ad_y + b(d_x + d_z), \qquad (7.21)$$
$$\sigma_z = -p + ad_z + b(d_x + d_y).$$

We next require the equation of continuity in rectangular coordinates, which is simply a statement of the fact that the salt is assumed to be in-incompressible, or the net amount of salt crossing the six surfaces of a rectangular element with sides Δx, Δy, and Δz is zero (Fig. 7.10). The net rate of flow across the sides parallel to the x axis is

$$\left[\left(u_y + \frac{\partial u_y}{\partial y}\Delta y\right) - u_y\right]\Delta x\,\Delta z = \frac{\partial u_y}{\partial y}\Delta x\,\Delta y\,\Delta z.$$

The sum of this contribution, and similar contributions from the sides parallel to the y axis and z axis, gives

$$\frac{\partial u_x}{\partial x} + \frac{\partial u_y}{\partial y} + \frac{\partial u_z}{\partial z} = d_x + d_y + d_z = 0.$$

Using this result in (7.21), and introducing the notation $a - b = 2\mu$, where μ is known as the coefficient of viscosity, we see that (7.21) reduces to

$$\sigma_x = -p + 2\mu\frac{\partial u_x}{\partial x}, \qquad \sigma_y = -p + 2\mu\frac{\partial u_y}{\partial y}, \qquad \sigma_z = -p + 2\mu\frac{\partial u_z}{\partial z}. \quad (7.22)$$

We now interpret this result in spherical coordinates. The rate of strain in the radial direction [compare (7.19) and Fig. 7.11] is simply $\partial u/\partial r$. The rate of strain in the tangential direction is given by (Fig. 7.11)

$$\lim_{\Delta\theta\to 0}\frac{u\sin\Delta\theta}{r\,\Delta\theta} = \frac{u}{r}.$$

Using these results in (7.22), with $\sigma_x = \sigma_r$, and $\sigma_y = \sigma_z = \sigma_t$, we see that

$$\sigma_r = -p + 2\mu\frac{\partial u}{\partial r}, \qquad \sigma_t = -p + 2\mu\frac{u}{r}. \qquad (7.23)$$

Since the rate of movement is extremely slow, we can assume that, at any instant, dynamical effects are negligible and we need consider only static equilibrium conditions. We consider the equilibrium of a small piece of salt between radii r and $r + \Delta r$, shown pictorially in Fig. 7.12a, where the plane $OABCD$ is redrawn in detail in Fig. 7.12b. The salt element has six faces, given by parts of two spheres of radii r and $r + \Delta r$, and four planes cutting each other at right angles, the angles between opposite planes being $\Delta\alpha$ (see Fig. 7.12b). The areas of the curved surfaces of radii r and $r + \Delta r$ are $(r\,\Delta\alpha)^2$ and $[(r + \Delta r)\,\Delta\alpha]^2$, with forces per unit area of $\sigma_r(r)$ and $\sigma_r(r + \Delta r)$, respectively. (Remember that the physical situation is assumed to be spherically symmetrical, so σ_r and σ_t depend only on r and t.) The net force in an outward

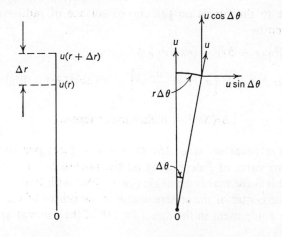

Fig. 7.11   Rate of strain in spherical coordinates.

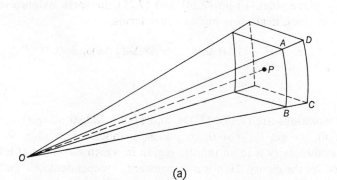

(a)

(b)

Fig. 7.12   Equilibrium of a salt element.

direction due to the forces on the curved surface of radii r and $r + \Delta r$ is therefore given by

$$[(r + \Delta r)\, \Delta\alpha]^2 \sigma_r(r + \Delta r) - (r\, \Delta\alpha)^2 \sigma_r(r)$$

$$= (r^2 + 2r\, \Delta r)(\Delta\alpha)^2 \left[\sigma_r(r) + \frac{\partial\sigma_r}{\partial r}\,\Delta r\right] - r^2(\Delta\alpha)^2 \sigma_r(r) + \text{higher-order terms}$$

$$= \left(2r\sigma_r + r^2\,\frac{\partial\sigma_r}{\partial r}\right)\Delta r(\Delta\alpha)^2 + \text{higher-order terms.} \tag{7.24}$$

The force at a point on side $ABCD$ is $\sigma_t(r + \xi\,\Delta r)$ per unit area, where $0 \le \xi \le 1$, the value of ξ depending on the precise point where the force is measured. This force makes an angle $(\frac{1}{2}\pi - \frac{1}{2}\Delta\alpha)$ with line OP in Fig. 7.12a, where O is the center of the sphere and P is the center of the curved face of radius r. The component in the direction OP of the force at any point of the face $ABCD$ is

$$-\sigma_t(r + \xi\,\Delta r)\sin\left(\tfrac{1}{2}\,\Delta\alpha\right) = -\tfrac{1}{2}\,\Delta\alpha\,\sigma_t(r) + \text{higher-order terms.} \tag{7.25}$$

The total contribution to the force in the direction OP is obtained by multiplying this by the area of $ABCD$, which is $r\,\Delta r\,\Delta\alpha$, and by a factor of 4 since there are four plane sides. From (7.24) and (7.25) the force balance in the radial direction gives, neglecting higher-order terms,

$$\left(2r\sigma_r + r^2\,\frac{\partial\sigma_r}{\partial r}\right)\Delta r(\Delta\alpha)^2 - 4r\,\Delta r\,\Delta\alpha(\tfrac{1}{2}\,\Delta\alpha)\sigma_t = 0$$

or
$$\frac{\partial\sigma_r}{\partial r} + \frac{2(\sigma_r - \sigma_t)}{r} = 0. \tag{7.26}$$

The basic equations are (7.18), (7.23), and (7.26). Substituting (7.18) and (7.23) in (7.26), we get $\partial p/\partial r = 0$, so $p = p(t)$, independent of r. We are assuming that the cavity is in an infinite region in which the stress at infinity is not affected by the cavity. Hence $p = \text{constant}$, independent of r and t.

Let the radius of the cavity at time t be $a(t)$. At the surface of the cavity, $\sigma_r = 0$. Hence the first equation in (7.23), together with (7.18), give

$$f(t) = -\frac{pa^3}{4\mu}.$$

Hence, by (7.18), the velocity of the surface of the cavity is given by

$$u(a, t) = -\frac{pa}{4\mu}.$$

But the velocity of the surface of the cavity is da/dt, so

$$\frac{da}{dt} = u(a, t) = -\frac{pa}{4\mu}.$$

Because p is a constant, this equation can be integrated to give

$$a = a_0 e^{-pt/4\mu},$$

where a_0 is the radius of the cavity at time $t = 0$. This equation gives the rate of closure since it gives the radius of the cavity in terms of the initial radius a_0 and the time t.

The time T in which the radius of the cavity is reduced by the factor $1/e = 0.368$ is determined by $pT/4\mu = 1$; that is,

$$T = \frac{4\mu}{p}.$$

The interval T is called the *relaxation time*. As might be expected, it increases with the viscosity μ and decreases with the surrounding pressure p. The pressure p is more or less proportional to the depth. The viscosity μ of salt under conditions existing in a salt dome must be determined by experiment. Experiments to check the validity of the above theory could be performed in the field by measuring the change with time of the volume of a cavity in a salt dome.

7.5 The Cigarette Problem[8]

Mathematics Used: Ordinary linear differential equations with constant coefficients.

Comment: A problem involving a distributed system is formulated in terms of a simple integral equation.

In this section we study the problem of filtration through a burning cigarette, which is a moving-boundary filtration problem. We make the following assumptions:

1. During steady inhalation (that is, constant velocity of air and burned gases being drawn through the cigarette, and constant rate of burning) a constant fraction a of any component Z in the tobacco that is burned at the tip is drawn through the cigarette, the remaining fraction $1 - a$ escaping into the air. Under normal smoking conditions a may be close to unity, but the assumption of arbitrary a does not essentially complicate the analysis.

2. With respect to filtration of component Z, the absorption coefficient of the tobacco is constant and equal to b. Similarly, if a filter tip is present, the absorption coefficient of the tip is constant and equal to β.

3. The rate of change in length due to burning is so slow that the time lag

---

[8] This section was suggested by an article by M. S. Klamkin, A Moving Boundary Filtration Problem or "The Cigarette Problem," *Am. Math. Monthly,* **64**, 710–715 (1957). Dr. Klamkin formulates the problem in terms of a first-order partial differential equation which he solves by guessing the form of the solution. (His equation can be solved by a systematic procedure by an elementary application of the Laplace transform.) We solve the problem here by formulating it in a different way, which leads to an ordinary instead of a partial differential equation. This paper was brought to the editor's attention by R. C. Buck.

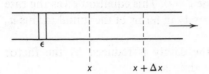

Fig. 7.13 Absorption by cigarette.

due to the finite rate of gas flow along the cigarette can be assumed to be negligible; that is, the deposition of the fraction a of a certain amount of component Z along the cigarette by filtration can be assumed to occur instantaneously with the burning of this amount at the tip.

We first study absorption of the component Z from the smoke passing along the cigarette. Denote distance along the cigarette by x, measured for the present purpose from any arbitrary zero. Suppose for simplicity that the smoke is moving along the cigarette with constant velocity, and consider a very thin slice of thickness ϵ, say, moving with the smoke (Fig. 7.13). Let the total weight of component Z in the slice when it passes position x be $w(x)$. The total weight at $x + \Delta x$ is then $w(x + \Delta x)$. Also, by definition of the absorption coefficient b, the weight removed from the slice as it moves from x to $x + \Delta x$ is $bw\,\Delta x$. Hence

$$w(x) - w(x + \Delta x) = bw\,\Delta x.$$

If we let Δx tend to zero, we obtain

$$\frac{dw}{dx} = -bw \quad \text{or} \quad w = w_0 e^{-bx}, \tag{7.27}$$

where w_0 is the value of w at $x = 0$. We have already noted that the weight deposited between x and $x + \Delta x$ is $bw\,\Delta x$; that is, the weight deposited per unit length at position x is given by

$$bw_0 e^{-bx}. \tag{7.28}$$

If the cigarette is cut off at $x = X$, it is clear physically that this does not affect the analysis from $x = 0$ to $x = X$, since there is no reflection from the end $x = X$ and the smoke goes through the plane $x = X$ in the same way, regardless of whether there is a cigarette or filter in $x \geq X$ or not. The weight of component Z that goes through the plane $x = X$ can be found by calculating the amount that would have been deposited from $x = X$ to infinity if the cigarette had been of infinite length; that is, from (7.28),

$$\int_X^\infty bw_0 e^{-bx}\,dx = w_0 e^{-bX}. \tag{7.29}$$

Similarly, if the cigarette has an absorption coefficient b in $0 \leq x \leq \xi$ and β in $\xi \leq x \leq X$, then instead of (7.29) we would have

$$w = \begin{cases} w_0 e^{-bx}, & 0 \leq x \leq \xi, \\ We^{-\beta x}, & \xi \leq x \leq X, \end{cases}$$

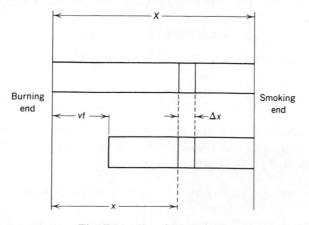

Fig. 7.14   Burning cigarette.

where the constant W is determined by the condition that w is continuous at $x = \xi$; that is,

$$w_0 e^{-b\xi} = W e^{-\beta\xi}$$

or

$$w = w_0 e^{-b\xi - \beta(x-\xi)}, \qquad \xi \le x \le X.$$

The weight deposited per unit length at the position x ($> \xi$) is given by

$$\beta w_0 e^{-b\xi - \beta(x-\xi)}, \tag{7.30}$$

and the weight that goes through the plane $x = X$ is

$$w_0 e^{-b\xi - \beta(X-\xi)}. \tag{7.31}$$

The ratio of the weight of component Z that passes through the plane $x = X$ when a filter is present [(7.31)], to that when no filter is present [(7.29)], is

$$e^{-(\beta - b)(X - \xi)}. \tag{7.32}$$

This depends only on the length of the filter, not on the length of the cigarette.

The actual situation is, of course, more complicated than the above analysis would indicate, and this we now consider. Suppose the cigarette is originally of length X, and that the tip burns at a velocity v, so the cigarette is of length $X - vt$ at time t (Fig. 7.14). Let $W(x, t)$ denote the weight of component Z per unit length of the cigarette at position x at time t, where x is always measured from the original position of the left (burning) end of the cigarette at $t = 0$ (Fig. 7.14). The weight of Z per unit length at the burning tip is $W(vt, t)$. In time Δt a length $v \Delta t$ of the cigarette is burned, containing $v \Delta t W(vt, t)$ of component Z, and of this

$$av \Delta t W(vt, t)$$

passes into the cigarette. The amount deposited between x and $x + \Delta x$ is, from (7.28),

$$abv \,\Delta t\, W(vt, t)e^{-b(x - vt)} \,\Delta x. \tag{7.33}$$

Hence the total weight deposited by absorption in time t between x and $x + \Delta x$ is

$$abv \int_0^t W(v\tau, \tau)e^{-b(x - vt)} \,d\tau \,\Delta x = w(x, t) \,\Delta x, \tag{7.34}$$

where this defines $w(x, t)$. The total weight in this section is obtained by adding $W(x, 0)\,\Delta x$ to this amount, and the result must equal $W(x, t)\,\Delta x$, by definition of $W(x, t)$. Hence

$$W(x, t) = W(x, 0) + abve^{-bx} \int_0^t W(v\tau, \tau)e^{bv\tau} \,d\tau. \tag{7.35}$$

We can obtain an equation from which $W(vt, t)$ can be determined by setting $x = vt$ in this equation. This gives

$$f(t) = W(vt, 0)e^{bvt} + abv \int_0^t f(\tau) \,d\tau, \tag{7.36}$$

where we have set

$$f(t) = W(vt, t)e^{bvt}. \tag{7.37}$$

Equation (7.36) is a simple integral equation which can be solved by differentiation. For simplicity we shall deal only with the case in which the initial concentration is a constant, independent of x, $W(x, 0) = W_0$. Then differentiation of (7.36) gives

$$\frac{df}{dt} - abvf = bvW_0e^{bvt}.$$

Solving this equation and using (7.37) we find

$$W(vt, t) = \frac{W_0}{1 - a} + Ae^{-b(1 - a)vt},$$

where A is an arbitrary constant that can be determined from the condition $W(0, 0) = W_0$. Hence

$$W(vt, t) = \frac{W_0}{1 - a} [1 - ae^{-b(1 - a)vt}]. \tag{7.38}$$

Substitution in (7.35) gives the final answer

$$W(x, t) = W_0 \left[1 + \frac{a}{1 - a} e^{-bx}(e^{bvt} - e^{abvt})\right].$$

If the length of the cigarette that is burned is denoted by ξ, so that $vt = \xi$, we have

$$W(x, t) = W_0 \left[1 + \frac{a}{1 - a} e^{-bx}(e^{b\xi} - e^{ab\xi})\right].$$

This is independent of the velocity v, as we should expect because of the third assumption made at the beginning of the section.

The weight of Z that will pass through the end of the cigarette at $x = X$ when the cigarette is smoked to $x = \xi$ is given, from (7.34), since t is equal to ξ/v, by

$$\int_X^\infty w(x, \xi/v)\, dx = ave^{-bX} \int_0^{\xi/v} W(v\tau, \tau)e^{bv\tau}\, d\tau$$

$$= \frac{aW_0}{b(1-a)} e^{-bX}(e^{b\xi} - e^{ab\xi}), \tag{7.39}$$

where we have used (7.38). If there is a filter tip in $\xi \leq x \leq X$ we have, when $x > \xi$, instead of (7.34), by using (7.30),

$$w(x, t) = a\beta v \int_0^t W(v\tau, \tau)e^{-b(\xi-vt)-\beta(x-\xi)}\, d\tau.$$

The weight that passes through $x = X$ is, instead of (7.39),

$$ave^{-\beta X + (\beta - b)\xi} \int_0^t W(v\tau, \tau)e^{bv\tau}\, d\tau, \tag{7.40}$$

where $W(v\tau, \tau)$ is the same as before.

The ratio of the weight of component Z that passes $x = X$ when a filter tip is present [(7.40)] to that when no filter is present [(7.39)], when both are smoked to $x = \xi$ [that is, $t = \xi/v$ in (7.40)], is

$$e^{-(\beta - b)(X - \xi)}.$$

This is precisely (7.32) and depends only on the length of the filter, not on the length of the cigarette.

As usual, the assumptions we have made have a determining effect on the result. We have assumed, for instance, that the cigarette is smoked to the same length whether a filter tip is present or not. One of the advantages of a filter tip, from the point of view of avoiding excessive inhalation of component Z, is that it prevents the cigarette being smoked to very short lengths. The effect of this could be investigated on the basis of the above analysis.

Chapter 8

The Mechanism of
Overthrust Faulting in Geology[1]

Mathematics Used: Simple algebra and trigonometry.

Comment: Quantitative examination of a simple model produces a paradox (Section 8.3) which is removed by improving the model.

8.1 Normal, Reverse, and Overthrust Faults

Consider the following experiment. A rectangular box is filled with loose dry sand. Embedded in the sand are three horizontal thin layers of material with a distinctive color, such as powdered plaster of paris, placed in the sand when the box was filled. A cross section of the sand, which can be imagined as viewed through a glass side of the box, is shown in Fig. 8.1a. The visible thin layers, denoted by lines AB, CD, and EF in the figure, have no significance except as markers to show sand movements.

The left end of the box can be moved horizontally, the right end being fixed. If the moveable end is moved to the left, the picture in Fig. 8.1b is obtained. A fairly sharp cleavage occurs, making a slope of about 60° with the horizontal. If the left end is moved to the right, a cleavage again occurs, but the angle of cleavage in this case is about 30°, as shown in Fig. 8.1c. Of

---

[1] This chapter is based on M. K. Hubbert and W. W. Rubey, Role of Fluid Pressure in Mechanics of Overthrust Faulting, *Bull. Geol. Soc. Am.*, **70**, 115–205 (1959). This paper gives an interesting account of the development of the authors' ideas, together with a historical survey of various unsuccessful attempts to explain the mechanism of overthrusting. For the discussion in Sections 8.1 and 8.2 see also M. K. Hubbert, Mechanical Basis for Certain Familiar Geologic Structures, *Bull. Geol. Soc. Am.*, **62**, 355–372 (1951).

This chapter suggested itself to the editor when he listened to a discussion between a panel of geologists and the Panel on Mathematics for the Physical Sciences and Engineering of CUPM in San Francisco in February 1964. During the discussion, the first paper mentioned above was quoted by one of the geologists, J. R. Balsley, Jr., Wesleyan University, Middletown, Conn., as an example of the way in which mathematics is being used in geology.

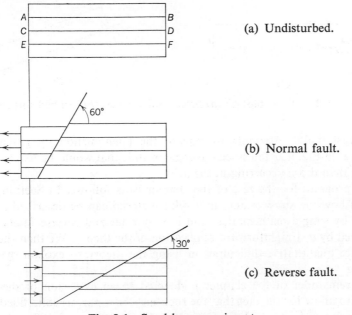

(a) Undisturbed.

(b) Normal fault.

(c) Reverse fault.

Fig. 8.1   Sand-box experiment.

course, the experimental pictures are not so neat or well defined as Fig. 8.1, but the general idea is correct.

Many rock structures are found in geology which fall under one of these two headings. Such sharp cleavages of rocks are called *faults*, and they fall into two classes, *normal faults*, corresponding to Fig. 8.1*b*, and *reverse faults*, corresponding to Fig. 8.1*c*. Not only is there a qualitative resemblance between the pictures given by the sand box and the appearance of faults in rocks, but the angles of 60° and 30° are also in reasonable agreement with those found in large-scale rock structures, the thickness of the rock being many hundreds of feet.

This chapter is also concerned with a difficulty that arises when attempts are made to explain another type of fault. In an *overthrust fault*, a large block of rock is displaced almost horizontally (that is, with dip less than, say, 5°) over a considerable distance. As an example of the magnitudes involved, a layer of rock 50 miles long may have been moved 10 or 20 miles horizontally.

The difficulty in giving a quantitative explanation of overthrust faulting can now be explained very simply. If we imagine that a block of rock is being pushed horizontally as in Fig. 8.2*a*, the idea is that fracture occurs along *AB*, and the upper block moves relative to the lower rock. However, simple calculations reproduced in Section 8.3 show that only blocks of comparatively short lengths *AB* would fracture as shown, along *AB*. If the simple theory is applied to the lengths of blocks that are actually observed, it appears that reverse faults such as those in Fig. 8.1*c* should have been produced, not

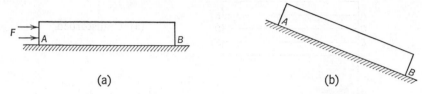

Fig. 8.2   Thrust blocks: (*a*) horizontal surface; (*b*) inclined surface.

overthrust faults. Attempts to explain the phenomenon by gravitational sliding as in Fig. 8.2*b* fail since the angle of slide that would be required is far greater than those occurring in the field.

The program for the rest of the chapter is as follows. In Section 8.2 we explain how the stress system in a solid material can be described approximately by simple mathematics, and how normal and reverse faults can be explained by a straightforward application of the theory. We then show why there are quantitative difficulties in using the theory to explain overthrust faulting.

The remainder of the chapter is devoted to an extension of the simple theory to allow for the fact that the rock may be a porous solid filled with a fluid under abnormally large pressures. This situation is often found in practice, for example, in oil wells. It is shown that the quantitative difficulties of the theory in explaining overthrust faulting can then be overcome. This does not, of course, prove that the modified theory is correct, but it removes the objections that decisively disprove the simple theory.

8.2   Mohr's Stress Circle, with Applications

Consider the state of stress in the box of sand in Fig. 8.1. In the undisturbed state, the vertical and horizontal normal stresses will be approximately equal, and the stress state will be hydrostatic with a normal stress σ per unit area on any surface, equal to the pressure of the overburden, or $\sigma = p = \rho g z$, where ρ is the bulk density of the sand, g the acceleration of gravity, and z the depth beneath the surface. If the moveable wall of the box is moved to the left (or right) as in Fig. 8.1*b* (or *c*), the vertical stress will remain unchanged, but the horizontal stress will decrease (increase). From symmetry there will be no shearing forces (forces parallel to a given surface, as opposed to normal

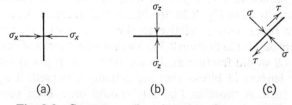

Fig. 8.3   Stresses on (imaginary) surfaces in sand.

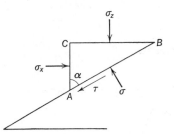

Fig. 8.4   Equilibrium of a small prism.

to the surface) on any (imaginary) vertical or horizontal surface in the sand. The forces on such surfaces are purely normal, as illustrated in Fig. 8.3, where $\sigma_x < \sigma_z$ for the situation in Fig. 8.1b and $\sigma_x > \sigma_z$ for Fig. 8.1c. The forces σ_x and σ_z are known as the *principal stresses*. Both normal and shear forces act on an inclined surface (Fig. 8.3c), and the relation between these and the principal stresses can be found by considering the equilibrium of a small right-triangular prism as in Fig. 8.4. The situation is two-dimensional and we can consider a unit length of the prism in a direction perpendicular to the plane of the paper. If the length of the hypotenuse of the prism is denoted by h, then by resolving forces horizontally and vertically, remembering that the stresses are forces per unit area and that $AC = h \cos \alpha$ and $BC = h \sin \alpha$, we obtain

$$(h \cos \alpha)\sigma_x - h\tau \sin \alpha - h\sigma \cos \alpha = 0,$$
$$(h \sin \alpha)\sigma_z + h\tau \cos \alpha - h\sigma \sin \alpha + \tfrac{1}{2}h^2\rho g \sin \alpha \cos \alpha = 0,$$

where the last term in the second equation is the gravitational force due to the weight of the prism. Dividing through by h and letting h tend to zero, this term vanishes (the weight of the prism is negligible compared with the surface forces for small h), and we obtain

$$\sigma_x \cos \alpha = \tau \sin \alpha + \sigma \cos \alpha,$$
$$\sigma_z \sin \alpha = -\tau \cos \alpha + \sigma \sin \alpha.$$

If these are solved for σ and τ we find, on simplifying, that

$$\sigma = \tfrac{1}{2}(\sigma_x + \sigma_z) + \tfrac{1}{2}(\sigma_x - \sigma_z) \cos 2\alpha, \tag{8.1}$$

$$\tau = \tfrac{1}{2}(\sigma_x - \sigma_z) \sin 2\alpha. \tag{8.2}$$

These equations can be interpreted geometrically by plotting σ against τ as in Fig. 8.5. For simplicity we assume $\sigma_x > \sigma_z$. Then for constant σ_x and σ_z, the locus of the point (σ, τ) as α goes from 0 to π is a circle with center $\tfrac{1}{2}(\sigma_x + \sigma_z)$ and radius $\tfrac{1}{2}(\sigma_x - \sigma_z)$, as shown. This circle is known as Mohr's circle, after the German engineer who first described it in 1882. Note that the angle α is the angle the surface makes with σ_z, the *least* principal stress. If $\sigma_x < \sigma_z$, the Mohr-circle diagram is still valid if the roles of σ_x and σ_z are interchanged; in this case σ is the angle the surface makes with σ_x.

We now require some additional knowledge of the properties of the material. Consider the experiment in Fig. 8.6. Sand is placed in a box whose upper half can be moved horizontally relative to the lower, producing a

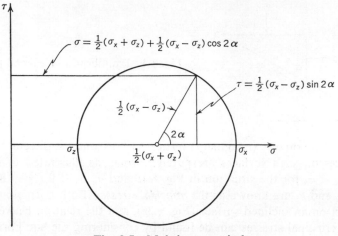

Fig. 8.5 Mohr's stress circle.

shearing stress in the sand along the dashed line. There are two forces acting along the interface, a normal force σ depending on the total normal force N and a shearing force τ depending on the force T acting to move the upper half of the box relative to the lower. If A is the area of the interface, $N = A\sigma$ and $T = A\tau$. Experimentally it is found that if N is fixed and T is increased from zero, no movement of the two halves relative to each other occurs until

$$\frac{T}{N} = \frac{\tau}{\sigma} = \text{constant} = \tan \phi, \tag{8.3}$$

where the constant is independent of N, and this defines $\tan \phi$.

If (8.3) is plotted in the Mohr diagram of Fig. 8.5, that is, the $\sigma\tau$ plane, we obtain a straight line making an angle ϕ with the σ axis, which illustrates the reason for introducing ϕ. Instead of moving the top of the box to the right in Fig. 8.6, we could equally have moved it to the left, and slippage would then have occurred when $\tau/\sigma = -\tan \phi$, corresponding to a line in the Mohr diagram making an angle $-\phi$ with the σ axis. These two straight lines are drawn in each of the parts of Fig. 8.8. They are called the *fracture lines*,

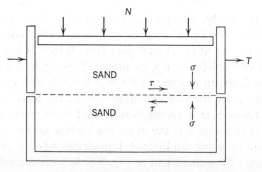

Fig. 8.6 Experiment for measuring τ/σ ratio for slippage.

because if any point lies between these lines, in the sector including the σ axis, $\tau/\sigma < \tan \phi$, and no fracture will occur. If a point lies outside these lines, then $\tau/\sigma > \tan \phi$, and fracture will occur before this state of stress can be reached.

Incidentally, it may be noted that ϕ is also the angle of repose of loose sand (Fig. 8.7). If w is the weight of a particle of loose sand lying on a slope making an angle β with the horizontal, then $\sigma = w \cos \beta$, $\tau = w \sin \beta$, and $\tau/\sigma = \tan \beta$. If $\beta = \phi$, the stresses lie on the line of fracture in the Mohr diagram. The angle ϕ gives the steepest slope at which loose sand will be stable.

Fig. 8.7   Loose sand at angle of repose.

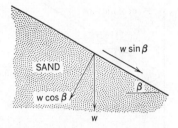

We can now deduce what will happen in the sand-box experiments in Fig. 8.1b and c. As we have said previously, the initial state of stress in the sand (Fig. 8.1a) is simply $\sigma_x = \sigma_z = \rho gz$, the hydrostatic pressure. If the moveable end is moved to the left as in Fig. 8.1b, the stress σ_z is unchanged, but the stress σ_x starts to decrease. On Mohr's diagram in Fig. 8.8b we have fixed the maximum stress σ_z and have shown a diminishing minimum stress with a Mohr's circle of increasing radius. Eventually the Mohr circle will become tangential to the fracture lines $\tau = \pm \sigma \tan \phi$, and fracture will occur. From the diagram (remembering the definition of α and Figs. 8.4 and 8.5), the planes along which fractures occur make angles α with the minimum principal stress σ_x which are given by

$$2\alpha = \pm (90 + \phi),$$

that is, $$\alpha = \pm (45 + \tfrac{1}{2}\phi) \tag{8.4}$$

Experimentally, for sand, ϕ is found to vary between 30 and 35°; this means that $|\alpha|$, the angle that lines of cleavage for normal faults make with the horizontal in loose sand should be about 60 to $62\tfrac{1}{2}°$, which agrees well with experiment. Similarly, for reverse faults, if the movable end of the box is moved to the right, as in Fig. 8.1c, the stress σ_z is unchanged, but σ_x increases. The Mohr circle becomes larger, as in Fig. 8.8c, until it is tangential to the lines of fracture. This occurs at precisely the angles (8.4), but in this case the minimum principal stress is σ_z, so fracture occurs at 60 to $62\tfrac{1}{2}°$ to the vertical, or $27\tfrac{1}{2}$ to 30° to the horizontal. The value observed experimentally is slightly lower, perhaps 25°. The main difference between the angles of normal and reverse faults is explained. The small discrepancy between the theoretical and experimental dips for reverse faults may be due to the fact that in the experiments the principal stresses are not precisely horizontal and vertical.

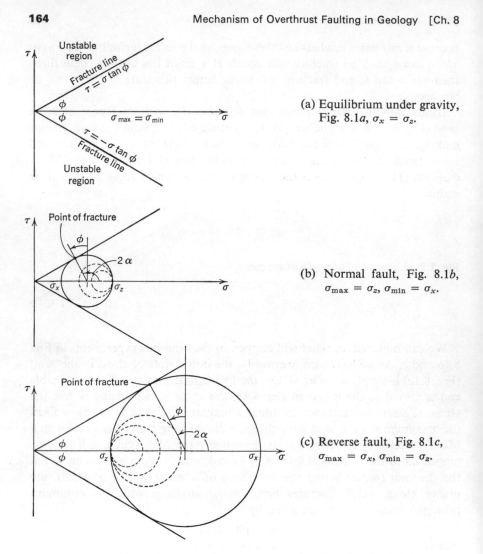

(a) Equilibrium under gravity, Fig. 8.1a, $\sigma_x = \sigma_z$.

(b) Normal fault, Fig. 8.1b, $\sigma_{max} = \sigma_z$, $\sigma_{min} = \sigma_x$.

(c) Reverse fault, Fig. 8.1c, $\sigma_{max} = \sigma_x$, $\sigma_{min} = \sigma_z$.

Fig. 8.8 Mohr's circle diagram for the situations in Fig. 8.1.

8.3   The Mechanical Paradox of Large Overthrusts

So far the theory has been concerned with a noncohesive material, loose sand. Rocks are cohesive, and the theory must be modified to take account of this. Mohr's circle represents a general property of a stress system, so it should need no modification. The other result we used was (8.3), which was a property of the material. Instead of this equation we simply write

$$\frac{\tau - \tau_0}{\sigma} = \tan \phi \qquad \text{or} \qquad \tau = \tau_0 + \sigma \tan \phi, \qquad (8.5)$$

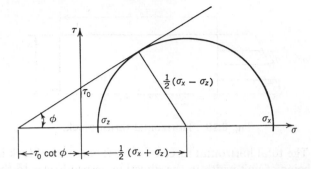

Fig. 8.9   The Mohr diagram when cohesion is present.

where τ_0 is a cohesive or initial shear stress that must be overcome before the material breaks along a fault line. This equation was first proposed by Coulomb in 1776, and is known as *Coulomb's law of failure*. It is, of course, not exactly correct, but it serves as an excellent first approximation to the behavior of rocks. When plotted on the Mohr diagram, as in Fig. 8.9, the lines of fracture have the same slope as before, but they cut the σ axis at the point $\sigma = -\tau \cot \phi$. The angles of normal and reverse faults are unchanged, so these do not depend on the cohesive strength of the rock. This is an important physical result which is not intuitively obvious (at least not to the editor!), but appears immediately from the mathematics, provided Coulomb's law of failure is correct.

We shall be interested in conditions corresponding to reverse faulting, where $\sigma_x > \sigma_z$, and in this case the relation between σ and τ for failure gives, from Fig. 8.9,

$$\tfrac{1}{2}(\sigma_x - \sigma_z) = [\tfrac{1}{2}(\sigma_x + \sigma_z) + \tau_0 \cot \phi] \sin \phi.$$

On simplifying,

$$\sigma_x = a + b\sigma_z, \tag{8.6}$$

where a and b are constants given by

$$b = \frac{1 + \sin \phi}{1 - \sin \phi}, \qquad a = 2\tau_0 \sqrt{b}. \tag{8.7}$$

The value of b is 3 if $\phi = 30°$.

With this background, suppose that we now apply to a horizontal block as large a horizontal force σ_x as possible, short of producing a reverse fault. This is given by (8.6), with σ_z produced by gravitational loading,

$$\sigma_z = kz, \tag{8.8}$$

where k is a constant. We proceed to show that if we make the natural assumption that $k = \rho g$, where ρ is the bulk density of the rock and g is the acceleration due to gravity, then only comparatively short blocks of rock can

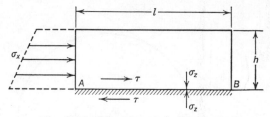

Fig. 8.10   Horizontal thrust block.

be moved. The total horizontal force on the left end of the block in Fig. 8.10 (the block being of unit width in the direction perpendicular to the paper) is

$$\int_0^h \sigma_x \, dz = ah + \tfrac{1}{2}bkh^2. \tag{8.9}$$

(Integration could be avoided by simply evaluating the area under the dashed force-depth curve in Fig. 8.10!)

Once the rock has been fractured along AB, the shear stress on the base will not depend on τ_0, and we shall have on the base simply

$$\tau = \sigma_z \tan \phi = kh \tan \phi, \tag{8.10}$$

where we have used (8.8) with $z = h$. The total resisting force is therefore $klh \tan \phi$, where l is the length of the block, and we must equate this to (8.9). Canceling h we obtain

$$kl \tan \phi = a + \tfrac{1}{2} bkh.$$

Hence

$$l = \left(\frac{a}{k} + \frac{1}{2} bh\right) \cot \phi.$$

If $\phi = 30°$ this becomes

$$l = \frac{6\tau_0}{k} + 2.6h. \tag{8.11}$$

A typical value of τ_0, found from experiment, is 2×10^8 dynes/cm². If we set $k = \rho g$, the value we would expect from the weight of the rock, where a representative value of the density is 2.31 g/cm³ and g is 980 dynes/gm, (8.11) is

$$l = (5.3 + 2.6h) \qquad \text{km,} \tag{8.12}$$

where h and l are measured in kilometers. The maximum length of an over-thrust block of rock 1 km thick would be about 8 km, and that for a block 6 km thick would be about 21 km. These are very much smaller than the values observed in practice.

8.4   The Beer-Can Experiment

The proposal of Hubbert and Rubey[2] is that internal pressure in fluid-filled porous rocks causes an uplifting effect which reduces the effective

[2] M. K. Hubbert and W. W. Rubey, Role of Fluid Pressure in Mechanics of Overthrust Faulting, *Bull. Geol. Soc. Am.*, **70**, 115–205 (1959).

pressure of a block of rock on its base, therefore making it easier to slide horizontally.

Perhaps the simplest way of explaining the theory from an elementary point of view is to describe a beer-can experiment attributed to M. A. Biot.[3] The end of an empty beer can in which holes are punched will be called the "open end," and the other end will be called the "closed end." The beer can is placed on a piece of wet glass. The glass is tilted until the critical angle ϕ is reached at which the can slides down the surface. This angle is independent of whether the open or closed end of the can is upward, since the can is sliding on its rim in each case. In an experiment the angle ϕ was found to be about 17°, so the coefficient of friction is approximately $\tan 17° \approx 0.3$. On reaching the edge of the glass, the can simply falls off (Fig. 8.11).

Fig. 8.11   The beer-can experiment.

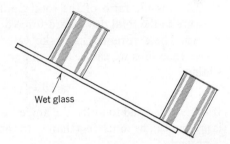

Wet glass

Next the can is chilled by placing it in the freezing compartment of a refrigerator, or a container of solid carbon dioxide, and the experiment is repeated. The can is first placed on the wet glass with its open end *upward*, and the experiment is repeated. The angle of sliding is found to be the same as before, indicating that the coefficient of friction is not temperature-sensitive. Finally, the can is placed on the wet glass with its open end *downward*. In this case it is found (perhaps after a little delay) that the can will slide when the angle of the glass is only 1 or 2°. The can slides down the whole length of the glass held at this very small angle, but stops abruptly when the open end protrudes beyond the edge.

The physical reason for this behavior is that as the cold can warms up, the air inside expands and causes the pressure to increase. This, in turn, partially supports the weight of the can, and therefore reduces the normal component of the force between the metal and the glass without affecting the tangential component. The can stops at the edge of the glass because the pressure is released.

[3] *Ibid.*, p. 161.

The mathematical theory of the experiment is as follows. Let F_n be the normal component of force exerted by the beer can on the glass and F_t the tangential component. Sliding will occur when

$$\frac{F_t}{F_n} = \tan \phi. \tag{8.13}$$

If θ is the angle of tilt of the glass, p the excess pressure of the air inside the can over that outside, A the area of the base of the can, and m its mass, then

$$F_t = mg \sin \theta, \tag{8.14}$$

$$F_n = mg \cos \theta - pA. \tag{8.15}$$

It is convenient to introduce λ defined by

$$pA = \lambda(mg \cos \theta), \tag{8.16}$$

so that λ is the ratio of the total uplift on the can by virtue of the excess pressure to the total downward force due to gravity when the excess pressure is zero. The constant λ can take values between zero and unity. From the above equations we can readily deduce that, when the can is on the point of sliding,

$$\tan \theta = (1 - \lambda) \tan \phi. \tag{8.17}$$

If λ is nearly equal to unity, the angle θ of sliding when excess internal pressure is present can be much less than ϕ, the angle of sliding when no excess pressure is present.

(It may be noted in passing that a striking example of substantially the same principle occurred in the design of the bearings of the 200-inch telescope at the Mount Palomar observatory. A 450-ton load was supported on the rims of boxes into which oil was pumped under pressure. Details and references can be found in the Hubbert-Rubey paper.[4])

8.5   The Effect of Internal Pressure on Fluid-Filled Porous Rocks

The rocks within a few kilometers of the earth's surface are porous and permeable, at least to some extent. The pores are filled with fluids, usually water, but sometimes with oil or gas or a mixture. The fluid is at a pressure p, which may be different from the pressures and stresses in the rock in which it is contained. If a rock is filled with water and permeable (that is, the pores are interconnected so that fluid can flow through the rock), the pressure of the water as a function of the depth z below the surface is usually closely approximated by the relation we should expect from hydrostatics,

$$p = \rho_w gz, \tag{8.18}$$

[4] *Ibid.*

where ρ_w is the density of water and g the acceleration due to gravity. However, sometimes pressures are encountered that are much greater than the above value. In a number of instances they have approached the magnitude

$$p = \rho g z, \tag{8.19}$$

where ρ is the bulk density of the fluid-saturated rock (which is, of course, considerably greater than ρ_w, the density of the water). This is the maximum value we should expect, since otherwise the fluid in the rock would tend to lift the overburden. A pressure-depth relation in accordance with (8.18) will be called a *normal* or *hydrostatic pressure*, whereas a pressure given by (8.19) will be called an *overburden* or *geostatic pressure variation*. An actual pressure variation that is greater than the normal pressure (8.18) will be called *abnormal*. A possible variation of pressure with depth when abnormal pressures exist is shown in Fig. 8.12.

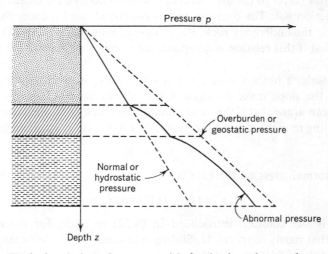

Fig. 8.12 Typical variation of pressure with depth when abnormal pressures exist.

The reader will immediately see the trend of the argument. If abnormal pressures occur which in effect partially support the overburden, the situation would be analogous to that in the beer-can experiment of Section 8.4. However, superficial analogies can be misleading, and we must try to formulate the situation mathematically, from first principles. The problem is to decide the effect of the pressure in the fluids in the pores on the mechanical properties of the rock.

In this connection, the crucial step in the argument in Section 8.3 was the statement that the vertical stress σ_z at depth z was given by (8.8),

$$\sigma_z = kz = \rho g z, \tag{8.20}$$

where ρ is the bulk density of the rock and fluids and g is the acceleration due to gravity. Hubbert and Rubey argue that since a fluid cannot support shear stresses, and the pores of the rock are interconnected, the vertical stress σ_z in the rock, which determines the shear stress τ at which the rock will fracture, should not be taken as the total stress due to the overburden. They appeal to both mathematical argument and experimental evidence to show that (8.20) should be replaced by

$$\sigma_z = \rho g z - p, \tag{8.21}$$

where p is the pressure in the fluid at depth z. If we introduce a constant λ such that $p = \lambda \rho g z$, then (8.21) becomes

$$\sigma_z = (1 - \lambda)\rho g z. \tag{8.22}$$

We shall not attempt to reproduce the arguments of Hubbert and Rubey in support of this conclusion. We content ourselves with saying that, if over-pressures exist, it would seem that there must be an impermeable (or almost impermeable) layer in the overburden, and this acts like the closed top of the can in Section 8.4. The overpressure is contained, and reduces the vertical stress σ_z on the underlying rock. Regardless of how we derive (8.22), the basic point is that if this relation is accepted, the paradox of Section 8.3 no longer exists.

We consider a block sliding down a slope under its own weight as in Fig. 8.2b. Let the slope make an angle θ with the horizontal, where θ is small. Then we can argue that if the total mass of the block is M, the component of force tending to move it down the plane, that is, the shear stress on the base, is

$$\tau = Mg \sin \theta, \tag{8.23}$$

and the normal stress on the base is

$$\sigma = (1 - \lambda)Mg \cos \theta, \tag{8.24}$$

where λ is the constant introduced in (8.22) to allow for the abnormal pressure that partly supports M. Sliding will occur when $\tau/\sigma = \tan \phi$, where ϕ is the angle of friction, and this gives

$$\tan \theta = (1 - \lambda) \tan \phi. \tag{8.25}$$

This is identical with (8.17), for the beer-can experiment. If $\phi = 30°$, this equation gives

λ:	0	0.6	0.8	0.9	0.95
θ:	30°	13°	6.6°	3.3°	1.6°

Since values of λ of 0.9 and 0.95 have been observed in practice, this means that a very significant reduction has been obtained in the angle at which a block will slide under its own weight.

It must be emphasized that the above argument would scarcely satisfy a mathematician, even if he accepted (8.22). He would object that we have performed some fast footwork in moving from (8.22), which involves a stress at a point, to an equation such as (8.24), which involves the total mass of the block. Also the expression (8.23) for the shear stress at the base of the block is not completely self-evident. The engineer might reply that it is "intuitively" clear that even if we made the argument more rigorous, this would not significantly affect the moral to be drawn from the above table.

If we are willing to accept fairly crude arguments of this type, it is a straight-forward matter to modify the formulas of Section 8.3 to take account of the abnormal pressure effect represented by (8.22), involving the introduction of the parameter λ. The reader is referred to the paper of Hubbert and Rubey[5] for details, but he is urged not to accept uncritically the mathematical equations deduced there. The difficulties lie not in the mathematics, as such, but in the idealized model. However, if the general argument concerning abnormal pressure is accepted, criticism of details will not affect the main conclusion: that the lengths of block that can be moved by horizontal forces are greater than the lengths calculated in Section 8.3 by a factor of 5 (or more) for values of λ equal to 0.9 (or more). Because values of 0.9 and more seem to occur in practice, this means that it would now be possible to move horizontally blocks of the lengths that occur in nature, and the paradox in Section 8.3 disappears. On the other hand, as pointed out earlier, this does not prove that the modified theory is in fact the correct explanation of the way in which overthrust faulting is produced.

8.6   Summary and Concluding Remarks

The discussion of normal and reverse faults in Sections 8.1 and 8.2 gives an instructive example of the use of simple mathematical and physical reasoning to explain natural phenomena. The physical motivation of the problem is that we wish to obtain insight into two types of faults that are commonly observed in nature. The idealization of the problem is to regard rock as an elastic material. Two basic results are required:

1. Normal and shear stresses can be described by the Mohr circle diagram.
2. The conditions for fracture can be approximated by Coulomb's law of fracture.

By using these results it is possible to obtain insight into the way in which normal and reverse faults occur.

When we attempt to use these ideas in Section 8.3 to explain overthrust faults, we immediately find that it is not possible to explain faults of the sizes that occur in nature by horizontal pushing or sliding under gravity. Hubbert and Rubey have introduced an hypothesis to account for the paradox, which depends on the experimental observation that abnormally large pressures are sometimes found in the fluids contained in the pores of rocks.

[5] *Ibid.*

Hubbert and Rubey make the following interesting comment[6]: "The results which we have just derived...are in substantial agreement with those reached by Harza[7] in a study of the significance of pore pressures in hydraulic structures (in particular, in dams). The fact that Harza's paper of 22 pages provoked 55 pages of dominantly adverse discussion, contributed by 21 authors, is eloquent evidence that the conclusions were not in accord with the majority opinion of the civil engineering profession—at least in the United States in 1949."

It seems quite clear to the editor of this book that many of the disagreements that arose in these discussions were caused by the fact that the arguments were not sufficiently precise and quantitative. The authors start from qualitative hypotheses which are not clearly stated and try to deduce conclusions by intuitive or common-sense reasoning. From a mathematician's point of view it will be necessary to understand much more clearly the stresses and stress interactions in the rocks and the contained fluids. It should then be possible to formulate a problem like that of the horizontal thrust block in Fig. 8.10 in terms of partial differential equations and specific boundary conditions. It will then be possible to produce detailed pictures of the pressure distribution in the fluids, the stresses in the rocks, and the deformation pattern. However, no matter how much sophisticated mathematics is used, the validity of the results will depend on the underlying physical model on which the mathematics is based.

[6] *Ibid.*, p. 135.

[7] L. F. Harza, *Trans. Am. Soc. Civil Engrs.*, **114**, 193–214, (1949); discussion, pp. 215–269; reply, pp. 269–289.

Chapter 9

Some Approximations in
Heat Transfer

Comment : In this chapter models based on physical intuition are used to obtain qualitative insight and approximate numerical results for problems involving heat conduction and heat convection.

9.1 Heat Conduction

Mathematics Used : Ordinary differential equations. (The formulation of a partial differential equation is incidental.)

Applications of mathematics abound in the theory of heat transfer,[1] including heat conduction, convection, and radiation. In this section we consider some problems involving heat conduction.

A rigorous treatment of heat-transfer problems involves extensive use of partial differential equations, but these will be avoided here, except in this section and in Section 9.3, where they are used to obtain exact solutions against which our approximate solutions can be checked. We shall be concerned mainly with developing approximate solutions of typical problems, to obtain qualitative insight, and rough quantitative answers. In heat conduction we shall use simply the principle of heat balance—that the increase in the quantity of heat in a solid must equal the amount of heat that has passed through the surface of the solid, assuming no heat is generated inside the solid.[2]

---

[1] Very many good textbooks exist; we cite only H. S. Carslaw and J. C. Jaeger, *Conduction of Heat in Solids*, 2nd ed., Oxford Univ. Press, New York, 1959; W. H. McAdams, *Heat Transmission*, 3rd ed., McGraw-Hill, New York, 1954; and E. R. Eckert and R. M. Drake, Jr., *Heat and Mass Transfer*, 2nd ed., McGraw-Hill, New York, 1959.

[2] After this chapter was written, the editor came across an article by T. R. Goodman in *Advances in Heat Transfer*, Vol. 1 (T. F. Irvine, Jr., and J. P. Hartnett, eds.), Academic, New York, 1964, pp. 51–122, in which methods similar to those used in Sections 9.1 to 9.3 are applied to a wide variety of problems.

Fourier's law for the conduction of heat, proposed in 1822, states that the amount of heat ΔQ which passes through an area A in time Δt is proportional to the temperature gradient across the surface. More precisely, if T is the temperature at any point in the solid, and n denotes distance normal to the area considered, then

$$\Delta Q = -kA\frac{dT}{dn}\Delta t, \tag{9.1}$$

where k is a constant depending on the properties of the solid, known as the *thermal conductivity*. The minus sign is necessary because, if we assume that the distance n is taken to be zero on A, and $T = T_0$ on A, with $T > T_0$ for $n < 0$, $t < T_0$ for $n > 0$, then dT/dn will be negative, whereas physically it is clear that the quantity of heat ΔQ transferred across the surface from $n < 0$ to $n > 0$ will be positive.

Consider a thin semi-infinite rod lying in $0 \le x < \infty$, which is initially at zero temperature. Assume that at $t = 0$ the end $x = 0$ is suddenly raised to a temperature T_0. The rod is assumed to have a constant cross section which for definiteness we can take to be circular and of unit area. We assume that the curved surface of the rod is insulated so that no heat is lost across the curved surface, and at any cross section $x = $ constant, the temperature can be assumed to be independent of the coordinates perpendicular to x.

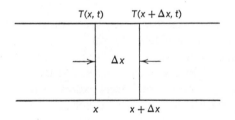

Fig. 9.1   Heat conduction in a rod.

We shall first establish the partial differential equation for heat flow in the rod (Fig. 9.1), although in fact we shall not make use of this equation in the remainder of this section. Consider a thin slice of the rod from x to $x + \Delta x$. Let $T(x, t)$ denote the temperature of the rod at position x at time t. The quantities of heat that flow in time Δt from left to right through the sections at x and $x + \Delta x$ are given, respectively, by

$$-k\frac{\partial T(x, t)}{\partial x}\Delta t \quad \text{and} \quad -k\frac{\partial T(x + \Delta x, t)}{\partial x}\Delta t.$$

The increase in the amount of heat in the slice from x to $x + \Delta x$ in time Δt is given, to a sufficient degree of approximation, by

$$\rho c\frac{\partial T(x, t)}{\partial t}\Delta x\,\Delta t,$$

where ρ is the density and c is the specific heat of the solid. Hence the heat balance—that the increase in the quantity of heat in the slice x to $x + \Delta x$ in time Δt must equal the net amount of heat that passes through the surface of the slice—gives

$$k \left[\frac{\partial T(x + \Delta x, t)}{\partial x} - \frac{\partial T(x, t)}{\partial x} \right] \Delta t = \rho c \frac{\partial T(x, t)}{\partial t} \Delta x \, \Delta t. \qquad (9.2a)$$

We have

$$T(x + \Delta x, t) = T(x, t) + \Delta x \frac{\partial T(x, t)}{\partial x} + O(\Delta x^2). \qquad (9.2b)$$

(The O-notation has been explained in connection with (7.12).)
  From (9.2a, b) we have

$$k \frac{\partial^2 T}{\partial x^2} + O(\Delta x) = \rho c \frac{\partial T}{\partial t}.$$

On letting Δx tend to zero this gives the partial differential equation for heat conduction in one dimension,

$$\kappa \frac{\partial^2 T}{\partial x^2} = \frac{\partial T}{\partial t},$$

where $\kappa = k/\rho c$. This must be solved subject to the initial condition

$$T = 0 \quad \text{at} \quad t = 0, \qquad 0 \leq x < \infty$$

and the boundary condition

$$T = T_0 \quad \text{at} \quad x = 0, \qquad t > 0$$

The exact solution of this problem can be found in the books mentioned at the beginning of this section, and we quote it for reference:

$$T = T_0 \left[1 - \text{erf} \frac{x}{2(\kappa t)^{1/2}} \right], \qquad (9.3)$$

where erf z is the error integral,

$$\text{erf } z = \frac{2}{\pi^{1/2}} \int_0^z e^{-u^2} \, du.$$

Values of erf z are

z:	0	0.2	0.4	0.6	0.8	1.0	1.2	∞
erf z:	0	0.223	0.428	0.604	0.742	0.843	0.910	1

  We now return to the main topic in the section, the approximate solution of problems in heat conduction. One of the reasons for establishing the partial differential equation above was to show that an exact treatment leads to an equation that is usually difficult to solve. Instead of proceeding this way, we

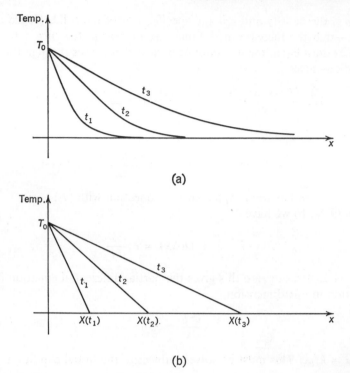

(a)

(b)

Fig. 9.2 Variation of temperature with distance for various times: (*a*) actual (intuitive and qualitative); (*b*) simplest approximation used.

use physical reasoning to obtain an approximate solution of various problems in heat conduction. In the problem above, involving heat flow in a semi-infinite solid, the argument proceeds as follows. Physically, it is clear that in this problem the temperature versus distance curves for various times $t_1 < t_2 < t_3 \cdots$ (which are what we wish to find) will look qualitatively like those in Fig. 9.2*a*. We know that for any given x we have $T > 0$ for $t > 0$ ("heat travels with an infinite velocity") but for any given x we also know that, for a given x, T will be very small for small t. For a given value of time t, it is reasonable to take $T = 0$ for $x \geq X(t)$, where $X(t)$ is some function we wish to determine. More specifically, as a first approximation, we assume the straight-line representation shown in Fig. 9.2*b*,

$$T(x, t) = \begin{cases} T_0 \left[1 - \dfrac{x}{X(t)} \right], & 0 \leq x \leq X(t), \\ 0, & x \geq X(t), \end{cases} \tag{9.4}$$

where $X(t)$ is a function of t that can be determined by the following argument. The total amount of heat H in the solid at time t is given by

$$H = \rho c T_0 \int_0^{X(t)} \left[1 - \frac{x}{X(t)} \right] dx = \tfrac{1}{2} \rho c T_0 X(t).$$

The rate at which heat is entering the solid is given by

$$-k\left(\frac{dT}{dx}\right)_{x=0} = \frac{kT_0}{X(t)}.$$

This must be equal to dH/dt, so

$$\tfrac{1}{2}\rho c T_0 \frac{dX}{dt} = \frac{kT_0}{X} \quad \text{or} \quad X\,dX = \frac{2k}{\rho c}\,dt;$$

that is,

$$\tfrac{1}{2}X^2 = \frac{2k}{\rho c}\,t,$$

where the constant of integration is zero, because $X = 0$ at $t = 0$. Hence $T(x, t)$ is given approximately by

$$T = T_0\left[1 - \frac{x}{2(\kappa t)^{1/2}}\right], \tag{9.5}$$

where $\kappa = k/\rho c$, as defined previously. The ratio T/T_0 is a function of only $\tfrac{1}{2}x/(\kappa t)^{1/2}$, as for the exact solution (9.3). The exact and approximate solutions are compared graphically in Fig. 9.3.

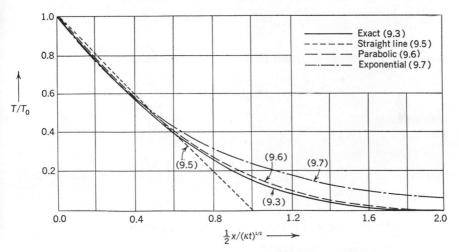

Fig. 9.3 Comparison of exact and approximate solutions.

The above approximate solution was obtained by the physical argument that the rate of change of the total amount of heat in the body is equal to the rate at which heat is entering the body. It is instructive to consider a purely mathematical argument that derives the same result from the partial differential equation $\kappa(\partial^2 T/\partial x^2) = \partial T/\partial t$. Integrate this equation with respect to x from $x = 0$ to infinity. Since $\partial T/\partial x$ tends to zero as x tends to infinity, we have

$$\kappa\left(\frac{\partial T}{\partial x}\right)_{x=0} = \frac{d}{dt}\int_0^\infty T(x, t)\,dx.$$

This equation involves only time t, so the derivative on the right side is ordinary, not partial. This equation is the mathematical statement of the physical argument in the first sentence of this paragraph. The approximate solution is obtained by replacing $T(x, t)$ in this equation by a guessed form involving precisely one unknown function of t [for example, $X(t)$ in (9.4)]. This leads to an ordinary differential equation in t from which the unknown function can be determined.

Instead of the straight-line approximation (9.4) we could use the more realistic representation

$$T = \begin{cases} T_0 \left[1 - \dfrac{x}{X(t)} \right]^2, & 0 \leq x \leq X(t), \\ 0, & x \geq X(t). \end{cases}$$

Following the same argument as before we find that

$$H = \rho c T_0 \int_0^{X(t)} \left[1 - \frac{x}{X(t)} \right]^2 dx = \tfrac{1}{3} \rho c T_0 X(t),$$

and the rate at which heat is entering the solid is given by

$$-k \left(\frac{dT}{dx} \right)_{x=0} = \frac{2kT_0}{X(t)}.$$

Hence the differential equation governing the heat balance is

$$X \frac{dX}{dt} = 6\kappa,$$

with solution

$$X(t) = \sqrt{3} \, [2(\kappa t)^{1/2}];$$

that is, $$T = T_0 \left\{ 1 - \frac{1}{\sqrt{3}} \left[\frac{x}{2(\kappa t)^{1/2}} \right] \right\}^2. \qquad (9.6)$$

This curve is also plotted on Fig. 9.3.

As a third attempt, consider the exponential approximation

$$T = T_0 e^{-A(t)x}.$$

Then $$H = \rho c T_0 \int_0^\infty e^{-A(t)x} \, dx = \frac{\rho c T_0}{A(t)}.$$

The rate at which heat is entering the solid is given by

$$-k \left(\frac{dT}{dx} \right)_{x=0} = kT_0 A(t).$$

The heat-balance equation is

$$-\frac{\rho c T_0}{A^2(t)} \frac{dA(t)}{dt} = kT_0 A(t) \qquad \text{or} \qquad -\frac{dA}{A^3} = \kappa \, dt,$$

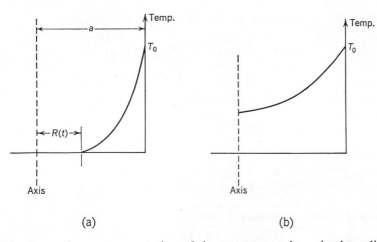

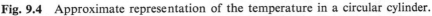

(a)   (b)

Fig. 9.4   Approximate representation of the temperature in a circular cylinder.

which gives

$$A(t) = (2\kappa t)^{-1/2}$$

and
$$T = T_0 \exp\{-\sqrt{2}\,[\tfrac{1}{2}x/(\kappa t)^{1/2}]\}. \tag{9.7}$$

This is plotted in Fig. 9.3.

From Fig. 9.3 it is clear that the parabolic approximation is superior to both the straight-line and exponential approximations.

The point of Sections 9.2 and 9.3 is that exactly the same method can be applied to much more complicated situations. Before going on to this, we examine one more relatively straightforward problem, the two-dimensional problem of the heating of an infinite cylinder of radius a. The cylinder lies in $0 \le r \le a$, $-\infty < z < \infty$. The temperature is independent of z and depends only on r and t. The cylinder is initially at temperature zero, with the surface temperature suddenly raised to a constant value T_0 at $t = 0$. We represent the temperature approximately as follows.

1. For $t \le t_0$ we choose a parabolic approximation,

$$T = \begin{cases} T_0\left[1 - \dfrac{a-r}{a - R(t)}\right]^2, & R(t) \le r \le a, \\ 0, & 0 \le r \le R(t), \end{cases} \tag{9.8}$$

where $R(0) = a$ and t_0 is the time such that $R(t_0) = 0$.

2. For $t \ge t_0$, since then $dT/dr = 0$ at $r = 0$, we choose

$$T = T_0[1 - A(t)(a^2 - r^2)], \tag{9.9}$$

where $A(t_0) = 1/a^2$. This agrees with (9.8) when $t = t_0$.

For $t \leq t_0$, the total heat in the cylinder, per unit length, is

$$H = 2\pi\rho c T_0 \int_{R(t)}^{a} r\left[1 - \frac{a - r}{a - R(t)}\right]^2 dr$$

$$= \tfrac{1}{6}\pi\rho c T_0[3a^2 - 2aR(t) - R^2(t)].$$

The heat flux per second outward over the surface $r = a$ is

$$-2\pi ak\left(\frac{dT}{dr}\right)_{r=a} = -\frac{4\pi akT_0}{a - R(t)}.$$

The heat-balance equation gives

$$-(a^2 - R^2)\, dR = +12a\kappa\, dt, \qquad \kappa = \frac{k}{\rho c}.$$

Integration yields, on using the condition $R = a$ at $t = 0$,

$$\tfrac{2}{3}a^3 - a^2R + \tfrac{1}{3}R^3 = 12a\kappa t. \tag{9.10}$$

The time t_0 was defined by the condition $R(t_0) = 0$, and (9.10) gives the result

$$\frac{\kappa t_0}{a^2} = \frac{1}{18}.$$

We now consider $t \geq t_0$. From (9.9) the total heat per unit length of the cylinder is

$$H = 2\pi\rho c T_0 \int_0^a [1 - A(t)(a^2 - r^2)]r\, dr$$

$$= \pi\rho c T_0 a^2[1 - \tfrac{1}{2}A(t)a^2].$$

The rate of loss of heat at $r = a$ is

$$-2\pi ak\left(\frac{dT}{dr}\right)_{r=a} = -4\pi a^2 k T_0 A(t).$$

The heat-balance equation leads to

$$\frac{dA(t)}{dt} = -8\frac{\kappa}{a^2} A(t);$$

that is, using the condition $A(t_0) = 1/a^2$,

$$A(t) = (1/a^2)e^{-8(\kappa/a^2)(t - t_0)}.$$

The temperature at the center of the rod ($r = 0$) is given by

$$T = \begin{cases} 0, & 0 \leq t \leq t_0, \\ T_0[1 - e^{-8(\kappa/a^2)(t - t_0)}], & t \geq t_0, \end{cases}$$

where $\kappa t_0/a^2 = 1/18$. This approximate solution is compared with the exact solution in Fig. 9.5. The qualitative behavior, including the dependence of T/t_0 on the single parameter $\kappa t/a^2$, is correct, but the quantitative agreement is not too satisfactory. This comparison is included as a reminder that the approximate methods of this section do not obviate the need for exact solutions.

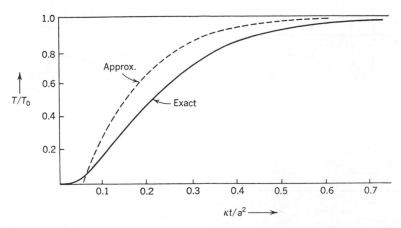

Fig. 9.5   Exact and approximate solutions for temperature on axis of cylinder.

There are, of course, many applications of the heat-conduction equation in engineering. One example was drawn to our attention by C. W. Suggs, Department of Agricultural Engineering, North Carolina State College,[3] in which experimental results are given for the change in temperature on the axis of a cylindrical mass of cucumbers that fell precisely on the "exact" curve in Fig. 9.5. Another example has been given by MacLean,[4] who shows that data on the unsteady heating of round, green southern pine timber can be correlated by using the theory of unsteady heat flow in circular cylinders.

In concluding this section we should point out that the methods developed above are valuable for preliminary investigations, particularly in connection with qualitative behavior. However, if an engineer wishes accurate numerical solutions of heat-conduction problems, he should go back to the partial-differential-equation formulation of the problem. The solutions will then involve finite-difference methods and an automatic computer, unless, of course, he can arrange for his problems to be among the few for which exact analytical solutions are available.

9.2   Ingot Solidification[5]

Mathematics Used: Simple differential equations.

Comment: An approximate solution is obtained very simply for a problem that is difficult to treat rigorously.

---

[3] Part of a doctoral thesis by C. E. Hood, Jr., "On the Apparent Thermal Conductivity of Bulked Cucumbers," North Carolina State College, Raleigh.

[4] J. D. MacLean, *Proc. Am. Wood-Preservers' Assoc.*, **26**, 197–219 (1930). This work was done at the Forest Products Laboratory, University of Wisconsin, Madison, Wis., with an acknowledgment to H. W. March, Department of Mathematics.

[5] The derivation of (9.13) was submitted by the College of Engineering, University of Illinois, Urbana, Ill., through Dean W. L. Everitt.

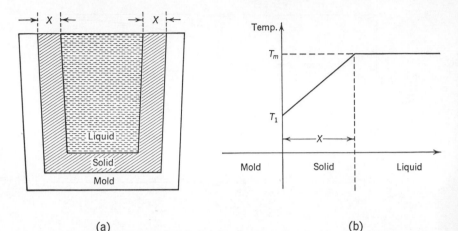

(a)   (b)

Fig. 9.6 Diagrammatic representation of ingot solidification.

When liquid metal is poured into a mold, the rate at which the thickness of the solidified crust increases is controlled by the rate at which the latent heat of freezing is removed by heat flow through the solid crust to the mold. It is assumed that the temperature of the liquid is its melting temperature T_m, and that the mold keeps the outside surface of the solid crust at a fixed temperature T_1, as in Fig. 9.6b.

Suppose the thickness of the crust is $X(t)$ at time t. The rate of heat flow through the solid crust is proportional to the temperature gradient in this crust:

$$J = k\frac{dT}{dx} = \frac{k(T_m - T_1)}{X}.$$

where k is the thermal conductivity of the solid metal. From equation (9.1) it can be seen that the units of k are cal/(cm²)(sec)(°C/cm), and J is then calculated in cal/(cm²)(sec). If the solid crust thickens by an amount Δx, the latent heat released at the solid-liquid interface per square centimeter of cross section is calculated as follows.

Let L be the latent heat of freezing in calories per gram, and ρ the density in grams per cubic centimeter, so that $L\rho$ is the heat released in calories per cubic centimeter. For each square centimeter of cross section, movement of the interface by Δx freezes a volume Δx, and the heat released is then $L\rho \Delta x$ cal/cm². Thus solidification at a rate dX/dt releases heat at a rate

$$L\rho \frac{dX}{dt} \quad \text{cal/(cm²)(sec).}$$

The actual value of dX/dt will be determined by how fast heat is conducted away from the interface where it is generated; that is, it will be determined by the condition

$$J = L\rho \frac{dX}{dt} \quad \text{or} \quad \frac{k(T_m - T_1)}{X} = L\rho \frac{dX}{dt}.$$

Then
$$X \, dX = K \, dt, \tag{9.11}$$

where
$$K = \frac{k(T_m - T_1)}{L\rho}. \tag{9.12}$$

All the factors that are material constants or experimental parameters are grouped in the single constant K. Integration of (9.11) yields

$$X^2 = 2Kt \quad \text{or} \quad X = (2Kt)^{1/2}, \tag{9.13}$$

where the constant of integration is zero because we assume that the thickness of the solid crust is zero at the start of the process; that is, $X = 0$ at $t = 0$.

An exact solution is known for the one-dimensional case of a liquid in $0 \le x < \infty$, initially at its melting point T_m, with the surface $x = 0$ held at temperature T_1, with $T_1 < T_m$.[6] If the interface between liquid and solid is at $x = X$ at time t, as above, the rigorous theory gives the result

$$X = 2\lambda(\kappa t)^{1/2}, \tag{9.14}$$

where κ is the thermal diffusivity of the solid, related to the thermal conductivity k, density ρ, and specific heat c by the relation $\kappa = k/\rho c$. Also λ is the solution of the transcendental equation

$$\lambda e^{\lambda^2} \, \text{erf} \, \lambda = \frac{c(T_m - T_1)}{L\pi^{1/2}}, \tag{9.15}$$

where

$$\text{erf} \, x = \frac{2}{\pi^{1/2}} \int_0^x e^{-u^2} \, du.$$

For small x we have $\text{erf} \, x \approx 2x/\pi^{1/2}$, and

$$\lambda^2 \approx \frac{c(T_m - T_1)}{2L}, \tag{9.16}$$

which, when substituted in (9.14), gives precisely the previous answer (9.12) and (9.13). This case applies, for example, to the freezing of water by conduction of heat into a region a few degrees below freezing point. On the other hand, for materials such as metals with high melting points, with surfaces maintained at room temperatures, the quantity on the right of (9.15) is usually of order unity, and the approximation (9.16), and, therefore, (9.12) and (9.13), is not very good. Nevertheless, the functional form of (9.13) is still correct, even though (9.12) for K is wrong. It is usually difficult to judge the range of validity of an approximate theory. This example illustrates both the utility and the limitations of an approximate theory.

[6] See, for example, H. S. Carslaw and J. C. Jaeger, *Conduction of Heat in Solids*, 2nd ed., Oxford Univ. Press, New York, 1959, pp. 285–286.

9.3   Thermal Explosions and Self-ignition[7]

Mathematics Used: Nonlinear ordinary differential equations.

Comment: An exact solution is obtained and compared with a solution derived by the approximate method developed in previous sections.

Consider a body in which a reaction liberates heat throughout the volume at a rate that increases with temperature. Also heat is lost from the surface of the body at a rate proportional to the difference between the surface temperature and the surrounding temperature. Two types of behavior are possible. In the first case, equilibrium is established with a relatively small temperature differential, which is, however, enough to conduct away the heat liberated. In the second case the heat is not conducted away rapidly enough, and the interior temperature rises to a high value. In most cases the transition between the two types of solution is sharp, and it is the object of the mathematics to show how this is possible. Obviously an increase in size favors the second type of solution, because of the lower surface-to-volume ratio.

An interesting example of this effect is the observation that stacks of sheets of plywood set up to cool after being dried at an elevated temperature may, instead, char, because of liberation of heat by an exothermic reaction. It should be noted that a similar situation exists for nuclear fission, with neutrons (which obey a diffusion equation) replacing heat.

We now describe an idealized situation in which the phenomenon just described can be examined mathematically. We imagine an infinite cylinder in which heat is being liberated, and we wish to find out under what conditions its temperature tends to a finite value as the time tends to infinity, as opposed to the case in which the temperature approaches infinity. (In the second case the mathematical model will break down at a finite time, owing to an explosion or combustion.) We shall approach the problem in two different ways, first, by an attack on the nonlinear partial differential equation (9.19) and, second, by an approximate method along the lines developed in previous sections. The agreement between the results of the two methods will be shown to be good.

For simplicity, if the infinite cylinder lies in $0 \leq r \leq a$, $-\infty < z < \infty$, we assume that all quantities are independent of z, so that the temperature depends only on r and t. Suppose heat is being liberated according to the Arrhenius law, namely, at a rate $Q \exp(-P/T)$ per unit volume, where Q

[7] This topic was suggested by material submitted by William Squire, Department of Aerospace Engineering, West Virginia University, Morgantown, W. Va. A more advanced treatment, with references, is given in W. Squire, A Mathematical Analysis of Self-Ignition, *Combust. Flame*, **7**, 1–8 (1963). Material has also been included from P. L. Chambré, On the Solution of the Poisson–Boltzmann Equation with Application to the Theory of Thermal Explosions, *J. Chem. Phys.*, **20**, 1795–1797 (1952).

and P are constants of the reaction liberating the heat and T is the absolute
temperature. If the temperature in the cylinder at radius r and time t is denoted
by $T(r, t)$, the equation for T can be set up by considering the heat balance in
a ring lying between r and $r + \Delta r$, in the following way, (see Fig. 9.7).

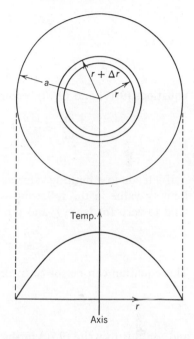

Fig. 9.7   Heat release in a circular cylinder.

Consider the time interval from t to $t + \Delta t$. Then

$$\begin{bmatrix} \text{Increase of heat} \\ \text{content of ring} \end{bmatrix} = \begin{bmatrix} \text{Net heat entering the ring} \\ \text{through its surfaces} \end{bmatrix} + \begin{bmatrix} \text{Heat produced by} \\ \text{the reaction} \end{bmatrix}.$$

In symbols, omitting Δt throughout,

$$\rho c \frac{\partial T}{\partial t} 2\pi r \, \Delta r = k \left[2\pi (r + \Delta r) \frac{\partial T(r + \Delta r, t)}{\partial r} - 2\pi r \frac{\partial T(r, t)}{\partial r} \right] + 2\pi r \, \Delta r \, Q e^{-P/T}.$$

Dividing through by Δr and letting Δr tend to zero, we find that

$$\rho c \frac{\partial T}{\partial t} = k \left(\frac{\partial^2 T}{\partial r^2} + \frac{1}{r} \frac{\partial T}{\partial r} \right) + Q e^{-P/T}. \tag{9.17}$$

This is a nonlinear partial differential equation which must be solved for T in
$0 \leq r \leq a$, with suitable initial conditions at $t = 0$ and boundary conditions
at $r = a$. We shall, in fact, suppose that the boundary $r = a$ is kept at a
constant temperature

$$T = T_0 \quad \text{at} \quad r = a, t > 0. \tag{9.18}$$

We shall make the simplifying assumption that T does not differ too much from T_0, so we can write, approximately,

$$\frac{1}{T} = \frac{1}{T_0}\left(1 + \frac{T - T_0}{T_0}\right)^{-1} \approx \frac{1}{T_0} - \frac{T - T_0}{T_0^2}.$$

Then
$$Qe^{-P/T} \approx Qe^{-P/T_0}e^{P(T - T_0)/T_0^2}.$$

If we set

$$T - T_0 = u, \qquad \frac{1}{k}Qe^{-P/T_0} = q, \qquad P/T_0^2 = p,$$

equations (9.17) and (9.18) become

$$\frac{1}{\kappa}\frac{\partial u}{\partial t} = \frac{\partial^2 u}{\partial r^2} + \frac{1}{r}\frac{\partial u}{\partial r} + qe^{pu}, \qquad \kappa = \frac{k}{\rho c}, \tag{9.19}$$

$$u = 0 \qquad \text{at } r = a.$$

If u tends to a limiting value as t tends to infinity, it is possible to find this limiting value in the following way. The quantity $\partial u/\partial t$ in (9.19) will then tend to zero for large t, and the limiting value of u, if it exists, will satisfy

$$\frac{d^2u}{dr^2} + \frac{1}{r}\frac{du}{dr} + qe^{pu} = 0. \tag{9.20}$$

This equation can be solved in the following way. Introduce

$$v = r\frac{du}{dr} \tag{9.21}$$

and use this to write (9.20) in the form

$$\frac{1}{r}\frac{dv}{dr} = -qe^{pu}. \tag{9.22}$$

Differentiation of this equation gives

$$\frac{d}{dr}\left(\frac{1}{r}\frac{dv}{dr}\right) = -qpe^{pu}\frac{du}{dr} = -qpe^{pu}\frac{v}{r}. \tag{9.23}$$

Elimination of e^{pu} between (9.22) and (9.23) yields

$$\frac{d}{dr}\left(\frac{1}{r}\frac{dv}{dr}\right) = \frac{pv}{r^2}\frac{dv}{dr},$$

or, after some manipulation,

$$\frac{d}{dr}\left(r\frac{dv}{dr} - 2v\right) = \frac{1}{2}p\frac{d(v^2)}{dr}.$$

On integrating and rearranging,

$$r\frac{dv}{dr} = \frac{v(pv + 4)}{2}, \tag{9.24a}$$

where the constant of integration is zero since $v = 0$ at $r = 0$. This equation can again be integrated by writing it in the form

$$\left(\frac{1}{v} - \frac{p}{pv + 4}\right) dv = 2\frac{dr}{r},$$

which gives

$$\log |v| - \log (pv + 4) = 2 \log r + \log A, \tag{9.24b}$$

where $\log A$ is a constant of integration. Note that it is clear from Fig. 9.7 and (9.21) that v is negative. Hence we must write

$$\int \frac{dv}{v} = \log |v|.$$

(This point is sometimes not emphasized in elementary work.) From the form of v deduced from Fig. 9.7 and (9.21) it is clear that dv/dr is negative. Hence from (9.24a) we see that $pv + 4$ is positive. Equation (9.24b) gives

$$\frac{|v|}{pv + 4} = Ar^2.$$

Since v is negative this means that

$$\frac{v}{pv + 4} = -Ar^2,$$

and on solving for v we find that

$$v = r\frac{du}{dr} = -\frac{4Ar^2}{1 + pAr^2},$$

where A is an arbitrary constant. Further integration gives

$$u = -\frac{2}{p} \log (1 + pAr^2) + B,$$

where B is another arbitrary constant. The condition $u = 0$ at $r = a$ gives B in terms of A, and we find

$$u = \frac{2}{p} \log \left(\frac{1 + pAa^2}{1 + pAr^2}\right). \tag{9.25}$$

To determine A we substitute this solution in the original equation (9.20). We find that (9.20) is satisfied identically if

$$8A = q(1 + pAa^2)^2.$$

If we set

$$pAa^2 = x, \qquad \frac{8}{qpa^2} = \alpha,$$

this quadratic in A becomes

$$x^2 + (2 - \alpha)x + 1 = 0.$$

From the form of the solution (9.25) it is clear that A must be real; that is, x must be real, so

$$(2 - \alpha)^2 - 4 \geq 0;$$

that is,

$$\alpha(\alpha - 4) \geq 0.$$

Since $\alpha > 0$, this means that $\alpha \geq 4$, or

$$qpa^2 \leq 2. \tag{9.26}$$

This is the condition that the temperature should tend to a finite value as t tends to infinity. Otherwise the solution tends to infinity with increasing time; that is, an explosion results, as discussed later and shown diagrammatically in Fig. 9.9. If $qpa^2 = 2$, then $x = 1$; that is, $pAa^2 = 1$, and (9.25) gives

$$u = \frac{2}{p} \log \left[\frac{2}{1 + (r/a)^2} \right].$$

The temperature at $r = 0$ is given by

$$u = \frac{2 \log 2}{p} \approx \frac{1.39}{p}. \tag{9.27}$$

We now approach the problem by an approximate method similar to that developed in Section 9.1. Suppose the temperature in the body is represented approximately by

$$T(r, t) = T_0 + \left[1 - \left(\frac{r}{a} \right)^2 \right] Y(t).$$

The basic equation is given by the relation

$$\begin{bmatrix} \text{Rate of increase} \\ \text{of total heat in} \\ \text{cylinder} \end{bmatrix} = \begin{bmatrix} \text{Total rate of} \\ \text{production of heat} \\ \text{by the reaction} \end{bmatrix} - \begin{bmatrix} \text{Heat lost} \\ \text{through the} \\ \text{outer boundary} \end{bmatrix}.$$

The rate of increase of the total heat in the cylinder, per unit length, is

$$\rho c \frac{dY(t)}{dt} \int_0^a \left[1 - \left(\frac{r}{a} \right)^2 \right] 2\pi r \, dr = \tfrac{1}{2}\pi a^2 \rho c \frac{dY(t)}{dt}. \tag{9.28}$$

The total rate of production of heat by the reaction is, per unit length of the cylinder,

$$I = \int_0^a 2\pi r Q e^{-P/T} \, dr. \tag{9.29}$$

We adopt the notation and approximations following (9.18):

$$Q e^{-P/T} \approx k q e^{p(T - T_0)}.$$

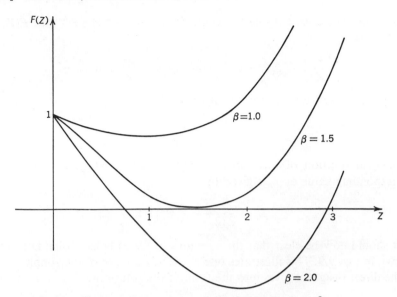

Fig. 9.8 $F(Z)$ plotted as a function of Z for various β.

Then (9.29) gives

$$I = 2\pi k q e^{pY} \int_0^a r e^{-pYr^2/a^2} \, dr = \pi k q a^2 \left(\frac{e^{pY} - 1}{pY}\right). \tag{9.30}$$

The rate of heat loss through the boundary $r = a$ is

$$-2\pi a k \left(\frac{dT}{dr}\right)_{r=a} = 4\pi k Y. \tag{9.31}$$

The heat-balance equation is, therefore, from (9.28), (9.30), and (9.31),

$$\tfrac{1}{2}a^2 \rho c \frac{dY}{dt} = k q a^2 \left(\frac{e^{pY} - 1}{pY}\right) - 4k Y.$$

If we set

$$pY = Z, \qquad \frac{4}{qpa^2} = \beta, \qquad \frac{\rho c}{2kqp} = \gamma,$$

this equation becomes

$$\gamma \frac{dZ}{dt} = \frac{e^Z - 1}{Z} - \beta Z = F(Z), \tag{9.32}$$

where this defines $F(Z)$.

The right side of this differential equation, $F(Z)$, is plotted as a function of Z for various β in Fig. 9.8. It is seen that for β less than a critical value β_0, the function $F(Z)$ is always positive. This means, from the differential equation, that Z will tend to infinity as t tends to infinity; that is, an explosion will occur. The critical value β_0 occurs for a value of Z such that $F(Z) = F'(Z) = 0$:

$$\frac{e^z - 1}{Z} - \beta_0 Z = 0, \qquad \frac{-e^z + 1}{Z^2} + \frac{e^z}{Z} - \beta_0 = 0.$$

On eliminating β_0 we find that Z satisfies

$$e^z = \frac{2}{2 - Z}.$$

Numerical solution of this equation gives, approximately, $Z = 1.59$. The corresponding value of β_0 is given by

$$\beta_0 = \frac{1}{Z(2 - Z)} \approx 1.54.$$

It should now be clear that the solutions of (9.32) behave qualitatively as shown in Fig. 9.9. This illustrates one of the advantages of the simple theory —the direct insight it gives into the form of the solutions.

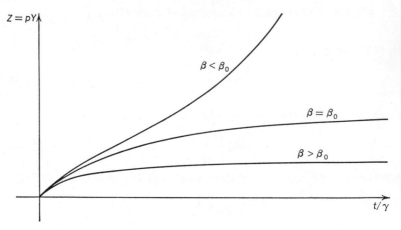

Fig. 9.9   Qualitative behavior of the solutions of (9.32).

It is of interest to compare the values of β_0 and the corresponding critical temperature as t tends to infinity, obtained from the approximate theory, with the exact values deduced earlier. The value $\beta_0 = 1.54$ corresponds to $qpa^2 = 4/1.54 = 2.6$, compared with the exact value of 2 [see (9.26)]. The value $Z = 1.59$ gives $Y = 1.59/p$, where Y corresponds to u defined previously, for which the critical value was given by (9.27) as $1.39/p$. The accuracy of the approximate solution is remarkably good considering the simplicity of the method.

If the reader wishes to exercise his ingenuity, he could try to obtain results corresponding to those given in this section for a plane (slab) geometry, and for a sphere.

9.4   A Class of Boundary-Layer Heat-Transfer Problems[8]

Comment: The unifying theme in the remainder of this chapter is the use of the idea of a boundary layer to obtain approximate formulas that correlate the four apparently different physical phenomena described in the second paragraph below.

Mathematics Used: Simple algebra and integration.

The general equations governing the transfer of heat in a moving fluid are extremely complicated. Nevertheless, considerable progress has been made in obtaining approximate solutions adequate for engineering applications. The basis of these approximate solutions is usually a physical picture that enables the salient features of the phenomenon to be expressed in terms of relatively simple mathematical equations. In particular, the physical concept we wish to exploit is the idea of the boundary layer—that certain phenomena which occur in fluids are determined by what happens in a thin layer of fluid near the surface of a solid body.

We consider four phenomena:

1. *Film condensation.* Suppose a vapor is in contact with a cool vertical wall, the temperature of the wall being below the temperature at which the vapor condenses. The vapor in contact with the wall will condense and form a thin film running down the surface of the wall, as illustrated in Fig. 9.10.

2. *Film boiling.* In a similar way, suppose a liquid is in contact with a surface that is hotter than the boiling point of the liquid, as in metal quenching, for instance. The surface will be completely covered by a thin vapor film as

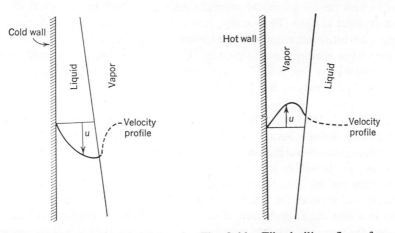

Fig. 9.10   Film condensation: flow of liquid film down a cool wall.

Fig. 9.11   Film boiling: flow of vapor film up a hot wall.

[8] The remainder of this chapter is based on (although it differs in some details from) H. W. Emmons, Natural Convection Heat Transfer Correlation, in *Studies in Mathematics and Mechanics* (presented to R. von Mises), Academic, New York, 1954, pp. 232–241.

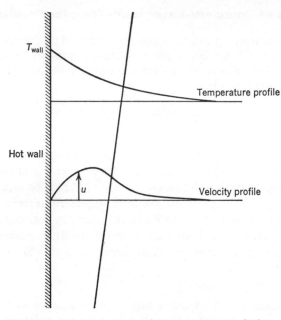

Fig. 9.12   Natural convection: no change of phase.

in Fig. 9.11. It is assumed that the gas moves vertically upward in the form of a thin film, and does not detach itself from the wall in the form of bubbles.

3. *Natural convection.*   Of course, the first two cases are really natural convection, in the sense that the heat transfer has caused density differences that in turn permit gravity to produce velocities which bring new fluid to the heat-transfer surface. Technically, however, natural convection has come to mean convection currents produced within a single phase by density differences arising from temperature differences. Consider a vertical plate with natural convection as in Fig. 9.12. The wall heats the fluid (liquid or vapor) near its surface. The density of this fluid therefore decreases, so that the fluid near the wall tends to rise. Again we use a boundary-layer picture of the liquid rising near the wall. The line dividing the layer in which movement takes place is not clearly defined because no change of phase takes place (compare the previous cases). Nevertheless, for certain ranges of parameters, the boundary layer is a fairly well defined physical entity.

4. *Film melting.*   Suppose a block of ice is set upon a very hot surface. The ice will melt at the hot surface and the water (or steam) produced will flow in a film out from under. If the hot surface is of sufficient conductivity to maintain an approximately uniform temperature, the ice will be supported on the melted film. This process is clearly like those already treated except that the motive force moving the fluid from under the block is provided by the weight of the ice block. This time Fig. 9.13 is appropriate. The film thickness Y might be expected to be roughly constant, since the additional heat transfer

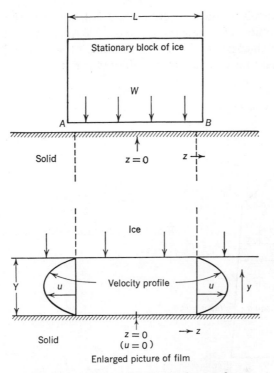

Fig. 9.13   Film melting on a hot surface.

across a thinner section of the film would produce increased melting, and vice versa. The mean velocity and flow increase from zero at the center of the block (by symmetry) to a maximum at the ends A and B (see Fig. 9.13).

In all four cases the problem is assumed to be two-dimensional; that is, Figs. 9.10 to 9.13 are cross sections, for a fixed (arbitrary) x, of a situation involving the three coordinates x, y, and z, in which the phenomenon is independent of x. Then y and z are coordinates in the planes of Figs. 9.10 to 9.13.

In practice we know the basic physical properties of the system, such as viscosity, density and heat conductivity of the fluid, difference in temperature between the wall and the fluid (or ice), length of the wall (or block of ice), and so on. The problem is to find an expression for the rate of heat transfer from the wall to the fluid (or to the block of ice).

9.5   Film Condensation and Film Boiling

We use a common method and common approximations to establish equations for each of the four phenomena listed in Section 9.4. Two basic relations are involved, one concerning heat balance, the other force balance. The ultimate object of the analysis is to deduce relations that can be used to correlate experimental results involving fluids of widely differing densities, viscosities, latent heats, and conductivities (see Fig. 9.16).

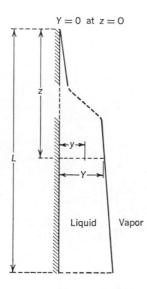

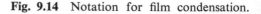

Fig. 9.14   Notation for film condensation.

1. *Film condensation* (Fig. 9.10).   We use the notation shown in Fig. 9.14. The thickness of the film at a distance z from the start of the film is denoted by Y. We have $Y = 0$ at $z = 0$. The total length of the film is L. Distance measured perpendicular to the wall is denoted by y. Let $u(y, z)$ denote the velocity at the point (y, z) of the fluid moving down the wall, and $U(z)$ denote the velocity at $y = Y$, that is, at the outer edge of the film. We use the physics of the situation to make a reasonable guess at how the velocity of the liquid in the film varies with y. The liquid should be at rest at the wall and have maximum velocity at the liquid-vapor interface. We assume a simple mathematical function with these properties—the following parabolic distribution of velocity (compare Fig. 9.10):

$$u(y, z) = U(z)\left(\frac{2y}{Y} - \frac{y^2}{Y^2}\right). \qquad (9.33)$$

The quantity $U(z)$ is the velocity at the liquid-vapor interface and can be found from the results derived below [see (9.37) and (9.40)]. Let $w(z)$ denote the mass flux per unit time across a cross section of the film at depth z,

$$w(z) = \rho \int_0^Y u(y, z)\, dy = \tfrac{2}{3}\rho U(z)\, Y, \qquad (9.34)$$

where ρ is the density of the liquid. In the film-condensation problem being considered, gravity is the force that moves the fluid in the film. The force on a slice of film of thickness δz is

$$\rho g \, Y \, \delta z, \tag{9.35}$$

where now, strictly speaking, ρ is the difference in density between the liquid and vapor, but we shall neglect the density of the vapor. If this force alone acted on the film it would accelerate as it moved. However, we assume that the film is so thin that viscosity is the main force opposing the gravitational force. The resistive force due to viscosity, per unit area of heat-transfer surface, is equal to the film fluid viscosity, μ, times a measure of the velocity gradient, which we take equal to the gradient at the wall:

$$\left[\frac{du(y, z)}{dy}\right]_{y=0} = \frac{2U(z)}{Y}. \tag{9.36}$$

Hence
$$\rho g \, Y \, \delta z = \frac{2\mu U(z) \, \delta z}{Y}. \tag{9.37}$$

Eliminating U between this equation and (9.34) we obtain

$$w(z) = \frac{\rho^2 g \, Y^3}{3\mu}. \tag{9.38}$$

We next consider heat transfer in the film. The heat flux per unit area per unit time is given by

$$\frac{k \, \Delta T}{Y},$$

where k is the thermal conductivity of the film fluid, $\Delta T = T - T_w$ the difference in temperature between the temperature T at the outer edge of the film (the boiling point of the fluid being condensed), and T_w the wall temperature. For each unit of heat transferred, a new mass of film material is produced. If λ is the latent heat of condensation, then in a length δz we have the balance

$$\lambda \, \delta w = \frac{k \, \Delta T}{Y} \, \delta z,$$

where δw is the change in flux per second corresponding to a change δz in z. Hence

$$\lambda \frac{dw}{dz} = \frac{k \, \Delta T}{Y}. \tag{9.39}$$

Substitution of (9.38) in (9.39) gives

$$Y^3 \frac{dY}{dz} = \frac{k\mu \, \Delta T}{\lambda \rho^2 g},$$

or, on integrating, using the condition that $Y = 0$ at $z = 0$,

$$Y = \left(\frac{4zk\mu \, \Delta T}{\lambda \rho^2 g}\right)^{1/4}. \tag{9.40}$$

This is an interesting intermediate result; it tells us how the film thickness varies with z. However, this cannot be readily measured, and we now obtain a relation between quantities that can be measured easily experimentally. If Q denotes the total heat transfer,

$$Q = k \, \Delta T \int_0^L \frac{1}{Y} \, dz = k \, \Delta T \left(\frac{64 \lambda \rho^2 g L^3}{81 k \mu \, \Delta T} \right)^{1/4}. \tag{9.41}$$

It is convenient to express this result in terms of the following nondimensional numbers:

$$\mathrm{Nu} = \text{Nusselt number} = \frac{Q}{k \, \Delta T}, \tag{9.42}$$

$$C = \text{convection number} = \frac{\lambda \rho^2 g L^3}{1.27 k \mu \, \Delta T}. \tag{9.43}$$

Then (9.41) becomes

$$\mathrm{Nu} = C^{1/4}. \tag{9.44}$$

2. *Film boiling* (Fig. 9.11).   The analysis of this case is basically similar to that given for film condensation. There are two differences (the notation is the same as in Fig. 9.14, assuming this figure is turned upside down; z is now measured positive upward from the bottom of the film).

In the case of film boiling, the vapor moves upward as in Fig. 9.11 (rather than downward as in Fig. 9.10). Since frictional forces act at both edges of the vapor film, we assume a parabolic distribution with maximum velocity in the center of the film,

$$u(y, z) = \frac{4 U(z) y (Y - y)}{Y^2},$$

so that

$$\int_0^Y u(y, z) \, dy = \tfrac{2}{3} U(z) Y,$$

as before, but, instead of (9.36),

$$\left(\frac{du}{dy} \right)_{y=0} = 4 \frac{U(z)}{Y}.$$

The density ρ that appears in (9.34) and (9.35) is no longer the same, or even approximately the same, in the two equations. Let ρ_v denote the density of the vapor and ρ_l the density of the liquid. Then the mass-flux equation (9.34) for film boiling becomes

$$w(z) = \tfrac{2}{3} \rho_v U(z) Y, \tag{9.45}$$

and the force expression (9.35) becomes

$$(\rho_l - \rho_v) g Y \, \delta z \approx \rho_l g Y \, \delta z. \tag{9.46}$$

Frictional forces resisting the flow now act on both sides of the film, so instead of (9.37) we have

$$\rho_l g Y = \frac{8\mu U(z)}{Y}.$$

(9.47)

Eliminating U between (9.45) and (9.47), we have, instead of (9.38),

$$w(z) = \frac{\rho_v \rho_l g Y^3}{12\mu}.$$

Equation (9.39) is unchanged, provided k is now interpreted as the thermal conductivity of the vapor. Proceeding as before we find, instead of (9.40),

$$Y = 2\left(\frac{zk\mu \Delta T}{\lambda \rho_v \rho_l g}\right)^{1/4}.$$

The theory given previously then leads to relation (9.44), $\mathrm{Nu} = \mathrm{C}^{1/4}$, as before, provided C is defined by

$$\mathrm{C} = \frac{16\lambda \rho_v \rho_l g L^3}{81 k\mu \Delta T} = \frac{\lambda \rho_v \rho_l g L^3}{5.06 k\mu \Delta T}.$$

9.6   Natural Convection, Film Melting, and Comparison with Experiment

3. *Natural convection* (Fig. 9.12).   The same basic principles can be applied as for film condensation and film boiling, but the boundary between the film and the main body of the fluid is not so well defined as in the previous cases, which makes it more difficult to estimate temperature and velocity profiles and to judge the validity of the theory. We suppose (quite arbitrarily) that the temperature varies linearly from the value at the wall to the value at the edge of the boundary layer, this latter temperature being that of the main body of the fluid. We assume also that the velocity in the boundary layer is given by

$$u(y, z) = A(z)\left(\frac{y}{Y} - q\,\frac{y^2}{Y^2}\right),$$

where q is a constant whose value lies between 0.5 and 1.0. The value of q is left arbitrary so that the effect of varying q can be seen later. These assumptions are illustrated in Fig. 9.15.

Following the same argument as before, instead of (9.34) we have

$$w(z) = \rho \int_0^Y u(y, z)\, dy = \rho A(z)\, Y(\tfrac{1}{2} - \tfrac{1}{3}q).$$

(9.48)

The force moving the fluid is now produced by buoyancy caused by temperature-induced density differences. If T is the temperature at (z, y), then

$$T_{\text{wall}} - T = \frac{\Delta T\, y}{Y}$$

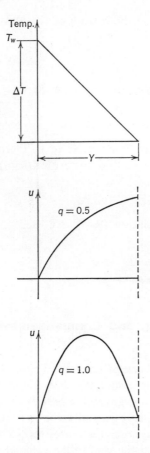

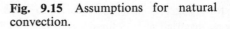

Fig. 9.15 Assumptions for natural convection.

and the total force at position z is

$$g\rho\beta \int_0^Y (T_{\text{wall}} - T)\, dy = \tfrac{1}{2}g\rho\beta \,\Delta T\, Y,$$

where β is the coefficient of thermal expansion. We also have

$$\left(\frac{du}{dy}\right)_{y=0} = \frac{A(z)}{Y}, \qquad -\left(\frac{du}{dy}\right)_{y=Y} = (2q - 1)\frac{A(z)}{Y}.$$

For the total shear stress we could decide to take only the stress at the wall $y = 0$, or to include the two stresses at $y = 0$ and $y = Y$. We shall write the shear stress

$$\frac{\sigma\mu A(z)}{Y},$$

where $\sigma = 1$ if only the wall stress is included, but $2q$ if both are included. Then, corresponding to (9.37) we have

$$\tfrac{1}{2}g\rho\beta \,\Delta T\, Y = \frac{\sigma\mu A(z)}{Y}.$$

Eliminating A between this equation and (9.48) we find

$$w(z) = \frac{\eta g \rho^2 \beta \, \Delta T \, Y^3}{\mu}, \qquad (9.49)$$

where
$$\eta = \frac{3 - 2q}{12\sigma}, \qquad \sigma = 1 \text{ or } 2q.$$

We next consider heat transfer in the film. The mass of fluid flowing along the plate is on the average heated to about one half the temperature difference ΔT. Hence

$$\tfrac{1}{2}\Delta Tc \, \delta w = \frac{k \, \Delta T}{Y} \, \delta z,$$

where c is the specific heat of the fluid; instead of (9.39) we have

$$\frac{dw}{dz} = \frac{2k}{cY}. \qquad (9.50)$$

From (9.49) and (9.50) we now obtain

$$Y^4 = \left(\frac{8}{3\eta}\right) \frac{k\mu z}{g\rho^2 \beta c \, \Delta T},$$

and we again obtain relation (9.44), $\mathrm{Nu} = C^{1/4}$, provided we define

$$C = \left(\frac{32\eta}{27}\right) \frac{g\rho^2 \beta c \, \Delta T L^3}{k\mu}.$$

If q varies from 0.5 to 1, and we take σ as either 1 or $2q$, the value of η can vary from 1/6 to 1/24. This is not as large a variation as might appear at first glance, because we take the fourth root of C, and the experimental points have a large scatter. Physically it seems reasonable to take a value in the middle range, say, $\eta = 1/12$, and then $32\eta/27$ is approximately 1/10. It is interesting to note that a more exact theory of Lorentz[9] gives exactly the same functional relation as that given above, with a value of 1/11 for the constant $32\eta/27$.

4. *Film melting* (Fig. 9.13).   The velocity variation across the film will be taken to be

$$u(y, z) = \frac{4U(z)y(Y - y)}{Y^2},$$

so that
$$w(z) = \rho \int_0^Y u(y, z) \, dy = \tfrac{2}{3}\rho U(z) Y, \qquad (9.51)$$

$$\left(\frac{du}{dy}\right)_{y=0} = 4 \frac{U(z)}{Y}.$$

[9] H. A. Lorentz, *Wied. Ann.*, **13**, 582 (1881). The more formal name of this journal is *Annalen der Physik und Chemie*; in the nineteenth century it was customary to refer to the journal by the name of its editor, who, from 1877 to 1899, was G. Wiedemann.

The pressure in the liquid for any value of z is approximately independent of y, and we denote this pressure by $p(z)$. The total force causing motion at any z is then approximately $-(dp/dz)Y$, and the force resisting motion is $8\mu U/Y$, so that

$$-\frac{dp(z)}{dz} = \frac{8\mu U(z)}{Y^2}. \tag{9.52}$$

The heat-balance equation (9.39) applies unchanged,

$$\lambda \frac{dw}{dz} = \frac{k\,\Delta T}{Y}. \tag{9.53}$$

Strictly speaking, relations (9.51) to (9.53) are not enough, and we should investigate the relation between p and U more carefully. However, this can be avoided if we assume Y is a constant independent of z, which seems reasonable on physical grounds because at points where Y is smaller there would be additional heat transfer which would tend to increase Y and vice versa. On the basis of this assumption, (9.53) would give

$$w(z) = \frac{k\,\Delta T}{\lambda Y}\, z,$$

where we now measure z from the center of the block (the block extends from $-\frac{1}{2}L$ to $+\frac{1}{2}L$). The constant of integration is zero, because (from symmetry) $w = 0$ at $z = 0$. From (9.51),

$$U(z) = \frac{3k\,\Delta T}{2\rho\lambda Y^2}\, z,$$

and, from (9.52),

$$p(z) = \frac{6\mu k\,\Delta T}{\rho\lambda Y^4}\,(\tfrac{1}{4}L^2 - z^2), \tag{9.54}$$

where the constant of integration is determined by the condition that $p = 0$ on $z = \pm\frac{1}{2}L$ (the liquid is in contact with the atmosphere).

The source of the pressure is, of course, the weight of the block, and in fact we must have

$$\int_{-L/2}^{L/2} p(z)\, dz = Mg.$$

Introducing (9.54) this gives

$$Y^4 = \frac{\mu k\,\Delta T L^3}{\rho\lambda Mg}.$$

In this case, since Y is a constant,

$$Q = \frac{k\,\Delta T L}{Y},$$

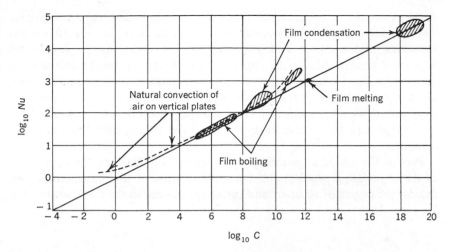

Fig. 9.16   Comparison of the relation $Nu = C^{1/4}$ (solid line) with some experimental results.

and we obtain (9.44), $Nu = C^{1/4}$, with

$$C = \frac{\rho \lambda M g L}{\mu k \, \Delta T}.$$

This concludes our discussion of film melting.

Some indication of the way in which the relation $Nu = C^{1/4}$ gives a very remarkable correlation with experimental results is shown in Fig. 9.16, which is somewhat diagrammatic. More detailed graphs can be found in the paper by Emmons.[10] Figure 9.16 indicates that the relation $Nu = C^{1/4}$ holds over a very wide range of Nu and C. Although the scatter of the experimental results is large, it is not excessive for the kind of scales that have to be used in a graph like that in Fig. 9.16. It is interesting that the reason for the deviation of the experimental curves for natural convection of air on vertical plates from the line $Nu = C^{1/4}$ for $C < 10^2$ is due to breakdown of the boundary-layer approximation; for $C > 10^9$ the deviation is due to the onset of turbulence.

9.7   Concluding Remarks

In the last three sections we have discussed some very complicated physical situations, using little more than algebra and elementary integration. The main moral of this example is probably that if we have a good physical idea, it is possible to go a long way with elementary mathematics. On the other

[10] H. W. Emmons, in *Studies in Mathematics and Mechanics* (presented to R. von Mises), Academic, New York, 1954, pp. 231–241.

hand, it should be remembered that many physical ideas that now appear obvious, for example, the boundary layer, can be clarified only after many laborious mathematical and experimental investigations to isolate the important factors. Also many engineering problems cannot be solved satisfactorily except by using high-powered mathematics. It is no accident that current papers in the *Transactions of the American Society of Mathematical Engineers* (Series C: *Journal of Heat Transfer*) are often filled with partial differential equations that have to be solved numerically by automatic computer.

Part of the art of engineering mathematics is to balance the complexity of the engineering problem and the sophistication of the mathematics used against the degree of accuracy and certainty required in the final conclusions.

Part IV

APPLICATIONS OF
LINEAR ALGEBRA

Chapter 10

Some Applications of
Matrix Algebra

Mathematics Used: The applications in this chapter require little more than elementary matrix manipulations, including matrix multiplication (especially the multiplication of partitioned matrices) and the idea of an inverse matrix.

Comment: All the developments in this chapter have been greatly influenced by the availability of automatic computers for performing laborious numerical calculations.

10.1 Summary

Perhaps the main objective of this chapter is to give some examples of the way in which matrix algebra often provides a systematic procedure for dealing with complicated algebraic and numerical calculations arising in connection with problems in the applied sciences. There are three main points to be illustrated:

1. The ease with which matrices can be used to organize and show the structure of complicated sets of relationships.
2. The utility of matrices in connection with automatic computers.
3. The way in which the matrix-plus-computer procedure often causes us to rethink the basic approach to a problem and come up with a more-or-less radical deviation from established techniques.[1]

Each of the three examples considered in this chapter illustrates all the above points.

---

[1] "Anyone who uses an automatic computer only to perform more quickly those calculations that he would have formerly carried out on a desk calculator is like a user of log tables who does nothing with a newly acquired desk calculator except add logarithms." (I am indebted to H. Eichhorn for this remark.)

1. In Section 10.2 we discuss a simple example of a matrix approach to the calculation of strains and stresses in pin-jointed frameworks. Some remarks on the problem of calculating frameworks by computer are made in Section 10.3.

2. In Section 10.4 we give a simple example of the matrix approach to the analysis of electrical networks. In Section 10.5 the results are used to show that it is impossible to produce a resistive network with a certain type of behavior, although intuitively it might seem that there is no reason why this should be so.

3. In Section 10.6 we consider the problem of making an accurate star map from overlapping photographs, each of which contains a large number of stars.

10.2   Plane Pin-Jointed Frameworks[2]

Mathematics Used: Simultaneous linear algebraic equations; matrix multiplication.

Comment: This section illustrates the power of matrices in elucidating the structure of systems of equations.

In this section we show how the calculation of strains and stresses in certain mechanical structures can be facilitated by using matrices. We shall first solve a simple problem "longhand," by writing out all the equations in detail. We then introduce matrices to express the manipulations in a compact form. This will enable us to appreciate some of the advantages of matrices—in particular, the ease with which the structure of the calculations can be seen and the utility of matrices in connection with automatic computing. Although we consider an almost trivial example from a very elementary point of view, the results should persuade the reader that the more complicated the problem, the greater the benefits that will be derived from the use of matrices.

Consider the simple plane framework in Fig. 10.1a. We assume that the frame is pin-jointed, which means that the members are connected to the wall, or connected together at A, by pins, in such a way that the ends are free to rotate. The forces at the joints are applied along the members, and no bending moments are transmitted. It is assumed that the weights of the members are negligible, and that the lengths of the members are such that, if the external forces F_1 and F_2 are zero, there are no stresses in the members.

The only information required about the behavior of an individual member is knowledge of its extension when a force is applied along its length. We assume Hooke's law—that the extension is linearly proportional to the force —so that

$$e = kT, \tag{10.1}$$

[2] This treatment of frameworks is taken from lecture notes on Matrix Calculations and Applications, by Ben Noble, The Mathematics Research Center, U.S. Army, University of Wisconsin, Madison, Wis., (mimeo.) 1964.

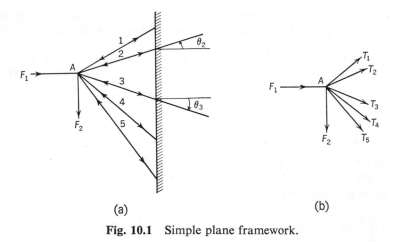

Fig. 10.1 Simple plane framework.

where T is the force (tension), e the extension, and k a factor of proportionality, assumed known. In fact, $k = l/AE$, where l is the length of the rod, A the area, and E the modulus of elasticity. The constant k is called the *flexibility* of the member; it is the extension of the member per unit force.

We number the members 1 to 5 as in Fig. 10.1a, and assume that the angle each member makes with the horizontal is given by θ_i $(i = 1, \ldots, 5)$. $(\theta_3, \theta_4,$ and θ_5 are negative in the example in Fig. 10.1a.) The changes in the θ_i produced by the application of forces are considered negligible. Let the flexibilities of the members be denoted by k_i, the tensions by T_i, and the extensions by e_i $(i = 1, \ldots, 5)$. The externally applied forces are denoted by F_1 and F_2 in the directions shown.

The equations of force equilibrium at joint A are obtained by resolving all forces horizontally and vertically. The arrows in Fig. 10.1a are intended to indicate that the tension in a rod is positive when the rod is being extended, negative when the rod is being compressed. The force diagram at point A is given by Fig. 10.1b, which leads to the following equations of equilibrium:

$$-T_1 \cos \theta_1 - T_2 \cos \theta_2 - \cdots - T_5 \cos \theta_5 = F_1,$$
$$T_1 \sin \theta_1 + T_2 \sin \theta_2 + \cdots + T_5 \sin \theta_5 = F_2. \tag{10.2}$$

Suppose that, when forces are applied to the framework, point A moves by a distance d_1 horizontally and d_2 vertically, measured in the same direction as the corresponding forces F_1 and F_2 (Fig. 10.1). Then the extensions e_i are given in terms of the d_i by

$$e_i = -d_1 \cos \theta_i + d_2 \sin \theta_i, \qquad i = 1, 2, \ldots, 5. \tag{10.3}$$

These equations simply state that the extension of the ith member is given by adding the components obtained by resolving d_1 and d_2 along the rods, taking account of signs. Alternatively, suppose that, when the framework is unstressed, point A has coordinates x_i and y_i measured from an origin fixed at the other end of the ith rod (a point on the wall). When the framework is stressed, the new position of A is given by $x_i + d_1$ and $y_i - d_2$. The original length of the ith rod is $l_i = (x_i^2 + y_i^2)^{1/2}$. The new length of the rod is given by

$$[(x_i + d_1)^2 + (y_i - d_2)^2]^{1/2} = [l_i^2 + 2(x_i d_1 - y_i d_2) + (d_1^2 + d_2^2)]^{1/2}$$
$$= l_i(1 + \delta_i)^{1/2}, \tag{10.4}$$

where
$$\delta_i = \frac{2(x_i d_1 - y_i d_2) + (d_1^2 + d_2^2)}{l_i^2}.$$

The quantities d_1 and d_2 are small compared with l_i, the length of the rod. From this assumption we see that δ_i is small compared with unity, and we can use the binomial theorem to expand $(1 + \delta_i)^{1/2}$ in the form $1 + \frac{1}{2}\delta_i + \cdots$. On dropping second-order terms we see that (10.4) gives

$$[(x_i + d_1)^2 + (y_i - d_2)^2]^{1/2} \approx l_i\left[1 + \frac{(x_i d_1 - y_i d_2)}{l_i^2}\right]$$

Hence
$$e_i = \frac{x_i d_1 - y_i d_2}{l_i}, \tag{10.5}$$

where we now use an equality sign since we assume that d_1 and d_2 are so small compared with l_i that higher-order terms are negligible. On consulting Fig. 10.1a we see that $x_i = -l_i \cos \theta_i$ and $y_i = -l_i \sin \theta_i$, so (10.5) agrees precisely with (10.3).

Equations (10.2) give relations between internal and external forces. Equations (10.3) give relations between internal and external displacements. To complete the solution we require relations between internal forces and internal displacements. These are given by writing Hooke's law (10.1) for each member:

$$e_i = k_i T_i, \qquad i = 1, 2, \ldots, 5. \tag{10.6}$$

Two methods of approach are commonly used to obtain the solution of (10.2), (10.3), and (10.6). In the remainder of this section we consider one of these, the *equilibrium method*. (We shall not consider the other standard approach, the *compatibility method*, in which the first step is to solve a statically determinate framework formed by removing redundant members from the original structure. We have mentioned only two of several possible methods of approach, all of which can be interpreted in matrix terms. The reader will realize that the matrix approach can be used to give a unified treatment of various methods for the calculation of structures.)

In the equilibrium method of approach we eliminate the unknown forces T_i, and derive simultaneous linear equations for the unknown displacements d_1 and d_2. From (10.3) and (10.6),

$$T_i = \frac{-d_1 \cos \theta_i + d_2 \sin \theta_i}{k_i}. \tag{10.7}$$

These values for T_i are then substituted in (10.2) to give two simultaneous equations for d_1 and d_2. Equations (10.2) are, using summation notation,

$$-\sum_{i=1}^{5} T_i \cos \theta_i = F_1,$$

$$\sum_{i=1}^{5} T_i \sin \theta_i = F_2.$$

Substitution for T_i from (10.7) gives

$$\begin{aligned} a_{11} d_1 + a_{12} d_2 &= F_1, \\ a_{21} d_1 + a_{22} d_2 &= F_2, \end{aligned} \tag{10.8}$$

where

$$a_{11} = \sum_{i=1}^{5} \frac{\cos^2 \theta_i}{k_i}, \qquad a_{22} = \sum_{i=1}^{5} \frac{\sin^2 \theta_i}{k_i}, \qquad a_{12} = a_{21} = -\sum_{i=1}^{5} \frac{\cos \theta_i \sin \theta_i}{k_i}.$$

The coefficients a_{11}, a_{22}, and $a_{12} = a_{21}$ are called the *stiffness coefficients* of the framework. A physical interpretation of a_{11} and a_{21} is that these are the forces required in the directions F_1 and F_2, respectively, to produce unit deflection d_1 and zero deflection d_2. Coefficients a_{12} and a_{22} can be interpreted similarly.

If equations (10.8) are solved to express d_1 and d_2 in terms of the forces, we obtain relations of the form

$$\begin{aligned} d_1 &= b_{11}F_1 + b_{12}F_2, \\ d_2 &= b_{21}F_1 + b_{22}F_2, \end{aligned}$$

where b_{11}, b_{22}, and $b_{12} = b_{21}$ are called the *flexibility coefficients* of the framework. For instance, if F_2 is zero, then b_{21} is the deflection in direction 2 produced by unit force in direction 1.

The equilibrium method of approach described above is particularly clear when expressed in terms of matrices. We define

$$\mathbf{t} = \begin{bmatrix} T_1 \\ T_2 \\ \vdots \\ T_5 \end{bmatrix}, \qquad \mathbf{e} = \begin{bmatrix} e_1 \\ e_2 \\ \vdots \\ e_5 \end{bmatrix}, \qquad \mathbf{f} = \begin{bmatrix} F_1 \\ F_2 \end{bmatrix}, \qquad \mathbf{d} = \begin{bmatrix} d_1 \\ d_2 \end{bmatrix},$$

$$\mathbf{C} = \begin{bmatrix} -\cos \theta_1 & -\cos \theta_2 & \cdots & -\cos \theta_5 \\ \sin \theta_1 & \sin \theta_2 & \cdots & \sin \theta_5 \end{bmatrix}, \tag{10.9}$$

$$\mathbf{K} = \begin{bmatrix} k_1 & 0 & \cdots & 0 \\ 0 & k_2 & \cdots & 0 \\ \vdots & \vdots & & \vdots \\ 0 & 0 & \cdots & k_5 \end{bmatrix}.$$

Then (10.2), (10.3), and (10.6) become, in matrix notation,

$$\mathbf{Ct} = \mathbf{f}, \tag{10.10}$$

$$\mathbf{e} = \mathbf{C}^T \mathbf{d}, \tag{10.11}$$

$$\mathbf{e} = \mathbf{Kt}. \tag{10.12}$$

The matrix $\mathbf{C}^T$ in (10.11) is precisely the transpose of the matrix $\mathbf{C}$ in (10.10). This relationship did not spring to our attention when we wrote out the original equations in the longhand forms (10.2) and (10.3). It is a bonus that we receive merely by writing everything in matrix notation. We can use this relationship as a check that we have written (10.2) and (10.3) correctly from physical reasoning. This is useful since it is easy to confuse signs. Alternatively, if we are sure that (10.2) is correct, we need not derive (10.3) from first principles.

In the equilibrium method of approach we wish to set up equations for $\mathbf{d}$. The $\mathbf{e}$ and $\mathbf{t}$ are unknown, so we eliminate them in the following way. From (10.10), (10.12), and (10.11) in succession,

$$\mathbf{f} = \mathbf{Ct} = \mathbf{CK}^{-1}\mathbf{e} = \mathbf{CK}^{-1}\mathbf{C}^T \mathbf{d};$$

that is,

$$(\mathbf{CK}^{-1}\mathbf{C}^T) \, \mathbf{d} = \mathbf{f}. \tag{10.13}$$

These are precisely (10.8). We are, of course, doing nothing new here; we are merely carrying out in matrix notation the same steps that we previously performed longhand. However the structure of the calculation is extremely clear. In addition, $\mathbf{K}$ is diagonal, $\mathbf{K}^{-1}$ is diagonal, and $\mathbf{CK}^{-1}\mathbf{C}^T$ is symmetrical, so we see immediately that we shall have $a_{12} = a_{21}$ in (10.8). This was found previously, because we computed a_{12} and a_{21} explicitly. However, we see from (10.13) that the symmetry of the matrix of coefficients is a basic property of this type of framework.

The reader should appreciate that, although we have confined our attention to a simple specific example, the same procedure can be carried through for more complicated structures. We always end up with a formula like (10.13), provided $\mathbf{C}$, $\mathbf{K}$, $\mathbf{d}$, and $\mathbf{f}$ are defined appropriately.

To conclude this section we remind the reader that we have considered only one possible method for using matrices to calculate strains and stresses in mechanical structures. A comprehensive treatment of the present state of the art has been given by Pestel and Leckie.[3]

10.3   The Application of Automatic Computers to Framework Calculation

Comment: This section illustrates the utility of matrices in connection with automatic computing.

[3] E. C. Pestel and F. A. Leckie, *Matrix Methods in Elastomechanics*, McGraw-Hill, New York, 1963.

We remind the reader of some elementary facts concerning automatic computers. A digital computer is a machine that can be instructed or programmed to carry out a sequence of logical steps and numerical calculations. Such a machine can be visualized as an *arithmetic unit*, which performs simple operations such as addition, multiplication, and division, and a "memory" or *store*, in which numbers and instructions can be stored. The memory can be regarded as a set of pigeonholes from which numbers and instructions can be produced, or in which numbers can be stored, at will.

To perform a calculation the computer must be provided with a set of instructions, or *program*. When solving a problem, the computer starts by storing the complete program in its memory. It then proceeds to obey the instructions in a sequence determined by the program. It is clear that if we wish to make the machine form the sum of products

$$ab + cd + ef + gh,$$

it would be laborious to have to tell the machine "Multiply a by b, c by d, e by f, g by h, and add the products." It is much easier to use suffix notation, labeling the numbers a_i, b_i, $(i = 1, \ldots, 4)$, in an obvious way, and say "Form the sum of the products $a_i b_i$, $i = 1, \ldots, 4$." Similarly, if we are dealing with two-dimensional arrays of numbers, it is convenient to arrange that these are rectangular. The machine can manipulate the arrays by systematic operations involving suffixes which run over values lying within fixed limits. This is essentially why matrices are indispensable when programming electronic computers.

We now make some remarks concerning the problem of calculating frameworks by computer. Before automatic computers were available, when all calculations had to be performed by hand, it was natural that emphasis was placed on methods that minimized the amount of calculation involved. This inevitably meant that special methods were invented for special types of problem. Many of the older textbooks are little more than collections of tricks for the easy solution of special types of framework. In particular, because the solution of simultaneous linear equations is laborious, many of these special methods were devised specifically to avoid the need for the formulation and solution of sets of equations, as such, although this may not have been the explicit motivation.

If calculations are to be performed by an automatic computer, the amount of calculation required is to some extent a secondary consideration. In particular, computers can easily solve systems of linear equations. In fact, this is such a routine operation on a computer that it may be preferable to use a method which formulates a problem in a way which leads to a set of linear equations, rather than go to the trouble of inventing an ingenious method that avoids the equations. The methods used for the analysis of frameworks by computer may seem cumbersome when applied to simple structures. On the other hand, it is possible to arrange that exactly the same methods apply no matter how complicated the structure. Although the formulas in Section 10.2 were developed for a very simple structure, they apply (if the matrices are defined appropriately) to structures of any degree of complexity.

Important considerations when deciding whether a method is suitable for an automatic computer are:

1. The method should be systematic and routine, so that it can be programmed easily for an automatic computer.

2. The method should be as general as possible, so that we do not need to make up a new program for each new framework.

Matrix methods admirably fulfill these requirements.

It is instructive to list the steps needed to calculate the strains and stresses in a pin-jointed framework by an automatic computer, using a method similar to that discussed in Section 10.2.

(1) The machine is given the following information:
  (a) The coordinates of the joints.
  (b) The coordinates of the supports.
  (c) The positions of the members, that is, the joints and the supports between which they are connected.
  (d) The properties of the members, for example, cross-sectional area and modulus of elasticity. The lengths of the members can be computed by the machine from (a) to (c), unless there is lack of fit, in which case the lengths must also be specified.
  (e) The nature of the supports, for example, rigid, constrained to move in one direction, etc.
  (f) The external forces.

(2) The machine will then compute
  (a) The stiffness coefficients of the members and hence the matrix **K** of stiffness coefficients.
  (b) The connection matrix **C**.

(3) The machine then multiplies matrices to obtain the simultaneous linear equations for the problem, depending on the precise method used.

(4) The machine solves the equations.

(5) The machine evaluates the stresses and deformations of individual members and any other required information.

(6) The end results are printed out.

To find the stresses and strains in a given structure, the engineer need concern himself only with step (1). It is difficult to see how the engineer could be provided with a simpler method for finding the stresses and strains in a given structure. However, two points should be noted.

1. The engineer will not see the details of the computations that take place inside the computer, so checks should be incorporated to ensure that the numerical procedures are as accurate as required, and that, in particular, no large numerical errors creep in because of ill-conditioning and other purely numerical troubles.

2. It should be emphasized that the above considerations are only a small part of the overall design problem facing the engineer. We have assumed that we are given the geometric configuration and cross-sectional areas of the members. In other words, we have assumed that most of the decisions regarding the design of the structure have already been made.

We conclude this section with a few comments on this second point.[4] There is, of course, no reason why the computer should not also take over much of the design procedure, such as the problem of deciding the best dimensions and combinations of structural members. We have deliberately confined our attention to the restricted problem of computing the strains and stresses in a given structure. It is a natural step to go on to consider the problem of programming a computer to deal with the more general design problem. This is allied to the optimization problems discussed in Chapters 2 and 3. We can state the design problem as follows. Certain materials are available with given properties such as modulus of elasticity, yield stress, coefficients of thermal expansion, and density. We wish to construct, from these materials, a structure that will withstand various loading conditions. In this form the problem is stated too broadly, because any number of designs can be produced to withstand given loading conditions, and we have given no reason to prefer one design to another. We therefore introduce some optimization criterion in the form of a merit factor which has to be minimized (or maximized). For instance, we may wish to produce the cheapest or lightest structure that will support given loads. In the case of Fig. 10.1, the problem might be to produce a framework connecting point A to the wall which will withstand forces F_1 and F_2, which lie within certain limits. We have to find angles θ_i $(i = 1, \ldots, n)$ and cross-sectional areas A_i $(i = 1, \ldots, n)$, where n is not known, that will give a strong enough framework at cheapest cost. The areas A_i will have to be large enough so that the beams do not buckle. This imposes inequalities which are a typical feature of this kind of optimization problem. Even from this brief and oversimplified account, the reader should see that we are placing the problem of calculating stresses and strains in structures in a much more general setting.

If computer techniques were the only method of calculating structures ever taught to the embryo engineer, there is obviously great danger that he would lose the intuitive "feel" for the behavior of a structure that is inculcated by the traditional methods of approach. On the other hand, by eliminating the need to spend time and effort on routine calculation, the computer

---

[4] These comments were suggested by material submitted by L. A. Schmit and R. H. Mallett, Engineering Division, Case Institute of Technology, Cleveland, Ohio. See also L. A. Schmit and T. P. Kichner, Synthesis of Material and Configuration Selection, *J. Struct. Div. Am. Soc. Civil Engrs.*, **88**(ST3), 79–102 (1962).

approach gives the designer more time, freedom, and opportunity to concentrate on optimization of the design, which is, after all, the crux of the
problem.

10.4 Kron's Fundamental Formula for the Mesh Analysis of an Electrical Network[5]

Mathematics Used: Simple matrix algebra.

Comment: In this method of approach to electrical networks, we distinguish between the properties of the individual elements and the
interconnections of the elements.

In this section we consider a system of resistors connected in any fashion
whatsoever, with electromotive forces in series with the resistors. As a specific
example we shall consider the bridge network in Fig. 10.2. The determination
of voltages and currents in a general network can be regarded as the basic
problem of electrical circuit theory. It is assumed that the reader is familiar
with Kirchhoff's two laws.

Kirchhoff's current law states that the sum of the currents entering and
leaving any node is algebraically zero. (A *node* of a network is any point to
which two or more impedances of the network are connected.)

Kirchhoff's voltage law states that the sum of the voltages (including
electromotive forces) around any closed circuit or loop in the network is
algebraically zero.

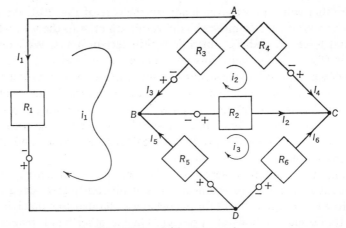

Fig. 10.2 Bridge network.

[5] This section is taken from lecture notes on Matrix Calculations and Applications,
by Ben Noble, Mathematics Research Center, U.S. Army, University of Wisconsin,
Madison, Wis., (mimeo.) 1964; an elementary reference is P. LeCorbeiller, *Matrix
Analysis of Electrical Networks*, Harvard Univ. Press, Cambridge, Mass., 1950.

One method for solving network problems is to write equations for loop currents by inspection. This is adequate for simple problems, but the writing of equations can become difficult if the network is complicated. (This is particularly true of networks containing mutual inductances, especially if these are moving relatively to each other, as in electric motors. However, we consider only linear resistive networks here.) The object of the following development is to provide a routine method for setting up the equations for any network, regardless of its complexity. We shall discuss only simple systems, but the method will deal with complicated systems without any change in principle. The key is to distinguish between the properties of the individual resistors and the interconnections of the resistors.

A *branch* of the network is defined as a resistor, or system of resistors, connected to the rest of the network by precisely two terminals (at nodes). For example, in Fig. 10.2, A and C are nodes, and AC, containing R_4, is a branch. A *loop* of the network is defined as any closed circuit, for example, $ABCA$. For clarity we number the steps in the argument.

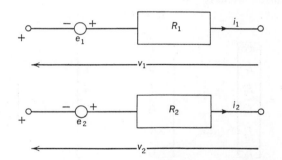

Fig. 10.3 Sign conventions for separate branches.

1. Suppose there are B branches (for example, $B = 6$ in Fig. 10.2). We establish B currents $I_1, I_2, \ldots, I_B$ in the branches, fixing the current directions arbitrarily. This merely means that we put an arrow along each branch, and this is then chosen as the direction in which positive current travels in the branch. We denote the B voltages across the branches by $v_1, v_2, \ldots, v_B$ and the B electromotive forces in the branches by $e_1, e_2, \ldots, e_B$, using the sign conventions shown in Fig. 10.3. The point here is that the signs of the voltages and electromotive forces are fixed whenever we choose the current directions.

2. Ohm's law gives, using the sign conventions established in step 1,

$$v_r + e_r = R_r I_r, \qquad r = 1, 2, \ldots, B.$$

In matrix notation,

$$\mathbf{v}_b + \mathbf{e} = \mathbf{R} \mathbf{i}_b, \tag{10.14}$$

where

$$\mathbf{R} = \begin{bmatrix} R_1 & 0 & \cdots & 0 \\ 0 & R_2 & \cdots & 0 \\ \vdots & \vdots & & \vdots \\ 0 & 0 & \cdots & R_B \end{bmatrix}, \quad \mathbf{v}_b = \begin{bmatrix} v_1 \\ v_2 \\ \vdots \\ v_B \end{bmatrix}, \quad \mathbf{e} = \begin{bmatrix} e_1 \\ e_2 \\ \vdots \\ e_B \end{bmatrix}, \quad \mathbf{i}_b = \begin{bmatrix} I_1 \\ I_2 \\ \vdots \\ I_B \end{bmatrix}.$$

3. We next choose independent loops in the network, as in the usual method for solving circuit problems. Suppose we require M mesh currents, $i_1, i_2, \ldots, i_M$ ($M = 3$ in Fig. 10.2). We can immediately write down relations between the I_r and the i_s. In the example in Fig. 10.2,

$$
\begin{aligned}
I_1 &= -i_1 \\
I_2 &= -i_2 + i_3 \\
I_3 &= i_1 - i_2 \\
I_4 &= i_2 \\
I_5 &= -i_1 + i_3 \\
I_6 &= - i_3.
\end{aligned}
$$

In matrix notation we have

$$\mathbf{i}_b = \mathbf{C} \mathbf{i}, \tag{10.15}$$

where

$$\mathbf{i}_b = \begin{bmatrix} I_1 \\ I_2 \\ I_3 \\ I_4 \\ I_5 \\ I_6 \end{bmatrix}, \quad \mathbf{C} = \begin{bmatrix} -1 & 0 & 0 \\ 0 & -1 & 1 \\ 1 & -1 & 0 \\ 0 & 1 & 0 \\ -1 & 0 & 1 \\ 0 & 0 & -1 \end{bmatrix}, \quad \mathbf{i} = \begin{bmatrix} i_1 \\ i_2 \\ i_3 \end{bmatrix}. \tag{10.16}$$

In a general network we have

$$
\begin{aligned}
I_1 &= C_{11}i_1 + C_{12}i_2 + \cdots + C_{1M}i_M, \\
&\ \vdots \\
I_B &= C_{B1}i_1 + C_{B2}i_2 + \cdots + C_{BM}i_M,
\end{aligned}
\tag{10.17}
$$

where

$C_{pq} = +1$ if branch p is contained in loop q and the branch and loop currents are assumed positive in the *same* direction,

$C_{pq} = -1$ if branch p is contained in loop q and branch and loop currents are assumed positive in *opposite* directions,

$C_{pq} = 0$ if branch p is *not* contained in loop q.

4. We next use the fact that the sum of the voltages around each mesh is zero (because each mesh forms a closed circuit). For the circuit in Fig. 10.2,

$$
\begin{aligned}
i_1 \text{ mesh:} \quad & -v_1 + v_3 - v_5 = 0 \\
i_2 \text{ mesh:} \quad & - v_2 - v_3 + v_4 = 0 \\
i_3 \text{ mesh:} \quad & v_2 + v_5 - v_6 = 0.
\end{aligned}
$$

In matrix notation this is

$$\mathbf{C}^T \mathbf{v}_b = \mathbf{0}, \tag{10.18}$$

where

$$\mathbf{C}^T = \begin{bmatrix} -1 & 0 & 1 & 0 & -1 & 0 \\ 0 & -1 & -1 & 1 & 0 & 0 \\ 0 & 1 & 0 & 0 & 1 & -1 \end{bmatrix},$$

as this matrix is precisely the transpose of $\mathbf{C}$ defined in (10.16). This is not accidental, as we see from the following argument. Suppose that in the general case

$$D_{11}v_1 + D_{12}v_2 + \cdots + D_{1B}v_B = 0,$$
$$\vdots$$
$$D_{M1}v_1 + D_{M2}v_2 + \cdots + D_{MB}v_B = 0.$$

Then the element D_{qp} is determined by the following rules:

$D_{qp} = +1$ if branch p is contained in loop q and the reference direction of branch p agrees with that of loop q,

$D_{qp} = -1$ if branch p is contained in loop q and the reference direction of branch p is the opposite to that of loop q,

$D_{qp} = 0$ if branch p is *not* contained in loop q.

These definitions show that if the equations are written, in matrix form, $\mathbf{Dv} = \mathbf{0}$, then $\mathbf{D}$ is the transpose of the matrix $\mathbf{C}$ whose elements were defined in step 3 in connection with (10.17).

5. The final step is to combine (10.14), (10.15), and (10.18). From (10.14) and (10.15) we have

$$\mathbf{v}_b + \mathbf{e} = \mathbf{RCi}.$$

Multiply through by $\mathbf{C}^T$, and use (10.18). This gives

$$\mathbf{C}^T \mathbf{RCi} = \mathbf{C}^T \mathbf{e}, \tag{10.19}$$

which are a set of M simultaneous equations for the M unknown loop currents. This is Kron's fundamental formula for the loop analysis of an electrical circuit.

As a simple example consider the circuit of Fig. 10.2. Then

$$\mathbf{R} = \begin{bmatrix} R_1 & 0 & \cdots & 0 \\ 0 & R_2 & \cdots & 0 \\ \vdots & \vdots & & \vdots \\ 0 & 0 & \cdots & R_6 \end{bmatrix},$$

and we have already written down $\mathbf{C}$ in (10.16). It is easily verified that

$$\mathbf{C}^T \mathbf{RC} = \begin{bmatrix} R_1 + R_3 + R_5 & -R_3 & -R_5 \\ -R_3 & R_2 + R_3 + R_4 & -R_2 \\ -R_5 & -R_2 & R_2 + R_5 + R_6 \end{bmatrix}.$$

The resulting equations for the loop currents, derived from using this result in (10.19), can be readily checked from first principles.

In the above example we considered a simple resistor network. The real usefulness of the method appears when we consider complicated systems, for example, alternating-current networks where mutual inductances are present, especially when there are asymmetric mutually induced voltages, as in electric motors. However, our purpose will have been achieved if the reader can see, however dimly, some of the potentialities of the method. The basic simplification and motivation is that problems connected with properties of the individual elements (steps 1 and 2) are divorced from problems concerning their interconnection (steps 3 and 4).

10.5   The Concavity of Resistance Functions[6]

Mathematics Used: Simple algebra (in the first half), matrix algebra (in the second half).

Comment: Mathematics is used to show that it is impossible to construct a resistor network with a certain property. This result was not originally intuitively obvious.

We first explain what is meant by functions being concave upward or downward. Consider a function $y = f(x)$ of a single variable x (Fig. 10.4). Graphically, suppose that we consider two points A and B on the curve. If

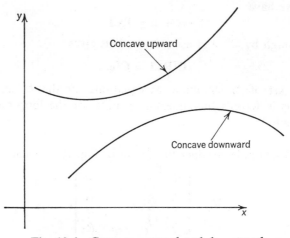

Fig. 10.4   Concave upward and downward.

[6] The original paper which suggested this section is by C. E. Shannon and D. W. Hagelbarger, Concavity of Resistance Functions, *J. Appl. Phys.*, **27**, 42–43 (1956), where an ingenious physical argument is used to establish the required result. A simplified proof is given by H. M. Melvin, *J. Appl. Phys.*, **27**, 658–659 (1956). I am indebted to C. A. Desoer for the matrix approach given in the second half of the section.

all the points on the straight line AB between A and B lie *below* (or coincide with) the curve, and this is true of all points A and B in the range of x considered, we say that $f(x)$ is *concave downward* in this range of x. Similarly, if all points on the straight line AB between A and B lie *above* (or coincide with) the curve for all A and B, we say that $f(x)$ is *concave upward* in this range. [Note that it is convenient to phrase our definition so that, if $y = f(x)$ is a straight line, it can be regarded as either concave upward or downward.] Mathematically, if A and B are the points (x', y') and (x'', y''), where $y' = f(x')$ and $y'' = f(x'')$, the line AB is given by

$$y = \frac{x'' - x}{x'' - x'} f(x') + \frac{x - x'}{x'' - x'} f(x''), \tag{10.20}$$

and, for a concave-downward curve, the right side of this equation must be less than or equal to $f(x)$ for $x' \le x \le x''$. If we introduce a parameter α defined by

$$\alpha = \frac{x - x'}{x'' - x'},$$

which implies

$$x = (1 - \alpha)x' + \alpha x'', \tag{10.21}$$

then, for a curve which is concave downward, the condition that $f(x)$ is greater than or equal to the right side of (10.20) is

$$f((1 - \alpha)x' + \alpha x'') \ge (1 - \alpha)f(x') + \alpha f(x''), \tag{10.22}$$

and for a concave downward function this must hold for $0 \le \alpha \le 1$.

We can now pose the problem we wish to consider in this section. As part of a computer, a rheostat or variable resistor was required which was a concave-upward function of the shaft angle. It was desired to do this by connecting fixed resistors and "linearly wound potentiometers" (variable resistors whose resistance is a linear function of the shaft angle). After some attempt to design a rheostat of this type, it became apparent that either it was impossible or that the designers were singularly inept. Rather than accept the second alternative, we show that a rheostat of this type must be concave downward. We first give an elementary proof, and then rephrase the proof in terms of matrices.

(It may help the reader if we interpolate an example at this point. Consider a circuit consisting of two resistors in parallel, a fixed resistor R_1 in parallel with a variable resistor xR_2, where x is a variable. The combined resistance R is given by

$$\frac{1}{R} = \frac{1}{R_1} + \frac{1}{xR_2} \quad \text{or} \quad R = \frac{xR_1R_2}{xR_2 + R_1}.$$

It is easy to see that R is a concave-downward function of x, because the graph of R against x increases from 0 to R_1 as x increases from 0 to infinity,

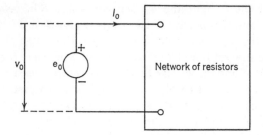

Fig. 10.5   Electromotive force connected to resistor network.

and the slope of the curve is monotone-decreasing. Alternatively we note that in this case R is a twice-differentiable function of x, and $d^2R/dx^2 \leq 0$ for $0 < x < \infty$, which implies that the curve is concave downward. We return to this argument at the end of this section.)

We assume that we are given a network of resistors which does not contain any sources of electromotive force. An electromotive force e_0 is connected to two nodes of the network, resulting in a current I_0 as in Fig. 10.5. The first result we require is

$$e_0 I_0 = \sum_{\text{branches}} R_s I_s^2, \tag{10.23}$$

where the sum is taken over the branches of the network in the box in Fig. 10.5. We use the same notation as in Section 10.4. There are B branches, with resistances and currents given by R_s and I_s, respectively, where $s = 1, 2, \ldots,$ B. If we are willing to accept a proof of (10.23) which relies on physical concepts familiar to the student of electrical networks, we need merely state that the left side of the equation represents the power delivered by the source of electromotive force to the network and the right side represents the power dissipated in the form of heat in the resistors. The equation is therefore simply a statement that the energy introduced into the network is equal to the energy dissipated in the network.

To prove (10.23) from first principles, consider a network of $B + 1$ branches consisting of the network in the box in Fig. 10.5, together with an extra branch containing the electromotive force e_0. This network will have $M + 1$ loops. We write Kirchhoff's voltage law for each of the loops,

$$\sum_{s \text{ in loop } k} v_s = 0, \tag{10.24}$$

where the sum is taken over all the branches s contained in loop k. Multiply this expression by the current i_k in the kth loop, and sum the result over all the loops,

$$\sum_{k=1}^{M+1} i_k \left(\sum_{s \text{ in loop } k} v_s \right) = 0. \tag{10.25}$$

Interchange orders of summation (the result should be clear if the reader visualizes what is happening):

$$\sum_{s=1}^{B+1} v_s \left(\sum_{k \text{ in branch } s} i_k \right) = 0, \tag{10.26}$$

where the inner sum is over all loop currents common to a given branch s. This inner sum is precisely I_s, the total current in the sth branch. Hence

$$\sum_{s=1}^{B+1} v_s I_s = 0. \tag{10.27}$$

For the branch containing the electromotive force, we have $v_0 = -e_0$; $v_s = R_s I_s$ for the remaining branches. Hence (10.23) follows immediately from (10.27). The argument leading to (10.27) is rephrased below in matrix terms.

The next result we require is the following. If the input current I_0 is fixed, and we consider all possible distributions of currents in the network that satisfy Kirchhoff's current law but not necessarily Kirchhoff's voltage law, then the actual current distribution minimizes the rate of heat generation in the network.[7]

To prove this theorem, select any closed circuit (or loop) $PQR \cdots P$ in the network, and let the currents and resistances in the branches $PQ, QR, \ldots$ be $x_1, x_2, \ldots$ and $R_1, R_2, \ldots$. Let the currents and resistances in those branches not included in this loop be denoted by $x_a, x_b, \ldots$ and $R_a, R_b, \ldots$. Then the total rate of heat production is

$$\sum R_a x_a^2 + \sum R_1 x_1^2, \tag{10.28}$$

where the notation is self-explanatory. A different arrangement of currents, which will still obey Kirchhoff's current law, can be obtained by supposing that all the branch currents in the loop $PQR \cdots P$ are increased by the same amount ϵ. The total rate of production of heat is now

$$\sum R_a x_a^2 + \sum R_1 (x_1 + \epsilon)^2. \tag{10.29}$$

If the currents $x_1, x_2, \ldots$ are those which actually occur, then by Kirchhoff's voltage law the sum of the voltage round the loop $PQR \cdots P$ is zero, or

$$\sum R_1 x_1 = 0.$$

Introducing this in (10.29), the rate of production of heat becomes

$$\left(\sum R_a x_a^2 + \sum R_1 x_1^2 \right) + \epsilon^2 \sum R_1.$$

The quantity in parentheses is the rate of production of heat when both Kirchhoff's laws are satisfied. Since $\epsilon^2 \sum R_1$ is an essentially positive quantity,

---

[7] We reproduce the proof given by J. Jeans, *The Mathematical Theory of Electricity and Magnetism*, Cambridge Univ. Press, New York, 1948, p. 322.

the actual rate of heat production is less than the rate when the current in the loop $PQR\cdots P$ is increased by ϵ.

The most general alteration that can be made in the actual system of currents, consistent with satisfaction of Kirchhoff's current law, is to alter all the loop currents. We have just discussed the case of altering one single loop current by an amount ϵ. In the general case the change in the rate of heat production will be

$$\sum R(x + \epsilon' + \epsilon'' + \cdots)^2 - \sum Rx^2 = \sum R(\epsilon' + \epsilon'' + \cdots)^2, \qquad (10.30)$$

where ϵ', ϵ'', ... are the additional currents flowing through the resistance R, the sum is now over all branches, and we have used Kirchhoff's voltage law around each of the loops. The quantity (10.30) is essentially positive, so any alteration in the current distribution increases the rate of heat production.

Now that we have established certain necessary preliminaries, we can prove quickly that resistance functions must be concave downward. Let $F(\mathbf{R})$ denote the resistance of the network in the box in Fig. 10.5, where $\mathbf{R}$ represents the B branch resistors R_s, $s = 1, 2, \ldots, B$. As previously explained, a linearly wound potentiometer is a resistor that varies from, say, R_s' to R_s'' as a linear function of a parameter α (proportional to the shaft angle),

$$R_s = (1 - \alpha)R_s' + \alpha R_s'', \qquad 0 \le \alpha \le 1. \qquad (10.31)$$

If the branch resistor R_s is fixed, we merely choose $R_s' = R_s'' = R_s$. Denote the sets of branch resistors R_s' and R_s'' ($s = 1$ to B) by $\mathbf{R}'$ and $\mathbf{R}''$. The required result, that $F(\mathbf{R})$ is a concave-downward function of α when R_s is defined by (10.31), implies that we wish to prove [compare (10.22)]

$$F((1 - \alpha)\mathbf{R}' + \alpha\mathbf{R}'') \ge (1 - \alpha)F(\mathbf{R}') + \alpha F(\mathbf{R}''). \qquad (10.32)$$

The resistance of the network in Fig. 10.5 is e_0/I_0. If the branch resistances are given by (10.31), then from (10.23) the resistance is

$$\frac{e_0}{I_0} = \sum [(1 - \alpha)R_s' + \alpha R_s'']\left(\frac{I_s}{I_0}\right)^2$$

$$= (1 - \alpha) \sum R_s' \left(\frac{I_s}{I_0}\right)^2 + \alpha \sum R_s'' \left(\frac{I_s}{I_0}\right)^2, \qquad (10.33)$$

where the sums are over the branches and I_s denotes the current in branch s [which has a resistance given by (10.31)] when the current and voltage laws of Kirchhoff are both satisfied. From the theorem proved above concerning the minimum rate of production of heat,

$$\sum R_s' I_s^2 \ge \sum R_s'(I_s')^2, \qquad (10.34)$$

$$\sum R_s'' I_s^2 \ge \sum R_s''(I_s'')^2, \qquad (10.35)$$

where I_s' and I_s'' refer to the actual currents in the networks with branch resistors R_s' and R_s'', where the current and voltage laws of Kirchhoff are both satisfied in these networks. (Note that I_s represents a current distribution for each of these networks which satisfies the current law, but not necessarily the voltage law.) On combining (10.33) to (10.35) to give

$$\sum \left[(1 - \alpha)R_s' + \alpha R_s'' \right] \left(\frac{I_s}{I_0} \right)^2 \geq (1 - \alpha) \sum R_s' \left(\frac{I_s'}{I_0} \right)^2 + \alpha \sum R_s'' \left(\frac{I_s''}{I_0} \right)^2, \quad (10.36)$$

and noting that

$$\sum R_s' \left(\frac{I_s'}{I_0} \right)^2, \quad \sum R_s'' \left(\frac{I_s''}{I_0} \right)^2$$

represent, respectively, the resistances of networks with branch resistors $\mathbf{R}'$ and $\mathbf{R}''$ instead of $\mathbf{R}$, we see that we have proved the required result (10.32)— that a resistance function must be concave downward.

The above derivation was rather long because it was necessary to establish several preliminary results by elementary methods. A more sophisticated (but essentially equivalent) proof is the following. Suppose the resistor network in the box in Fig. 10.5 has B branches with branch currents $\mathbf{i}_b$ and M loops with loop currents $\mathbf{i}$, as in Section 10.4, with a connection matrix $\mathbf{C}$ and a $B \times B$ diagonal resistance matrix $\mathbf{R}$. Let the electromotive force e_0 and the current I_0 in Fig. 10.5 form a $(B + 1)$th branch with zero resistance in this branch. Form an $(M + 1)$th loop such that the $(B + 1)$th branch occurs in the $(M + 1)$th loop, and in no other loop. Denote the branch current, loop current, and connection and resistance matrices of this new network by $\hat{\mathbf{i}}_b$, $\hat{\mathbf{i}}$, $\hat{\mathbf{C}}$, $\hat{\mathbf{R}}$, respectively, so that

$$\hat{\mathbf{i}}_b = \begin{bmatrix} I_0 \\ \mathbf{i}_b \end{bmatrix}, \quad \hat{\mathbf{i}} = \begin{bmatrix} I_0 \\ \mathbf{i} \end{bmatrix}, \quad \hat{\mathbf{C}} = \begin{bmatrix} 1 & 0 \\ \mathbf{p} & \mathbf{C} \end{bmatrix}, \quad \hat{\mathbf{R}} = \begin{bmatrix} 0 & 0 \\ 0 & \mathbf{R} \end{bmatrix}, \quad (10.37)$$

where $\mathbf{p}$ is a $B \times 1$ column matrix determined by the choice of the $(M + 1)$th loop. We shall use the basic matrix relations developed in Section 10.4, (10.14), (10.15), and (10.18). In the present context these are

$$\hat{\mathbf{v}}_b + \hat{\mathbf{e}} = \hat{\mathbf{R}}\hat{\mathbf{i}}_b, \quad (10.38)$$

$$\hat{\mathbf{i}}_b = \hat{\mathbf{C}}\hat{\mathbf{i}} \quad (10.39)$$

$$\hat{\mathbf{C}}^T \hat{\mathbf{v}}_b = 0. \quad (10.40)$$

In these equations, since the only electromotive force is e_0 in the $(B + 1)$th branch, and this branch has no resistance,

$$\hat{\mathbf{e}} = \begin{bmatrix} e_0 \\ 0 \end{bmatrix}, \quad \hat{\mathbf{v}}_b = \begin{bmatrix} -e_0 \\ \mathbf{v}_b \end{bmatrix}. \quad (10.41)$$

Substituting (10.37) and (10.41) in (10.38) to (10.40), we obtain

$$\mathbf{v}_b = \mathbf{R}\mathbf{i}_b, \quad (10.42)$$

$$\mathbf{i}_b = I_0\mathbf{p} + \mathbf{C}\mathbf{i}, \quad (10.43)$$

$$e_0 = \mathbf{p}^T\mathbf{v}_b, \quad \mathbf{C}^T\mathbf{v}_b = 0. \quad (10.44)$$

In the following manipulations we are guided by the minimum-rate-of-dissipation-of-heat argument presented previously. To obtain the basic result (10.23) from our matrix approach, we see that the right side of (10.23) is, in fact, $i_b^T \mathbf{R} i_b$. This leads us to multiply (10.42) by i_b^T, which gives

$$i_b^T \mathbf{R} i_b = i_b^T \mathbf{v}_b = I_0 \mathbf{p}^T \mathbf{v}_b + i^T \mathbf{C}^T \mathbf{v}_b = e_0 I_0, \tag{10.45}$$

where we have used (10.43) and (10.44). This is precisely (10.23).

Suppose next that the loop currents are changed from i to $i + \delta i$, and that the branch currents then change from i_b to $i_b + \delta i_b$, keeping I_0 constant. From (10.43), which is also valid for the new currents, we see that

$$\delta i_b = \mathbf{C} \, \delta i. \tag{10.46}$$

From (10.46), (10.42), and (10.44),

$$\delta i_b^T \mathbf{R} i_b = \delta i^T \mathbf{C}^T \mathbf{v}_b = 0.$$

Hence,

$$(i_b + \delta i_b)^T \mathbf{R}(i_b + \delta i_b) - i_b^T \mathbf{R} i_b = 2\delta i_b^T \mathbf{R} i_b + \delta i_b^T \mathbf{R} \, \delta i_b.$$
$$= \delta i_b^T \mathbf{R} \, \delta i_b, \tag{10.47}$$

where the quantity on the right is positive if δi_b is nonzero, as can be seen immediately if this expression is written out in full, since $\mathbf{R}$ is a diagonal matrix and resistances are positive. Equations (10.47) and (10.30) are the same, and the above argument is simply the matrix proof that any alteration in the current distribution (I_0 being kept constant) increases the rate of heat production.

The argument now goes precisely as before. [Compare the argument following (10.33) with that given below.] From (10.45) the resistance of a network with branch resistors $(1 - \alpha)\mathbf{R}' + \alpha \mathbf{R}''$ is given by

$$\frac{e_0}{I_0} = \frac{i_b^T[(1 - \alpha)\mathbf{R}' + \alpha \mathbf{R}'']i_b}{I_0^2} = \frac{(1 - \alpha)i_b^T \mathbf{R}' i_b}{I_0^2} + \frac{\alpha i_b^T \mathbf{R}'' i_b}{I_0^2}. \tag{10.48}$$

By the argument in the last paragraph we have

$$i_b^T \mathbf{R}' i_b \geq i_b'^T \mathbf{R}' i_b', \qquad i_b^T \mathbf{R}'' i_b \geq i_b''^T \mathbf{R}'' i_b'', \tag{10.49}$$

where i_b' and i_b'' are the actual currents in the networks with resistances $\mathbf{R}'$ and $\mathbf{R}''$. Combining (10.48) and (10.49) we obtain a result that is in fact precisely (10.36), obtained previously by a more elementary but much less elegant argument. This proves by a matrix method that the resistance function must be concave downward.

We conclude this section by pointing out that the result could have been obtained by straightforward but uninspiring differentiation, in the following way. The fundamental equation for the complete circuit in Fig. 10.5, corresponding to (10.19), is $\hat{\mathbf{C}}^T \hat{\mathbf{R}} \hat{\mathbf{C}} \hat{i} = \hat{\mathbf{C}}^T \hat{e}$. Introducing the expressions in (10.37) and (10.41) and multiplying out, we find

$$\begin{bmatrix} z_0 & \mathbf{z}^T \\ \mathbf{z} & \mathbf{Z} \end{bmatrix} \begin{bmatrix} I_0 \\ i \end{bmatrix} = \begin{bmatrix} e_0 \\ 0 \end{bmatrix}, \tag{10.50}$$

where $\qquad z_0 = \mathbf{p}^T \mathbf{Rp}, \qquad \mathbf{z} = \mathbf{C}^T \mathbf{Rp}, \qquad \mathbf{Z} = \mathbf{C}^T \mathbf{RC}.$ $\qquad$ (10.51)

Separating out the equations in (10.50), we find

$$z_0 I_0 + \mathbf{z}^T \mathbf{i} = e_0,$$
$$\mathbf{z} I_0 + \mathbf{Z} \mathbf{i} = \mathbf{0}.$$

The second equation gives $\mathbf{i} = -\mathbf{Z}^{-1} \mathbf{z} I_0$, and substituting this in the first equation we see that the resistance of the network is given by

$$R = \frac{e_0}{I_0} = z_0 - \mathbf{z}^T \mathbf{Z}^{-1} \mathbf{z}. \qquad (10.52)$$

To show that this is concave downward we need only show (as in the special example discussed previously), that $d^2 R/d\alpha^2 \leq 0$ for $0 \leq \alpha \leq 1$. This is easy to prove since, remembering that $\mathbf{R} = (1 - \alpha)\mathbf{R}' + \alpha \mathbf{R}''$, we see from (10.51) that z_0, $\mathbf{z}$, and $\mathbf{Z}$ are linear functions of α. Differentiating the relation $\mathbf{Z}^{-1}\mathbf{Z} = \mathbf{I}$ with respect to α, we see that

$$\frac{d\mathbf{Z}^{-1}}{d\alpha} = -\mathbf{Z}^{-1}\left(\frac{d\mathbf{Z}}{d\alpha}\right)\mathbf{Z}^{-1} = -\mathbf{Z}^{-1}\mathbf{C}^T(\mathbf{R}'' - \mathbf{R}')\mathbf{C}\mathbf{Z}^{-1}.$$

With this hint it is left to the reader to form $d^2 R/d\alpha^2$ from (10.52) and show that this second derivative is essentially negative. This provides another proof of the concavity of resistance functions.

10.6   The Determination of Star Positions from Photographs[8]

Mathematics Used: Matrix algebra, especially partitioned matrices; the solution of linear equations by least squares.

Comment: The availability of automatic computers has suggested a new approach to the problem of deducing accurate star positions from overlapping photographs. Matrix notation is used to clarify the structure of a complicated system of linear equations.

In this section we wish to consider one of the problems involved in deducing the positions of celestial objects such as stars from measurements of the relative coordinates of their images on photographic plates. The position of a star is usually specified by giving its (angular) spherical coordinates, at a

---

[8] The inspiration for this section came from a lecture given by H. Eichhorn during a visit of several members of the Army Map Service to the Mathematics Research Center, U.S. Army, University of Wisconsin, Madison, Wis., May 1965. Some relevant papers are H. Eichhorn, Modern Developments and Problems in Photographic Astrometry, *Photogrammetric Engineering*, **1964**, 771–780; H. Eichhorn, Über die Reduktion von photographischen Sternpositionen und Eigenbewegungen, *Astron. Nachr.*, **285**, 233–237 (1960); and W. H. Jeffreys, On Computational Techniques for Photographic Astrometry with Overlapping Plates, *Astron. J.*, **68**, 111–113 (1963).

certain instant of time, with reference to a given system of coordinates, for example, a system with its origin at the center of the earth and fixed relative to the distant stars. In technical terms the "angular spherical coordinates" might be, for example, the right ascension and declination.

The over-all situation is, of course, extremely complicated. Although stars can be regarded as points, the images of stars on a photographic plate will be dots of a certain size and shape, depending on the effects of the atmosphere, the spectra and intensities of the stars, the quality of the optical equipment, and so on. The accuracy of the transformation of measurements taken from a photographic plate, into numbers specifying positions of stars in the sky, will depend on the accuracy with which the photograph has been measured and the accuracy of our knowledge of the properties of the optical system and the geometry of the configuration represented by "sky + optical system + plate."

Suppose an arbitrary rectangular coordinate system is fixed on the plate. (This can be chosen to suit the convenience of the investigator, but details do not concern us here.) Let the coordinates of a star on the plate, relative to this coordinate system, be denoted by (x, y). The relation between the measured coordinate of the star, and its right ascension α and declination δ, is given by a known functional relationship of the form

$$\alpha = f(x, y; \mathbf{u}), \qquad \delta = g(x, y; \mathbf{v}), \tag{10.53}$$

where

$$\mathbf{u} = \begin{bmatrix} u_1 \\ \vdots \\ u_p \end{bmatrix}, \qquad \mathbf{v} = \begin{bmatrix} v_1 \\ \vdots \\ v_p \end{bmatrix}.$$

The vectors $\mathbf{u}$ and $\mathbf{v}$ represent sets of parameters that depend on the coordinate system chosen on the plate and on the geometry of the transformation from the sky, via the optical system, to the photographic plate. These parameters are the same for all stars on a given photograph, and they are called *plate constants*. They are not known beforehand. In theory it might be possible to calculate $\mathbf{u}$ and $\mathbf{v}$ from knowledge of the geometry of the system, but it would be extremely difficult to do this with sufficient accuracy. In practice we use an indirect method to deduce $\mathbf{u}$ and $\mathbf{v}$ from the positions of certain reference, or *catalog* stars. The aim of this section is to first describe how the plate constants $\mathbf{u}$ and $\mathbf{v}$ can be determined when only one photographic plate is available, and then to generalize the method to the situation in which several overlapping plates are available.

The functional relationships f and g in (10.53) can usually be approximated sufficiently closely by assuming that α and δ are power series in x and y:

$$\begin{aligned} \alpha &= u_1 + u_2 x + u_3 y + u_4 x^2 + u_5 xy + \cdots, \\ \delta &= v_1 + v_2 x + v_3 y + v_4 x^2 + v_5 xy + \cdots. \end{aligned} \tag{10.54}$$

Although the relation between α, δ and x, y is nonlinear, the unknown parameters $\mathbf{u}$ and $\mathbf{v}$ enter linearly, and this is why we can use matrix notation directly. We assume that there are p terms in each of these series, and introduce the $p \times 1$ row matrix

$$\mathbf{x} = [1, x, y, x^2, xy, \ldots].$$

Then (10.54) can be written

$$\begin{bmatrix} \alpha \\ \delta \end{bmatrix} = \begin{bmatrix} \mathbf{x} & \mathbf{0} \\ \mathbf{0} & \mathbf{x} \end{bmatrix} \begin{bmatrix} \mathbf{u} \\ \mathbf{v} \end{bmatrix}. \tag{10.55}$$

Now suppose there are n stars with right ascensions α_i and declinations δ_i, and that the coordinates of these stars on the photographic plate are given by (x_i, y_i). Introduce the notation

$$\mathbf{y}_i = \begin{bmatrix} \alpha_i \\ \delta_i \end{bmatrix}, \qquad \mathbf{h}_i = \begin{bmatrix} \mathbf{x}_i & \mathbf{0} \\ \mathbf{0} & \mathbf{x}_i \end{bmatrix}, \qquad \mathbf{t} = \begin{bmatrix} \mathbf{u} \\ \mathbf{v} \end{bmatrix},$$

where $\mathbf{x}_i$ denotes $\mathbf{x}$ with x, y replaced by x_i, y_i. Equation (10.55) then gives

$$\mathbf{y}_i = \mathbf{h}_i \mathbf{t}, \qquad i = 1, \ldots, n. \tag{10.56}$$

Note that $\mathbf{t}$ is independent of i. Equations (10.56) represent $2n$ relations between $2n + 2p$ unknowns. Suppose now that we consider only catalog stars for which estimates of α_i, and δ_i, that is, $\mathbf{y}_i$, are available, say $\mathbf{k}_i$. If these were known exactly, we should merely substitute them in (10.56) to obtain

$$\mathbf{h}_i \mathbf{t} = \mathbf{k}_i, \qquad i = 1, \ldots, n. \tag{10.57}$$

These are a system of $2n$ equations in $2p$ unknowns. If we choose $n = p$, these can be solved directly. If we choose $n > p$, we shall in general have an inconsistent set of equations [since the $\mathbf{h}_i$ depend on the (x_i, y_i), which are not known exactly, and in any case the relation (10.54) is approximate]. These inconsistent equations must be solved approximately by least squares. However, the estimates $\mathbf{k}_i$ of $\mathbf{y}_i$ are subject to error, and it is better to consider the system

$$\mathbf{y}_i = \begin{cases} \mathbf{h}_i \mathbf{t}, & i = 1, \ldots, n. \tag{10.58} \\ \mathbf{k}_i, & i = 1, \ldots, n. \tag{10.59} \end{cases}$$

These are $4n$ equations in $2n + 2p$ unknowns. If we choose $n > p$, there are more equations than unknowns, and the system must be solved approximately by least squares. We digress at this point to remind the reader about the method.

Suppose we wish to solve approximately the following system of linear equations by the method of least squares:

$$\sum_{j=1}^{n} a_{ij} x_j = b_i, \qquad i = 1, \ldots, m, \tag{10.60}$$

where $m > n$, so there are more equations than unknowns. In general it will not be possible to find x_j to satisfy these equations exactly. We define errors or residuals, r_s, by the equation

$$r_s = b_s - \sum_{j=1}^{n} a_{sj} x_j.$$

We then minimize the weighted sum of squares of the residuals,

$$S = \sum_{s=1}^{m} w_s r_s^2, \tag{10.61}$$

where the w_s are weights chosen in a more or less arbitrary way, depending on the importance attached to the various equations. If all the equations are equally important, all the w_s are taken equal to unity. If one equation is regarded as more important than the others (for example, if the position of one star can be measured very accurately on the photograph, or if its catalog coordinates are known very accurately), a large weight can be attached to this equation compared to the others. The sum of squares of residuals, S, is minimized by setting

$$\frac{\partial S}{\partial x_i} = 0$$

for $i = 1, 2, \ldots, n$ in turn. From (10.61) this gives

$$\sum_{s=1}^{m} w_s \left(b_s - \sum_{j=1}^{n} a_{sj} x_j \right) a_{si} = 0, \qquad i = 1, 2, \ldots, n,$$

or

$$\sum_{j=1}^{n} \left(\sum_{s=1}^{m} w_s a_{si} a_{sj} \right) x_j = \sum_{s=1}^{m} w_s a_{si} b_s. \tag{10.62}$$

If equations (10.60) are written in matrix notation, in the usual way, as

$$\mathbf{Ax} = \mathbf{b}, \tag{10.63}$$

and $\mathbf{W}$ is the diagonal matrix whose ith diagonal element is w_i, then equations (10.62) are simply

$$(\mathbf{A}^T \mathbf{W} \mathbf{A})x = \mathbf{A}^T \mathbf{W} \mathbf{b}. \tag{10.64}$$

This is a set of n equations in n unknowns, obtained by multiplying the original set (10.63) first by $\mathbf{W}$ and then by the transpose of $\mathbf{A}$. We have assumed implicitly that the rank of $\mathbf{A}$ is n, so these equations have a unique solution.

We are now in a position to conclude our discussion of the first phase of the star problem. In partitioned matrix notation, the equations of the problem are, from (10.58) and (10.59),

$$\begin{bmatrix} \mathbf{I} & \mathbf{0} \\ \mathbf{I} & -\mathbf{B} \end{bmatrix} \begin{bmatrix} \mathbf{y} \\ \mathbf{t} \end{bmatrix} = \begin{bmatrix} \mathbf{k} \\ \mathbf{0} \end{bmatrix}, \tag{10.65}$$

where we have introduced

$$
\mathbf{y} = \begin{bmatrix} \mathbf{y}_1 \\ \mathbf{y}_2 \\ \vdots \\ \mathbf{y}_n \end{bmatrix}, \qquad \mathbf{k} = \begin{bmatrix} \mathbf{k}_1 \\ \mathbf{k}_2 \\ \vdots \\ \mathbf{k}_n \end{bmatrix}, \qquad \mathbf{B} = \begin{bmatrix} \mathbf{h}_1 \\ \mathbf{h}_2 \\ \vdots \\ \mathbf{h}_n \end{bmatrix}.
$$

Introducing a weighting matrix,

$$
\mathbf{W} = \begin{bmatrix} \mathbf{W}_1 & \mathbf{0} \\ \mathbf{0} & \mathbf{W}_2 \end{bmatrix},
$$

where $\mathbf{W}_1$ and $\mathbf{W}_2$ are $2n \times 2n$ diagonal matrices, the procedure leading from (10.63) to (10.64) gives the following least-squares system for (10.65):

$$
\begin{bmatrix} \mathbf{I} & \mathbf{I} \\ \mathbf{0} & -\mathbf{B}^T \end{bmatrix} \begin{bmatrix} \mathbf{W}_1 & \mathbf{0} \\ \mathbf{0} & \mathbf{W}_2 \end{bmatrix} \begin{bmatrix} \mathbf{I} & \mathbf{0} \\ \mathbf{I} & -\mathbf{B} \end{bmatrix} \begin{bmatrix} \mathbf{y} \\ \mathbf{t} \end{bmatrix} = \begin{bmatrix} \mathbf{W}_1 \mathbf{k} \\ \mathbf{0} \end{bmatrix}.
$$

Multiplying out, we find the following system of equations for $\mathbf{y}$ and $\mathbf{t}$:

$$
(\mathbf{W}_1 + \mathbf{W}_2)\mathbf{y} - \mathbf{W}_2\mathbf{B}\mathbf{t} = \mathbf{W}_1\mathbf{k}, \tag{10.66}
$$

$$
-\mathbf{B}^T\mathbf{W}_2 y + \mathbf{B}^T\mathbf{W}_2\mathbf{B}\mathbf{t} = \mathbf{0}. \tag{10.67}
$$

The matrix $\mathbf{W}_1 + \mathbf{W}_2$ is diagonal and nonsingular, so it can be inverted easily. Solving the first equation for $\mathbf{y}$ and substituting in the second, we see that

$$
\mathbf{B}^T\mathbf{D}\mathbf{B}\mathbf{t} = \mathbf{B}^T\mathbf{D}\mathbf{k}, \tag{10.68}
$$

where $\mathbf{D}$ is a simple diagonal matrix,

$$
\mathbf{D} = \mathbf{W}_1\mathbf{W}_2(\mathbf{W}_1 + \mathbf{W}_2)^{-1}.
$$

This means that $\mathbf{t}$ can be found by solving a set of $2p$ equations in $2p$ unknowns, (10.68). When $\mathbf{t}$ is found, corrected values for the celestial coordinates of the catalog stars can be obtained from (10.66). The celestial coordinates of noncatalog stars can be found by substituting the corresponding values of (x_i, y_i) in (10.54), using the optimum value of $\mathbf{t}$ that has just been determined.

Having built up the necessary background, we can now state the main problem we wish to consider in this section. If a region of the sky is covered by more than one photographic plate, the above procedure will give slightly different celestial coordinates for a given star from the measurements obtained from each plate. We could, of course, simply average the various estimates, with appropriate weighting, but it is possible to do better than this. We shall describe a procedure in which all the available information is used simultaneously, to give unique coordinates for each star. The method is practicable only if an electronic computer is available.

To fix our ideas, consider Fig. 10.6, which represents two overlapping photographs of stars. There are twelve stars in all, seven on plate 1, nine on plate 2, and four stars are common to both plates. Suppose estimates of the positions of the five stars 2, 5, 6, 10, and 11 are known from outside sources, for example, catalogs. It is required to obtain improved estimates of the

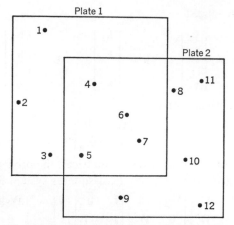

Fig. 10.6   Overlapping star photographs.

positions of these five stars, together with estimates of the positions of the rest of the stars, from data obtained by measuring the photographs.

In the general situation, a region of the sky will be covered by plates in such a way that every plate overlaps at least one other plate at least partially. Suppose in the general case there are m stars numbered $i = 1, 2, \ldots, m$, and q photographic plates numbered $j = 1, 2, \ldots, q$. Denote the coordinates of the ith star on the jth plate $x_i^{(j)}$ and $y_i^{(j)}$, measured relative to an arbitrary coordinate system, different for each plate.

We wish to find the right ascension α_i and the declination δ_i of each star. These are related to $x_i^{(j)}$ and $y_i^{(j)}$ by a relation that is different for each plate; it depends on j. This has already been discussed in detail in connection with (10.53) to (10.56), where we considered the case of a single plate. When there are q plates, the previous discussion applies, provided equations (10.56) are replaced by

$$\mathbf{y}_i = \mathbf{h}_i^{(j)}\mathbf{t}_j, \tag{10.69}$$

where this is the equation relating α_i and δ_i for the ith star to the plate constants $\mathbf{t}_j$ of the jth plate, the known matrix $\mathbf{h}_i^{(j)}$ being of the same form as $\mathbf{h}_i$ in (10.56) except that x_i and y_i are replaced by $x_i^{(j)}$ and $y_i^{(j)}$, the coordinates of the ith star measured on the jth plate.

It is now necessary to consider the catalog and noncatalog stars separately. For the catalog stars 2, 5, 6, 10, and 11 in the specific example of Fig. 10.6, we have

$$
\begin{aligned}
\mathbf{y}_2 &= \mathbf{h}_2^{(1)}\mathbf{t}_1 \\
\mathbf{y}_5 &= \mathbf{h}_5^{(1)}\mathbf{t}_1 \\
\mathbf{y}_5 &= \quad\quad \mathbf{h}_5^{(2)}\mathbf{t}_2 \\
\mathbf{y}_6 &= \mathbf{h}_6^{(1)}\mathbf{t}_1 \\
\mathbf{y}_6 &= \quad\quad \mathbf{h}_6^{(2)}\mathbf{t}_2 \\
\mathbf{y}_{10} &= \quad\quad \mathbf{h}_{10}^{(2)}\mathbf{t}_2 \\
\mathbf{y}_{11} &= \quad\quad \mathbf{h}_{11}^{(2)}\mathbf{t}_2.
\end{aligned}
$$

In a more compact notation this is

$$\mathbf{Ey = Pt,} \qquad (10.70)$$

where

$$
\mathbf{E} =
\begin{bmatrix}
I & 0 & 0 & 0 & 0 \\
0 & I & 0 & 0 & 0 \\
0 & I & 0 & 0 & 0 \\
0 & 0 & I & 0 & 0 \\
0 & 0 & I & 0 & 0 \\
0 & 0 & 0 & I & 0 \\
0 & 0 & 0 & 0 & I
\end{bmatrix},
\qquad
\mathbf{P} =
\begin{bmatrix}
h_2^{(1)} & 0 \\
h_5^{(1)} & 0 \\
0 & h_5^{(2)} \\
h_6^{(1)} & 0 \\
0 & h_6^{(2)} \\
0 & h_{10}^{(2)} \\
0 & h_{11}^{(2)}
\end{bmatrix},
\qquad
\mathbf{y} =
\begin{bmatrix}
y_2 \\
y_5 \\
y_6 \\
y_{10} \\
y_{11}
\end{bmatrix},
\qquad
\mathbf{t} =
\begin{bmatrix}
t_1 \\
t_2
\end{bmatrix}.
$$

One important property of the matrix $\mathbf{E}$ is that if $\mathbf{D}$ is a square diagonal (partitioned) matrix, $\mathbf{E}^T\mathbf{D}\mathbf{E}$ is a square diagonal matrix.

The noncatalog stars can be considered in exactly the same way. The equation analogous to (10.70) is

$$
\mathbf{FY = Qt,} \qquad \text{where} \quad
\mathbf{Y} =
\begin{bmatrix}
y_1 \\
y_3 \\
y_4 \\
y_7 \\
y_8 \\
y_9 \\
y_{12}
\end{bmatrix}.
\qquad (10.71)
$$

The matrices $\mathbf{F}$ and $\mathbf{Q}$ are similar in form to $\mathbf{E}$ and $\mathbf{P}$, respectively. In the example in Fig. 10.6, the partitioned forms of $\mathbf{F}$ and $\mathbf{Q}$ are of orders 9×7 and 9×2. The matrix $\mathbf{F}$ has the same property as $\mathbf{E}$—that $\mathbf{F}^T\mathbf{D}\mathbf{F}$ is diagonal, where $\mathbf{D}$ is an arbitrary diagonal matrix.

Equations (10.59) are true for the catalog stars; that is, in the notation introduced in (10.65) we have $\mathbf{y = k}$, where $\mathbf{k}$ is a given vector. Writing this equation, together with (10.70) and (10.71), as a single equation, we obtain

$$
\begin{bmatrix}
I & 0 & 0 \\
E & 0 & -P \\
0 & F & -Q
\end{bmatrix}
\begin{bmatrix}
y \\
Y \\
t
\end{bmatrix}
=
\begin{bmatrix}
k \\
0 \\
0
\end{bmatrix}.
\qquad (10.72)
$$

Generalizing the least-squares procedure following (10.65), we introduce a weighting matrix

$$
\mathbf{W} =
\begin{bmatrix}
W_1 & 0 & 0 \\
0 & W_2 & 0 \\
0 & 0 & W_3
\end{bmatrix}.
$$

The least-squares equations are obtained by multiplying (10.72) by $\mathbf{W}$ and then by the transpose of the partitioned coefficient matrix. Multiplying out we obtain

$$\begin{bmatrix} \mathbf{K} & \mathbf{0} & -\mathbf{R} \\ \mathbf{0} & \mathbf{L} & -\mathbf{S} \\ -\mathbf{R}^T & -\mathbf{S}^T & \mathbf{M} \end{bmatrix} \begin{bmatrix} \mathbf{y} \\ \mathbf{Y} \\ \mathbf{t} \end{bmatrix} = \begin{bmatrix} \mathbf{W}_1\mathbf{k} \\ \mathbf{0} \\ \mathbf{0} \end{bmatrix}, \tag{10.73}$$

where

$$\mathbf{K} = \mathbf{W}_1 + \mathbf{E}^T\mathbf{W}_2\mathbf{E}, \qquad \mathbf{L} = \mathbf{F}^T\mathbf{W}_3\mathbf{F}, \qquad \mathbf{M} = \mathbf{P}^T\mathbf{W}_2\mathbf{P} + \mathbf{Q}^T\mathbf{W}_3\mathbf{Q},$$
$$\mathbf{R} = \mathbf{E}^T\mathbf{W}_2\mathbf{P}, \qquad \mathbf{S} = \mathbf{F}^T\mathbf{W}_3\mathbf{Q}.$$

From remarks made previously, the matrices $\mathbf{K}$ and $\mathbf{L}$ are both diagonal, and can be inverted directly. Hence it is practicable to eliminate $\mathbf{y}$ and $\mathbf{Y}$ from (10.73) in the following way. Writing the three sets of equations in (10.73) separately, the first two give

$$\mathbf{y} = \mathbf{K}^{-1}\mathbf{W}_1\mathbf{k} + \mathbf{K}^{-1}\mathbf{R}\mathbf{t}, \qquad \mathbf{Y} = \mathbf{L}^{-1}\mathbf{S}\mathbf{t}.$$

Substitution in the third set obtained from (10.73) gives

$$(\mathbf{M} - \mathbf{R}^T\mathbf{K}^{-1}\mathbf{R} - \mathbf{S}^T\mathbf{L}^{-1}\mathbf{S})\mathbf{t} = \mathbf{R}^T\mathbf{K}^{-1}\mathbf{k}.$$

This is a set of equations involving only the plate constants $\mathbf{t}$. Note that formulation of the equations involves only matrix multiplications and the inversion of diagonal matrices.

As an example of the order of magnitude of the computational problem involved, consider the question of producing a map of the stars in the southern hemisphere by this method. We might have 800 photographic plates with about 250 stars on each plate, 25 of these catalog stars. If each plate involves six plate constants, we should need to solve about 4800 equations in 4800 unknowns. The coefficient matrix contains a considerable number of zeros, and it would seem that the procedure is practicable. However, the data-handling problems involved when handling information about hundreds of thousands of stars becomes formidable. Also, everyone knows about problems of ill-conditioning which occur when solving large systems of linear equations. These are purely numerical difficulties caused by round-off error in the computer. The applied scientist dealing with this type of problem has to balance the increased accuracy obtained by the above method of approach against the inevitable and inherent inaccuracies that creep in when the system of equations becomes too large.

To conclude this section we remind the reader that the above problem is a good example of the way in which matrix notation clarifies the structure of a complicated set of equations. Moreover, it is only because automatic computers are available that we think of doing the problem in the way described in the second half of this section.

Chapter 11

Some Applications of Linear Dependence, Elementary Row Operations, and Rank

11.1 Mathematical Prerequisites

In this chapter we present some applications of the ideas of linear dependence, elementary row operations, and rank. It is assumed that the reader is familiar with the following concepts.

A set of matrices $\mathbf{v}_1, \mathbf{v}_2, \ldots, \mathbf{v}_n$ (which, in particular, may be row or column vectors) are said to be linearly dependent if there exists numbers $\alpha_1, \alpha_2, \ldots, \alpha_n$, not all zero, such that

$$\alpha_1 \mathbf{v}_1 + \alpha_2 \mathbf{v}_2 + \cdots + \alpha_n \mathbf{v}_n = \mathbf{0}.$$

Three types of elementary operations or transformations on the rows of a general $m \times n$ matrix can be defined:

1. Interchange of two rows.
2. Multiplication of the elements of any row by a nonzero scalar.
3. Addition to any row of a multiple of any other row.

If $\mathbf{A}$ is a nonsingular square matrix (that is, det $\mathbf{A} \neq 0$), then $\mathbf{A}$ can be converted into the identity matrix by elementary row operations alone. If $\mathbf{A}$ is an $m \times n$ matrix with rank r ($\neq 0$), $r \leq \min(m, n)$, then $\mathbf{A}$ can be transformed, by elementary row operations and column interchanges, into a matrix of the form

$$\begin{bmatrix} \mathbf{I}_r & \mathbf{B}_r \\ \mathbf{0}_1 & \mathbf{0}_2 \end{bmatrix},$$

where $\mathbf{I}_r$ is the $r \times r$ unit matrix, $\mathbf{B}_r$ is an $r \times (n - r)$ matrix, and $\mathbf{0}_1$ and $\mathbf{0}_2$ are, respectively, $(m - r) \times r$ and $(m - r) \times (n - r)$ null matrices. (If elementary column operations are allowed, we can replace $\mathbf{B}_r$ by a null matrix.)

If we have a set of m homogeneous equations in n unknowns, represented by $\mathbf{A}\mathbf{x} = \mathbf{0}$, where $m \le n$, and $\mathbf{A}$ has rank r, the equations possess exactly $n - r$ sets of linearly independent (nonzero) solutions.

11.2   Examples from Dimensional Analysis[1]

Engineering Context: Fluid flow ; heat transfer in tubes.

Mathematics Used: Linear dependence and elementary row operations on a matrix.

A typical problem that arises in dimensional analysis is the following. A fluid-flow situation depends upon the velocity V, density ρ, diameter D, gravity g, and viscosity μ. In terms of the usual fundamental quantities mass M, length L, and time T, the dimensions of the physical quantities are

Quantity:	V	ρ	D	g	μ
Dimensions:	LT^{-1}	ML^{-3}	L	LT^{-2}	$ML^{-1}T^{-1}$

It is required to find whether it is possible to formulate nondimensional products of the form

$$V^a \rho^b D^c g^d \mu^e,$$

and, if so, to find as many independent products as possible. By saying that the product is nondimensional, we mean that when each quantity is replaced by its dimensions, as shown in the above table, then the sum of the exponents of each dimension is zero. In other words, we require

$$(LT^{-1})^a (ML^{-3})^b L^c (LT^{-2})^d (ML^{-1}T^{-1})^e = M^0 L^0 T^0.$$

Hence the following three equations must be satisfied:

(From powers of M)	$b + e$	$= 0,$
(From powers of L)	$a - 3b + c + d - e$	$= 0,$ (11.1)
(From powers of T)	$-a - 2d - e$	$= 0.$

There are three equations in five unknowns, and the number of independent solutions depends on the rank of the matrix of coefficients,

$$\begin{bmatrix} 0 & 1 & 0 & 0 & 1 \\ 1 & -3 & 1 & 1 & -1 \\ -1 & 0 & 0 & -2 & -1 \end{bmatrix}.$$

---

[1] The first example in this section was submitted by the School of Engineering, Mississippi State University, State College, Miss. (through Dean H. C. Simrall), and the second by John Mahoney, Department of Chemical Engineering, West Virginia University, Morgantown, W. Va.

If we interchange the first and second rows, and add multiples of the first and second rows to the last row to reduce the first two elements of the last row to zero, the matrix becomes

$$\begin{bmatrix} 1 & -3 & 1 & 1 & -1 \\ 0 & 1 & 0 & 0 & 1 \\ 0 & 0 & 1 & -1 & 1 \end{bmatrix}. \qquad (11.2)$$

There are three nonzero rows, so the rank of this matrix is 3, and the original equations have $5 - 3 = 2$ independent solutions. Two unknowns in (11.1) can be chosen arbitrarily, provided the 3×3 matrix left by omitting the columns corresponding to these unknowns in (11.2) is nonsingular. In this case the three remaining unknowns can be expressed in terms of the two arbitrarily chosen unknowns. Thus from examination of the matrix it is clear that it is not permissible to choose b and e arbitrarily (since the matrix obtained by omitting the second and fifth columns in (11.2) is obviously singular), but we can choose d and e arbitrarily. If we set $d = 0$, $e = 1$, and $d = 1$, $e = 0$ as two separate selections, this results in the two combinations

$$\frac{V\rho D}{\mu} \quad \text{and} \quad \frac{Dg}{V^2}.$$

The first combination is the well-known *Reynolds number*, and the second is the inverse of the *Froude number*.

As a second example, consider the heating or cooling of a fluid flowing through a heated or cooled tube. The heat-transfer coefficient h is defined as

$$Q = hA(\theta_1 - \theta_2), \qquad (11.3)$$

where Q is the quantity of heat per unit time transferred from temperature θ_1 to θ_2 and A is the area. Quantity of heat has the dimensions of energy, ML^2T^{-2}, so if $[h]$ denotes the dimensions of h and Θ denotes the independent-dimensional-quantity temperature, (11.3) gives

$$ML^2T^{-3} = [h]L^2\Theta \quad \text{or} \quad [h] = MT^{-3}\Theta^{-1}.$$

We assume we are considering a situation in which the heat transfer is governed by a thin film of fluid near the surface of the tube. The heat conductivity k of the tube is therefore involved. The film thickness depends on the mass velocity G of the fluid, tube diameter D, and viscosity μ. The bulk temperature of the stream depends on the specific heat c_p, which should therefore also be included. The dimensions of these quantities are

Quantity:	G	D	μ	c_p	k
Dimension:	$ML^{-2}T^{-1}$	L	$ML^{-1}T^{-1}$	$L^2T^{-2}\Theta^{-1}$	$MLT^{-3}\Theta^{-1}$

The discussion up to this point has been concerned entirely with the physical aspects of the problem.

We now wish to form as many independent dimensionless products of the following form as possible:

$$h^a G^b D^c \mu^d c_p^e k^f.$$

The procedure described previously leads to the following equations:

$$
\begin{array}{llr}
\text{(From powers of } M) & a + b + d + f & = 0, \\
\text{(From powers of } L) & -2b + c - d + 2e + f & = 0, \\
\text{(From powers of } T) & -3a - b - d - 2e - 3f & = 0, \\
\text{(From powers of } \Theta) & -a - e - f & = 0.
\end{array}
\qquad (11.4)
$$

The matrix of coefficients is

$$
\begin{bmatrix}
1 & 1 & 0 & 1 & 0 & 1 \\
0 & -2 & 1 & -1 & 2 & 1 \\
-3 & -1 & 0 & -1 & -2 & -3 \\
-1 & 0 & 0 & 0 & -1 & -1
\end{bmatrix}
$$

By systematic row operations, using the first row to reduce the first elements in the third and fourth rows to zero, and so on, this matrix can be reduced to the form

$$
\begin{bmatrix}
1 & 1 & 0 & 1 & 0 & 1 \\
0 & -2 & 1 & -1 & 2 & 1 \\
0 & 0 & 1 & 1 & 0 & 1 \\
0 & 0 & 0 & 0 & 0 & 0
\end{bmatrix}.
$$

Further row operations produce a diagonal matrix in the upper left,

$$
\begin{bmatrix}
1 & 0 & 0 & 0 & 1 & 1 \\
0 & -2 & 0 & -2 & 2 & 0 \\
0 & 0 & 1 & 1 & 0 & 1 \\
0 & 0 & 0 & 0 & 0 & 0
\end{bmatrix}.
\qquad (11.5)
$$

The rank of the matrix is 3, so the original equations (11.4) have $6 - 3$ independent solutions. In fact, from (11.5),

$$
\begin{aligned}
a &= -e - f, \\
b &= -d + e, \\
c &= -d - f,
\end{aligned}
$$

and d, e, and f can be chosen arbitrarily. If we choose $d = 1$, $e = f = 0$, we have $a = 0$, $b = -1$, and $c = -1$. Similarly, $d = f = 0$, $e = 1$ gives $a = -1$,

$b = 1$, and $c = 0$, and $d = e = 0, f = 1$ gives $a = -1, b = 0$, and $c = -1$.
These yield the dimensionless quantities

$$\alpha = \frac{\mu}{GD}, \qquad \beta = \frac{c_p G}{h}, \qquad \gamma = \frac{k}{hD}.$$

Equivalent sets are obtained by multiplying or dividing these quantities. In engineering work the quantities usually used are

$$\frac{1}{\alpha} = \frac{GD}{\mu}, \qquad \frac{\alpha\beta}{\gamma} = \frac{c_p \mu}{k},$$

and either $1/\beta$ or $1/\gamma$.

Of course, the results in this section could have been obtained (and usually are obtained) without introducing matrices or the idea of the rank of a matrix, simply by solving the sets of equations (11.1) and (11.4) directly. The virtue of the matrix approach is that it gives a clear idea of the structure of the calculation and a systematic calculation procedure. As usual, the more complicated the situation, the more useful the matrix method of approach will be.

11.3   An Example from Radiative Heat Transfer[2]

Mathematics Used: Gaussian elimination.

We consider radiation of heat from the walls into the interior of a cylindrical enclosure. Three independent surfaces are involved: the two flat ends we call surfaces 1 and 2, and the curved surface 3. We are interested in the *shape factors*, defined as the fraction of the total radiant energy leaving surface a that is incident on surface b, denoted by F_{ab}. In this example there are three surfaces, so there are $3^2 = 9$ shape factors. The shape factors are quantities that could be determined from the geometry of the enclosure by integration. However, relations exist between the various shape factors, and it is not necessary to compute all the shape factors independent of each other. By linear algebra it is possible to find easily the maximum number of independent shape factors—that is, the minimum number it is necessary to compute.

In the example of the cylindrical enclosure we have the following relations:

1. Since all the energy leaving a surface is incident on one of the surfaces of the enclosure,

$$F_{11} + F_{12} + F_{13} = 1, \tag{11.6}$$

$$F_{21} + F_{22} + F_{23} = 1, \tag{11.7}$$

$$F_{31} + F_{32} + F_{33} = 1. \tag{11.8}$$

---

[2] Submitted by the School of Engineering, Mississippi State University, State College, Miss., through Dean H. C. Simrall.

2. Since surfaces 1 and 2 are flat, they cannot receive radiation from themselves. Hence

$$F_{11} = 0, \tag{11.9}$$

$$F_{22} = 0. \tag{11.10}$$

3. Reciprocal relations exist. We need to know the areas of the various surfaces. If A_1 and A_2 are the areas of the flat ends, A_3 the area of the cylindrical surface, r the radius, and l the length of the cylinder, then

$$A_1 = A_2 = \pi r^2, \qquad A_3 = 2\pi r l.$$

The reciprocity relations are

$$A_1 F_{12} = A_2 F_{21} \qquad \text{or} \qquad F_{12} = F_{21}, \tag{11.11}$$

$$A_1 F_{13} = A_3 F_{31} \qquad \text{or} \qquad F_{13} = \left(\frac{2l}{r}\right) F_{31}, \tag{11.12}$$

$$A_2 F_{23} = A_3 F_{32} \qquad \text{or} \qquad F_{23} = \left(\frac{2l}{r}\right) F_{32}. \tag{11.13}$$

4. From symmetry,

$$F_{13} = F_{23}, \tag{11.14}$$

$$F_{31} = F_{32}. \tag{11.15}$$

These equations are 10 relations among 9 unknowns. It is necessary to check that the equations are consistent, and to express the 9 shape factors in terms of as small a number of independent shape factors as possible. In a complicated example it would probably be convenient to use matrix notation and perform elementary row operations to reduce the matrix to canonical form. However, in this example it is simple to solve the equations directly. From (11.6) and (11.9),

$$F_{13} = 1 - F_{12}.$$

From (11.7), (11.10), and (11.11),

$$F_{23} = 1 - F_{21} = 1 - F_{12}.$$

From (11.8),

$$F_{33} = 1 - 2F_{31} = 1 - \left(\frac{r}{l}\right) F_{13} = 1 - \left(\frac{r}{l}\right)(1 - F_{12}).$$

By proceeding this way, all the shape factors can be expressed in terms of F_{12}, and it is readily checked that the resulting expressions satisfy all the equations. Hence the above analysis shows that if F_{12} is determined by some method that lies outside the scope of the present considerations, all the other shape factors can be deduced.

11.4   Linear Dependence and Chemical Reactions (Stoichiometry)[3]

Mathematics Used: Determination of the rank of a matrix by elementary row operations.

Comment: The numerical example at the end of the section illustrates that, if round-off errors are present, numbers below a certain limit must be interpreted as zero.

The chemical reaction $A + 2B \rightleftharpoons C + D$ stands for the reaction in which 1 molecule of A and 2 of B react together to form 1 of C and 1 of D. A molecule has a definite mass called the *molecular weight*, and a number of grams (or pounds) of a substance equal to its molecular weight is called 1 gram (or pound) mole. It follows that 1 mole of any substance contains the same number of molecules—a rather large one—and hence the chemical equation might be interpreted: 1 mole of A reacts with 2 moles of B to give 1 mole each of C and D. It is convenient to write the reaction equation symbolically in the form

$$\alpha_1 A_1 + \alpha_2 A_2 + \alpha_3 A_3 + \alpha_4 A_4 = 0, \tag{11.16}$$

where A_1, A_2, A_3, and A_4 stand for the chemical species A, B, C, and D and the α_i are the *stoichiometric coefficients*; that is, they are simply the coefficients of the A_i in (11.16). Positive values are given to coefficients of species that are regarded as products of the reaction, negative values to species that are used up. In the above case we could take $\alpha_1 = -1$, $\alpha_2 = -2$, $\alpha_3 = 1$, and $\alpha_4 = 1$. These coefficients are not, of course, unique, since they can be multiplied by any constant factor. However their ratios are unique.

As an example consider a mixture of CO, H_2, and CH_4 fed to a furnace where it is burned with oxygen to form CO, CO_2, and H_2O. To make sure no reaction is overlooked, we write down all the reactions that could possibly be relevant, and obtain

$$CO + \tfrac{1}{2}O_2 \rightarrow CO_2 \qquad \text{(only reaction of CO)},$$
$$H_2 + \tfrac{1}{2}O_2 \rightarrow H_2O \qquad \text{(only reaction of } H_2\text{)},$$
$$CH_4 + 2O_2 \rightarrow CO_2 + 2H_2O \qquad \text{(complete combustion of } CH_4\text{)},$$
$$CH_4 + \tfrac{3}{2}O_2 \rightarrow CO + 2H_2O \qquad \text{(partial combustion of } CH_4\text{)}.$$

We wish to find out whether any of these equations are simply combinations of the others. The answer in this particular case is evident by inspection, but

[3] The first example in this section was contributed by John Mahoney, Department of Chemical Engineering, West Virginia University, Morgantown, W. Va. The remainder of the section is based on material contributed by Rutherford Aris, Department of Chemical Engineering, University of Minnesota, Minneapolis, Minn. A reference is R. Aris and R. H. S. Mah, The Independence of Chemical Reactions, *Ind. Eng. Chem. Fundamentals*, **2**, 90–94 (1963).

the method we use is of general applicability. We write the formulas as in (11.16)

$$-CO - \tfrac{1}{2}O_2 + CO_2 = 0,$$
$$-H_2 - \tfrac{1}{2}O_2 + H_2O = 0,$$
$$-CH_4 - 2O_2 + CO_2 + 2H_2O = 0,$$
$$-CH_4 - \tfrac{3}{2}O_2 + CO + 2H_2O = 0. \tag{11.17}$$

We then form the matrix of coefficients:

$$\begin{array}{cccccc} CO & H_2 & CH_4 & O_2 & CO_2 & H_2O \end{array}$$

$$\begin{bmatrix} -1 & 0 & 0 & -\tfrac{1}{2} & 1 & 0 \\ 0 & -1 & 0 & -\tfrac{1}{2} & 0 & 1 \\ 0 & 0 & -1 & -2 & 1 & 2 \\ 1 & 0 & -1 & -\tfrac{3}{2} & 0 & 2 \end{bmatrix}. \tag{11.18}$$

We wish to find the rank of this matrix. By inspection we see that the 3×3 matrix on the upper left has a nonzero determinant and zeros below the diagonal. We reduce the first three elements in the last row to zero by adding the first row to the fourth and subtracting the third row. It is found that all the elements in the resulting fourth row are zero, so the rank of the matrix is 3. Only three independent reactions are needed to describe the reaction system, and these could be taken as the first three equations in (11.17). It is left to the reader to show that alternatively the first or third equations could be deleted from the set, but that the second equation cannot be omitted. [Explain these statements in terms of the structure of the matrix (11.18).]

Linear algebra is useful in answering several other questions connected with equations such as (11.16) or (11.17). Suppose first, for simplicity, that only one reaction is producing the composition changes in a mixture of S species $A_1, A_2, \ldots, A_S$. Let $a_1, a_2, \ldots, a_S$ be concentrations of each species in moles per unit volume at a given time. Let $a_i(0)$ denote the initial concentrations. Suppose the volume does not change during the reaction. The change in the number of moles of each species will be proportional to the stoichiometric coefficients α_j, where the reaction is written symbolically as

$$\sum_{j=1}^{S} \alpha_j A_j = 0.$$

This means that

$$\frac{a_j(t) - a_j(0)}{\alpha_j} = \xi(t), \text{ say, for all } j,$$

where this defines the parameter ξ which is called the *extent* of the reaction.

If R independent reactions are involved,

$$\sum_{j=1}^{S} \alpha_{ij} A_j = 0, \qquad i = 1, 2, \ldots, R, \tag{11.19}$$

where α_{ij} is the stoichiometric coefficient for the jth species in the ith reaction, and if c_{ij} denotes the change in concentration of the jth species due to the ith reaction, the c_{ij} are proportional to the α_{ij} for any given reaction (that is, for a given i):

$$c_{ij} = \xi_i \alpha_{ij},$$

where the ξ_i are constants called the *extents* of the ith reaction. Also,

$$a_j = a_j(0) + \sum_{i=1}^{R} c_{ij}$$

$$= a_j(0) + \sum_{i=1}^{R} \xi_i \alpha_{ij}, \quad j = 1, 2, \ldots, S. \tag{11.20}$$

By a set of reactions equivalent to the original R independent reactions in (11.19), we mean a new set of reactions from which (11.19) can be recovered by taking sums of multiples of the equations for the new set of reactions. For instance, when considering the reactions (11.17), we showed that the first, second, fourth, the first, second, third, and the second, third, fourth equations all give equivalent sets of reactions. We can ask the following questions.

1. What reactions are equivalent to (11.19) and how are the extents of the new sets of equations related to the extents of the original set?

To answer this let $\boldsymbol{\alpha} = [\alpha_{ij}]$, the $R \times S$ matrix whose (i, j)th element is α_{ij}; let $\mathbf{A}$, $\mathbf{a}$, and $\mathbf{a}(0)$ be $S \times 1$ column vectors with jth elements A_j, a_j, and $a_j(0)$, respectively; and let $\boldsymbol{\xi}$ be the $R \times 1$ column vector whose ith element is ξ_i. Then (11.19) and (11.20) can be written, in matrix notation,

$$\boldsymbol{\alpha}\mathbf{A} = \mathbf{0}, \tag{11.21}$$

$$\mathbf{a}^T = \mathbf{a}^T(0) + \boldsymbol{\xi}^T\boldsymbol{\alpha}. \tag{11.22}$$

The reactions (11.19) are independent, so the rank of $\boldsymbol{\alpha}$ is R. Denote an equivalent set of reactions by $\boldsymbol{\alpha}^*\mathbf{A} = \mathbf{0}$, where $\boldsymbol{\alpha}^*$ is an $R \times S$ matrix with rank R. If this set of equations is to be equivalent to the original set (11.21), there must exist an $R \times R$ nonsingular matrix $\mathbf{U}$ such that $\mathbf{U}\boldsymbol{\alpha}^*\mathbf{A} = \mathbf{0} \equiv \boldsymbol{\alpha}\mathbf{A} = \mathbf{0}$, identically in $\mathbf{A}$, which implies that

$$\mathbf{U}\boldsymbol{\alpha}^* = \boldsymbol{\alpha}. \tag{11.23}$$

Introducing this in (11.22) we see that

$$\mathbf{a}^T = \mathbf{a}^T(0) + \boldsymbol{\xi}^T\mathbf{U}\boldsymbol{\alpha}^* = \mathbf{a}^T(0) + (\mathbf{U}^T\boldsymbol{\xi})^T\boldsymbol{\alpha}^*.$$

Hence the new $R \times 1$ column vector of extents is $\mathbf{U}^T\boldsymbol{\xi}$.

2. What linear combinations of the concentrations (that is, sums of the form $\gamma_1 a_1 + \gamma_2 a_2 + \cdots + \gamma_S a_S$, for suitable constants γ_j) are left unchanged by the set of reactions, and how many combinations of this kind are there?

To answer this let γ be an $S \times 1$ column vector orthogonal to the rows of α, that is, such that

$$\alpha\gamma = 0. \tag{11.24}$$

Postmultiplying (11.22) by γ we have

$$a^T\gamma = a^T(0)\gamma.$$

If the jth element of γ is γ_j, this means that the quantity

$$\sum_{j=1}^{S} \gamma_j a_j = \sum_{j=1}^{S} \gamma_j a_j(0)$$

is an invariant of the reaction. Since α is an $R \times S$ matrix of rank R, there will be $S - R$ independent sets of solutions of (11.24), because (11.24) can be regarded as a set of homogeneous simultaneous linear equations for the unknown vector γ.

To conclude this section, suppose that we do not know the number of independent reactions R in a system for which (11.20) is true,

$$a_j(t) - a_j(0) = \sum_{i=1}^{R} \xi_i(t)\alpha_{ij}, \qquad j = 1, 2, \ldots, S, \tag{11.25}$$

where the α_{ij} are, of course, constants, independent of time t. We wish to determine the value of R from experimental results. Let $\mathbf{B}$ denote the $R \times S$ matrix with (i, j)th element α_{ij}. Let $\mathbf{a}$ denote the $S \times 1$ column matrix with jth elements $a_j(t) - a_j(0)$, and let $\mathbf{e}$ denote the $R \times 1$ column matrix with ith element $\xi_i(t)$. Then, in matrix notation, (11.25) is

$$\mathbf{a} = \mathbf{B}^T\mathbf{e}. \tag{11.26}$$

The matrix $\mathbf{a}$ can be determined experimentally for any required value of time t. Suppose $\mathbf{a}$ is determined experimentally for $Q = S + K$ $(K \geq 0)$ values of time t, giving (known) vectors $\mathbf{a}_1, \mathbf{a}_2, \ldots, \mathbf{a}_Q$, and let the corresponding (unknown) vectors $\mathbf{e}$ be denoted $\mathbf{e}_1, \mathbf{e}_2, \ldots, \mathbf{e}_Q$. Let $\mathbf{F}$ and $\mathbf{E}$ denote the $S \times Q$ and $R \times Q$ matrices whose rth columns are $\mathbf{a}_r$ and $\mathbf{e}_r$, respectively. Then we have, from (11.26),

$$\mathbf{F} = \mathbf{B}^T\mathbf{E},$$

where $\mathbf{F}$ is known and $\mathbf{B}$ and $\mathbf{E}$ are unknown. By hypothesis the rank of $\mathbf{B}$ is R (since there are R *independent* reactions). The matrix $\mathbf{E}$ has R rows, so its rank must be less than or equal to R. However, the rank of $\mathbf{E}$ cannot be less than R since the last row of E could then be written as a linear combination of the first $R - 1$ rows; that is, for each of the times t_k $(k = 1$ to $Q)$ for which measurements have been made we could write

$$\xi_k(t_k) = \sum_{i=1}^{R-1} c_i \xi_i(t_k),$$

where the c_i are constants independent of the t_k. Substituting this result in (11.25), with $t = t_k$ ($k = 1$ to Q), we find

$$a_j(t_k) - a_j(0) = \sum_{i=1}^{R-1} \xi_i(t_k)(\alpha_{ij} + c_i \alpha_{Rj}),$$

which means that there are only $R - 1$ independent reactions, which contradicts the original assumption of R independent reactions. Hence the rank of $\mathbf{E}$ is R.

Summing up the situation at this stage of the argument, we have

$$\mathbf{F} = \mathbf{B}^T \mathbf{E},$$

where $\mathbf{F}$ is a known $S \times Q$ matrix, $\mathbf{B}^T$ an unknown $S \times R$ matrix, and $\mathbf{E}$ an unknown $R \times Q$ matrix, with $S \geq R$ and $Q \geq R$. The ranks of $\mathbf{B}^T$ and $\mathbf{E}$ are both R. We now assert that the rank of $\mathbf{F}$ is R. For it follows from the definition of rank that elementary row operations on $\mathbf{B}^T$ and column operations on E can be used to reduce $\mathbf{B}^T$ and $\mathbf{E}$ to the forms

$$\begin{bmatrix} \mathbf{G} \\ \mathbf{0} \end{bmatrix} \quad \text{and} \quad [\mathbf{H} \quad \mathbf{0}],$$

respectively, where $\mathbf{G}$ and $\mathbf{H}$ are nonsingular. This means that elementary row and column operations can be used to reduce the product $\mathbf{B}^T \mathbf{E}$ to the form

$$\begin{bmatrix} \mathbf{G} \\ \mathbf{0} \end{bmatrix} [\mathbf{H} \quad \mathbf{0}] = \begin{bmatrix} \mathbf{GH} & \mathbf{0} \\ \mathbf{0} & \mathbf{0} \end{bmatrix}.$$

The matrix $\mathbf{GH}$ is nonsingular, so the rank of $\mathbf{B}^T \mathbf{E}$, that is, $\mathbf{F}$, is R. The matrix $\mathbf{F}$ is known, so its rank can be found, and thus the unknown number of reactions R can be found.

As an example, consider the following set of observations made at five instants of time on a reaction involving five species,[4]

$$F = \begin{bmatrix} 1.02 & 2.03 & 4.20 & 6.63 & 10.21 \\ -1.25 & -2.35 & -4.64 & -7.59 & -12.39 \\ -1.17 & -1.96 & -3.46 & -6.21 & -11.71 \\ 0.45 & 0.62 & 0.91 & 1.93 & 4.40 \\ 0.44 & 0.61 & 0.89 & 1.95 & 4.41 \end{bmatrix}.$$

These are experimental results with errors of at most 0.01.

To find the rank, we reduce the matrix to upper triangular form by elementary row operations and column interchanges, choosing the largest

[4] The figures are taken from R. Aris and R. H. S. Mah, *Ind. Eng. Chem. Fundamentals*, **2**, 90–94 (1936); these authors obtained the original matrix from results by J. Beek, given in *Advances in Chemical Engineering*, Vol. 3, Academic, New York, 1962, pp. 204–272.

pivot at each stage. The first step is to bring the numerically largest element (-12.39) to the top left-hand position in the matrix, giving

$$\begin{bmatrix} -12.39 & -1.25 & -2.35 & -4.64 & -7.59 \\ 10.21 & 1.02 & 2.03 & 4.20 & 6.63 \\ -11.71 & -1.17 & -1.96 & -3.46 & -6.21 \\ 4.40 & 0.45 & 0.62 & 0.91 & 1.93 \\ 4.41 & 0.44 & 0.61 & 0.89 & 1.95 \end{bmatrix}. \qquad (11.27)$$

We now divide the first row by -12.39 and use the result to reduce the remaining elements in the first column to zero, obtaining

$$\begin{bmatrix} 1 & 0.101 & 0.190 & 0.375 & 0.613 \\ 0 & -0.010 & 0.094 & 0.376 & 0.376 \\ 0 & 0.011 & 0.261 & 0.925 & 0.963 \\ 0 & 0.006 & -0.215 & -0.738 & -0.765 \\ 0 & -0.005 & -0.226 & -0.762 & -0.752 \end{bmatrix}. \qquad (11.28)$$

If the elements in the matrix (11.27) are denoted by a_{ij}, the typical element in (11.28) is given by

$$a_{ij} - \frac{a_{i1}a_{1j}}{a_{11}}, \qquad i > 1, j > 1.$$

If the largest error in any a_{ij} is less than ϵ, it is easy to see that the largest error in the elements of (11.28) is therefore less than

$$\left(1 + \left|\frac{a_{i1}}{a_{11}}\right|\right)\left(1 + \left|\frac{a_{1j}}{a_{11}}\right|\right)\epsilon.$$

In the above example, the maximum value of this quantity is

$$\left(1 + \frac{11.71}{12.39}\right)\left(1 + \frac{7.59}{12.39}\right)(0.01) \approx 0.031.$$

Hence the elements of (11.28) in the last four rows have errors of at most 0.031.

The above procedure is repeated, bringing the largest element (0.963) into the second row–second column position, dividing the new second row by 0.963, and using the result to reduce the remaining elements in the second column, below the diagonal, to zero. The result is

$$\begin{bmatrix} 1 & 0.613 & 0.101 & 0.190 & 0.375 \\ 0 & 1 & 0.102 & 0.271 & 0.961 \\ 0 & 0 & -0.015 & -0.008 & 0.016 \\ 0 & 0 & 0.015 & 0.007 & -0.003 \\ 0 & 0 & 0.004 & -0.023 & -0.040 \end{bmatrix}.$$

The maximum possible error in the elements in the last three rows can be investigated as before, and is found to be 0.109. The elements in the last three rows are all less than this quantity, so to all intents and purposes they are zero. Hence the rank of the matrix is 2. The implication is that there are only two independent reactions in the original chemical process.

The lesson of the above example, from a purely mathematical point of view, is that when errors are present in the elements of a matrix, we cannot directly apply the strict method for determination of rank r—that row operations on the matrix will reduce all except r of the rows to zero. The same comment, of course, applies to the practical determination of the rank of a matrix with exact coefficients, if rounding errors are introduced during the reduction to canonical form.

(The analysis leading to a rank of 2 in the above example is relatively crude. The author of this book has not found a satisfactory treatment in the literature to the problem of the determination of rank when errors are present.)

11.5   The Reduction of Systems of Differential Equations to Canonical Form[5]

Mathematics Used: Elementary row operations on matrices.

Comment: Matrices are often useful in elucidating the structure of complicated systems.

The idea of reducing a matrix to a standard, or *canonical*, form by row operations can be applied to simplify systems of differential equations. We illustrate by considering two examples that arise in connection with chemical reactions.

A chemical reaction is governed by the equations

$$A_1 + A_2 \xrightarrow{k_1} A_3,$$

$$A_3 + A_2 \xrightarrow{k_2} A_4,$$

$$A_5 + A_2 \xrightarrow{k_3} A_6,$$

$$A_6 + A_2 \xrightarrow{k_4} A_7,$$

where A_4 is the desired product and A_6 and A_7 are undesirable byproducts. These reactions are assumed to proceed at constant volume and temperature.

[5] The material in this section and the next is contained in a paper by W. F. Ames, Canonical Forms for Nonlinear Kinetic Differential Equations, *Ind. & Eng. Chem. Fundamentals*, **1**, 214–218 (1962), © American Chemical Society; used by permission. Submitted from the School of Engineering, University of Delaware, Newark, Del.

Furthermore, it is assumed that the rate of change of the concentration of each substance in any given reaction is proportional to the product of the concentrations of the substances being used up in the reaction, the same rate constant applying to each substance in any given reaction. If x_i is the concentration of A_i in moles per unit volume and k_i is the rate constant in liters per gram-mole second, the differential equations for the chemical reactions are

$$\frac{dx_1}{dt} = -k_1 x_1 x_2, \tag{11.29}$$

$$\frac{dx_2}{dt} = -k_1 x_1 x_2 - k_2 x_2 x_3 - k_3 x_2 x_5 - k_4 x_2 x_6, \tag{11.30}$$

$$\frac{dx_3}{dt} = k_1 x_1 x_2 - k_2 x_2 x_3, \tag{11.31}$$

$$\frac{dx_4}{dt} = k_2 x_2 x_3, \tag{11.32}$$

$$\frac{dx_5}{dt} = -k_3 x_2 x_5, \tag{11.33}$$

$$\frac{dx_6}{dt} = k_3 x_2 x_5 - k_4 x_2 x_6, \tag{11.34}$$

$$\frac{dx_7}{dt} = k_4 x_2 x_6. \tag{11.35}$$

The system has four independent reactions, so only four independent equations are required to describe the reaction. It is often possible to find the redundant equations by inspection, but in complicated cases it is usually preferable to proceed systematically as described below. It is useful to bear in mind the "dead-end" variables—the products of the reaction that do not themselves react. In this case the dead-end variables are clearly x_4 and x_7.

We arrange this system in matrix form, symbolically, in the following way:

$$
\begin{array}{cccc}
d/dt & x_1x_2 & x_2x_3 & x_2x_5 & x_2x_6
\end{array}
$$

$$
\begin{bmatrix} x_1 \\ x_2 \\ x_3 \\ x_4 \\ x_5 \\ x_6 \\ x_7 \end{bmatrix}
=
\begin{bmatrix}
-k_1 & 0 & 0 & 0 \\
-k_1 & -k_2 & -k_3 & -k_4 \\
k_1 & -k_2 & 0 & 0 \\
0 & k_2 & 0 & 0 \\
0 & 0 & -k_3 & 0 \\
0 & 0 & k_3 & -k_4 \\
0 & 0 & 0 & k_4
\end{bmatrix}. \tag{11.36}
$$

We now wish to reduce the matrix on the right to diagonal form by elementary row operations. The element in the upper left corner is nonzero. (If it had been zero, a nonzero element could have been transferred into this position by interchanging two rows.) The remaining nonzero elements in the first column can be reduced to zero by adding or subtracting elements of the first row. Thus (11.36) becomes

$$
\frac{d}{dt}
\begin{bmatrix}
x_1 \\
x_2 - x_1 \\
x_3 + x_1 \\
x_4 \\
x_5 \\
x_6 \\
x_7
\end{bmatrix}
=
\begin{array}{cccc}
x_1x_2 & x_2x_3 & x_2x_5 & x_2x_6 \\
\end{array}
\begin{bmatrix}
-k_1 & 0 & 0 & 0 \\
0 & -k_2 & -k_3 & -k_4 \\
0 & -k_2 & 0 & 0 \\
0 & k_2 & 0 & 0 \\
0 & 0 & -k_3 & 0 \\
0 & 0 & k_3 & -k_4 \\
0 & 0 & 0 & k_4
\end{bmatrix}.
\tag{11.37}
$$

By inspection we see that the simplest way to obtain a diagonal matrix (remembering that we should not consider the dead-end variables x_4 and x_7) is to use the third row in (11.37) as the second row in a new matrix, the fifth row in (11.37) as the new third row, and the sum of the fifth and sixth rows in (11.37) as the new fourth row. This gives the new system,

$$
\frac{d}{dt}
\begin{bmatrix}
x_1 \\
x_3 + x_1 \\
x_5 \\
x_5 + x_6 \\
x_2 - x_1 \\
x_4 \\
x_7
\end{bmatrix}
=
\begin{array}{cccc}
x_1x_2 & x_2x_3 & x_2x_5 & x_2x_6 \\
\end{array}
\begin{bmatrix}
-k_1 & 0 & 0 & 0 \\
0 & -k_2 & 0 & 0 \\
0 & 0 & -k_3 & 0 \\
0 & 0 & 0 & -k_4 \\
0 & -k_2 & -k_3 & -k_4 \\
0 & k_2 & 0 & 0 \\
0 & 0 & 0 & k_4
\end{bmatrix}.
$$

On reducing the last three rows to zero, we finally obtain

$$
\frac{d}{dt}
\begin{bmatrix}
x_1 \\
x_1 + x_3 \\
x_1 \\
x_5 + x_6 \\
X \\
x_1 + x_3 + x_4 \\
x_5 + x_6 + x_7
\end{bmatrix}
=
\begin{array}{cccc}
x_1x_2 & x_2x_3 & x_2x_5 & x_2x_6 \\
\end{array}
\begin{bmatrix}
-k_1 & 0 & 0 & 0 \\
0 & -k_2 & 0 & 0 \\
0 & 0 & -k_3 & 0 \\
0 & 0 & 0 & -k_4 \\
0 & 0 & 0 & 0 \\
0 & 0 & 0 & 0 \\
0 & 0 & 0 & 0
\end{bmatrix},
\tag{11.38}
$$

where $X = -2x_1 + x_2 - x_3 - 2x_5 - x_6$.

The fifth equation is simply $dX/dt = 0$, or $X = $ constant,

$$-2x_1 + x_2 - x_3 - 2x_5 - x_6 = c_2.$$

Similarly, the last two equations give

$$x_1 + x_3 + x_4 = c_4, \qquad x_5 + x_6 + x_7 = c_7,$$

where c_2, c_4, and c_7 are constants that can be determined from the initial conditions.

The remaining equations in (11.38) are

$$\frac{dx_1}{dt} = -k_1 x_1 x_2, \tag{11.39}$$

$$\frac{d(x_1 + x_3)}{dt} = -k_2 x_2 x_3, \tag{11.40}$$

$$\frac{dx_5}{dt} = -k_3 x_2 x_5, \tag{11.41}$$

$$\frac{d(x_5 + x_6)}{dt} = -k_4 x_2 x_6. \tag{11.42}$$

These are the four independent equations that we wish to find. They can be solved by dividing the equations in pairs. Thus from (11.39) and (11.40) we obtain

$$\frac{dx_3}{dx_1} + 1 = \left(\frac{k_2}{k_1}\right)\left(\frac{x_3}{x_1}\right).$$

This can be solved by standard techniques to yield a relation between x_1 and x_3. Relations between x_1 and x_5 can be obtained from (11.39) and (11.41) and between x_5 and x_6 from (11.41) and (11.42). Details can be found in the paper by Ames.[6]

11.6   Reduction of a Nonlinear System of Differential Equations to Canonical Form

Mathematics Used: Elementary row operations on matrices.

Although the set of equations (11.29) to (11.35) were apparently nonlinear, they can be reduced to linear form by introducing a new independent variable τ defined by setting $d\tau/dt = x_2$. We now show that the same method can be applied to more complicated systems of nonlinear equations. An example

[6] W. F. Ames, Canonical Forms for Nonlinear Kinetic Differential Equations, *Ind. & Eng. Chem. Fundamentals*, **1**, 214–218 (1962).

considered in the paper of Ames[7] deals with the gas-phase pyrolysis of toluene, which is governed by the chemical equations

$$A_1 \xrightarrow{k_1} A_2 + A_3,$$

$$A_3 + A_1 \xrightarrow{k_2} A_2 + A_4,$$

$$A_3 + A_1 \xrightarrow{k_3} A_5 + A_6,$$

$$A_6 + A_1 \xrightarrow{k_4} A_2 + A_7,$$

$$A_2 + A_2 \xrightarrow{k_5} A_3.$$

Again setting x_i = concentration of A_i and k_i = rate constant as shown, the kinetic differential equations become

$$\frac{dx_1}{dt} = -k_1x_1 - k_2x_1x_3 - k_3x_1x_3 - k_4x_1x_6, \tag{11.43}$$

$$\frac{dx_2}{dt} = k_1x_1 + k_2x_1x_3 + k_4x_1x_6 - k_5x_2^2, \tag{11.44}$$

$$\frac{dx_3}{dt} = k_1x_1 - k_2x_1x_3 - k_3x_1x_3 + k_5x_2^2, \tag{11.45}$$

$$\frac{dx_4}{dt} = k_2x_1x_3, \tag{11.46}$$

$$\frac{dx_5}{dt} = k_3x_1x_3, \tag{11.47}$$

$$\frac{dx_6}{dt} = k_3x_1x_3 - k_4x_1x_6, \tag{11.48}$$

$$\frac{dx_7}{dt} = k_4x_1x_6. \tag{11.49}$$

In the matrix form adopted in Section 11.5, these equations read

$$
\begin{array}{cccc}
d/dt & x_1 & x_1x_6 & x_2^2 & x_1x_3 \\
\end{array}
$$

$$
\begin{bmatrix} x_1 \\ x_2 \\ x_3 \\ x_4 \\ x_5 \\ x_6 \\ x_7 \end{bmatrix} =
\begin{bmatrix}
-k_1 & -k_4 & 0 & -k_2 - k_3 \\
k_1 & k_4 & -k_5 & k_2 \\
k_1 & 0 & k_5 & -k_2 - k_3 \\
0 & 0 & 0 & k_2 \\
0 & 0 & 0 & k_3 \\
0 & -k_4 & 0 & k_3 \\
0 & k_4 & 0 & 0
\end{bmatrix}. \tag{11.50}
$$

[7] *Ibid.*

From either the chemical equations or the differential equations it is clear that the dead-end variables are x_4, x_5, and x_7. With these in mind, application of elementary row transformations yields the following reduced form of (11.50), after rearrangement of rows:

$$
\begin{array}{c}
\begin{array}{cccc}
d/dt \qquad\qquad\qquad & x_1 & x_1 x_6 & x_2^2 & x_1 x_3
\end{array}\\
\begin{bmatrix} x_1 - x_6 - \frac{1}{2}U \\ x_6 + \beta U \\ x_1 + x_2 - \beta U \\ U \\ x_5 + \beta U \\ x_4 + (k_2/k_3)\beta U \\ x_7 + x_6 + \beta U \end{bmatrix}
=
\begin{bmatrix}
-k_1 & 0 & 0 & 0 \\
0 & -k_4 & 0 & 0 \\
0 & 0 & -k_5 & 0 \\
0 & 0 & 0 & -2(k_2 + 2k_3) \\
0 & 0 & 0 & 0 \\
0 & 0 & 0 & 0 \\
0 & 0 & 0 & 0
\end{bmatrix},
\end{array}
$$

where $U = 2x_1 + x_2 + x_3 - x_6$ and $\beta = \frac{1}{2}k_3/(k_2 + 2k_3)$. From the last three equations we obtain

$$
\begin{aligned}
x_7 &= c_7 - x_6 - \beta U, \\
x_4 &= c_4 - (k_2/k_3)\beta U, \\
x_5 &= c_5 - \beta U.
\end{aligned}
$$

A canonical set of differential equations has the form

$$
\frac{d(x_1 - x_6 - \frac{1}{2}U)}{dt} = -k_1 x_1,
$$

$$
\frac{d(x_6 + \beta U)}{dt} = -k_4 x_1 x_6,
$$

$$
\frac{d(x_1 + x_2 - \beta U)}{dt} = -k_5 x_2^2,
$$

$$
\frac{dU}{dt} = -2(k_2 + 2k_3)x_1 x_3.
$$

The general procedure can be summarized as follows:

1. Write the equations in "matrix" form.
2. Develop a canonical form by elementary row operations. (This canonical form is, of course, generally not unique.)

The objective is to write the equations in as simple a form as possible. The advantage of the present approach derives mainly from the convenience of matrix notation. We are not doing anything that could not be done "long-hand," but the repeated writing out of formulas in detail often degenerates into a meaningless mess of algebra. Matrix notation enables the manipulations to be carried out in a relatively straightforward and clear way.

Chapter 12

The Structure and Analysis of
Linear Chemical Reaction Systems[1]

12.1 The Basic Problem

Mathematics Used: A system of linear ordinary differential equations with constant coefficients is solved by linear algebra, using the eigenvalues and eigenvectors of a matrix.

Comment: This chapter is intended to illustrate that relatively sophisticated mathematics can sometimes be of great help in the interpretation and analysis of experimental results.

In chemistry we often encounter highly coupled systems of chemical reactions involving several chemical species. (The word *species* is a general term used to denote distinct chemical elements or compounds.) It is an important purpose of chemical kinetics to explore and describe the relations between the amounts of the various species during the course of the reaction, and to relate the concentration changes to a minimal number of concentration-independent parameters that characterize the reaction system. As is well known from previous attempts, the behavior of even linear systems containing as few as three reacting species is sufficiently complicated to make their basic dynamic behavior difficult to visualize.

In this chapter we discuss the structure of a certain class of linear reactions. By structure we mean qualitative and quantitative features common to large

[1] This chapter is based on a paper by J. Wei and C. D. Prater of the Socony Mobil Oil Co. Research Department, Paulsboro, N.J., The Structure and Analysis of Complex Reaction Systems, *Advances in Catalysis*, Vol. 13, Academic, New York, 1962, pp. 203–392, where much additional material and discussion can be found. See also the summary article by J. Wei and C. D. Prater, A New Approach to First-Order Chemical Reaction Systems, *Am. Inst. Chem. Eng. J.*, **9**, 77–81 (1963). It was the submission of this paper by J. Wei, School of Engineering and Applied Science, Princeton University, Princeton, N.J., that led to this chapter.

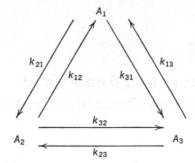

Fig. 12.1   General three-component monomolecular reaction.

well-defined classes of systems. This approach leads to two related but independent results. First, descriptive models and analyses are developed that create a sound basis for understanding the macroscopic behavior of a wide variety of dynamic systems. Second, these descriptive models and the procedures obtained from them lead to a new and powerful method for obtaining the rate parameters from experimental data.

In a chemical reaction the reaction rates of the various species A_i $(i = 1, 2, \ldots, n)$ are defined as the rates of change of the concentrations. Thus if the concentration of A_i is denoted, in suitable units, by a_i, the reaction rate is da_i/dt. From the laws governing the chemical reaction it is possible to set up differential equations satisfied by the a_i of the form

$$\frac{da_i}{dt} = \sum_j k_{ij} a_1^{\alpha_{1j}} a_2^{\alpha_{2j}} \cdots \alpha_n^{\alpha_{nj}},$$

where the k_{ij} and α_{pj} are constants. We shall be concerned entirely with the special class of system in which the equations are linear,

$$\frac{da_i}{dt} = \sum_{j=1}^{n} k_{ij} a_j, \qquad i = 1, 2, \ldots, n. \tag{12.1}$$

In chemical terminology this corresponds to monomolecular reactions in which the coupling between each pair of species is by first-order reactions only. (Note that the reactions considered in Sections 11.5 and 11.6 were of the form $k_{ij} a_i a_j$, involving products of the concentrations.) In passing we note that the analysis in this chapter will also apply to nonlinear systems of the form

$$\frac{da_i}{dt} = \phi(a_1, \ldots, a_n) \sum_{j=1}^{n} k_{ij} a_j, \qquad i = 1, 2, \ldots, n. \tag{12.2}$$

The general three-component monomolecular reaction is represented diagrammatically by Fig. 12.1. The rate constant for the reaction converting the ith species into the jth species is denoted by k_{ji}; that is, $A_i \to A_j$ is associated with k_{ji}. The equations for this system are therefore given by

$$\frac{da_1}{dt} = -(k_{21} + k_{31})a_1 + k_{12}a_2 + k_{13}a_3,$$

$$\frac{da_2}{dt} = +k_{21}a_1 - (k_{12} + k_{32})a_2 + k_{23}a_3, \tag{12.3}$$

$$\frac{da_3}{dt} = +k_{31}a_1 + k_{32}a_2 - (k_{13} + k_{23})a_3.$$

The negative term on the right of the ith equation is the sum of the reaction rates away from the ith species, and the remaining terms are the reaction rates of each jth species back to the ith species. Adding these equations we see that

$$\frac{d(a_1 + a_2 + a_3)}{dt} = 0$$

or
$$a_1 + a_2 + a_3 = \text{constant}; \tag{12.4}$$

that is, the sum of the concentrations is a constant, independent of time.

In deriving (12.4) we have made use of the fact that the sum of the coefficients of a_j on the right of (12.3) is zero for $j = 1, 2, 3$. This important feature of the structure of the matrix of rate constants generalizes to n-component systems. In the terminology of (12.2) we have

$$\sum_{i=1}^{n} k_{ij} = 0, \qquad j = 1, 2, \ldots, n$$

or
$$k_{jj} = -\sum_{i=1}^{n}{}' k_{ij}, \qquad j = 1, 2, \ldots, n, \tag{12.5}$$

where the prime denotes that the term $i = j$ is omitted from the sum.

The solution of the system (12.3) is of the following form, which we justify later:

$$a_1 = c_{11} + c_{12}e^{-\mu t} + c_{13}e^{-\nu t},$$

$$a_2 = c_{21} + c_{22}e^{-\mu t} + c_{23}e^{-\nu t}, \tag{12.6}$$

$$a_3 = c_{31} + c_{32}e^{-\mu t} + c_{33}e^{-\nu t},$$

where μ, ν, and the c_{ij} are constant parameters related to the rate constants and initial concentrations. Standard procedures are available for calculating μ, ν, and the c_{ij} if the rate factors and initial concentrations are known. However, the basic problem we wish to consider is much more difficult.

The basic problem (first form). It is assumed that the variations of $a_i(t)$ with time are known from experimental results. It is required to determine the rate constants k_{ij}.

When first confronted with this problem it is natural to suggest that we should use the known form of equations (12.6) to find μ, ν, and the c_{ij}, and then to deduce the k_{ij} from these constants. However, curve fitting when the data involve more than a single exponential is fraught with hazards, especially when the data are subject to random experimental error. Although the constants obtained may give a solution that fits the experimental data of composition versus time, used for their evaluation, as satisfactorily as the true solution, their values may have little resemblance to the true values, and they may be useless for predicting the course of the reaction for initial compositions differing appreciably from that used in the evaluation of the constants.

The difficulty does not arise from the formulation of the equations governing the phenomenon, since the formulation is clear and definite, or from the mathematical solution as such, since this is straightforward. The difficulty arises from the fact that if we are not careful the procedure we propose for determination of the reaction rates may be ill-conditioned in the sense in which this term is used in numerical analysis—that small changes in the given data [the $a_i(t)$] may produce large changes in the deduced reaction rates.

We conclude this section by making an important general remark, related to the comments made in the last two paragraphs. If an experimenter performs a series of experiments, yielding the $a_i(t)$ as functions of t for various initial conditions, there is no guarantee that the resulting data will be convenient to determine the rate constants. It is essential that the theory be used to design the experiments, and the statement of the problem should be rephrased in the following way:

The basic problem (*second form*).   Describe a procedure by means of which we can choose suitable initial concentrations $a_i(0)$ for a series of experiments, from the results of which the rate constants k_{ij} can be conveniently and accurately determined.

12.2   Some Properties of the Matrix of Rate Constants

For simplicity we confine our attention to the three-component system described by equations (12.3). (The method generalizes to n-component systems, although the geometric description in Section 12.3 will not be so simple.) In matrix notation, equations (12.3) can be written in the form

$$\frac{d\mathbf{a}}{dt} = \mathbf{Ka}, \tag{12.7}$$

where

$$\mathbf{a} = \begin{bmatrix} a_1 \\ a_2 \\ a_3 \end{bmatrix}, \quad \mathbf{K} = \begin{bmatrix} -(k_{21} + k_{31}) & k_{12} & k_{13} \\ k_{21} & -(k_{12} + k_{32}) & k_{23} \\ k_{31} & k_{32} & -(k_{13} + k_{23}) \end{bmatrix}.$$

This system has three important properties which we use extensively later.

1. From (12.4) the sum of the a_i is a constant. The equations are homogeneous, as this constant can be taken to be unity without loss of generality,

$$a_1 + a_2 + a_3 = 1. \tag{12.8}$$

2. Since concentration cannot be negative,

$$a_i \geq 0, \qquad i = 1, 2, 3. \tag{12.9}$$

3. In *reversible* reactions (which we consider here), it is known that

$$k_{ij}a_j(\infty) = k_{ji}a_i(\infty). \tag{12.10}$$

The physical interpretation of this equation is that, in the limit of large time, the total rate of conversion of species A_j into A_i is equal to the total rate of conversion of A_i into A_j. We do not allow, in the equilibrium state, "circular" reactions in which A_i is converted into A_j, A_j into A_k, and A_k into A_i. Mathematically, instead of having $n(n - 1)$ independent rate constants k_{ij}, we have only $\frac{1}{2}n(n - 1)$, in the general n-component reaction. In the chemical literature, the result (12.10) is referred to as the *principle of detailed balancing*, or the *principle of microscopic reversibility*. Irreversible reactions also exist, for which (12.10) is not true, and these are also considered by Wei and Prater.[2]

The matrix **K** in (12.7) is not in general symmetric, but the properties of symmetric matrices are so convenient that we transform (12.7) to a system with a symmetric matrix. This can be done by using property 3, given by (12.10). Suppose **P** is a nonsingular 3×3 diagonal matrix. We premultiply (12.7) by **P** and rewrite the result in the form

$$\frac{d(\mathbf{Pa})}{dt} = (\mathbf{PKP}^{-1})(\mathbf{Pa}). \tag{12.11}$$

If the diagonal elements of **P** are denoted by p_i, the (i, j)th and (j, i)th elements of $\mathbf{PKP}^{-1}$ are, respectively,

$$p_i k_{ij} p_j^{-1} \quad \text{and} \quad p_j k_{ji} p_i^{-1}. \tag{12.12}$$

To make $\mathbf{PKP}^{-1}$ symmetric we require that

$$p_i k_{ij} p_j^{-1} = p_j k_{ji} p_i^{-1};$$

that is,

$$k_{ij} p_j^{-2} = k_{ji} p_i^{-2}.$$

[2] J. Wei and C. D. Prater in *Advances in Catalysis*, Vol. 13, Academic, New York, 1962, pp. 203–392.

From (12.10) this relation is clearly satisfied if we choose $p_i^{-2} = a_i(\infty)$. We therefore introduce the diagonal matrix whose ith element is $a_i(\infty)$,

$$\mathbf{D} = \begin{bmatrix} a_1(\infty) & 0 & 0 \\ 0 & a_2(\infty) & 0 \\ 0 & 0 & a_3(\infty) \end{bmatrix}.$$

Then $\mathbf{P} = \mathbf{D}^{-1/2}$, and from (12.11) the system (12.7) can be written[3]

$$\frac{d\mathbf{z}}{dt} = \mathbf{M}\mathbf{z}, \tag{12.13}$$

where $$\mathbf{z} = \mathbf{D}^{-1/2}\mathbf{a}, \qquad \mathbf{M} = \mathbf{D}^{-1/2}\mathbf{K}\mathbf{D}^{1/2} \tag{12.14}$$

and $\mathbf{M}$ is symmetrical.

Since $\mathbf{M}$ is symmetrical it follows immediately that its eigenvalues are real. Suppose that the eigenvalues and corresponding eigenvectors are denoted by λ_i and $\mathbf{z}_i$, respectively. Then

$$\mathbf{M}\mathbf{z}_i = \lambda_i\mathbf{z}_i, \tag{12.15}$$

and, premultiplying by $\mathbf{z}_i^T$,

$$\lambda_i = \frac{\mathbf{z}_i^T\mathbf{M}\mathbf{z}_i}{\mathbf{z}_i^T\mathbf{z}_i}.$$

We show that $\mathbf{z}_i^T\mathbf{M}\mathbf{z}_i \le 0$, so all the eigenvalues are negative or zero. We show in fact that $\mathbf{u}^T\mathbf{M}\mathbf{u} \le 0$ for any vector $\mathbf{u}$. From (12.12), remembering that $p_i = [a_i(\infty)]^{-1/2}$, the general element of $\mathbf{M}$ is

$$m_{ij} = p_i k_{ij} p_j^{-1} = k_{ij}[a_j(\infty)/a_i(\infty)]^{1/2} = (k_{ij}k_{ji})^{1/2}.$$

Hence, if the general element of $\mathbf{u}$ is u_i,

$$\mathbf{u}^T\mathbf{M}\mathbf{u} = \sum_{i=1}^{3}\sum_{j=1}^{3} u_i m_{ij} u_j$$

$$= u_1[-(k_{21} + k_{31})u_1 + (k_{12}k_{21})^{1/2}u_2 + (k_{13}k_{31})^{1/2}u_3]$$
$$+ \text{two similar terms}$$

$$= -[(u_1\sqrt{k_{21}} - u_2\sqrt{k_{12}})^2 + \text{two similar terms}]$$
$$\le 0.$$

This is the required result.

The sum of the elements in each column of $\mathbf{K}$ is zero; this implies det $\mathbf{K} = 0$, so det $\mathbf{M} = 0$, and zero is an eigenvalue of $\mathbf{M}$. Suppose, therefore, that the eigenvalues of $\mathbf{M}$ are $\lambda_1 = 0$, $\lambda_2 = -\mu$, and $\lambda_3 = -\nu$, where for simplicity we suppose that μ and ν are distinct, and $\mu > 0$ and $\nu > 0$. Denote the

---

[3] We do not follow the notation of Wei and Prater in detail, but adopt the notation that arises naturally from the way in which we develop the problem.

corresponding eigenvectors by z_i, and let Z denote the following 3×3 matrix:

$$Z = [z_1 \quad z_2 \quad z_3]$$

Since M is symmetrical and the eigenvalues are distinct, the eigenvectors are orthogonal, $z_i^T z_i = 0$ $(i \neq j)$. It is assumed that the z_i are normalized so that $z_i^T z_i = 1$, and then

$$Z^T Z = I = Z Z^T. \tag{12.16}$$

In the usual way,

$$MZ = [Mz_1 \quad Mz_2 \quad Mz_3] = Z\Lambda,$$

where

$$\Lambda = \begin{bmatrix} \lambda_1 & 0 & 0 \\ 0 & \lambda_2 & 0 \\ 0 & 0 & \lambda_3 \end{bmatrix} = - \begin{bmatrix} 0 & 0 & 0 \\ 0 & \mu & 0 \\ 0 & 0 & \nu \end{bmatrix} \tag{12.17}$$

and

$$Z^T M Z = \Lambda. \tag{12.18}$$

On applying these results to the system (12.13), we multiply (12.13) by Z^T and rewrite in the form

$$\frac{d(Z^T z)}{dt} = (Z^T M Z)(Z^T z). \tag{12.19}$$

If we define

$$Z^T z = y = \begin{bmatrix} y_1 \\ y_2 \\ y_3 \end{bmatrix}, \tag{12.20}$$

(12.19) becomes

$$\frac{dy}{dt} = \Lambda y,$$

or, in components,

$$\frac{dy_1}{dt} = 0, \qquad \frac{dy_2}{dt} = -\mu y_2, \qquad \frac{dy_3}{dt} = -\nu y_3.$$

Hence

$$y_1 = b_1, \qquad y_2 = b_2 e^{-\mu t}, \qquad y_3 = b_3 e^{-\nu t}, \tag{12.21}$$

where b_1, b_2, and b_3 are arbitrary constants. From (12.14), (12.16), and (12.20), which imply $a = D^{1/2} z$ and $z = Z y$, we see that

$$a = D^{1/2} Z y = D^{1/2} Z \begin{bmatrix} b_1 \\ b_2 e^{-\mu t} \\ b_3 e^{-\nu t} \end{bmatrix}. \tag{12.22}$$

We have now justified the form of solution stated in (12.6), Section 12.1.

We note that $\mathbf{M}\mathbf{z}_i = \lambda_i\mathbf{z}_i$, so that, from (12.14),

$$\mathbf{K}(\mathbf{D}^{1/2}\mathbf{z}_i) = \lambda_i(\mathbf{D}^{1/2}\mathbf{z}_i).$$

If we define

$$\mathbf{w}_i = \mathbf{D}^{1/2}\mathbf{z}_i, \tag{12.23}$$

which fixes the $\mathbf{w}_i$ uniquely, since the $\mathbf{z}_i$ are normalized so that $\mathbf{z}_i^T\mathbf{z}_i = 1$, then

$$\mathbf{K}\mathbf{w}_i = \lambda_i\mathbf{w}_i, \tag{12.24}$$

and (12.22) can be written, on performing the multiplication on the right,

$$\mathbf{a} = b_1\mathbf{w}_1 + b_2\mathbf{w}_2 e^{-\mu t} + b_3\mathbf{w}_3 e^{-\nu t}. \tag{12.25}$$

On introducing the 3×3 matrix

$$\mathbf{W} = [\mathbf{w}_1 \quad \mathbf{w}_2 \quad \mathbf{w}_3], \tag{12.26}$$

(12.22) can be written

$$\mathbf{a} = \mathbf{W} \begin{bmatrix} b_1 \\ b_2 e^{-\mu t} \\ b_3 e^{-\nu t} \end{bmatrix}.$$

Multiplying both sides by $\mathbf{W}^{-1}$ and setting

$$\mathbf{W}^{-1}\mathbf{a} = \boldsymbol{\alpha} = \begin{bmatrix} \alpha_1 \\ \alpha_2 \\ \alpha_3 \end{bmatrix},$$

we see that

$$\alpha_1 = b_1, \qquad \alpha_2 = b_2 e^{-\mu t}, \qquad \alpha_3 = b_3 e^{-\nu t}.$$

By taking logarithms of the last two equations and eliminating t, we see that

$$\log \alpha_2 - \frac{\mu}{\nu} \log \alpha_3 = \log b_2 - \frac{\mu}{\nu} \log b_3. \tag{12.27}$$

The situation we shall encounter in Section 12.4 is that the matrix $\mathbf{W}$ will be deduced from experimental results, so $\mathbf{W}$ and $\mathbf{W}^{-1}$ are known. From a given set of experimental results for the variation of $\mathbf{a}$ with time, we can deduce $\boldsymbol{\alpha} = \mathbf{W}^{-1}\mathbf{a}$, so α_2 and α_3 are known as functions of the time. Hence, from (12.27), if $\log \alpha_2$ is plotted against $\log \alpha_3$, since the right side of (12.27) is a constant independent of the time, the resulting curve will be a straight line, and the slope of this line will give the ratio μ/ν of the eigenvalues.

12.3   A Geometric Interpretation for the Case of Three Species

We shall make essential use of two properties of the a_i given in (12.8) and (12.9), which we repeat for convenience:

$$a_1 + a_2 + a_3 = 1, \tag{12.28}$$

$$a_i \geq 0, \qquad i = 1, 2, 3. \tag{12.29}$$

If the concentrations a_i are plotted along rectangular x, y, and z axes, the composition of a mixture at any instant defines a point (a_1, a_2, a_3) in the three-dimensional space. From (12.28) the point lies on a plane that passes through the points $(1, 0, 0)$, $(0, 1, 0)$, and $(0, 0, 1)$. The constraints given by (12.29) further confine the point to the equilateral triangle defined by the part of the plane lying in the positive octant of the coordinate system, as shown by ABC in Fig. 12.2.

The equilateral triangle ABC will be called the *reaction triangle*, and the plane in which it lies, the *reaction plane*. As the reaction proceeds, the composition point moves in the reaction plane toward an equilibrium point with components $[a_1(\infty), a_2(\infty), a_3(\infty)]$, which we denote by $\mathbf{a}(\infty)$ for brevity. The path the composition point $\mathbf{a}$ traces out in the reaction plane, starting from an initial point $[a_1(0), a_2(0), a_3(0)]$, $\mathbf{a}(0)$ for short, is called the *reaction path*.

We first state that the equilibrium point $\mathbf{a}(\infty)$ is independent of the initial point $\mathbf{a}(0)$. This can be seen in the following way. Since the rate constants k_{ij} are independent of the initial conditions, (12.10) shows that the ratios

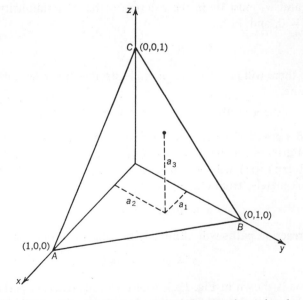

Fig. 12.2   The reaction plane and the reaction triangle.

$a_i(\infty)/a_j(\infty)$ are constant, independent of the initial conditions. Since the sum of the $a_i(\infty)$ is unity, from (12.28), the $a_i(\infty)$ are constants, independent of the initial conditions.

The reaction paths are given by (12.25),

$$\mathbf{a} = b_1\mathbf{w}_1 + b_2\mathbf{w}_2 e^{-\mu t} + b_3\mathbf{w}_3 e^{-vt}, \qquad (12.30)$$

where the $\mathbf{w}_i$ are fixed vectors defined by (12.23). We should expect that the constants b_1, b_2, and b_3 would be determined by the initial concentrations $a_i(0)$. However, b_1 is independent of the initial concentrations, for if we let t tend to infinity in (12.30) we obtain

$$\mathbf{a}(\infty) = b_1\mathbf{w}_1, \qquad (12.31)$$

and both $\mathbf{a}(\infty)$ and $\mathbf{w}_1$ are independent of the initial concentrations. The constant b_1 can be determined from the definition (12.23) of $\mathbf{w}_1$. Since $\mathbf{w}_1 = \mathbf{D}^{1/2}\mathbf{z}_1$ and $\mathbf{z}_1^T\mathbf{z}_1 = 1$, we must have $\mathbf{w}_1^T\mathbf{D}^{-1}\mathbf{w}_1 = 1$. Since $\mathbf{D}$ is a diagonal matrix whose ith diagonal element is $a_i(\infty)$, we have $1 = \mathbf{w}_1^T\mathbf{D}^{-1}\mathbf{w}_1 = b_1^{-2}\mathbf{a}^T(\infty)\mathbf{D}^{-1}\mathbf{a}(\infty) = b_1^{-2}$, so $b_1 = 1$, and

$$\mathbf{w}_1 = \mathbf{a}(\infty) = \begin{bmatrix} a_1(\infty) \\ a_2(\infty) \\ a_3(\infty) \end{bmatrix}, \qquad (12.32)$$

$$\mathbf{a} = \mathbf{a}(\infty) + b_2\mathbf{w}_2 e^{-\mu t} + b_3\mathbf{w}_3 e^{-vt}. \qquad (12.33)$$

Since the points $\mathbf{a}$ and $\mathbf{a}(\infty)$ lie on the reaction plane, the vectors representing $\mathbf{w}_2$ and $\mathbf{w}_3$ must lie in the reaction plane. For simplicity we assume that $\mu \neq v \neq 0$, and, in fact,

$$v > \mu > 0. \qquad (12.34)$$

In this case there will be only two possible straight-line reaction paths in the reaction plane,

$$\mathbf{a} = \mathbf{a}(\infty) + \rho\mathbf{w}_2, \qquad \mathbf{a} = \mathbf{a}(\infty) + \tau\mathbf{w}_3,$$

where ρ and τ are time-dependent parameters. All other paths will in general be curved. Furthermore, when we are near the equilibrium point (t large) the exponential $\exp(-vt)$ will be much smaller than $\exp(-\mu t)$, and we shall have, approximately, from (12.33),

$$\mathbf{a} = \mathbf{a}(\infty) + b_2\mathbf{w}_2 e^{-\mu t};$$

that is, all reaction paths will ultimately be tangent to the line

$$\mathbf{a} = \mathbf{a}(\infty) + \rho\mathbf{w}_2. \qquad (12.35)$$

The situation is shown in Fig. 12.3, where various reaction paths are shown for a typical reaction for which numerical results are presented in Section 12.4.

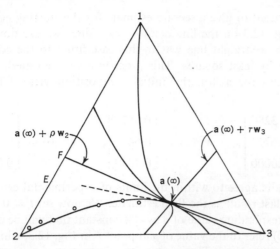

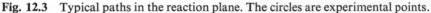

Fig. 12.3 Typical paths in the reaction plane. The circles are experimental points.

12.4 A Numerical Example (Butene Isomerization over Pure Alumina Catalyst)

The theory given in Sections 12.2 and 12.3 suggests a procedure for the determination of the rate constants which we now describe, together with numerical results obtained experimentally by Lago and Hoag.[4]

The first step is to carry out an experiment with arbitrarily chosen initial concentrations. This will lead to the determination of $\mathbf{a}(\infty)$, that is, $\mathbf{w}_1$ [equation (12.32)]. Thus Lago and Hoag, starting with $a_1 = 0$, $a_2 = 1$, and $a_3 = 0$, found

$$\mathbf{a}(\infty) = \mathbf{w}_1 = \begin{bmatrix} 0.1436 \\ 0.3213 \\ 0.5351 \end{bmatrix}. \tag{12.36}$$

Typical experimental results could be those shown by small circles in Fig. 12.3.

As noted in Section 12.3, the reaction path is tangent to the straight line $\mathbf{a}(\infty) + \rho\mathbf{w}_2$ at $\mathbf{a}(\infty)$. This suggests that the position of this straight line can be estimated from the approximately straight position of the reaction path near equilibrium. In the case considered by Lago and Hoag, their first experiment gave results near equilibrium which, when extrapolated, yielded the dashed line in Fig. 12.3 as an estimate for $\mathbf{a}(\infty) + \rho\mathbf{w}_2$, through the composition point E, that is, $(0.26, 0.76, 0)$. This was used as a new starting composition for a second experiment, and the resulting reaction path near

[4] Discussed by J. Wei and C. D. Prater in *Advances in Catalysis*, Vol. 13, Academic, New York, 1962, pp. 203–392.

equilibrium was used to give a second estimate for the starting composition at point F in Fig. 12.3 on the line $\mathbf{a}(\infty) + \rho\mathbf{w}_2$. Since we are now near the straight-line path, a straight line was in this case fitted to the composition near equilibrium by least squares. This procedure was repeated, giving the following estimates for $\mathbf{a}^{(r)}(0)$, the initial composition yielded by the rth experiment:

$$\mathbf{a}^{(2)}(0) = \begin{bmatrix} 0.3286 \\ 0.6714 \\ 0.0000 \end{bmatrix}, \qquad \mathbf{a}^{(3)}(0) = \begin{bmatrix} 0.3510 \\ 0.6490 \\ 0.0000 \end{bmatrix}, \qquad \mathbf{a}^{(4)}(0) = \begin{bmatrix} 0.3492 \\ 0.6508 \\ 0.0000 \end{bmatrix}.$$

The last two results agree to within the limits of experimental error, and we shall choose the last result as the final estimate. We now set $t = 0$ in (12.35), denoting the corresponding value of ρ by c, a constant that will be determined later. Also let $\mathbf{a}(0)$ refer to the value of $\mathbf{a}$ at point F in Fig. 12.3, which we take to be given by $\mathbf{a}^{(4)}(0)$ above. Then

$$c\mathbf{w}_2 = \mathbf{a}(0) - \mathbf{a}(\infty) = \begin{bmatrix} 0.3492 \\ 0.6508 \\ 0.0000 \end{bmatrix} - \begin{bmatrix} 0.1436 \\ 0.3213 \\ 0.5351 \end{bmatrix} = \begin{bmatrix} 0.2056 \\ 0.3295 \\ -0.5351 \end{bmatrix}. \quad (12.37)$$

We now exploit the definition (12.23) of $\mathbf{w}_i$, that is $\mathbf{w}_i = \mathbf{D}^{1/2}\mathbf{z}_i$, where $\mathbf{z}_i^T\mathbf{z}_i = 1$, $\mathbf{z}_i^T\mathbf{z}_j = 0$ $(i \neq j)$, and

$$\mathbf{D} = \begin{bmatrix} a_1(\infty) & 0 & 0 \\ 0 & a_2(\infty) & 0 \\ 0 & 0 & a_3(\infty) \end{bmatrix} = \begin{bmatrix} 0.1436 & 0 & 0 \\ 0 & 0.3213 & 0 \\ 0 & 0 & 0.5351 \end{bmatrix},$$

$$\mathbf{D}^{1/2} = \begin{bmatrix} 0.3789 & 0 & 0 \\ 0 & 0.5668 & 0 \\ 0 & 0 & 0.7315 \end{bmatrix}, \qquad \mathbf{D}^{-1/2} = \begin{bmatrix} 2.6389 & 0 & 0 \\ 0 & 1.7642 & 0 \\ 0 & 0 & 1.3670 \end{bmatrix}.$$

Since $\mathbf{z}_i = \mathbf{D}^{-1/2}\mathbf{w}_i$, we find

$$\mathbf{z}_1 = \begin{bmatrix} 0.3789 \\ 0.5668 \\ 0.7315 \end{bmatrix}, \qquad \mathbf{z}_2 = \frac{1}{c}\begin{bmatrix} 0.5426 \\ 0.5812 \\ -0.7315 \end{bmatrix}. \quad (12.38)$$

We can verify that $\mathbf{z}_1^T\mathbf{z}_1 = 1$ to four decimal places, which must be the case, since $\mathbf{w}_i = \mathbf{a}(\infty)$, and the sum of the elements of $\mathbf{a}(\infty)$ is unity. To determine the constant c we use the property $\mathbf{z}_2^T\mathbf{z}_2 = 1$, which gives $c = (1.1673)^{1/2}$, and then

$$\mathbf{z}_2 = \begin{bmatrix} 0.5022 \\ 0.5380 \\ -0.6771 \end{bmatrix}. \quad (12.39)$$

The vectors z_1 and z_2 should be orthogonal, since they are eigenvectors corresponding to distinct eigenvalues of a symmetric matrix $\mathbf{M}$. We can, in fact, check numerically from (12.38) that $z_2^T z_1 = 0$, but this is not surprising since

$$z_2^T z_1 = w_2^T D^{-1} w_1 = w_2^T \begin{bmatrix} 1 \\ 1 \\ 1 \end{bmatrix} = 0,$$

where we have used the facts that $w_1 = a(\infty)$ and that the sum of the elements of w_2 is zero, [since the sums of the elements of $a(0)$ and $a(\infty)$ in (12.37) are each unity].

To find z_3 we use the orthogonality relations $z_1^T z_3 = 0$ and $z_2^T z_3 = 0$. We first form a vector $\mathbf{u}$ orthogonal to z_1. This can be done, for instance, by taking the first element of $\mathbf{u}$ equal to minus the second element of z_1, the second element of $\mathbf{u}$ to be the first element of z_1, and the third element of $\mathbf{u}$ to be zero:

$$\mathbf{u} = \begin{bmatrix} -0.5668 \\ 0.3789 \\ 0.0000 \end{bmatrix}.$$

We then set

$$p z_3 = \mathbf{u} + q z_2, \tag{12.40}$$

where q is a constant chosen to make z_3 orthogonal to z_2 and p is a constant that will be determined by the normalization $z_3^T z_3 = 1$. Multiplying this equation by z_2^T we see that

$$q = -z_2^T \mathbf{u} = 0.08080.$$

Then (12.40) gives

$$z_3 = \frac{1}{p} \begin{bmatrix} -0.5262 \\ 0.4224 \\ -0.0547 \end{bmatrix},$$

where p can be determined from the relation $z_3^T z_3 = 1$. This gives $p = (0.4584)^{1/2}$, and we find

$$z_3 = \begin{bmatrix} -0.7773 \\ 0.6239 \\ -0.0808 \end{bmatrix}.$$

The vectors w_2 and w_3 can now be found from the relation $w_i = D^{1/2} z_i$, and the final result is

$$\mathbf{W} = [\mathbf{w}_1 \quad \mathbf{w}_2 \quad \mathbf{w}_3] = \begin{bmatrix} 0.1436 & 0.1903 & -0.2945 \\ 0.3213 & 0.3049 & 0.3536 \\ 0.5351 & -0.4953 & -0.0591 \end{bmatrix}. \tag{12.41}$$

We remind the reader that, as introduced in Section 12.2, $Z = [z_1, z_2, z_3]$, so $W = D^{1/2}Z$. Also $ZZ^T = I$, so $WZ^TD^{-1/2} = I$, and therefore

$$W^{-1} = Z^TD^{-1/2} = W^TD^{-1}. \tag{12.42}$$

Also, from (12.24), (12.17), we have $KW = W\Lambda$,   or

$$K = W\Lambda W^{-1} = W\Lambda W^TD^{-1}. \tag{12.43}$$

The matrices W and D are known. As pointed out at the end of Section 12.2, it is easy to determine the ratio μ/ν from experimental data, since, if we have a set of experimental results for the variation of the composition **a** with time, we need only form $W^{-1}a = \alpha$, with components $(\alpha_1, \alpha_2, \alpha_3)$, say, and then a plot of $\log \alpha_2$ against $\log \alpha_3$ should give a straight line from which μ/ν can be deduced. A detailed analysis of a set of experimental results obtained by Lago and Hoag is given in the paper by Wei and Prater,[5] where it is found that $\mu/\nu = 0.4769$. We define

$$\Lambda^* = - \begin{bmatrix} 0 & 0 & 0 \\ 0 & 0.4769 & 0 \\ 0 & 0 & 1.0000 \end{bmatrix},$$

which is in fact Λ divided by ν, where ν is not known. However, if we define [compare (12.43)]

$$K^* = W\Lambda^*W^TD^{-1},$$

we shall obtain the relative rate constants, which is usually what is required in practice. On performing the numerical work we find

$$K^* = \begin{bmatrix} -0.7245 & 0.2381 & 0.0515 \\ 0.5327 & -0.5273 & 0.1736 \\ 0.1918 & 0.2892 & -0.2251 \end{bmatrix}.$$

It is convenient to make one of the relative constants unity. If we divide all the elements in this matrix by 0.0515 we find

$$\begin{bmatrix} -14.06 & 4.62 & 1.00 \\ 10.34 & -10.24 & 3.37 \\ 3.72 & 5.62 & -4.37 \end{bmatrix}.$$

In terms of Fig. 12.1 we obtain Fig. 12.4.

[5] *Ibid.*, p. 255.

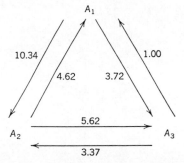

Fig. 12.4   Numerical results for rate constants.

We have now accomplished the objective stated at the end of §12.1. We have outlined a procedure by means of which experiments can be designed in such a way that the rate constants k_{ij} can be conveniently and accurately determined.

Part V

APPLICATIONS OF PROBABILITY THEORY

Chapter 13

Some Miscellaneous Applications of Simple Probability

13.1 Summary

In this chapter we present a selection of problems involving simple probability. The following summary indicates the theory we shall use.

1. In Section 13.2 it is shown that, perhaps surprisingly, certain experimental results derived from speech data can be fitted by a distribution function derived from the theory of repeated independent Bernoulli trials. This section is inserted at the beginning of this chapter to illustrate that if a phenomenon is to be regarded as statistical in nature, one of the first steps must be to describe the data by a frequency distribution. This will involve the checking of theory against experiment, and vice versa.

2. Sections 13.3 and 13.8 involve little more than the idea that the probability that two independent results should both occur is the product of the probabilities that each should separately occur.

3. Section 13.4 uses only the idea of a probability distribution function.

4. Section 13.5 is an application of independent Bernoulli trials.

5. Section 13.6 is an application of the normal distribution. Section 13.7 is an application of the bivariate normal distribution function.

6. Section 13.9 is included because it is an unusual application of simple ideas in probability, solving completely deterministic problems by turning them into games of chance.

Applications of the binomial and Poisson distributions are given in later chapters.

13.2   The Analysis of Speech Dynamics[1]

Mathematics Used : The theory of repeated independent Bernoulli trials.

The properties that describe speech as it occurs in a conversation between two people can be described only on a statistical basis, because the events occurring in a conversation do not occur in a deterministic manner. To characterize speech patterns, various parameters might be considered, such as loudness, variation with time, frequency distribution of the sound, and so on. Here we examine one small aspect of "on-off" patterns. In general these might include, for a single speaker, an analysis of the periods of talking and the periods of silence, and, for two speakers, an analysis also of periods of "double-talking," in which both speakers talk at once, and "mutual-silence" intervals.

The occurrence and lengths of events may be determined by examining the states of the conversation at successive instants of time. An illustration of the type of data provided by examination of a speech record of *one particular talker*, engaged in a conversation which lasted about $3\frac{1}{4}$ minutes, is shown in Fig. 13.1. The conversation was resolved into 5-millisecond (msec) segments, and each sampling of the speech simply represents whether speech was present in that segment or not. A talking state is recorded when speech is present at any time in the period, a silent state when speech is absent. Gaps of silence lasting less than 75 msec are considered as speech, to correct for the apparent absence of speech during stop consonants. (Further study has suggested that a longer fill-in time, such as 200 msec, would be more appropriate.) After these short gaps of silence have been filled in, speech bursts less than or equal to 40 msec are thrown away, to compensate for miscellaneous extraneous short bursts of noise, for example, impulse noise. Thus every period of speech must be longer than 40 msec.

A period of time during which speech is taking place continuously is known as a *talkspurt*. Analysis of the speech record in the manner just described gives a frequency distribution for the frequency of occurrence of talkspurts of various lengths. The corresponding cumulative distribution function gives the fraction of talkspurts with lengths less than a certain period of time. This fraction is plotted in Fig. 13.1. (The actual analysis of the record was carried out by an automatic computer.)

To describe the distribution function mathematically, we make the hypothesis that if the speaker is talking, the probability that he will be talking in the next 5 msec is a constant p, regardless of how long he has already been talking. Suppose speech has occurred for our minimum period of 40 msec. The probability that it will stop in the next 5 msec is $q = 1 - p$, and the probability that it will carry on for precisely another k intervals is

[1] This is taken from a manuscript with this title by P. T. Brady and N. W. Shrimpton, Bell Telephone Laboratories, Murray Hill, N.J., drawn to our attention by E. E. David.

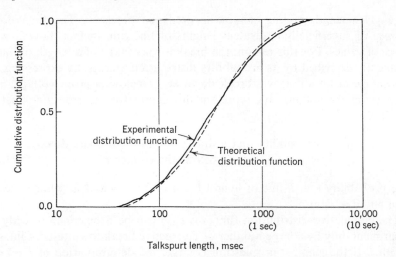

Fig. 13.1   Talkspurt distribution function for one speaker.

qp^{k-1}. The cumulative distribution function, which is the probability of obtaining j units of conversation or less over and above the 40-msec starting period, is

$$\sum_{k=1}^{j} qp^{k-1} = 1 - p^{j}. \tag{13.1}$$

An experimental value for p is easily found; one need only take a frequency count of the probability that if speech is occurring in a certain 5-msec interval, it does not occur in the next. The value of p found in this way was 0.98894.

The theoretical curve (13.1) can now be plotted directly, and it is shown by the dashed line in Fig. 13.1. For example, at 600 msec, $(600 - 40)/5 = 112$ units of speech have occurred beyond the 40-msec minimum, and the theoretical distribution-function value is

$$1 - (0.98894)^{112} = 0.7341.$$

As shown in Fig. 13.1, the agreement between theory and experiment is remarkable.

13.3   The Breakdown Voltage of Long Transmission Lines[2]

Mathematics Used: Basic probability theory.

The electrical breakdown voltage of long lengths of transmission line is of great importance to telephone companies. The exact breakdown voltage

[2] This section was contributed by W. Lechleider, Bell Telephone Laboratories, Murray Hill, N.J.

of a given length of line cannot be predicted precisely. The breakdown voltage of superficially equivalent lengths of line can, in fact, have a wide range of values. For this reason, the breakdown voltage of a length of line is frequently described by its probability distribution, that is, by expressing the percentage of lines that will break down at, or below, a given voltage, as a function of the voltage. We represent this cumulative distribution function by $F_l(v)$:

$$F_l(v) = \text{probability that a line of length } l \text{ will break down,}$$
$$\text{electrically, at, or below, the voltage } v. \tag{13.2}$$

The probability that a line of length l will break down at a voltage greater than v is $1 - F_l(v)$.

The cumulative distribution function $F_l(v)$ can be determined directly by experiment only by a large number of destructive breakdown tests of lines of length l. If the length l in question is large, the determination of $F_l(v)$ can be a costly and cumbersome procedure. The usual method used in design is to measure the breakdown voltage of short lengths of line and from this determine the cumulative probability distribution for breakdown of short lengths, say, $F_s(v)$, where s is the length of the short section. This is then used to predict the performance of long lengths of the same kind of line.

The relation between $F_s(v)$ and $F_l(v)$ can be determined theoretically by probability theory, using only a plausible assumption concerning the relation between the probability of breakdown of the two lengths of line. Suppose a long length of line of length l is composed of N sections of length s, so that

$$l = Ns. \tag{13.3}$$

We assume that the breakdown voltages of the short sections are statistically independent of each other but have the same cumulative distribution function $F_s(v)$. This assumption, when applied to a length of multipair cable, is equivalent to saying that all the pairs have been manufactured by a process that has only random variables affecting the quality of the individual pairs and that no accident such as crushing, for example, has occurred during cabling.

Clearly the long length of line will break down when the weakest section of length s, in the long line, breaks down. Thus the probability that the breakdown voltage of the long line is greater than v is equal to the probability that each of the sections of length s comprising the long length has a breakdown voltage greater than v; that is, since the sections are assumed to be independent,

$$\text{prob } (v_l > v) = [\text{prob } (v_s > v)]^N, \tag{13.4}$$

where v_l is the breakdown voltage of the long line and v_s is the breakdown voltage of the short line.

Substitution of (13.2) in (13.4) gives

$$1 - F_l(v) = [1 - F_s(v)]^N;$$

that is
$$F_l(v) = 1 - [1 - F_s(v)]^{l/s}. \tag{13.5}$$

This is the required formula, relating the probability distribution for lines of length l to that for lines of length s.

We have not assumed that l is much larger than s. For example, we could have $l = 2s$. However, we have assumed that l is an integer multiple of s and it is desirable to remove this restriction. Suppose l and s are both multiples of some length Δ, and let v_Δ denote the breakdown voltage for a line of length Δ. Then the same argument that led to (13.4) gives

$$\text{prob}(v_l > v) = [\text{prob}(v_\Delta > v)]^{l/\Delta},$$
$$\text{prob}(v_s > v) = [\text{prob}(v_\Delta > v)]^{s/\Delta},$$
so
$$\text{prob}(v_l > v) = [\text{prob}(v_s > v)]^{l/s},$$

which is (13.4) without the restriction that l/s is integral. Since Δ can be arbitrarily small, (13.5) is true for arbitrary l/s.

13.4   Minimization of Error in Telegraphy[3]

Mathematics Used: The idea of a probability distribution function.

In Morse telegraphy two possible signals can be transmitted: a *dot*, lasting one time unit, and a *dash*, lasting three time units. (We ignore here the spaces between symbols, letters, and words, which are represented by *no* transmission for various lengths of time.) Owing to faulty keying by the operator, noise in the transmission channel, or other unpredictable causes, the received signal may have a duration, which we denote by Δ, of other than one or three time units. In fact, the duration of the received signal is described by two probability-density distributions: $p_\bullet(\Delta)$, which denotes the distribution of the received duration when the transmission was meant to be a dot, and $p_-(\Delta)$, which denotes the distribution when the transmission was meant to be a dash. To be specific we assume that the triangular distributions in Fig. 13.2 illustrate how the duration deviates from the ideal for the two signals. In each case the total area under the probability curve is, of course, unity.

It is possible for the two distributions to overlap. For example, in the illustration given, the two distributions are both nonzero in the range $1.5 < \Delta < 1.75$. If the received signal has a duration falling in the range of overlap, it could have been caused by either a dot or a dash. For such a situation it is clearly impossible to determine the true meaning, dot or dash,

---

[3] This example was contributed by G. L. Turin, Department of Electrical Engineering, University of California, Berkeley, Calif.

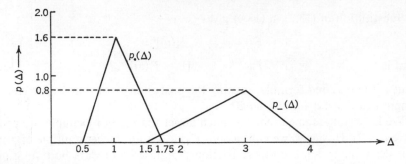

Fig. 13.2 Distributions of deviations of lengths of dots and dashes from means.

without the possibility of making an error. The essence of receiver design is to formulate a decision rule (which will then be mechanized in a piece of equipment) to minimize the probability that an error is made.

Suppose a rule of the following form is chosen: For a certain given number D, if $\Delta > D$ we decide a dash was intended, and if $\Delta \leq D$ we decide a dot was intended. (This type of rule turns out to be best in a wide class of cases, of which the case illustrated above is one.) The minimization of the probability of error then reduces to choosing the best value of D. To find D we proceed as follows. Write an expression for P_e, the probability of error, in terms of: $P_\bullet$, the probability that a dot was meant; P_-, the probability that a dash was meant; D, the "decision level"; and the probability densities $p_\bullet(\Delta)$ and $p_-(\Delta)$ described above. Differentiate the expression for P_e with respect to D so as to find the condition that D must satisfy for P_e to be a minimum. This will give the required optimum value of D. We can also find the probability of error corresponding to the optimum D.

The probability of error P_e is given by the following argument. If a dot was sent, an error occurs if $\Delta > D$; the probability of this event is $\int_D^\infty p_\bullet(\Delta)\, d\Delta$. If a dash was sent, the probability of error is, similarly, $\int_0^D p_-(\Delta)\, d\Delta$. The overall probability of error is, therefore,

$$P_e = P_\bullet \int_D^\infty p_\bullet(\Delta)\, d\Delta + P_- \int_0^D p_-(\Delta)\, d\Delta.$$

Differentiating with respect to D and setting the result equal to zero to give the stationary values of D, we find

$$\frac{dP_e}{dD} = -P_\bullet p_\bullet(D) + P_- p_-(D) = 0.$$

Hence the optimum D satisfies the equation

$$\frac{p_\bullet(D)}{p_-(D)} = \frac{P_-}{P_\bullet}. \tag{13.6}$$

Further, for the solution to be a minimum rather than a stationary value or a maximum, we must have

$$\frac{d^2P_e}{dD^2} = -P_\bullet p'_\bullet(D) + P_- p'_-(D) > 0 \tag{13.7}$$

for D satisfying (13.6). (Of course, in many cases it will be obvious by inspection whether we have a minimum or a maximum.)

As a particular case, if $P_\bullet = P_- = \frac{1}{2}$, the optimum D must satisfy $p_\bullet(D) = p_-(D)$. For the triangular distributions of Fig. 13.2 this equality gives

$$1.6\left[1 - \frac{1}{0.75}(D - 1)\right] = 0.8\left[\frac{1}{1.5}(D - 1.5)\right],$$

which has the solution $D = 1.70$. For this value of D, $p'_\bullet(D)$ is negative and $p'_-(D)$ is positive, so, from (13.7), d^2P_e/dD^2 is clearly positive, as required for a minimum. Also, on evaluating areas of triangles, we see that

$$\int_D^\infty p_\bullet(\Delta)\, d\Delta = \frac{0.05}{2}\left[\frac{1.6}{0.75}(0.05)\right] = 0.0027,$$

$$\int_0^D p_-(\Delta)\, d\Delta = \frac{0.20}{2}\left[\frac{0.8}{1.5}(0.20)\right] = 0.0107.$$

Thus
$$P_e = \frac{0.0027 + 0.0107}{2} = 0.0067;$$

that is, a mistake will be made in $\frac{2}{3}$ of 1% of the pulses (dots or dashes) transmitted.

13.5 A Simplified Statistical Model for Missile Launching[4]

Mathematics Used: Simple probability, including the theory of repeated independent Bernoulli trials.

In this section we estimate the number of days it takes to launch three vehicles from two launching pads. In particular we wish to take account of the delays that can occur during countdown. The delay model assumed is very simple and there is no claim that it is realistic. However the basic method of attack can be generalized to deal with more realistic situations.

The following situation is assumed.

1. Two vehicles are erected simultaneously on two launch pads, and the countdown proceeds on one vehicle.

2. When the countdown has been successfully completed on the first vehicle, the countdown on the second vehicle is initiated the following day.

[4] This section is based on a submitted contribution: C. B. Solloway, A Simplified Statistical Model for Missile Launching, *Tech. Rept. 32–431* (Part III), Jet Propulsion Laboratory, California Institute of Technology, Pasadena, Calif., July 1963.

3. Simultaneously, the vacated pad is immediately cleaned and prepared for the third vehicle. There is a fixed period of R days delay after a launching before the same pad may be utilized for a second launch attempt (the turnaround time).

4. After the third vehicle has been erected on the vacated pad, the countdown procedure is not initiated until the day after the second vehicle is launched.

5. Each vehicle is independent of, and identical with, the others. On any single countdown attempt, there is a probability p of a successful completion, and a probability $q = 1 - p$ of a failure. It is assumed that a successful countdown attempt can be completed in a day, and that any failure leads to a 1-day delay, that is, that any failure results in the termination of that countdown attempt and a new attempt, from the beginning, on the following day.

6. The failure to complete a countdown does not affect subsequent attempts in any way; the trials are independent from day to day as well as from vehicle to vehicle.

With these assumptions, the probability of the first successful countdown on the kth trial for any vehicle is clearly

$$pq^{k-1}, \qquad k = 1, 2, \ldots. \tag{13.8}$$

Suppose now that we label the pads 1 and 2, and the first vehicle on each pad by the same number; the standby vehicle is labeled 3. Then there is only one possible way in which the vehicles may be launched—1, 2, 3. However, there are two distinct and mutually exclusive cases to consider:

Case	Event
A	No. 2 goes before turnaround time is completed.
B	No. 2 goes at, or after, completion of turnaround time.

Given case A, the probability of three successful countdowns in N days is

$$P(N \text{ days} \mid \text{case } A) = \sum_{k=1}^{N-R-1} \sum_{m=1}^{R-1} P \begin{cases} \text{No. 1 took } k \text{ trials,} \\ \text{No. 2 took } m \text{ trials,} \\ \text{No. 3 took } N - k - R \text{ trials,} \end{cases} \tag{13.9}$$

where the limits for m and k can be understood from

$$\longleftarrow \text{———————} N \text{ days} \text{———————} \longrightarrow$$

k days	R days	$N - R - k$ days
No. 1	No. 2	No. 3

Since we assume in case A that the No. 2 vehicle goes before turnaround is completed, the limits on m are $1 \leq m \leq R - 1$. The earliest No. 3 will go is the first day after its countdown is started. The firings of Nos. 1 and 3 are always separated by the R days required to set up No. 3, so that at most

$N - R - 1$ trials are available to No. 1, that is, $1 \le k \le N - R - 1$. Equation (13.9) gives

$$P(N \text{ days} \mid \text{case } A) = \sum_{k=1}^{N-R-1} \sum_{m=1}^{R-1} (pq^{k-1})(pq^{m-1})(pq^{N-k-R-1})$$

$$= p^3 q^{N-R-2}(N - R - 1) \sum_{m=1}^{R-1} q^{m-1}$$

$$= p^2 q^{N-R-2}(N - R - 1)(1 - q^{R-1}). \qquad (13.10)$$

Similarly, for case B, we have

$$P(N \text{ days} \mid \text{case } B) = \sum_{k=1}^{N-R-1} \sum_{m=R}^{N-k-1} P \begin{cases} \text{No. 1 took } k \text{ trials,} \\ \text{No. 2 took } m \text{ trials,} \\ \text{No. 3 took } N - k - m \text{ trials,} \end{cases} \qquad (13.11)$$

where, as before, the limits are easily deduced from

$$\longleftarrow \overline{\qquad N \text{ days} \qquad} \longrightarrow$$

k days	$m(\ge R)$ days	$N - k - m$ days
No. 1	No. 2	No. 3

This means that at most $N - R - 1$ days are available for No. 1, as in case A, so $1 \le k \le N - R - 1$. Also, if No. 1 takes k days, then at most $N - k - 1$ days are available for No. 2, since No. 3 takes at least 1 day to launch, and $m \ge R$, so the range for m is $R \le m \le N - k - 1$. Hence (13.11) gives

$$P(N \text{ days} \mid \text{case } B) = \sum_{k=1}^{N-R-1} \sum_{m=R}^{N-k-1} (pq^{k-1})(pq^{m-1})(pq^{N-k-m-1})$$

$$= p^3 q^{N-3} \sum_{k=1}^{N-R-1} (N - R - k)$$

$$= p^3 q^{N-3}[(N - R)(N - R - 1) - \tfrac{1}{2}(N - R - 1)(N - R)]$$

$$= \tfrac{1}{2} p^3 q^{N-3}(N - R)(N - R - 1). \qquad (13.12)$$

The probability $f(N)$ of completing the third countdown on the Nth day is given by the sum of (13.10) and (13.12). To obtain the mean and variance, it is convenient to obtain the moment-generating function, which has a reasonably simple form:

$$M(\theta) = \sum_{s=R+2}^{\infty} e^{\theta s} f(s) = e^{\theta(R+2)} \left[\frac{p^2(1 - q^{R-1})}{(1 - e^\theta q)^2} + \frac{p^3 q^{R-1}}{(1 - e^\theta q)^3} \right].$$

The reason for introducing the generating function here is merely that many of the properties of the probability distribution can be obtained directly from it. Thus the mean value of $f(x)$ is given by

$$\mu_N = \left(\frac{dM}{d\theta} \right)_{\theta=0} = \sum_{s=R+2}^{\infty} sf(s).$$

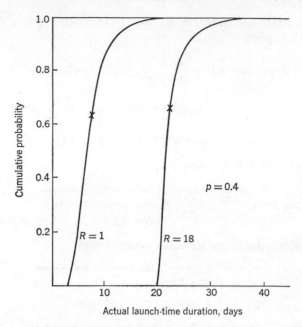

Fig. 13.3 Probability of launching all three vehicles within a certain time.

In the above case we find that the mean μ_N is given by

$$\mu_N = (R + 2) + \frac{2q}{p} + \frac{q^R}{p}. \tag{13.13}$$

The cumulative distribution function for N is defined as the probability of completing the third countdown on or before the Nth day,

$$F(N) = \sum_{s = R + 2}^{N} f(s).$$

A graph of the cumulative probability function against the launch-time duration is given in Fig. 13.3 for $p = 0.4$ and $R = 1$ day and 18 days. The average number of days taken to launch all three vehicles (denoted by crosses) are 7.5 and 23, respectively. The median number of days (that is, the number of days such that the probability is 0.5 that the vehicles will be launched on or before that day) is approximately 6 in the first case, 22 in the second.

In most practical cases R is quite large. For example, a realistic R might be about 18 days, which is the reason $R = 18$ was chosen in Fig. 13.3. In such a case, q^R and q^N (but not, of course, q^{N-R}) can be small compared with unity, even for quite large values of q (that is, for quite small probabilities p). Then the probability of failing to launch No. 2 in the turnaround time is very small, and we can neglect case B altogether. This considerably simplifies $f(N)$, which becomes

$$f(N) \approx p^2 q^{N-R-2}(N - R - 1).$$

The mean launch time becomes, from (13.13),

$$\mu_N = (R + 2) + \frac{2q}{p}.$$

This concludes our discussion of a simplified statistical model for missile launching.

13.6   A Problem of Tape Alignment[5]

Mathematics Used: Mean, variance, and normal distribution.

A 100-ft steel tape is used to measure the distance between two points. Small errors in aligning the tape make the observed distance greater than the true distance; that is, a positive error is incurred in the measured distance. We shall show, for example, that if the alignment errors (Fig. 13.4) e_1, e_2, e_3, ... are small random errors, each with a standard deviation of 0.5 ft and zero mean, then the error incurred in a measured distance of 8,000 ft lies between 0.07 and 0.13 ft with 95% probability.

Let L denote the length of the tape, e_k the error in aligning the kth leg of the measurement, l_k the measured length of the kth leg, and θ_k the angle it makes with the direct line joining the two points whose distance apart is required. Then, using Pythagoras,

$$l_k = (L^2 - e_k^2)^{1/2} = L\left[1 - \left(\frac{e_k}{L}\right)^2\right]^{1/2} \approx L\left[1 - \frac{1}{2}\left(\frac{e_k}{L}\right)^2\right];$$

that is

$$l_k \approx L - \frac{e_k^2}{2L},$$

neglecting higher-order terms in the series expansion of the square root since e_k^2/L is small. Since l_k is taken to be L, the length of the kth leg is *overestimated* by an amount $e_k^2/2L$. For n tape lengths the total error is

$$\delta = \frac{1}{2L}\sum_{r=1}^{n} e_r^2. \tag{13.14}$$

It is assumed that the random errors $e_1, \ldots, e_n$ are independent. (Since, for example, the sum of the e_i is zero, the errors are not strictly independent, but this is of no practical significance if n is large, because of the way in which the measurements are carried out in practice, by trying to align the tape along

[5] This example was contributed by the College of Engineering, University of Illinois, Urbana, Ill., through Dean W. L. Everitt.

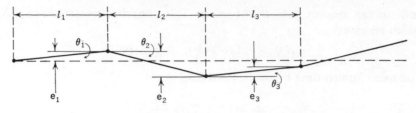

$$e_k = \text{error in aligning the } k\text{th leg of the measurement}$$

Fig. 13.4   Error in tape alignment.

the line joining the two objects that are far apart. However, it would seem to be difficult to set up a realistic model to take this into account.) The random errors therefore constitute a random sample from a normal distribution with mean zero, and variance σ^2, assumed to be known.

To obtain the statistical behavior of δ we need to know the behavior of the e_i^2. Suppose we have m numbers x_i with zero mean and variance σ^2,

$$\sigma^2 = \frac{1}{m} \sum_{i=1}^{m} x_i^2.$$

If we denote the mean of the x_i^2 by X, then

$$X = \frac{1}{m} \sum_{i=1}^{m} x_i^2 = \sigma^2,$$

and the variance of the x_i^2 is given by

$$v^2 = \frac{1}{m} \sum_{i=1}^{m} (x_i^2 - X)^2 = \frac{1}{m} \sum_{i=1}^{m} x_i^4 - \frac{2X}{m} \sum_{i=1}^{m} x_i^2 + X^2$$

$$= \frac{1}{m} \sum_{i=1}^{m} x_i^4 - \sigma^4.$$

The sum of x_i^4 divided by m in the last line of this equation is simply the fourth moment of the x_i. If we now assume that the x_i are normally distributed with mean zero and variance σ^2, the fourth moment is $3\sigma^4$ (see below), so the variance of the x_i^2 is given by $v^2 = 3\sigma^4 - \sigma^4 = 2\sigma^4$.

A more sophisticated method of deriving this result is the following. Suppose the frequency distribution of a variable x is given by $f(x)$, $-\infty < x < \infty$, so that its cumulative distribution function is

$$F(\xi) = \int_{-\infty}^{\xi} f(x)\, dx,$$

where $F(\xi)$ is the probability that x is less than ξ. We now consider the frequency distribution of $y = x^2$. The probability that y is less than, say, η $(\eta > 0)$ is the probability that $-\sqrt{\eta} < x < \sqrt{\eta}$, that is,

$$G(\eta) = \int_{-\sqrt{\eta}}^{+\sqrt{\eta}} f(x)\, dx,$$

where $G(\eta)$ is the cumulative distribution function of y. The frequency distribution function for y is

$$\left(\frac{dG}{d\eta}\right)_{\eta=y} = \frac{f(\sqrt{y}) + f(-\sqrt{y})}{2\sqrt{y}} = g(y), \text{ say,}$$

where this defines $g(y)$. The mean $\bar{y}$ of y is given by

$$\bar{y} = \int_0^\infty yg(y)\, dy = \tfrac{1}{2} \int_0^\infty y^{1/2}[f(\sqrt{y}) + f(-\sqrt{y})]\, dy$$

$$= \int_0^\infty u^2[f(u) + f(-u)]\, du = \int_{-\infty}^\infty u^2 f(u)\, du = \mu_2,$$

where μ_2 denotes the second moment of $f(x)$ about the origin. The variance ν^2 of y is given by

$$\nu^2 = \int_0^\infty (y - \bar{y})^2 g(y)\, dy$$

$$= \tfrac{1}{2} \int_0^\infty (y^{3/2} - 2y^{1/2}\bar{y} + \bar{y}^2 y^{-1/2})[f(\sqrt{y}) + f(-\sqrt{y})]\, dy$$

$$= \int_{-\infty}^\infty u^4 f(u)\, du - 2\mu_2\bar{y} + \bar{y}^2 = \mu_4 - \mu_2^2,$$

where μ_4 denotes the fourth moment of $f(x)$ about the origin. For the normal distribution we have

$$f(x) = \frac{1}{(2\pi)^{1/2}\sigma} e^{-(x/\sigma)^2/2},$$

and it is easy to show that $\mu_2 = \sigma^2$ and $\mu_4 = 3\sigma^4$, which lead to $\bar{y} = \sigma^2$ and $\nu^2 = 2\sigma^4$, as before.

We now return to the original problem. The mean of the e_r is zero. Denote the variance of the e_r by σ^2. Then from the results in the last two paragraphs, the mean of the e_r^2 is σ^2 and their variance is $2\sigma^4$. The quantity δ in (13.14) is the sum of n independent variables. By the central limit theorem δ will behave, for large n, like a normal variate with

$$\text{Mean} = \frac{1}{2L} n(\text{mean of the } e_r^2) = \frac{n\sigma^2}{2L},$$

$$\text{Variance} = \frac{1}{4L^2} n(\text{variance of the } e_r^2) = \frac{2n\sigma^4}{4L^2},$$

$$\text{Standard deviation} = (\text{variance})^{1/2} = \frac{(2n)^{1/2}\sigma^2}{2L}.$$

These formulas constitute the required answer.

In the specific case mentioned in the first paragraph of this section we have $L = 100$, $n = 8000/100 = 80$, and the standard deviation of the e_r is 0.5; that is, $\sigma^2 = (0.5)^2 = 0.25$. Hence

$$\text{Mean} = (80)(0.25)/200 = 0.1,$$
$$\text{Standard deviation} = (160)^{1/2}(0.25)/200 = 0.0158.$$

The 95% confidence limits are 1.95 times the standard deviation, or $(1.95)(0.0158) = 0.03$ ft. Hence the error lies in the range 0.1 ± 0.03 ft with 95% probability, as quoted previously.

13.7   Survival of Communication Facilities During Nuclear Attack[6]

Mathematics Used: Bivariate normal distribution.

It is required to construct a communication facility in the form of a long buried telephone cable that will withstand the effects of nuclear explosions. The communication link passes near several potential targets. The link itself is not considered a likely target since, with a limited number of weapons, the attacker will concentrate on other targets of greater importance (see Fig. 13.5).

The peak overpressure resulting from an explosion is commonly used as a criterion of potential mechanical damage to buried equipment. The overpressure is greatest at the center of an explosion and falls off as a function of the distance. We shall use the following in later numerical work:

$$
\begin{array}{lcccc}
\text{Range from explosion (miles):} & 3.1 & 1.9 & 1.5 & 1.2 \\
\text{Overpressure (psi):} & 30 & 100 & 200 & 400
\end{array}
\qquad (13.15)
$$

The communication link will be considered damaged if there is a hit within a distance D on either side of the link, where D is determined from (13.15), once the critical overpressure is fixed (see Fig. 13.5).

For any particular target it is assumed that the distribution of hits is approximated by a bivariate normal distribution with $\sigma_1 = \sigma_2 = \sigma$ and $\mu_1 = \mu_2 = 0$. Let x_1 and x_2 be the coordinates of a hit relative to the target. Assuming x_1 and x_2 independent, we have the density function

$$f(x_1, x_2) = \frac{1}{2\pi\sigma^2} \exp\left[-\frac{1}{2}\left(\frac{x_1^2}{\sigma^2} + \frac{x_2^2}{\sigma^2} \right) \right].$$

Let p represent the probability of damage to the communication link due to an attack on a target at distance d from the link. The link will be damaged if the weapon hits within a distance D of the link. Thus the probability of a hit

[6] This section is based on a contribution by A. G. Vedejs, Bell Telephone Laboratories, Murray Hill, N.J.

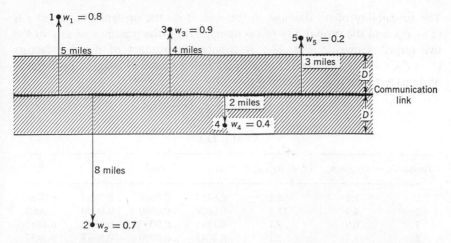

Fig. 13.5 Diagrammatic representation of communication link. A hit in the shaded zone results in damage to the link.

within the zone of damage to the link, in the event the target is attacked, is

$$p = \frac{1}{2\pi\sigma^2} \int_{d-D}^{d+D} \int_{-\infty}^{\infty} \exp\left[-\frac{1}{2}\left(\frac{x_1^2}{\sigma^2} + \frac{x_2^2}{\sigma^2}\right)\right] dx_1 \, dx_2. \qquad (13.16)$$

It is assumed that the link is essentially straight over a distance sufficiently great that the integration from $-\infty$ to ∞ is justified. In practice, if the terminals of the straight section are further than 3σ from the point closest to the target, the error introduced by this assumption is negligible. On setting $x_1 = \sigma u$, $x_2 = \sigma v$ in (13.16), and evaluating the infinite integral in v by a standard result, we find that

$$p = \frac{1}{(2\pi)^{1/2}} \int_{(d-D)/\sigma}^{(d+D)/\sigma} e^{-u^2/2} \, du$$

$$= I[(d + D)/\sigma] - I[(d - D)/\sigma] \qquad (13.17)$$

where

$$I(x) = \frac{1}{(2\pi)^{1/2}} \int_{x}^{\infty} e^{-u^2/2} \, du,$$

and this is simply the area under the standard normal distribution to the right of the lower limit, which can be looked up in tables.

There is one more complicating factor. Usually the number of weapons is less than the number of potential targets. We can take account of this by weighting each target in accordance with its estimated tactical significance. The sum of the weights of all targets is equal to the number of weapons. Let w_i be the weight assigned to target i, and let p_i be the probability that a weapon aimed at target i will damage the link. Then the probability of damage to the link due to the presence of target i is given by

$$P_i = w_i p_i.$$

The probability of no damage to the link from the presence of target i is $(1 - P_i)$, and the probability of no damage from the presence of any of the five targets shown in Fig. 13.5 is simply the product of the five factors $(1 - P_i)$, $i = 1$ to 5, since the targets are independent. Hence the probability of damage to the link is given by

$$1 - (1 - P_1)(1 - P_2)(1 - P_3)(1 - P_4)(1 - P_5). \qquad (13.18)$$

TABLE 13.1

Target	$(d_i - D)/\sigma = \alpha_i$	$(d_i + D)/\sigma = \beta_i$	$I(\alpha_i)$	$I(\beta_i)$	p_i	P_i
1	1.9	8.1	0.0287	0.0000	0.0287	0.0230
2	4.9	11.1	0.0000	0.0000	0.0000	0.0000
3	0.9	7.1	0.1841	0.0000	0.1841	0.1657
4	-1.1	5.1	0.8643	0.0000	0.8643	0.3457
5	-0.1	6.1	0.5398	0.0000	0.5398	0.0108

As a numerical example, we have Table 13.1 for the case of 30-psi over-pressure, assuming $\sigma = 1$ mile, $D = 3.1$ miles, and using the distances and weights shown in Fig. 13.5. (The shaded area in Fig. 13.5 corresponds to the case $D = 2.5$ miles.) From these figures and (13.18) we find that the probability of damage to the link is 0.4725. The corresponding figures for 100, 200, and 400 psi are, respectively, 0.2196, 0.1401, and 0.0933. These are the results we wish to obtain from the analysis.

Information of this type, together with estimates of the relative costs of providing increased protection (that is, increasing the overpressure the link can withstand), can be used as a basis for the engineering design, although of course many more factors and possibilities would have to be taken into account.

13.8   The Minimization of the Cost of a Digital Device (the Juke-Box Problem)[7]

Mathematics Used: Simple probability theory.

In digital systems, data is stored, transmitted, and recorded in k-state devices, that is, a device which can exist in k different states. Thus an on-off relay is a two-state device; a counter that records $+1$, 0, and -1 is a three-state device; a counter that records the digits $0, 1, \ldots, 9$ is a ten-state device. Typically the *cost* of a k-state device is proportional to k. Given r of these k-state devices, there are $m = k^r$ possible *messages* that can be stored, at a

---

[7] This example was contributed by S. Golomb, Department of Electrical Engineering, University of Southern California, Los Angeles, Calif.

cost of $n = rk$. How should k be picked to maximize the ratio m/n of data capacity to cost?

A colloquial formulation of this problem is as follows. A juke box has two rows of twelve buttons each, for selecting records. Since one button is chosen from the first row, and one from the second, we are dealing with two twelve-state devices, and there are 12^2 possible selections. If the juke-box manufacturer wishes to maximize the number of possible selections for a fixed number of buttons, and can arrange the buttons in several rows (a selection then consisting of choosing one button from each row), how should the buttons be arranged to maximize the total number of selections?

On returning to the mathematical formulation of this problem, as given in the previous paragraph, we see that we have to maximize the ratio of data capacity to cost, which we denote by:

$$f(k) = \frac{m}{n} = \frac{k^r}{rk} = \frac{k^{n/k}}{n} = \frac{1}{n}(k^{1/k})^n,$$

where n is a fixed (given) number. The optimum value of k will not therefore depend on n. In fact, since k must be an integer, we need consider only the following table:

k:	2	3	4	5
$k^{1/k}$:	1.41	1.46	1.41	1.38

Hence $k = 3$ is the best integer and $k = 2$ and $k = 4$ are tied for runner-up. [If k were a continuous variable, the optimum value would be given by $d(k^{1/k})/dk = 0$, which yields $k = e = 2.718\ldots$.]

In the juke-box example, we can ennumerate the various possibilities as follows. The total number of buttons is 24 ($= n$).

Buttons in a row (k):	12	8	6	4	3	2
Number of rows ($r = n/k$):	2	3	4	6	8	12
Total number of choices (k^r):	144	512	1296	4096	6561	4096

From the table we confirm that the design which gives the maximum number of possibilities is the case $k = 3$, involving 8 rows of buttons. However, this would not give a satisfactory juke-box design since it is undesirable to ask a person to punch eight buttons to perform a simple operation such as selecting a record. The juke-box manufacturer might compromise by using three rows of eight buttons, which would give him more than three times the number of choices available compared with two rows of twelve. The moral is that the problem is incorrectly formulated if we merely ask "What is the maximum number of choices?" We must ask "What is the optimum number of choices, subject to the limitations of the people who will operate the juke box?"

In a similar way, if we are constructing a digital device, we must remember that our original assumption, that the cost of a k-state device is proportional to k, is often not true, in that two-state devices are often proportionately cheaper than our assumption would indicate. Since there is not too much difference in the values of $f(2)$ and $f(3)$, it may be cheaper in practice simply to use two-state devices.

13.9   The Monte Carlo Method[8]

Mathematics Used: Simple probability theory.

The idea of the Monte Carlo method is that if we are presented with a problem that can be stated precisely in analytical form and we wish to solve the problem numerically, we may be able to replace the analytical problem by another problem in statistics or probability such that the numerical answer to the new problem is the same as the numerical answer to the original problem. The new probability problem is solved by playing games of chance on an automatic computer.

As a simple example consider the problem of evaluating an integral:

$$I = \int_a^b f(x) \, dx.$$

We can make a game of chance out of this problem (Fig. 13.6a) by first embedding the shaded area in the rectangle $abBA$, and then standing back and throwing darts at the rectangle. The darts should be thrown "at random," not aiming at any particular part of the target. We keep score by

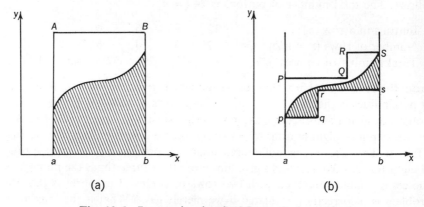

(a)   (b)

Fig. 13.6   Integration by the Monte Carlo method.

[8] This is abstracted, in modified form, from notes submitted by J. H. Cashman, Mechanical Engineering Department, University of Detroit, Detroit, Mich. See also the chapter by G. W. Brown in *Modern Mathematics for the Engineer* (E. F. Beckenbach, ed.), McGraw-Hill, New York, 1956.

counting as successes the number of times the dart hits below the curve, and as failures the number of times the dart hits above the curve. After sufficient throws, the ratio of successes to the total number of throws will give an estimate of the ratio of the area under the curve (the desired quantity) to the area of the rectangle $abBA$, which is known. The greater the number of throws, the better the estimate. The problem of integration has been replaced by a game whose main disadvantage is that it must be played a very great number of times before an accurate estimate of the area can be obtained. The only practicable way to play the game is to make an automatic computer do it. The coordinates corresponding to one throw of the dart are obtained by getting the computer to choose two random numbers in the ranges ab and aA.

It is obviously important to use as many devices as possible to reduce the time involved in playing the game on a computer. We mention two of these:

1. Instead of using the shaded area in Fig. 13.6a embedded in the total area $abBA$, we could use the shaded area in Fig. 13.6b, embedded in the area $pqrsSRQP$. This is an example of a *variance-reducing* technique.
2. To avoid evaluating $f(x)$ for every trial (which could be extremely expensive in computer time), we evaluate $f(x)$ at equidistant points and then represent $f(x)$ by an interpolation formula.

This technique is usually not preferable to straightforward numerical integration methods for one-dimensional integrals, but it may be preferable for multiple integrals.

We now consider a completely different type of application of Monte Carlo methods. The object of the procedure we describe is to solve the finite difference equations (13.22) in order to solve the differential equation (13.24) approximately. Discussion of the precise motivation is postponed until after we describe the method.

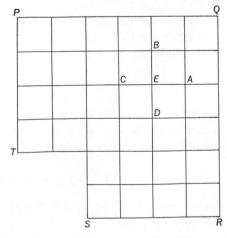

Fig. 13.7 Solution of Laplace's equation by the Monte Carlo method.

Suppose a square mesh is superimposed on a rectangular region, with the sides of the region coinciding with lines of the mesh (Fig. 13.7). We distinguish "interior" points of the mesh from "boundary" points lying on $PQRST$. We consider "dots" that move from one point of the mesh to a neighboring point according to a random law—that a dot at, say, E in Fig. 13.7 will move to one of the points A, B, C, or D with a probability $\frac{1}{4}$ of moving to each of these points. A dot moving through the network in this way is said to perform a *random walk*.

Suppose points of the mesh are identified by integer coordinates m and n, where $m = 1, 2, 3, \ldots$ denotes horizontal distance and n denotes vertical distance. Boundary points are identified by suffixes: (m_i, n_i), $i = 1, 2, \ldots$. Consider a dot starting from a point (m, n). This dot will eventually reach a boundary point, and then we assume that the random walk terminates. By repeating the random walk a large number of times, starting from the point (m, n) in each case, we can determine experimentally the probability $P_i(m, n)$ that a dot starting at (m, n) will terminate at the boundary point (m_i, n_i). At point E in Fig. 13.7, for which none of the neighboring points $ABCD$ are boundary points, we have

$$P_i(m, n) = \tfrac{1}{4}[P_i(m + 1, n) + P_i(m - 1, n) + P_i(m, n + 1) + P_i(m, n - 1)].$$
$$(13.19)$$

The reason for this is that, of all the random walks originating at (m, n), one fourth become new random walks originating at each of the four neighboring points of the set. Hence a dot originating at E in Fig. 13.7 and going to point D, for example, will have a probability $\tfrac{1}{4}P_i(m, n - 1)$ of reaching the boundary point i. At a point such as A in Fig. 13.7, which has its right-hand neighbor on a boundary, we have

$$P_i(m, n) = \tfrac{1}{4}[1 + P_i(m - 1, n) + P_i(m, n + 1) + P_i(m, n - 1)]$$

if point i is in fact the point on the boundary to the right of A, because the probability is $1/4$ that a dot at (m, n) will go to the boundary point on the right. However, if point i is *not* the boundary point to the right of A, we have

$$P_i(m, n) = \tfrac{1}{4}[P_i(m - 1, n) + P_i(m, n + 1) + P_i(m, n - 1)],$$

since, in this case the dot can reach boundary point i only by going up or down or to the left. If we agree that with each boundary point or pair of boundary points we associate the probabilities

$$P_i(m_i, n_i) = 1, \quad P_i(m_j, n_j) = 0, \qquad i \neq j, \tag{13.20}$$

we see that (13.19) holds for all interior points, regardless of whether they are near boundaries.

We next assume that we are given a set of "boundary values," or a set of numbers u_i, the number u_i being associated with boundary point i. Consider, for a fixed interior point (m, n), the weighted sum

$$V(m, n) = \sum_j u_j P_j(m, n), \tag{13.21}$$

where the value u_i is associated with boundary point i. Then $V(m, n)$ is the expected value for random walks starting at point (m, n). From (13.19) and (13.21) it is clear that $V(m, n)$ satisfies the difference equation

$$V(m, n) = \tfrac{1}{4}[V(m + 1, n) + V(m - 1, n) + V(m, n + 1) + V(m, n - 1)]. \tag{13.22}$$

Also, from (13.20) and (13.21),

$$V(m_i, n_i) = u_i. \tag{13.23}$$

Hence we have obtained a method for solving the partial difference equation (13.22) with boundary conditions (13.23) by playing the following game of chance.

Consider a dot at point (m, n). Trace its path through the network by making it move at random on the mesh, with equal probability of going left, right, up, or down, at each step. It will finally arrive at a boundary point. Repeat this procedure a large number of times. Then the probabilities P_i which we require are the ratios of the number of times the dot arrived at boundary point i divided by the total number of runs.

The flow diagram in Fig. 13.8 can be used to play the game on a computer. The random-step direction is determined by first generating two random digits α and β; that is, select two numbers at random from $0, 1, 2, \ldots, 9$.[9] We then make decisions with regard to the direction of the step as given in Table 13.2. The remainder of the flow diagram should be self-explanatory.

TABLE 13.2

α	β	Δ_x	Δ_y
≥ 5	≥ 5	1	0
< 5	≥ 5	0	1
≥ 5	< 5	0	-1
< 5	< 5	-1	0

The reason we often wish, in practice, to solve large systems of linear equations of the form (13.19) is that the steady-state distribution of many

---

[9] Methods of choosing random numbers are discussed, for example, in K. D. Tocher, *The Art of Simulation*, Van Nostrand, Princeton, N.J., 1963.

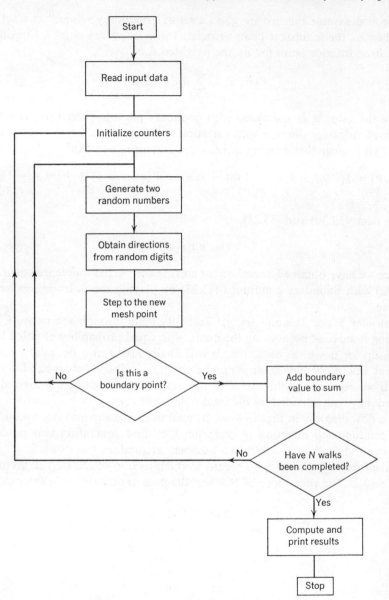

Fig. 13.8   Flow diagram for random walk.

field quantities, such as temperature, pressure, and electrical potential, are often governed by Laplace's equation,

$$\frac{\partial^2 \phi}{\partial x^2} + \frac{\partial^2 \phi}{\partial y^2} = 0. \tag{13.24}$$

If we wish to solve this equation in a given region with values of ϕ specified on the boundary of the region, a common procedure is to cover the region with a square mesh (Fig. 13.7). If the mesh size is h, then at point E in Fig. 13.7, replacing the derivatives by difference approximations,

$$\frac{\partial^2 \phi}{\partial x^2} \approx \frac{\phi_A - 2\phi_E + \phi_C}{h^2}, \qquad \frac{\partial^2 \phi}{\partial y^2} \approx \frac{\phi_B - 2\phi_E + \phi_D}{h^2}.$$

Hence (13.24) can be replaced approximately by

$$(\phi_A - 2\phi_E + \phi_C) + (\phi_B - 2\phi_E + \phi_D) = 0$$

or

$$\phi_E = \tfrac{1}{4}(\phi_A + \phi_B + \phi_C + \phi_D).$$

This is precisely (13.19).

As a practical example, it was required to solve (13.24) in $0 \le x \le 5$, $0 \le y \le 3$, with $\phi = 0$ on $x = 5$, $0 \le y \le 3$, and $\phi = 1$ on the remaining three sides. The region was divided into 1,500 squares by a mesh of side 0.1. A Monte Carlo procedure estimated ϕ at $x = 3$, $y = 1$ to be 0.84 after 100 runs. In this case the exact ϕ could be found analytically, and is 0.864. The number of steps required for each run is about $\tfrac{1}{2}m^2$, where m is the average number of mesh points to be traversed to reach the boundary. If we estimate $m = 20$ in this case, each run takes about 200 steps, or 20,000 steps for 100 runs. It is obvious why a computer is required to play the game. Of course, various improvements would be incorporated in practice to save labor, and it is possible to check accuracy by computing the variance as the runs progress. Nevertheless, the amount of work involved in accumulating statistical results means that only under certain circumstances is the Monte Carlo process efficient compared with more direct processes.

Chapter 14

A Probabilistic Model of
a Conveyor System [1]

14.1 An Idealized Model of a Conveyor

Comment: The first six sections of this chapter are devoted to a single problem. A model is set up on the basis of certain listed assumptions, the model is analyzed mathematically, competing proposals for improving the performance are evaluated, and the validity and effects of the assumptions are considered.

Mathematics Used: Simple theory of repeated independent Bernoulli trials.

A factory, taken in its totality, is an extremely complicated entity. If we were interested in reducing the costs of production directly associated with a given product, we might try to clarify our ideas by deciding first to examine various factors separately. Without trying to be exhaustive, we might list the following factors:

1. The raw material.
2. The operations at the work stations, converting the raw material into the finished product.
3. Material handling, e.g., transportation from one point to another, storage, etc.
4. Inspection of the final product.

We shall confine our attention to one small aspect of the handling of material. This is a fertile field for cost reduction because at least two handlings

---

[1] This chapter (except Section 14.7) is a slightly condensed and modified version of an article by H. E. Mayer, Jr., An Introduction to Conveyor Theory, *Western Electric Engineer*, **4**, 42–47 (1960), drawn to our attention by J. C. Merriam, Western Electric Co.

occur for every work station the material or product passes through, and further handlings are necessitated by inspections, storages, and delays.

One popular solution to the handling problem is the conveyor. In our model the term *conveyor* will refer to an overhead hook-carrier trolley conveyor which functions in the following way. The conveyor carries production away from a number of work stations. We imagine an endless band to which hooks are attached at equal intervals. The band is moving at a constant speed and any given hook passes each of the work stations in turn. If, as a hook passes a given work station, a worker completes a work cycle, the worker will place the product on the hook if it is empty. If, however, a product is already hanging on the hook (having been placed there when the hook passed a previous work station), the worker must either wait for an empty hook, or dispose of the product in some other way.

It will be assumed that the workers are working independent of each other, so that the action of one will not influence the action of the others. It is purely a matter of chance whether one or more workers will attempt to load a given hook. The development of the mathematical description of the model must therefore be based on probability theory.

The object of developing a mathematical model is to help us to understand how and why the system behaves as it does. In particular, we shall be able to make a quantitative comparative study of different proposals for improving the system.

In the usual way, it is essential to simplify the real situation by setting up an idealized model that contains only the important features of the physical system. To describe the operation of the man-machine system more specifically, and to provide a basis for the analysis, the following assumptions are stated. (The validity and effects of the assumptions are discussed in Section 14.5.)

1. The conveyor speed is constant and uninterrupted during periods of productive work.
2. All conveyor hooks are empty before arrival at the first work station.
3. There are n stations; the work-cycle times at all stations are equal.
4. At any given station the work cycle time is a constant, and each worker works independently of the others.
5. Only one conveyor hook is available to a worker when he tries to place his product on a hook at the end of a work cycle. (The spacing of hooks is such that when one hook is within his reach, the neighboring ones are not; conversely, there is always one hook within his reach.)
6. If the worker finds the hook he wishes to use already loaded to capacity, he places his product on the floor and immediately resumes work. (A worker on incentive does not wait for an empty hook.)
7. Once production is placed on the floor it is eliminated from consideration. (This is reasonable, because we are aiming at a situation in which very little production is placed on the floor. If a large amount were to be placed

on the floor, we should certainly need to consider how to deal with it, but we assume that conditions are adjusted so that this does not occur. In other words, we do not need to deal with *bad* performance in a realistic way.)

14.2 The Mathematical Analysis of the Model by Probability Considerations

Let h be the number of hooks that pass a work station during a work cycle. From assumption 1 this is a constant, independent of time. Then the probability p that an attempt is made to load a hook is a constant $1/h$, and the probability q that no attempt is made to load a hook is $1 - p$. (Since it is certain that an attempt at loading either is or is not made, we have $p + q = 1$).

We illustrate the way in which the binomial distribution governs the situation by considering the special case in which there are precisely three work stations. The activities at the work stations are independent of each other, so the probability that no attempt is made to load a given hook as it passes the three work stations is q^3, and the probability that an attempt is made to load the hook as it passes each of the three stations is p^3. Consider the probability that exactly one attempt is made to load a hook. This attempt might be made by the first work station and not by the others, or it might be made by the second and not by the others, or by the third and not by the others. Because the activities at the work stations are independent of each other, the probability for each of the three outcomes is found by taking the product of the separate probabilities that constitute each outcome. This gives pqq, qpq, and qqp. As the outcomes are mutually exclusive, the probability that any one of them occurs is found by taking the sum of the probabilities for each outcome. Therefore the probability that exactly one attempt is made to load a given hook is

$$pqq + qpq + qqp = 3pq^2.$$

We see that the probabilities of 3, 2, 1, and 0 attempts to load a given hook are, respectively, p^3, $3pq^2$, $3p^2q$, and q^3, and these are, in fact, the successive terms in the binomial expansion

$$(p + q)^3 = p^3 + 3p^2q + 3pq^2 + q^3.$$

In general, when there are n work stations, the probabilities of $n, n - 1, \ldots$ attempts to load a given hook are given by the successive terms in the binomial expansion

$$(p + q)^n = p^n + \binom{n}{1}p^{n-1}q + \binom{n}{2}p^{n-2}q^2 + \cdots + \binom{n}{n-1}pq^{n-1} + q^n,$$

where
$$\binom{n}{k} = \frac{n!}{k!\,(n-k)!} = \binom{n}{n-k},$$

and this is the number of ways that k successes can be obtained in n independent trials.

The performance of the conveyor can now be assessed. Ideal performance would result if, at any loading point, the conveyor accepted a product without causing rehandling by, or delays to, the operator. It seems reasonable, then, to consider the quantity of production not readily accepted, if any, in relation to the total production, as a satisfactory index of performance. Therefore, we define a measure-of-demerit to be equal to the quantity of production not readily accepted, divided by the total production. Let

   D = measure-of-demerit,
   F = quantity of production not accepted by the conveyor (placed on the floor during the shift or period of production),
   N = total number of units produced during the shift.

Then
$$D = \frac{F}{N}. \tag{14.1}$$

Ideal performance yields a measure-of-demerit equal to zero, and a conveyor which accepts nothing would yield a value of unity. The measure-of-demerit for all other situations would assume values between zero and unity.

We deduce a formula for D in terms of the following data:

1. Conveyor:
   (a) The conveyor speed is a constant at s hooks per minute.
   (b) The capacity of each hook is one unit of production.
2. Worker and work station:
   (a) There are n identical work stations.
   (b) At each work station a worker, working independent of the others, completes a unit of production in a work cycle of w minutes.

We have previously introduced the quantity h, the number of hooks that pass a given work station in a work cycle, and therefore

$$h = sw. \tag{14.2}$$

Consider a total period of production, or shift time, of R work cycles, or Rw minutes. It is clear that the quantity R will not enter into the final formula for D since D is defined in terms of F and N [see (14.1)], and both F and N are simply proportional to R. The total number of units produced during the shift is then

$$N = Rn.$$

The total number of hooks that pass a work station during a shift is Rh. We have seen above that the probability that no attempt is made to load a given hook as it passes all n work stations is given by q^n, where

$$q = 1 - p = 1 - \frac{1}{h}.$$

Hence the expected total number of hooks that are loaded is

$$Rh(1 - q^n).$$

Since $N = Rn$ units are produced, we see that the number of units left on the floor [the quantity denoted by F in (14.1)] is

$$F = R[n - h(1 - q^n)].$$

Hence from (14.1),

$$D = \frac{F}{N} = 1 - \frac{h}{n}\left[1 - \left(1 - \frac{1}{h}\right)^n\right]. \tag{14.3}$$

If n/h is small, say, less than one half, we can write approximately, using the binomial theorem,

$$\left(1 - \frac{1}{h}\right)^n \approx 1 - \frac{n}{h} + \frac{n(n - 1)}{2h^2}.$$

Substituting this result in (14.3) we obtain, for $n \le 2h$,

$$D \approx \frac{n - 1}{2h}. \tag{14.4}$$

14.3   An Application to an Example

We now consider an actual example. It was proposed to install a hook-type conveyor to remove products from 10 identical work stations ($n = 10$), knowing that each work cycle takes 2 minutes ($w = 2$). Suppose the total working time in a shift is 400 minutes, so that each worker produces 200 units and the total production is 2,000 units. On the basis of 2,000 units of production, the designer thought that arranging for 4,000 hooks to pass through the system per shift ($h = 20$) would be more than adequate. However, since the installation, the workers have complained that not enough hooks were available, and that an excessive number of units have to be placed on the floor.

We assume that an engineer assigned to study the problem has worked out the theory in Section 14.2 on the basis that the assumptions in Section 14.1 are reasonable. (This point is discussed further in Section 14.5 below.) The first thing to do, then, is to check whether the quantitative predictions of the theory check with the results actually found in practice.

We work out, from first principles, some consequences of the theory. Twenty hooks pass a work station during the 2-minute work cycle. Of the 20 hooks, 1 will be offered a product; therefore, the probability that an attempt at loading a hook is made at a work station is $\frac{1}{20}$. Consequently the probability that no attempt is made is $\frac{19}{20} = 0.95$. The probability that a hook passes all work stations and is offered no product is $(0.95)^{10} = 0.5987$. Hence, since a total of 4,000 hooks passes through the system, the expected number of empty hooks that pass through the system is

$$(4,000)(0.5987) = 2,395.$$

If 2,395 of the available 4,000 hooks are empty, the difference

$$4,000 - 2,395 = 1,605$$

represents the expected number of loaded hooks. However, if 2,000 units are produced, the difference

$$2,000 - 1,605 = 395$$

represents the expected number of units which are not accepted by the conveyor. Hence the measure-of-demerit is given by

$$D = \frac{395}{2,000} = 0.1975.$$

In other words, about 20% of the production was not accepted by the conveyor, and, therefore, required rehandling.

This figure could have been obtained from (14.3):

$$D = 1 - \frac{20}{10}\left[1 - \left(1 - \frac{1}{20}\right)^{10}\right] = 1 - 2[1 - (0.95)^{10}].$$

It is of interest to note that the approximate equation (14.4) gives an estimate of D equal to $\frac{9}{40} = 0.225$.

The 20% nonacceptance of production is an average figure for all 10 work stations. Because all hooks arrive empty at the first station, the conveyor will always accept its output. The interference in loading starts at the second work station and gets worse as the hooks travel down the line. The probability that the hook which arrives at the rth work station is loaded is given by

$$1 - (0.95)^{r-1}.$$

For example, the probability that a hook is loaded at the tenth (last) work station is $1 - (0.95)^9 = 0.3698$. Hence 36.98% of the production from the last work station, or 74 units, is placed on the floor.

Quantitative predictions, for example, that there are a total of 395 units on the floor per shift and 74 units on the floor from the tenth work station, substantiate the complaint that excessive numbers of units have to be placed on the floor. These figures, and similar estimates for the other work stations, are easily checked experimentally. If they occur, approximately, in practice, this will give us some confidence in the applicability of the model to the real situation. Assuming that the validity of the model has been checked in this way, we can go on to discuss the relative merits of proposals for improving the performance of the system. (It is obviously important that we should check the applicability of the theory before using it to make recommendations for improving the system!)

14.4   The Evaluation of Competing Proposals for Improving Performance

We can now evaluate proposals for improving the performance of the system, on the assumption that the theory of Section 14.3 is applicable. Believing that an increase in the number of hooks will alleviate the problem we make the following alternative proposals:

1. Double the capacity of each hook (or place two hooks where one existed before).
2. Double the speed of the conveyor.

At first sight it might seem that both proposals accomplish the same thing—provide twice the number of hooks during a shift. However we shall determine whether the two proposals are equivalent on the basis of our idealized model.

The first proposal does not change the probabilities of success or failure from their original values of 0.05 and 0.95, respectively. However, because a hook location may now carry two units, overloading does not begin until an attempt is made to place three or more units on the same location.

The probability that a pair of hooks passes all the work stations and is offered no product is, as before, $(0.95)^{10} = 0.5987$. The probability that a pair of hooks passes all work stations and is offered exactly one product is

$$\binom{10}{1}(0.05)^1(0.95)^9 = 0.3151.$$

Hence the total number of empty hooks that pass through the system is given by

$$4{,}000[(2)(0.5987) + (1)(0.3151)] = 6{,}050,$$

where 4,000 is the total number of hook locations.

If 6,050 of 8,000 available hooks are empty, 1,950 $(8{,}000 - 6{,}050)$ are loaded. Therefore, if 2,000 units are produced, 50 $(2{,}000 - 1{,}950)$ are not accepted by the conveyor. Hence the measure of demerit is

$$D = \frac{50}{2{,}000} = 0.025.$$

In other words, 2.5% of the production is not accepted now by the conveyor. If this is compared with the figure of 20% for the original scheme, we see that doubling the capacity at each position has produced a large increase in efficiency.

We can obtain a simple formula for D by proceeding as at the end of Section 14.2. The probability that a pair of hooks passes all work stations and is offered no product is q^n, and the probability that a pair of hooks is offered exactly one product is npq^{n-1}. The total number of hook locations is Rh, so the number of empty hooks is

$$Rh[2q^n + npq^{n-1}].$$

The number of units carried by the conveyor is

$$2Rh - Rh[2q^n + npq^{n-1}].$$

Hence the number of units left on the floor (F) is

$$Rn - 2Rh + Rh[2q^n + npq^{n-1}].$$

The measure-of-demerit is, therefore, this quantity divided by Rn, which gives

$$D = 1 - \frac{h}{n}[2 - 2q^n - npq^{n-1}].$$

Remembering that $q = 1 - (1/h)$, and assuming $n \leq 2h$, we find approximately, using the binomial theorem,

$$q^n \approx 1 - \frac{n}{h} + \frac{n(n-1)}{2h^2} - \frac{n(n-1)(n-2)}{6h^3},$$

$$q^{n-1} \approx 1 - \frac{n-1}{h} + \frac{(n-1)(n-2)}{2h^2}.$$

Substitution in the above formula for D gives

$$D \approx \frac{(n-1)(n-2)}{6h^2}.$$

For the example considered at the beginning of the section we have $n = 10$, $h = 20$, so $D \approx (9)(8)/(6)(400) = 0.03$, compared with the value 0.025 calculated above.

We now examine the second proposal listed at the beginning of the section, doubling the speed of the conveyor. This doubles the value of h, the number of hooks passing a work station during a work cycle, so the new value of h is 40. The probability p that an attempt is made to load a hook is now $1 - p = 0.975 = q$. As before, the number of work stations is $n = 10$. The approximate formula (14.4) for the measure-of-demerit gives $D \approx 9/80 = 0.111$, or 11.1%. The exact formula (14.3) gives

$$D = 1 - 4[1 - (0.975)^{10}] = 0.105.$$

Hence 10.5% of the production is not accepted now by the conveyor. This is an improvement of about 2:1 over the original system.

Proposal (1) to double the hook capacity, gives $D = 0.025$ and proposal (2) gives $D = 0.105$, compared with the original $D = 0.20$. Proposal (1) is obviously much better than (2), which at first sight is surprising, because it seems that both proposals accomplish the same thing. If we leave the speed unchanged and provide two hooks where one existed before, we provide twice as many hooks during the shift. If we double the speed of the conveyor we also provide twice as many hooks during the shift.

It is important that we should not leave the comparison at this point, but try to understand precisely why the factors of improvement should turn out to be so different, in spite of the fact that the two proposals seem to be superficially similar. Examining the basic assumptions listed at the end of Section 14.1, we find that the basic difference between the two schemes is connected with assumptions 5 and 6:

5. Precisely one hook location is within reach of the worker at any instant.
6. If the worker finds this hook location loaded, he places his product on the floor.

Suppose that instead of placing two hooks where one existed before, as in proposal (1), we double the total number of hooks by halving the original spacing between hooks, still keeping the speed of the conveyor the same as before. Then assumptions 5 and 6 become:

5′. Precisely two hook locations are within reach of the worker at any instant.
6′. If the worker finds that both of the hooks within his reach are loaded, he places his product on the floor.

Clearly the measure-of-demerit of this system will be precisely as for proposal (1).

The basic reason proposal (2) does not result in much improvement is that when the system is speeded up there is still only one hook within the worker's reach at any time. In proposal (1), or the alternative just described, there are always two hooks within his reach.

The number of hooks available to a worker depends not only on the number of hooks instantaneously within his reach, but also on how long he is willing to wait for an empty hook. We have assumed that the worker is not willing to wait any time at all, but in practice he will probably take a finite time to decide whether to place his product on a hook or on the floor. If the interval between hooks is not too infrequent, he may be willing to wait a small length of time if he sees that although the nearest hook is loaded, the next approaching hook is empty. If we admit this possibility, the previous analysis will underestimate the benefits of speeding up the conveyor, because speeding up the system will give the worker a better chance of obtaining an empty hook during a fixed waiting period.

This discussion has been included to emphasize that the results obtained by mathematical reasoning always depend crucially on the initial assumptions.

14.5   Evaluation of Assumptions

Each of the assumptions made in Section 14.1 was introduced essentially to simplify the picture, to facilitate the application of mathematics. It is important to examine these assumptions critically to clarify the departure from reality that each assumption has created.

Assumption 1 simply means that we confine our attention to the steady-state activity of the conveyor, when it is working normally.

Assumption 2 eliminates the need to consider complications that would arise if the conveyor were simultaneously used for other purposes, for example, conveying raw material or unfinished products to the work stations. In cases such as these it would be necessary to adopt a more complicated model.

Assumption 3 specifies that the same activity is performed at all work stations, and that all the workers take the same time to perform this activity. Small differences in work-cycle time between workers will not affect the main picture, but if groups of workers have significantly different work-cycle times (because, for example, they are performing different jobs), it will be necessary to examine a more complicated model.

The first part of assumption 4, that the work cycle time is a constant at any given work station, is an approximation. Cycle times will vary about an average, depending on the time of day, the effort being made by the worker, and so on. If work cycles fluctuate, the conveyor performance will be worse than we have calculated on the basis of a constant work-cycle time, since a temporary increase in output will mean that more units will go on the floor, and this will not be altogether compensated for by fewer units going on the floor during periods of temporarily reduced output.

The second part of assumption 4, the independence of workers, justifies the probabilistic approach and the use of the binomial theorem. If the workers perform in some systematic way (for example, if they perform their tasks in a definite time, starting and finishing at known instants), then a deterministic approach would be required, because we would be dealing with a completely different problem. The assumption of the independence of the workers is much more likely to be true if the workers are physically separated (for example, by machinery or partitions).

Assumption 5 is somewhat arbitrary. In a real situation a designer would find it difficult, impracticable, or even undesirable to arrange that there is one and only one hook accessible at any one instant. The number of accessible hooks will depend on such factors as the size of the product, the freedom of movement of the worker, the hook spacing, and the conveyor speed. The importance of the number of accessible hooks should be clear from the discussion at the end of Section 14.4. The method given there for analyzing the situation when two hooks are accessible can clearly be extended to the general case in which an arbitrary number of hooks are accessible.

Assumption 6 simplifies the analysis considerably because it eliminates any need to consider waiting times. If the worker had to wait for the first empty hook, we should be involved in some difficult (or at least laborious) probability calculations. Assumption 7 is not realistic because production placed on the floor must be removed sometime, and the conveyor would be used to remove it. Whenever the floored production is placed on the conveyor, hooks that were empty become loaded, causing additional production to be placed on the floor. Obviously assumption 7 (like 6) is adopted to simplify the analysis. It would, of course, be possible to take account of the factors that we have deliberately eliminated in making assumptions 6 and 7 by developing a more complicated model, but we shall not attempt to do this here.

It can be argued that the primary objects of the theory are:

(a) To design a system which will ensure that most of the time an empty hook will be within reach of a worker.
(b) To provide a method for evaluating competing proposals for improving a given system.

For these purposes it can be argued that it does not matter much which methods are used to deal with the situation that arises when no empty hook is within reach. Therefore, we choose the simplest assumptions we can think of (or, more accurately, the assumptions that lead to the simplest mathematics). These are assumptions 6 and 7 in Section 14.1. However, if the worker is willing to wait a certain time to see if an empty hook appears, these assumptions will underestimate the benefits of speeding up the conveyor, for speeding up the conveyor will give the worker a greater chance of obtaining an empty hook during a given waiting period.

14.6   Summary and Concluding Remarks

Section 14.1 described a simplified model setup for a hook conveyor system. This was analyzed by probability considerations in Section 14.2.

In Section 14.3 it was found that in a specified example the conveyor system was not entirely satisfactory, even though 4,000 hooks were available for 2,000 products. The apparently surplus empty hooks were not always at the place needed, because of the element of chance in the loading process.

In Section 14.4 two competing proposals for improving performance were examined. Although the proposals seemed similar, it turned out that one produced a much greater improvement than the other. However, this conclusion depended essentially on two of the assumptions (5 and 6) on which the model was based.

The basic assumptions were further examined in Section 14.5.

It is important to emphasize that it is precisely because the behavior of an individual worker cannot be predicted exactly that we go to the other extreme and assume that the workers behave independently and randomly. The model can predict what will happen because it is based on probability considerations, even though unpredictable "human factors" are involved.

The fact that so many limitations are implicit in the model should not worry an applied scientist or engineer. We are accustomed to assuming that members are rigid, surfaces are smooth, materials are homogeneous, and so on. The important thing in this connection is to have enough judgment to know whether the assumptions are likely to be satisfied to a sufficient degree of approximation.

The model discussed here can be extended in various ways. We can study the real situation more exactly by making the model more complicated. We can also use similar types of model to discuss other kinds of situation. For example, problems involving belt conveyors may be investigated in the same way by considering units of belt area occupied by the product as the basis for establishing the necessary probabilities.

Although we have ignored economics in the example, the real question of the relative costs of various proposals may be evaluated after determining just what the proposal means to the operational characteristics of the system. The last sentence in the paper by Mayer[2] states: "It is anticipated that the economic gains that may be realized through increased efficiency in conveyor design may provide incentive to cause extensions of the previous theory to be developed."

The object of including this elementary analysis of one type of conveyor is to illustrate two of the objectives of using mathematics in engineering problems.

(a) The value of quantitative as opposed to qualitative information, both in the original design and in comparing alternative designs.

(b) The clarification of the underlying factors determining the performance of a system that is forced on us whenever we try to analyze the system mathematically.

Mathematics plays an essential role, but engineering judgment is also important in connection with isolating the factors that must be incorporated in the model, and neglecting nonessentials.

14.7 A Postscript on the Storage and Retrieval of Material[3]

Mathematics Used: Simple probability theory.

In this section we mention briefly another kind of factory problem, some aspects of which can be analyzed by simple probability theory. Material for manufacturing operations must be available when required. This means that stores must be maintained. There are many factors involved, such as building

[2] H. E. Mayer, Jr., *Western Electric Engineer*, **4**, 42–47 (1960).
[3] This section is based on part of a submitted article: H. E. Mayer, Jr., Storage and Retrieval of Material, *Western Electric Engineer*, **5**, 42–48 (1961).

investment (floor space), inventory investment, equipment, and labor. We consider only one small segment of the overall problem.

Consider an *order-picker*, by which we mean a person who walks along a line of storage cells, depositing or retrieving material as required. Suppose the cells are numbered $1, 2, 3, \ldots, N$, where the origin, zero, is the point at which the incoming material is received (or outgoing material is released). To simplify the analysis we make the following assumptions.

1. All the storage cells are identical, and all the loads deposited in or retrieved from single cells are equivalent. (This means that we do not need to worry about storing special items in certain cells.)

2. A single trip of the order-picker consists of starting from the origin zero, moving to one or more cells, and returning to the origin. The work involved can be taken to be proportional to the distance traveled by the order-picker. The cells are assumed to be equally spaced along a line, so the work involved in going from the origin to cell p is proportional to p and the work involved in going from cell p to cell q is proportional to $|p - q|$. A factor of proportionality can be ignored, because we shall be interested only in comparing different modes of operation.

3. In assuming that the work involved can be taken to be proportional to the distance traveled, we are implicitly assuming that the bookkeeping or paperwork connected with storage or retrieval is being handled independent of the order-picker. The way in which the associated information is handled must obviously be taken into account in any complete analysis of storage-and-retrieval systems, but this aspect will be ignored here.

4. The operation of the order-picker is assumed to be continuous; that is, he has no waiting periods. This means that there is always an excess of material waiting to be stored, or a surplus of orders for the retrieval of material waiting to be executed. If the order-picker has random waiting periods, the analysis becomes much more complicated.

5. When depositing material in, or retrieving material from, storage, the locations visited by the order-picker are determined by drawing, at random, a storage cell from the population of cells, there being a known probability that any given cell is chosen. It is this assumption that requires us to use probability theory to analyze the situation.

6. The material is handled in the form of unit loads; that is, all loads intended for (or retrieved from) single cells are identical. Typical modes of operation would be

(a) Single load working, in which the order-picker *either* deposits a unit load in storage *or* retrieves a unit load from storage.

(b) Double load working, in which the order-picker deposits two unit loads in different cells chosen at random, or retrieves two loads, or deposits one load and retrieves another load (the two locations being assumed independent). The work involved in each of these three operations is assumed to be the same.

As an example we compare the time required for single and double load working, assuming the cells are visited at random by the order-picker, the probability of visiting any cell being the same, independent of the position of the cell. We use two fundamental notions from probability theory:

1. The expected value of a random variable may be determined if its probability distribution is known.
2. The expected value of a sum is equal to the sum of the individual expected values.

To evaluate the expected time T_1 required for a single cycle of operation, let t_0 be the time required by the order-picker to go from one cell to the next, assumed to be the same for all cells. The time required to go from the origin to the first cell is also assumed to be t_0, and the time spent at the origin and at the cells when depositing or retrieving material is assumed to be negligible. Then

$$T_1 = 2E(n)t_0,$$

where $E(n)$[4] is the expected value of the cell number to which the order-picker goes from the origin, to deposit or retrieve material,

$$E(n) = \sum_{n=1}^{N} nP(n),$$

where there are N cells and $P(n)$ is the probability that the order-picker goes to cell n. Because the cells are visited with equal probability,

$$P(n) = \frac{1}{N} \quad \text{and} \quad E(n) = \frac{1}{N} \sum_{n=1}^{N} n = \tfrac{1}{2}(N + 1).$$

Hence
$$T_1 = (N + 1)t_0. \tag{14.5}$$

Double load working involves traveling from the origin to one of the cells, then to another cell, then returning to the origin. The expected times for traveling from the origin to the first cell, and from the second cell back to the origin, will be the same as those found above, so the expected time T_2 for double load working is given by

$$T_2 = T_1 + E(d)t_0, \tag{14.6}$$

where $E(d)$ is the expected difference in cell numbers between the first and second cells visited by the order-picker. To evaluate $E(d)$ we require the probability that $|n_i - n_j| = d$ for $d = 1, 2, \ldots, N - 1$. There are N ways of choosing a number n_i, and then $N - 1$ ways of choosing a second number

---

[4] To prevent confusion, it is perhaps worthwhile to point out that the notation $E(n)$ for the expected value of n is *not* analogous to the notation $f(x)$ for a function of x. The quantity $E(n)$ is a function of N and not of n, which is a "dummy variable."

n_j ($\neq n_i$), that is, $N(N - 1)$ equally likely ways of choosing $|n_i - n_j|$. Of these $|n_i - n_j|$, exactly $2(N - d)$ will have $|n_i - n_j| = d$. Hence

$$P(|n_i - n_j| = d) = \frac{2(N - d)}{N(N - 1)}, \qquad d = 1, 2, \ldots, N - 1.$$

Hence

$$E(d) = \sum_{d=1}^{N-1} dP(|n_i - n_j| = d) = \sum_{d=1}^{N-1} \frac{2d(N - d)}{N(N - 1)} = \frac{1}{3}(N + 1). \quad (14.7)$$

From (14.5) to (14.7) we see that

$$T_2 = \tfrac{4}{3}(N + 1)t_0.$$

To compare single and double load working we need to compare T_2 with $2T_1$ because single load working requires twice as many trips as double load working to deal with the same number of loads, that is, we compare $\tfrac{4}{3}(N + 1)t_0$ with $2(N + 1)t_0$, so double load working requires $\tfrac{2}{3}$ of the time of single load working. However, this figure is based on the assumption that the time spent at the origin or at the cells is negligible compared with the traveling time, and the full factor $\tfrac{2}{3}$ may not be attainable in practice, for this and for other reasons. Nevertheless, it is useful to know what the ideal improvement factor is.

In this section we have analyzed an extremely simple situation, but it should be clear that the same method can be extended to deal with much more complicated problems, for example, when the cells are visited with unequal but known probabilities, or when the cells are arranged in two or three dimensions.

Chapter 15

Waiting-Line and Traffic Problems[1]

15.1 Introduction

A typical situation considered in waiting-line theory is the following. A flow of customers requiring service arrives "at random" at a service facility within which there are one or more servers. Each customer is serviced by one of the servers. A typical question is: How long would each customer expect to spend waiting in a queue? The terms "customers," "servers," and "service facility" are to be understood in a broad sense, as illustrated in the following examples.

1. Machines require attention from time to time (starting, loading, unloading, servicing, and so on). How many machines should be assigned to each operator, the operator being able to attend to only one machine at a time? Here the machine is the customer and the operator is the server.

2. Items of work (the customers) come into a testing department or a typing pool, the number of items that can be dealt with being limited by the number of workers (servers) in the department.

3. There are numerous waiting-line problems in connection with telephone exchanges.[2] Thus there may be a fixed number of telephone lines between two places and a fixed amount of central office equipment. A certain number of subscribers make calls at random. Are there enough lines and switching facilities to prevent undue inconvenience?

4. There are, similarly, many waiting-line problems in connection with road traffic. If the customers are pedestrians waiting to cross the road, service is available only when a sufficiently large gap occurs in the traffic.

---

[1] An interesting introduction to this type of problem, using only basic probability theory and elementary calculus, is given in D. R. Cox and W. L. Smith, *Queues*, Methuen, London, and Wiley, New York, 1961.

[2] See, for example, T. C. Fry, *Probability and Its Engineering Uses*, 2nd ed., Van Nostrand, Princeton, N.J., 1965.

5. The customers can be items in a store waiting to be withdrawn by the servers. The service is withdrawal of the item from the store. Not more than a limited number of items can be stored at once, owing to lack of space and overhead cost. If the demand for an item is random, what is the connection with the maximum content of the store, the frequency with which the stock of items is renewed, and the chance that the store will be found empty when a call for a fresh item is made?[3]

The most we can do here is to introduce the reader to the treatment of one or two typical examples. In Section 15.2 we discuss the random distribution of points on a line, which is standard course work. The details of the derivations are not required in the remainder of this chapter. They are included to indicate the fundamental importance of the Poisson and exponential distributions in this subject. A simple traffic problem is discussed in Section 15.3. Sections 15.4 to 15.6 are devoted to a more extended treatment of a waiting-line problem in a factory. A method of simulating waiting-line problems by computer is discussed in Section 15.7.

15.2   Completely Random Arrivals

Mathematics Used: Limits. Simple probability theory, leading to the Poisson and exponential distributions.

It is convenient to derive here, for future reference (although it is a piece of standard book work),[4] some of the mathematical properties of a completely random arrival pattern. This pattern of arrivals is defined as follows. Suppose the average rate of arrival of customers is α, and suppose that for any short time interval t to $t + \Delta t$ the probability that no customers arrive is $1 - \alpha \Delta t + o(\Delta t)$, that one customer arrives is $\alpha \Delta t + o(\Delta t)$, and, therefore, that two or more customers arrive is $o(\Delta t)$, where $o(\Delta t)$ denotes quantities that become negligible compared with Δt as Δt tends to zero. Also, what happens in the interval t to $t + \Delta t$ is assumed to be statistically independent of the arrival or nonarrival of customers in any time interval not overlapping $(t, t + \Delta t)$.

We deduce an expression for the probability distribution of the number of customers arriving in a time period of fixed length T. Divide the period T into m intervals each of length Δt, $m \Delta t = T$. The probability that a single customer arrives in one of these intervals is $\alpha \Delta t + o(\Delta t)$, and the probability that no customer arrives is $1 - \alpha \Delta t + o(\Delta t)$. The numbers of customers to arrive in different intervals are statistically independent, and the probability that two or more customers arrive in any interval is $o(\Delta t)$. Hence, by the

---

[3] Some references to these and other applications of waiting-line theory can be found in F. S. Hillier, The Application of Waiting-Line Theory to Industrial Problems, *J. Ind. Eng.*, **15**, 3–8 (1964).

[4] D. R. Cox and W. L. Smith, *Queues*, Methuen, London, and Wiley, New York, 1961, pp. 5–12.

binomial law, the probability that precisely r customers arrive in the whole period is

$$\frac{m!}{r!\,(m-r)!}\,[\alpha\,\Delta t + o(\Delta t)]^r[1 - \alpha\,\Delta t + o(\Delta t)]^{m-r} + o(\Delta t\,).$$

We wish to find the limit of this expression as Δt tends to zero. We can then neglect $o(\Delta t)$ terms. On setting $\Delta t = T/m$ we see that we require

$$\lim_{m\to\infty} \frac{(\alpha T)^r}{r!}\,\frac{m!}{m^r(m-r)!}\left(1 - \frac{\alpha T}{m}\right)^{m-r}. \tag{15.1}$$

Now
$$\frac{m!}{m^r(m-r)!} = \left(1 - \frac{1}{m}\right)\left(1 - \frac{2}{m}\right)\cdots\left(1 - \frac{r-1}{m}\right),$$

and, since r is fixed, the number of bracketed terms is fixed, and the limit of this quantity as m tends to infinity is just unity. Also,

$$\lim_{m\to\infty}\left(1 - \frac{\alpha T}{m}\right)^{m-r} = \lim_{m\to\infty}\left(1 - \frac{\alpha T}{m}\right)^m \lim_{m\to\infty}\left(1 - \frac{\alpha T}{m}\right)^{-r} = e^{-\alpha T},$$

where the second limit is unity since r is fixed, and the fact that the first limit is an exponential is a standard result. Hence (15.1) gives the result that the probability that precisely r customers arrive during a period T is given by

$$\frac{(\alpha T)^r}{r!}\,e^{-\alpha T}, \qquad r = 0, 1, 2, \ldots. \tag{15.2}$$

This is simply the Poisson distribution.

Instead of considering the number of customers arriving during a fixed period of time T, it is sometimes useful to consider the distribution of time intervals between consecutive arrivals. Let

$$F(t) = \text{prob (interval between arrivals is} \geq t),$$

and let $f(t)$ denote the probability distribution that the time interval between successive arrivals is t:

$$f(t)\,\Delta t = \text{prob (time interval between successive arrivals is between}$$
$$t \text{ and } t + \Delta t).$$

Then
$$F(t) - F(t + \Delta t) = f(t)\,\Delta t$$

or
$$F(t) = \int_t^\infty f(u)\,du. \tag{15.3}$$

The basic relation we require is simply:

$$F(t) = \text{prob (interval between arrivals is} \geq t)$$
$$= \text{prob (there are no arrivals in a period } t)$$
$$= e^{-\alpha t},$$

where the last line has been obtained by setting $r = 0$ in (15.2). Hence

$$\int_t^\infty f(u)\, du = e^{-\alpha t}.$$

Differentiation gives

$$f(t) = \alpha e^{-\alpha t}. \tag{15.4}$$

This is the exponential distribution giving the probability distribution for a time interval t between successive arrivals. It is a continuous distribution, whereas the Poisson distribution is discrete.

Another derivation of this result, this time not using the Poisson distribution, is the following. Let

$$g(t) = \text{prob (no customer arrives between } t_0 \text{ and } t_0 + t).$$

Then

$$
\begin{aligned}
g(t + \Delta t) &= \text{prob (no customer arrives between } t_0 \text{ and } t_0 + t + \Delta t) \\
&= g(t)\, \text{prob (no customer arrives between } t_0 + t \text{ and} \\
&\qquad t_0 + t + \Delta t) \\
&= g(t)[1 - \alpha\, \Delta t + o(\Delta t)],
\end{aligned}
$$

where the second line comes from the product law for the probability of independent events, the events being independent, from the definition of random series. Then

$$g(t + \Delta t) - g(t) = -\alpha g(t)\, \Delta t + o(\Delta t).$$

Dividing by Δt and letting Δt tend to zero, we find

$$\frac{dg}{dt} = -\alpha g$$

or

$$g = a e^{-\alpha t}.$$

By definition of $g(t)$ we have $g(0) = 1$, so that $a = 1$ and

$$g(t) = e^{-\alpha t}.$$

The probability density function $f(t)$ of the interval between successive arrivals is, therefore, given by

$$
\begin{aligned}
f(t)\, \Delta t &= \text{prob (interval lies between } t \text{ and } t + \Delta t) \\
&= g(t) - g(t + \Delta t).
\end{aligned}
$$

On letting Δt tend to zero,

$$f(t) = -\frac{dg}{dt} = \alpha e^{-\alpha t},$$

which of course agrees with (15.4).

From the derivation in the last paragraph it is clear that the distribution (15.4) refers to the interval between successive arrivals, or to the interval from an arbitrary fixed instant to the next arrival. That these two distributions

Fig. 15.1   Random series of arrivals.

should be the same may appear paradoxical at first sight, but it is in fact a natural consequence of the initial assumption that whether or not an arrival occurs in one interval is independent of what happens in other intervals. Hence whether the starting point corresponds to an arrival or not can have no effect on the subsequent occurrences, and in particular on the length of time elapsing before the next arrival.

The exponential distribution is greatest for zero interval length ($t = 0$) and decreases as the interval length t increases. Hence short intervals are relatively frequent, and as a result random series tend to "clump" rather more than one might at first expect (Fig. 15.1).

15.3   A Traffic Problem: Safe Gaps at School Crossings[5]

Mathematics Used: Poisson distribution.

Comment: Note the check of the assumptions against experiment in Fig. 15.2.

It is always extremely important to check experimentally, if possible, that the assumptions on which a statistical analysis is based are sound. We wish to apply a theory similar to that developed in the last section to the passage of motor vehicles along a highway. The first step is to check whether in fact the distribution of cars along the highway can be considered random. There are all sorts of reasons why this might not be true. It is perhaps surprising that in many cases the hypothesis of random distribution is in reasonable agreement with experiment.

Suppose that

$$P(t) = \text{prob (no vehicle passes a certain point in a time interval } t) \quad (15.5)$$

If measurement shows that N cars pass the point over a total period of time T where N is large (say, greater than 100), the mean number of cars per time interval t is Nt/T. Hence, by the Poisson distribution [(15.2) with $r = 0$],

$$P(t) = e^{-Nt/T}. \quad (15.6)$$

[5] This section is based on D. L. Gerlough, *Use of Poisson Distribution in Highway Traffic*, Eno Foundation for Highway Traffic Control, Saugatuck, Conn., 1955. The discussion of safe gaps at school crossings is based on: Report on Warrants for Traffic Officers at School Intersections, *Proc. Inst. Traffic Engrs.*, **18**, 118–130 (1947). The last example was drawn to our attention by the College of Engineering, University of Illinois, Urbana, Ill., through Dean W. L. Everitt.

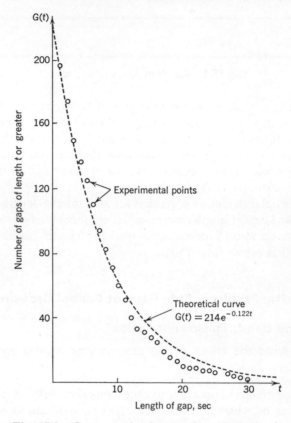

Fig. 15.2 Gaps on the Arroyo Seco Freeway, in
one lane, in one period of 1753 sec in an afternoon,
October 1950.

The function $P(t)$ is also the probability that there is a gap of at least t sec
between the vehicle that has just passed and the next vehicle. Hence

$$G(t) = (\text{expected number of gaps} \geq t) = NP(t) = Ne^{-Nt/T}. \quad (15.7)$$

Figure 15.2 is a comparison of theory and experiment for one observation
period of 1,753 sec on the Arroyo Seco Freeway, during which 214 cars
passed. Then the theory predicts

$$G(t) = 214e^{-214t/1753} = 214e^{-0.122t}.$$

The agreement between theory and experiment is reasonably good.

We now use a similar analysis to study the natural gaps in traffic at school
crossings. Suppose that at a crossing the width of the street is D ft and that the
walking speed of a child is 3.5 ft/sec, so that a child takes $t = D/3.5$ sec to
cross the street. We wish to arrange at least one opportunity of crossing the
street per minute, on the average, assuming that the automobile traffic flow

past the crossing is governed by a Poisson distribution, as previously described. If the flow rate is N vehicles per hour, it is required to determine the maximum traffic flow rate N_{max} that would be allowed, assuming cars pass randomly, and still allow one opportunity of crossing per minute, on the average. The significance of N_{max} is that any survey showing a traffic rate in excess of N_{max} would be a justification for installing some kind of control at the crossing.

To solve this problem, let

p = prob (no vehicle passes in a given interval of t sec),
t = number of seconds a child takes to cross the road ($= D/3.5$ in the above example),
τ = time interval in which we wish there to be at least one interval of length t free of vehicles ($= 60$ sec), and
R = flow rate of vehicles per second ($= N/3,600$).

(Note that the original formulation involved width of road, walking speed, and seconds, minutes, and hours. To avoid confusion we isolate essential factors by introducing suitable notation. The special values are reintroduced at the end.)

The expected number of vehicles per time interval t is Rt. Hence the probability that no vehicle will pass in a given interval of t sec is, from (15.2) with $r = 0$,

$$p = e^{-Rt}. \tag{15.8}$$

If we consider k successive intervals of length t, we expect that kp of these will be free of vehicles. To obtain, on the average, one interval free of vehicles, we need to consider k intervals, where k is given by $kp = 1$; that is, $k = 1/p$. These will occupy a time kt, and this is the time we have defined as τ,

$$\tau = kt = \frac{t}{p}. \tag{15.9}$$

The argument used to establish this equation is not exact because we have assumed successive independent intervals of time t, whereas, of course, a child would cross at any suitably large gap in the traffic. However, any deductions from our formulas will be on the safe side, since our reasoning underestimates the number of crossing periods available.

Combining (15.8) and (15.9) we obtain

$$t = \tau e^{-Rt}.$$

Take the logarithm of both sides to the base 10,

$$\log_{10}\left(\frac{t}{\tau}\right) = -Rt \log_{10} e.$$

Introduce the previous notation,

$$t = \frac{D}{3.5}, \qquad \tau = 60, \qquad R = \frac{N}{3,600}.$$

From the statement of the problem, N is in fact the critical number of vehicles per hour that must not be exceeded. Hence, finally,

$$N_{max} = \frac{1}{D} \, 29{,}000(2.322 - \log_{10} D), \tag{15.10}$$

where D is the width of the road in feet. This gives

Width of street, D (ft):	25	50	75
Max. flow rate, N_{max} (autos/hr):	1,072	361	173

One of the interesting things about these results is that they show how critical the street width is on the problem of pedestrian crossing. The permissible flow rate decreases sharply with increasing street width. The results indicate how important crossing controls for school children must be for large highways, which are liable to have heavy traffic. Even if traffic is not heavy, the wider highways offer surprisingly greater hazard. Equation (15.10) has been adopted by the Joint Committee of the Institute of Traffic Engineers and the International Association of Chiefs of Police.

15.4   A Waiting-Line Problem in an Aircraft Factory[6]

Mathematics Used: Poisson and exponential distributions; difference equations.

Comment: This section and the following two are concerned with a waiting-line problem. Again note the experimental check of the assumptions in Figs. 15.3 and 15.4. The conclusion is that it is desirable to provide more service facilities than might appear necessary at first sight.

A study was made to determine the number of clerks to be assigned to the tool-crib counters in use in a Boeing factory area. These cribs store a variety of tools required by the mechanics in the shops and in the assembly lines. There are about 60 of them scattered throughout three plants, each employing anywhere from one to five clerks. The number of clerks that should be assigned to each crib has been long argued about, two conflicting pressures applying: one, the complaints of foremen when they felt that their mechanics were waiting too long in line, which led to more clerks; the other, the pressure of management to reduce overhead, which led to fewer.

---

[6] Sections 15.4 and 15.6 are a condensed version of part of an article by G. Brigham, On a Congestion Problem in an Aircraft Factory, *Operations Res.*, **3**, 412–428 (1955). This is reprinted in E. H. Bowman and R. B. Fetter (eds.), *Analyses of Industrial Operations*, Irwin, Homewood, Ill., 1959, in which reprints of many other papers containing interesting applications of elementary mathematics to industrial problems can be found.

The argument, of course, revolves around the time spent waiting, both by the mechanics and the clerks. Given the tool cribs as they are laid out, the efficiency of the clerks, and the present production lines, the mechanics will arrive in a certain fashion, and the clerks will take a certain time to wait on them. The "slack," so to speak, with which we can work is then the combined waiting time of the clerks and the mechanics, which can be varied by changing the number of clerks. However, in most cases these times are not equally valuable; hence their cost is a better measure of the loss incurred than the times themselves.

To evaluate the waiting times requires knowing the following characteristics of the queue:

(a) the distribution of serving times;
(b) the distribution of arrival times;
(c) the type of service, whether random or not;
(d) the number of clerks (the variable we can control).

The first step was to obtain data on these factors. The serving times can be checked by sampling. An observer simply watches the people at the counter and measures, with a stop watch for example, the length of time taken to serve a man. An example of a distribution curve of serving times observed experimentally in this way, compared with a theoretical exponential

TABLE 15.1

Mean serving time $= 50.5$ sec

Theoretical values are given
by $475e^{-t/50.5}$

t	Actual	Theoretical
0	475	475
10	392	384
20	294	315
30	224	258
40	174	212
50	135	174
60	104	143
70	89	117
80	76	96
90	71	79
100	61	65
110	56	53
120	41	43
130	32	36
140	31	29
150	29	24

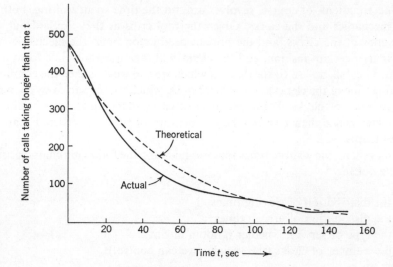

Fig. 15.3 Distribution of serving times.

distribution, is shown in Fig. 15.3 and Table 15.1. The agreement shows that it is reasonable to assume an exponential distribution for serving times.

The number of arrivals at the tool cribs per unit time were also observed. An example of the numbers of arrivals per mean serving time observed experimentally for one tool crib, compared with the numbers to be expected theoretically, is shown in Fig. 15.4 and Table 15.2. The agreement shows that it is reasonable to assume a random rate of arrival.

TABLE 15.2

Average number of arrivals
per mean serving time = 1.43

Theoretical values are given
by $976e^{-1.43}(1.43)^k/k!$

k	Actual	Theoretical
0	272	233
1	306	334
2	213	239
3	117	114
4	44	41
5	12	12
6	6	3
7	5	1
8	1	0

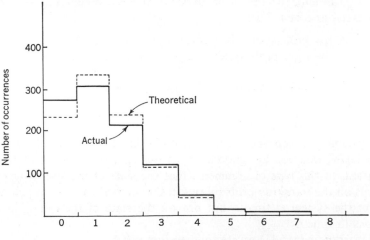

Number of arrivals per mean serving time, k

Fig. 15.4   Distribution of arrivals: solid line, actual; dashed line, theoretical.

On the basis of the agreement between experimental and theoretical distributions in Figs. 15.3 and 15.4 and Tables 15.1 and 15.2, we can conclude that it is reasonable to make the following assumptions:

1. The probability that there will be an arrival in time t to $t + \Delta t$ is $\alpha \Delta t$, to first order, where α is a constant.
2. The probability that a customer will depart (the servicing being finished) is $\beta \Delta t$, to first order, where β is a constant.

In the next section we use these assumptions to construct a theory from which the average waiting time and other parameters of the process can be computed.

15.5   Formulas Required for the Factory Problem

We first consider a simple example. Suppose that if the system is in state A at time t, the probability that it will switch to state B in the interval t to $t + \Delta t$ is, to first order, $\alpha \Delta t$, independent of what happens at any other time. [In Section 15.2 we should have written this probability as $\alpha \Delta t + o(\Delta t)$. From now on we shall omit explicit mention of small-order terms, although we use such phrases as "to the first order" to indicate that they have been omitted. We are interested only in the limiting case, where Δt tends to zero.] The probability that the system in state A stays in state A is $1 - \alpha \Delta t$, to first order. Similarly, for transition from state B to state A, suppose the probability is $\beta \Delta t$, so there is probability $1 - \beta \Delta t$ that the system stays in state B in the time interval t to $t + \Delta t$.

Let $p_A(t)$ and $p_B(t)$ denote the probabilities that the system is in state A or B, respectively, at time t. Then

$$p_A(t + \Delta t) = \text{prob (system is in state } A \text{ at time } t + \Delta t)$$
$$= p_A(t) \cdot \text{prob (system stays in state } A \text{ in the interval } t \text{ to}$$
$$t + \Delta t)$$
$$+ p_B(t) \cdot \text{prob (system changes from state } B \text{ to state } A \text{ in the}$$
$$\text{interval)}$$
$$= p_A(t)(1 - \alpha \Delta t) + p_B(t)\beta \Delta t. \tag{15.11}$$

The probability of two or more transitions in time Δt is of order $(\Delta t)^2$, by the product law, and can be ignored in setting up the above equation. It is important, in this type of argument, that the state of the system at $t + \Delta t$ depends on the transition probabilities in the interval t to $t + \Delta t$ and on the state of the system at time t, but not on the state of the system at times previous to time t.

On rearranging (15.11) we see that, to first order,

$$p_A(t + \Delta t) - p_A(t) = [-\alpha p_A(t) + \beta p_B(t)] \Delta t.$$

On dividing by Δt and letting Δt tend to zero, we find

$$\frac{dp_A}{dt} = -\alpha p_A + \beta p_B. \tag{15.12}$$

Precisely the same type of argument applied to p_B gives

$$\frac{dp_B}{dt} = \alpha p_A - \beta p_B. \tag{15.13}$$

We shall be interested only in steady-state conditions. Then

$$\frac{dp_A}{dt} = \frac{dp_B}{dt} = 0,$$

and (15.12) and (15.13) reduce to the single equation

$$\alpha p_A - \beta p_B = 0. \tag{15.14}$$

Since the system must be in one of the states A or B, we have

$$p_A + p_B = 1. \tag{15.15}$$

We now have two equations, (15.14) and (15.15), for p_A and p_B, which can be solved to give

$$p_A = \frac{\beta}{\alpha + \beta}, \qquad p_B = \frac{\alpha}{\alpha + \beta}.$$

We extend this argument to the case, where there are m servers and a queue of any length can form. This might appear at first sight to be much more complicated than the above simple problem, but in fact the principles involved are no more difficult; only the algebra is more complicated. If there are n customers at the service facility we say that the system is "in state n." Two cases arise:

(a) If $n \leq m$, all the customers are being served.
(b) If $n > m$, then m customers are being served, while $n - m$ are waiting for service.

In accordance with the experimental results in Section 16.4 we make the following assumptions:

1. The probability that there will be an arrival between t and $t + \Delta t$ is $\alpha \Delta t$, independent of t.
2. The probability that any one customer departs (having been served) in the time interval t to $t + \Delta t$ is $\beta \Delta t$, where β is a constant, independent of t. In applying this second assumption we distinguish two cases:
    (a) If $n \leq m$ customers are being served, the probability that one customer departs in the interval t to $t + \Delta t$ is $n\beta \Delta t$.
    (b) If $n \geq m$ customers are being served, the probability that one customer departs in the interval t to $t + \Delta t$ is $m\beta \Delta t$.

Let $p_n(t)$ denote the probability that the system is in state n at time t. Then simple bookkeeping gives the result:

$$p_n(t + \Delta t) = p_n(t) \cdot \text{prob (system stays in state } n \text{ in the interval } t \text{ to } t + \Delta t)$$
$$+ p_{n-1}(t) \cdot \text{prob (system moves from state } n - 1 \text{ to state } n)$$
$$+ p_{n+1}(t) \cdot \text{prob (system moves from state } n + 1 \text{ to state } n).$$

$$(15.16)$$

Also

prob (system stays in state n in the interval t to $t + \Delta t$)
$$= \text{prob (system does not move to state } n + 1)$$
$$\times \text{prob (system does not move to state } n - 1).$$

This expression can be simplified by neglecting second-order terms. Thus if $n \geq m$, we have

prob (system stays in state n in interval Δt) $= (1 - m\beta \Delta t)(1 - \alpha \Delta t)$
$$= 1 - (\alpha + m\beta) \Delta t + o(\Delta t).$$

Equation (15.16) can take various forms, which we proceed to enumerate.

1. $n \geq m$:

$$p_n(t + \Delta t) = p_n(t)[1 - (\alpha + m\beta) \Delta t] + p_{n-1}(t)\alpha \Delta t + p_{n+1}(t)m\beta \Delta t.$$

We assume steady-state conditions, so $p_n(t + \Delta t) = p_n(t)$, and this gives

$$\alpha p_{n-1} - (\alpha + m\beta)p_n + m\beta p_{n+1} = 0. \qquad (15.17)$$

2. $0 < n < m$: Omitting details, the equation corresponding to (15.17) is

$$\alpha p_{n-1} - (\alpha + n\beta)p_n + (n + 1)\beta p_{n+1} = 0. \qquad (15.18)$$

3. $n = 0$: Since a system in state 0 can go only to state 1,

$$-\alpha p_0 + \beta p_1 = 0. \qquad (15.19)$$

It is easy to guess the form of the solution of (15.18) and (15.19) by inspection of the first few cases. If we set $\mu = \alpha/\beta$, then (15.19) gives $p_1 = \mu p_0$, and from (15.18) with $n = 1, 2, 3, \ldots$ in succession, dividing by β in each case for convenience,

$$2p_2 = (\mu + 1)p_1 - \mu p_0 = \mu p_1 + (p_1 - \mu p_0) = \mu p_1,$$
$$3p_3 = (\mu + 2)p_2 - \mu p_1 = \mu p_2 + (2p_2 - \mu p_1) = \mu p_2,$$
$$4p_4 = (\mu + 3)p_3 - \mu p_2 = \mu p_3 + (3p_3 - \mu p_2) = \mu p_3, \ldots,$$

and so on. This indicates that, in general,

$$p_k = \frac{1}{k}\,\mu p_{k-1}, \qquad k = 1, 2, \ldots, m; \qquad (15.20)$$

that is

$$p_k = \frac{\mu^k}{k!}\,p_0, \qquad k = 1, 2, \ldots, m. \qquad (15.21)$$

This solution can be verified easily by direct substitution in (15.18).

To find p_k for $k > m$, it is necessary to solve (15.17). We again proceed by inspection of the first few cases. For convenience divide (15.17) by $m\beta$ and set $\rho = \alpha/m\beta$. We first note that, since $m\rho = \mu$, equation (15.20) gives

$$p_m = \rho p_{m-1}.$$

Then from (15.17), for $n = m, m + 1, m + 2, \ldots$, in succession,

$$p_{m+1} = (1 + \rho)p_m - \rho p_{m-1} = \rho p_m + (p_m - \rho p_{m-1}) = \rho p_m,$$
$$p_{m+2} = (1 + \rho)p_{m+1} - \rho p_m = \rho p_{m+1} + (p_{m+1} - \rho p_m) = \rho p_{m+1},$$

and in general

$$p_{m+r} = \rho p_{m+r-1} = \rho^r p_m. \qquad (15.22)$$

In order that p_{m+r} tend to zero as r tends to infinity (that is, in order that queues of infinite length do not form), it is necessary that $\rho < 1$, that is, $m\beta > \alpha$. This merely states that the maximum possible rate of departures should be greater than the rate of arrivals. The necessity for this condition is clear on physical grounds. The value of p_m is known from (15.21) so that (15.22) gives

$$p_k = \frac{m^m}{m!}\,\rho^k p_0, \qquad k = m, m + 1, \ldots. \qquad (15.23)$$

To complete the solution we need to determine the value of p_0. This is done by using the condition that because the system must be in one of the possible states, the sum of the probabilities must be unity,

$$\sum_{k=0}^{\infty} p_k = 1.$$

On substituting the values of p_k from (15.21) and (15.23), we find

$$p_0 = \frac{1}{S},$$

where $\quad S = 1 + \mu + \frac{\mu^2}{2!} + \cdots + \frac{\mu^{m-1}}{(m-1)!} + \frac{m^m}{m!} \rho^m + \rho^{m+1} + \cdots$

$$= 1 + \mu + \frac{\mu^2}{2!} + \cdots + \frac{\mu^{m-1}}{(m-1)!} + \frac{m^m \rho^m}{m!(1-\rho)}. \tag{15.24}$$

Hence the final answer is

$$p_n = \begin{cases} S^{-1} \dfrac{\mu^n}{n!}, & 0 \le n \le m, \\[2mm] S^{-1} \dfrac{m^m}{m!} \rho^n, & n \ge m, \end{cases} \tag{15.25}$$

where $\rho = \alpha/m\beta$, $\mu = m\rho = \alpha/\beta$, and S is given by (15.24).

It is convenient to introduce a probability P defined as the probability that all clerks are busy. From this definition, and (15.25),

$$P = \sum_{n=m}^{\infty} p_n = S^{-1} \frac{m^m}{m!} \sum_{n=m}^{\infty} \rho^n = S^{-1} \frac{m^m \rho^m}{m!(1-\rho)};$$

that is, on writing P as a function of m and μ,

$$P = P(m, \mu) = S^{-1} \frac{\mu^m}{(m-1)!\,(m-\mu)}. \tag{15.26}$$

In a total time τ hours, there are precisely k customers during $p_k \tau$ hours. Hence, since none of the customers need to wait if $k \le m$, and exactly m of the customers are being served at any time if $k > m$, there are precisely r customers waiting during $p_{m+r} \tau$ of the τ hours. Hence the total number of customer hours spent waiting is, using (15.25),

$$\tau \sum_{r=1}^{\infty} r p_{m+r} = \tau S^{-1} \frac{m^m}{m!} \sum_{r=1}^{\infty} r \rho^{m+r} = \tau S^{-1} \frac{m^m \rho^{m+1}}{m!\,(1-\rho)^2}.$$

Hence, remembering that $\mu = m\rho$, the number of customer hours spent waiting out of a total of τ hours is

$$\frac{\tau P \rho}{1-\rho} = \frac{\tau P \mu}{m-\mu}. \tag{15.27}$$

This result enables us to complete the discussion of the factory problem started in Section 15.4.

15.6   The Factory Problem (concluded)

We assume, in the problem of Section 15.4, that the following quantities are either known directly or determined experimentally:

h = mean serving time (hours),
m = number of clerks,
T = length of the working day (hours),
N = total number of arrivals (customers) in 1 day,
r_m = cost of the excess waiting time of a mechanic (customer) per hour,
r_s = cost of the idle time of a server (clerk) per hour.

Note that the term "cost" here does not mean simply the hourly wage rate but includes overhead costs such as the cost of machinery, loss of profit if the mechanic could have been working, and so on. Hence r_m is usually somewhat greater than r_s.

To link these quantities with the parameters α, β, and μ introduced previously, we note first that the probability of a server finishing service in an interval Δt is $\beta \Delta t$; that is, β is the reciprocal of the mean serving time, $\beta = 1/h$. Also the probability of an arrival in an interval Δt is $\alpha \Delta t$, so α is the reciprocal of the mean time between arrivals, $\alpha = N/T$. Hence

$$\mu = \frac{\alpha}{\beta} = \frac{Nh}{T}. \tag{15.28}$$

Note that μ is the average number of arrivals per mean service time.

The total time that the clerks are on duty is mT hours, but of this only Nh hours is spent serving, so the waiting time of the clerks is

$$(mT - Nh) \qquad \text{hours.}$$

From (15.27) the customers are waiting for a time

$$\frac{TP\mu}{m - \mu} \qquad \text{hours.}$$

Hence the cost C of waiting time is

$$C = r_s(mT - Nh) + \frac{r_m TP\mu}{m - \mu}.$$

This can be written in a more convenient form by dividing through by $r_s T$,

$$C' = \left(\frac{C}{r_s T}\right) = m - \mu + \frac{rP\mu}{m - \mu},$$

where now $r = r_m/r_s$, the ratio of the effective cost of a mechanic to a clerk per unit time and C' is a "normalized" cost (which is directly related to the actual cost C), because we wish to consider how the cost varies with m when r_s and T are fixed. From (15.26) we see that P is a function of m and μ, so

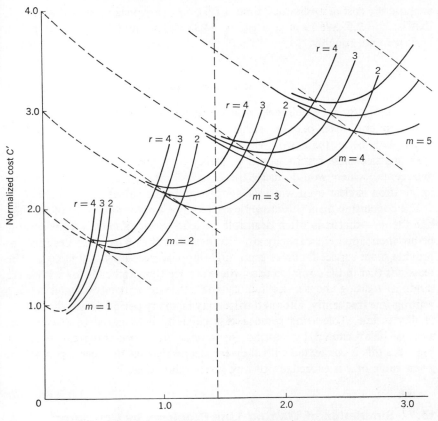

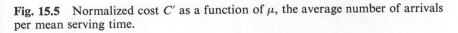

Fig. 15.5   Normalized cost C' as a function of μ, the average number of arrivals per mean serving time.

that there are only two parameters characterizing the variation, namely r and μ, and it is easy to illustrate the situation graphically, as in Fig. 15.5.

As shown in Fig. 15.5, for fixed r and m, the curve of C' against μ is J-shaped with $C' = m$ at $\mu = 0$, reaching a minimum for some value of μ less than m, and tending to infinity as μ tends to m. For various m we obtain various curves. Because we are interested in minimum C', we have drawn only the bottoms of the curves. For each m there are various curves corresponding to different r, the ratio of the effective cost of a mechanic to that of a clerk.

As an example consider the situation for which experimental information was plotted in Figs. 15.3 and 15.4. The average time required by a clerk to serve a mechanic was about 50 sec, and one mechanic arrived every 35 sec, on the average. Obviously at least two clerks are required. At first sight it might seem that two clerks would be enough, since two mechanics arrive every 70 sec and two clerks can deal with two mechanics in 50 sec. However, suppose the cost of mechanics' time is 2.5 times as expensive as that of clerks; that is, $r = 2.5$. We have $\mu = \alpha/\beta = 50/35 = 1.43$ and, on consulting Fig. 16.5, we find, roughly,

m:	2	3	4	5
C':	4.0	2.0	2.6	3.6

This indicates very definitely that three clerks should be assigned to the tool crib and that, perhaps somewhat surprising, four clerks would be appreciably better than two.

In practice these results would probably be expressed in terms of dollars and cents, which would make them more impressive, but the practical implication is clear even when we simply quote the values of C'.

The conclusion from this example seems to be a common lesson of waiting-line theory—that it is often desirable to load service facilities considerably below their apparent capacity or, alternatively, that it is often desirable to provide more service facilities than might appear necessary at first sight. The reason is that in the common case where service time and calls for service are random, loading the service facility too close to capacity creates a long waiting-line frequently, although there may be many periods when the serving facility is idle. Tolerating some excess capacity is essential to prevent the average delay caused by waiting for service from becoming excessive. In Fig. 15.5 this is connected with the very steep way that the curves rise once a given value of μ is exceeded, for any given value of m.

15.7   Simulation of Waiting-Line Problems by Computer[7]

Mathematics Used: Frequency distributions ; flow charts.

An exact mathematical solution of a waiting-line problem, as in the last few sections, is possible only in very special circumstances. When the process is very complicated and when no mathematical solution is available, it may be advisable to study the system by reconstructing its behavior experimentally on a computer using service times, arrival times, and so on, derived from random numbers. This is particularly useful when an answer is required for specific clearly defined conditions, so that we can ask a definite question of the computer. The procedure is obviously related to the Monte Carlo methods described in Section 13.9. The term *simulation* is usually used when the process is a close model of the real system, and *Monte Carlo method* when there is no very direct connection with the original system, but this is not a universally accepted terminology. Sometimes the Monte Carlo method is used to describe any method in which random numbers are used.

[7] This section is based on an article by Norman Nielsen, Monte Carlo Solutions to Waiting-Line Problems, *The Pentagon*, **23**, 28–39 (1963).

We note first that a random number y, uniformly distributed over the range $0 \le y < 1$, can be used to produce observations independently distributed with any frequency distribution $f(x)$, that is, such that the probability that x lies between x and $x + \Delta x$ is $f(x) \Delta x$. We introduce the cumulative distribution function

$$F(x) = \int_{-\infty}^{x} f(u)\, du.$$

Let $y_1, y_2, y_3, \ldots$ be numbers independently and uniformly distributed in $0 \le y < 1$, and let $x_1, x_2, x_3, \ldots$ be the corresponding numbers such that $y_i = F(x_i)$. Then we assert that the x_i are the required random numbers with frequency distribution $f(x)$. For x lies in $x + \Delta x$ if y lies in $y + \Delta y$, where, neglecting first-order terms,

$$y + \Delta y = F(x + \Delta x) = F(x) + F'(x)\,\Delta x = F(x) + f(x)\,\Delta x;$$

that is, $\Delta y = f(x)\,\Delta x$. The probability of x lying in x to $x + \Delta x$ is the same as the probability of y lying in y to $y + \Delta y$, which is precisely Δy, that is, $f(x)\,\Delta x$, exactly as required.

As an example, suppose that we require exponentially distributed quantities $x \ge 0$ with mean γ. Then, from (15.4),

$$f(x) = \begin{cases} (1/\gamma)e^{-x/\gamma}, & x > 0, \\ 0, & x < 0, \end{cases}$$

so that
$$F(x) = \frac{1}{\gamma} \int_0^x e^{-t/\gamma}\, dt = 1 - e^{-x/\gamma}.$$

If y_i are numbers randomly and uniformly distributed in $0 \le y < 1$, we find the corresponding x_i from

$$y_i = 1 - e^{-x_i/\gamma};$$

that is
$$x_i = -\gamma \log (1 - y_i).$$

The numbers $1 - y_i$ are also uniformly distributed in $(0, 1)$, so we finally have the result: If z_i are numbers uniformly distributed in $0 < z_i \le 1$,

$$x_i = -\gamma \log z_i$$

are numbers with an exponential distribution, mean γ, in $(0, \infty)$.

Note that this procedure can be used even if the distribution function $F(x)$ is empirical, which means that simulation procedures are not limited to distributions with simple analytical expressions.

As a specific example we now consider the problem of simulating the operation of a gasoline service station. The assumptions made may not be entirely realistic, but the example will illustrate the principles involved. Suppose there are m pumps (with m attendants) and that the mean service time is known and is the same for all pumps. Suppose also that the mean

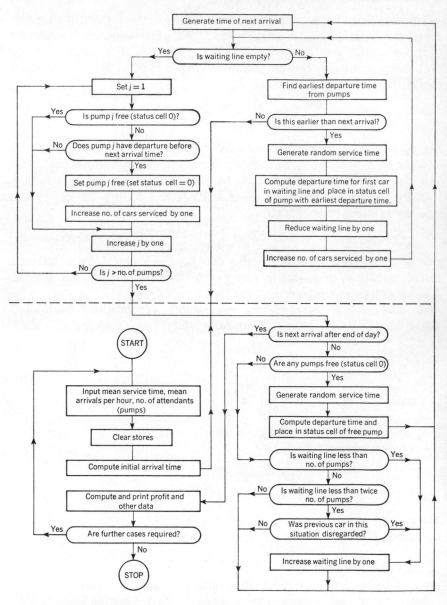

Fig. 15.6   Flow chart for simulation of gas service station.

number of cars that pass the station per hour and might stop for service is known. These will be called "arrivals," although they may not all stop at the station. If there are n cars stopped at the station, then if $n \leq m$ it is assumed that m are being serviced and $n - m$ form a *waiting line*. (Note that in the terminology of this example we do not include in the waiting line the *m* cars being serviced.) Suppose that whether a car stops or not is governed by the following rules:

1. If $n < 2m$ (that is, either all cars are being serviced, or the waiting line is less than m), a passing car will stop.
2. If $2m \leq n < 3m$, half the passing cars will stop. We shall alternately accept and reject passing cars, but an alternative would be to stop these cars on a random basis, with 50% probability that such a car will stop.
3. If $n \geq 3m$, no passing cars stop.

A possible computer flow chart is shown in Fig. 15.6. This is essentially the same as Neilsen's[8] although it may seem different because of rearrangement.

Each pump is given a "status cell," which is merely a store or memory position in the computer in which is placed a zero if no car is being serviced at the pump. Otherwise, the time at which the car being serviced will leave is placed in the status cell. Whether a pump is free or not is easily checked by seeing whether its status cell contains a zero or not.

The service times are assumed to be exponentially distributed, and these are generated by the random procedure described previously. The key number is the time of the next arrival (the time when the next car *might* stop). This is generated from the known time of the last arrival (corresponding, of course, to a car that did not necessarily stop) by adding a random exponentially distributed time, the mean being the known average time interval between cars.

When we generate a new arrival time, we first decide what has happened in the meantime—how many cars have been serviced since the last arrival, and, at the new arrival time, how many are being serviced, and how many cars are awaiting service. This is accomplished in the top half of the flow chart in Fig. 15.6 above the dashed line. It is seen that this part of the flow chart divides into two columns. The left-hand column deals with the case $n \leq m$ (that is, no waiting line, or all cars are being serviced), and the right-hand column deals with the case $n > m$ (that is, there are cars in the waiting line). In this part of the flow chart we do nothing about the car whose arrival time has been generated in the box at the top of the flow chart. In the bottom right of the flow chart we decide whether this car will stop or not. The bottom left of the flow chart is concerned with starting and stopping the program.

The sequence of operations in the flow chart is therefore as follows. The program starts in the bottom left quarter of Fig. 15.6 where the computer is given the basic data for a run and computes an initial (random) arrival time. The program than moves to the bottom right quarter of the flow chart, where at this point the phrase "next arrival" refers to the initial arrival, the time of which has just been computed. The program will compute a departure time, place this in the status cell of a pump, and move to the top of the flow chart where it computes the time of the second arrival. We describe the general situation from this point onwards. Suppose that the time of the kth arrival is

[8] *Ibid.*

given by $t = t_k$, and that the next arrival is the nth. When the time t_n is generated in the box at the top of the flow chart, the information in the computer will refer to $t = t_{n-1}$. The computer updates its information to $t = t_n$ in one of two ways, depending on whether the waiting-line is empty or not. If the waiting-line is empty, the computer runs through the pumps by setting $j = 1, 2, \ldots$ in turn until j is greater than the number of pumps. The program then moves to the bottom right of the flow chart where it is decided whether the arrival at $t = t_n$ can be serviced, or whether it must join the waiting-line. If the waiting-line is not empty, we find the earliest departure time from the pumps, say T. If $T \leq t_n$, the corresponding car leaves before $t = t_n$, and a car from the waiting line is serviced. This is repeated until either the waiting-line is empty or $T > t_n$. In this latter case the program moves to the bottom right of the flow chart and decides whether the arrival at $t = t_n$ will join the waiting line or will not stop at the garage. Successive arrivals are dealt with in this way until an arrival occurs after the end of the day, in which case the program is terminated. (There is no claim that this is the most efficient flow chart for this problem.)

At this point we have probably only whetted the appetite of the engineering reader, who would wish us to go on and discuss computer runs and conclusions to be drawn from the results of these runs. However, we adopt the point of view that the procedure itself has now been described in detail, and the application of the procedure can be left to the imagination of the reader.

We conclude with two comments:

1. In queuing problems it is common to find that the results have a large degree of variability. When analytical methods are used, this causes no difficulty, because the mean and standard deviation can be computed explicitly. In simulation procedures it is necessary to design the simulation so that statistical information concerning the variability can be deduced from the results themselves. In the above example this would involve an analysis of how the results vary from one hour to another, and it would also involve repeating the simulation several times. To obtain reliable results from data that are inherently liable to considerable statistical fluctuation, it may in fact be necessary to repeat the simulation many times.

2. It is obvious that one of the great disadvantages of simulation methods is that each numerical result refers to one special system, whereas an analytical formula gives us the behavior of a whole range of systems. Thus it would be troublesome, to say the least, to derive a diagram like Fig. 15.5 by simulation on a computer alone. On the other hand, simulation enables us to solve problems that are not amenable to exact solution. As usual in engineering analysis, the best compromise may be to find a theoretical solution for a system which resembles the one being studied as closely as possible, and then to examine the differences between the predictions of this theory and results found by simulation of a more realistic model, for typical or important values of the parameters.

Chapter 16

Random Plane Networks and Needle-Shaped Crystals

Comment : The two examples considered in this chapter are interesting illustrations of the way in which problems that are not amenable to exact theoretical analysis can be tackled by a combination of ingenuity, elementary mathematics, and numerical experimentation.

16.1 Random Plane Networks[1]

Engineering Context : Typical examples are the spread of contagious diseases and communication networks of short-range radio stations.

To construct a random plane network we first pick points at random from the infinite plane with an average density of D points per unit area. Next join each pair of points by a line if and only if the pair is separated by a distance less than some given constant R.

The random plane network can be used to represent an infinite communication network of short-range radio stations, each of which has range R. The random plane network falls into separate sets of connected components. A radio station can relay messages to any other station in the same component, but there is no communication between different connected sets.

Another application is to the study of the spread of a contagious disease. Points represent individuals susceptible to the disease. If sick individuals infect all others within distance R, the disease spreads along lines of the network.

Figure 16.1 shows two networks obtained for different values of R. It is convenient to work in terms of the nondimensional parameter $E = \pi R^2 D$, which is the average number of points in a circle of radius R. Figure 16.1 was

---

[1] The treatment in this and the following two sections is a slightly abridged version of a submitted article: E. N. Gilbert, Bell Telephone Laboratories, Murray Hill, N.J., Random Plane Networks, *J. Soc. Ind. Appl. Math.*, **9**, 533–543 (1961).

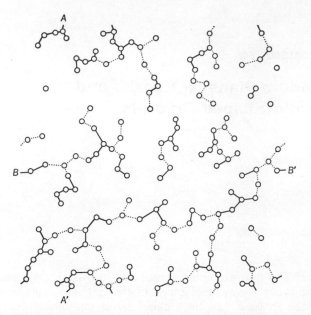

Fig. 16.1   Random plane network: solid lines, connections when $E = 1.8$; dashed lines, additional
connections when $E = 4.7$.

constructed by first picking points at random in a rectangular area with a
density corresponding to $E = 1.8$. If points were separated by less than R,
they were joined by a solid line, as indicated in Fig. 16.1. Additional points
were chosen at random until the density reached a value corresponding to
$E = 4.7$. The dashed lines in Fig. 16.1 show the additional connections
obtained from these new points. Naturally the components for $E = 4.7$ are
bigger than those for $E = 1.8$, but there is even a qualitative difference. The
small components of the $E = 1.8$ network are so merged together in the
$E = 4.7$ network that most of the points belong to a single large component.
(The points A and A', B and B' are supposed to be connected for a reason
explained in the third paragraph of Section 16.3.) This example suggests that
if similar random networks are constructed in the infinite plane, there would
be a component with infinitely many points when $E = 4.7$, but not when
$E = 1.8$.

Let $P(N)$ denote the probability that a point belongs to a component
containing at least $N - 1$ additional points. If E is very small, then most of
the points are isolated, and $P(N)$ tends to zero as N tends to infinity. However, the phenomenon noted above, that most of the points belong to a single
large component when $E = 4.7$, suggests that in this case there is a component
with infinitely many points in the infinite plane. Then the limit

$$\lim_{N \to \infty} P(N) = P(\infty)$$

need not be zero. It represents the probability of belonging to an infinite component.

In the next section we show that $P(\infty) = 0$ when $E < 1.64$, and we indicate that $P(\infty) > 0$ when E is sufficiently large. Thus there exists a critical value E_c which is the largest value of E for which $P(\infty) = 0$. A computer simulation is described in Section 16.3, and calculations suggest that E_c is approximately 3.2.

In the communication model, the network provides only local communication if $E \leq E_c$, and provides some long-distance communication if $E > E_c$. In the disease model, a widespread epidemic can occur only if $E > E_c$.

16.2   Theoretical Arguments Concerning the Critical Value of *E*

Mathematics Used : Simple probability ; Poisson distribution.

Comment : Note the use of approximate models and analogies.

The component containing a given point Q might have been constructed step by step as follows. First pick the points directly connected to Q. These are found by a random process of density D points per unit area in the circle $A(1)$ of radius R centered at Q. These points, if any, will be said to belong to the *first generation* of descendants of Q. Continuing, the *second-generation* points are to be chosen within distance R of first-generation points, but more than distance R away from Q. In general, in choosing generation $n + 1$, draw the set $A(n + 1)$ of all points lying within distance R of a point of generation n and not in $A(1), A(2), \ldots, A(n)$. Then generation $n + 1$ is obtained by a random process of density D in the set $A(n + 1)$. If at some generation the random process produces no points, the construction stops and the component is finite.

A related but simpler construction, which will be called construction B, proceeds as follows. Construct the first generation as before. Suppose the nth generation has been found and call its points $q_1, q_2, \ldots, q_k$. Construct circles $C_1, C_2, \ldots, C_k$ of radius R and centered at $q_1, q_2, \ldots, q_k$. Pick points independently from $C_1, C_2, \ldots, C_k$ by random processes of density D. These points form generation $n + 1$.

Clearly the probability of obtaining N or more points by process B is greater than $P(N)$. In fact, the component in the random network might have been constructed by process B, deleting at each step any new point that belongs to any circle C_i considered in the same or earlier generations.

Construction B is a simple branching process of the type that occurs in connection with the breeding of animals, and we consider this problem first. Suppose all animals of a certain species are alike, and that the probability of any animal having exactly k offspring is denoted by p_k. Let q_n denote the probability that the species dies out by the nth generation, there being precisely one animal to start with, so that $q_1 = p_0$. Suppose q_n is known for any given n. We then compute q_{n+1} by the following argument. If in the first generation there were k offspring, each of these can be thought of as new heads of family, and if the original family dies out by the $(n + 1)$th generation, this means that the families of each of the k offspring has died out by the nth generation. Since the k families reproduce independently of each other, the probability that they all die out is q_n^k. The probability of k offspring in the first generation is p_k, so

$$q_{n+1} = \sum_{k=0}^{\infty} p_k q_n^k. \tag{16.1}$$

If we introduce the generating function

$$f(x) = \sum_{k=0}^{\infty} p_k x^k, \tag{16.2}$$

equation (16.1) is

$$q_{n+1} = f(q_n). \tag{16.3}$$

Letting n tend to infinity, (16.3) gives

$$q = f(q), \tag{16.4}$$

where q is the limit of q_n as n tends to infinity. Since all the p_k are positive we see that $f(x) \geq 0, f'(x) \geq 0$, and $f''(x) \geq 0$ in $0 < x \leq 1$. Also, from (16.2), $f(0) = p_0$ and $f(1) = 1$ since the sum of the p_k is unity. Hence the curve

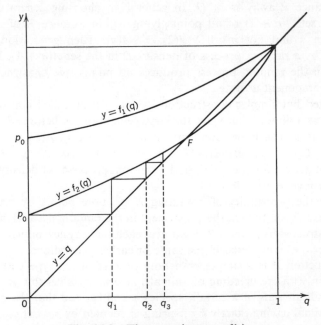

Fig. 16.2   The equation $q = f(q)$.

$y = f(q)$ looks like either $y = f_1(q)$ or $y = f_2(q)$ in Fig. 16.2. In the case of the curve $y = f_2(q)$, this cuts $y = q$ at a point F between $q = 0$ and 1. We know that $q_1 = p_0$, and from (16.3), $q_2 = f(q_1), q_3 = f(q_2), \ldots$, which corresponds to the graphical procedure shown for finding $q_2, q_3, \ldots$ in succession. Clearly q_n is tending to the value of q corresponding to the point F which is less than unity, so there is a nonzero probability that the species will survive. On the other hand, the curve $y = f_1(q)$ does not cut $y = q$ between 0 and 1, the value of q is unity, and there is zero probability that the species will survive. The situation can be summarized as follows:

$$\text{If } f'(q) > 1 \text{ at } q = 1, \text{ then a root } q < 1 \text{ exists,}$$
$$\text{If } f'(q) \le 1 \text{ at } q = 1, \text{ then no root } q < 1 \text{ exists.} \tag{16.5}$$

We now apply this analysis to the construction B mentioned previously. The density of points per unit area is D and the radius of the circles used is R. Hence the probable number of points in one of the circles C_i is $\pi R^2 D = E$, the parameter introduced previously. The probability of finding precisely k points in one of the circles is given by the Poisson distribution

$$p_k = \frac{E^k e^{-E}}{k!}. \tag{16.6}$$

The corresponding generating function (16.2) is given by

$$f(x) = \sum_{k=0}^{\infty} \frac{(Ex)^k e^{-E}}{k!} = e^{(x-1)E}.$$

Equation (16.4) is then

$$q = e^{(q-1)E}.$$

The value of E for which $f'(q) = 1$ at $q = 1$ is given by

$$E[e^{(q-1)E}]_{q=1} = 1;$$

that is, $E = 1$. From (16.5) this means that no root $q < 1$ exists (that is, no infinite network exists) if $E < 1$. But from our procedure, the probability of obtaining an infinite network by construction B is greater than the corresponding probability for a random plane network. Hence no infinite component can occur in the random plane network if $E < 1$, so the critical value of E is greater than or equal to unity, $E_c \ge 1$.

This estimate can be improved by a simple refinement B^* of construction B which replaces the circles C_i of radius R by certain lune-shaped figures. Note that circles C_i and C_i' surrounding a point Q_i and its descendant Q_i' in

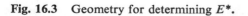

Fig. 16.3 Geometry for determining E^*.

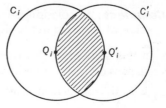

the next generation always intersect in an area which is at least as great as that shown shaded in Fig. 16.3; a simple calculation shows this to be $(2\pi/3 - \sqrt{3}/2)R^2$. This area would be forbidden to descendants of Q_i' in the random-plane network. The remaining part of C_i' is a lune of area $(\pi/3 + \sqrt{3}/2)R^2$. In the construction B^* the descendants of Q_i are picked by a random process of density D in this lune. The probability of finding a point in one of the lunes is now

$$E^* = \left(\frac{\pi}{3} + \frac{\sqrt{3}}{2}\right)R^2 D = \frac{E}{1.64},$$

where E is the parameter $\pi R^2 D$ defined previously.

In construction B^* the first generation has a number of offspring governed by the Poisson law with mean E, but subsequent generations have numbers of offspring governed by the Poisson law with mean E^*. The species will die out if all descendants of the first generation die out, regardless of what has happened in producing the first generation. Hence the species will die out (no infinite network exists) if $E^* < 1$, that is, $E < 1.64$. Following the same argument as before, this means that the critical value of E is greater than or equal to 1.64:

$$E_c \geq 1.64.$$

Gilbert[2] gives two arguments to provide upper bounds for E_c:

1. On the basis of an analogy between random plane networks as defined above, and random networks devised as models of porous media through which fluid seeps, although the two kinds of network are not identical, a correspondence is used to show that

$$E_c \leq 17.4.$$

2. A game called Hex is played on a honeycomb pattern of hexagonal cells, and it is known that one and only one of the players can obtain a connected path through the network. This is used to show that arbitrarily large connected networks can be found when $E \geq 10.9$ (although this is different from proving that $E_c \leq 10.9$).

Neither of these arguments is very satisfactory. However, it is possible to determine E_c experimentally by computer, as discussed in Section 16.3.

16.3   An Experimental Determination of the Critical Value of E

Comment: Simulation on a digital computer is used to determine the value of a parameter which cannot be found from the existing theory.

In this section we describe how an automatic computer can be used to simulate the construction of random plane networks in a large square.

[2] E. N. Gilbert, Random Plane Networks, *J. Soc. Ind. Appl. Math.*, **9**, 533–543 (1961).

It is easy to pick a random point in a square $0 \le x < 1, 0 \le y < 1$, since we need only pick two random numbers in the range $(0, 1)$, excluding 1, and use these as the coordinates of the point. In a typical computer run, the range R and area A of the square were fixed parameters. We wish to obtain a series of networks for a range of values of E, and much computing time can be saved by using old networks as parts of new networks with higher E. Starting with a network of just one point, the computer adds points one at a time to obtain networks with increasing values of E. As each point is added, its distances from each of the points already present are computed. If any of these distances is less than R, the new point belongs to a connected component of the net. As the points are added and E reaches the eleven values 0.5, 1.0, 1.5, ..., 5.0 in turn, information is printed out concerning the size distribution of the connected components.

Points near the edges of a square tend to belong to small components because connection paths that go outside the square are missing. To offset these edge effects, the computation identified opposite sides of the square, making the square topologically equivalent to a torus. This is why we were careful to specify in the last paragraph that the square was $0 \le x < 1$, $0 \le y < 1$, with equality included at zero but excluded at unity. In Fig. 16.1 the points A and A', B and B', etc., are supposed to be connected.

In programming this experiment, it is important to avoid using a storage unit for each pair of points for the sole purpose of remembering whether or not the pair of points is joined by a line, because this would require an impossibly large store. It is also desirable to compute the distance between each pair of points at most once. Both objectives can be achieved by storing the components in the computer as lists. We describe one possible way of doing this.

We label the points $1, 2, \ldots, i, \ldots$ as they are found in sequence by the computer. Associated with each point are coordinates (x_i, y_i). We number the connected components $1, 2, \ldots, r, \ldots$ as they are found, where by "connected component" we include also those single points which are at distances greater than R from any other point. Each point i will therefore be in some component which we denote by $r(i)$. Thus the first point goes in the first component, $r(1) = 1$. When the second point is computed, if it is within R of the first, the machine sets $r(2) = 1$, but if it is not within R of the first, this point starts a second component, $r(2)$ is set equal to 2. When the third point is found, if it is within R of the first, $r(3) = 1$; if it is within R of the second, $r(3) = 2$; and if it is not within R of either, $r(3) = 3$. There is one more possibility. If it is within R of both points 1 and 2, points 1, 2, and 3 are all in the same component. We have $r(1) = r(2) = r(3) = 1$, and component 2 is now nonexistent.

The general procedure should now be clear. To add the jth point to the network the computer first finds its coordinates (x_j, y_j) by selecting two random numbers as previously described. It then computes $d_{i,j}$, the distance between this new jth point and each of the previous points, $i = 1, 2, \ldots, j - 1$, in turn. The first time this distance is less than R, say when $i = k$, the machine sets $r(j) = r(k)$. If for some later point $i = m$ the distance $d_{m,j}$ is also less than R but $r(m)$ is not the same as $r(j)$, all points with the component number $r(m)$ [that is, in the same component as m] are given the component number $r(k)$ [that is, the components corresponding to $r(m)$ and $r(k)$ are combined into one single component since they are now connected by the point j]. For any given value of E, the number of components with N points can be calculated, $N = 1, 2, \ldots$, and hence the fraction of points in components of size greater than or equal to N, and also the fraction of points in the largest component.

To give an idea of the computer time involved, a case involving 1,000 points takes 2 minutes, and 2,000 points takes 7 minutes, on an IBM 7090.

As an example of the computer results, Fig. 16.4 gives the fraction of points in the largest component in 11 experimental runs for various values of E. (The computer results are described in more detail in the article by Gilbert.[3])

In a random plane network, a point has probability $P(\infty)$ of belonging to a component of maximum size. This follows immediately when $E_c < E$, in which case a component with an infinite number of points occurs. Also, when $E \leq E_c$, an infinite component has probability zero, and yet arbitrarily large finite component sizes have nonzero probabilities. In the computer simulation the fraction of points belonging to the component of largest size was used as an estimate of $P(\infty)$. For each value of E, these estimates from 11 networks were averaged to give a point on the solid curve shown in Fig. 16.4.

The computer only produced finite square approximations to random plane networks, so the values plotted in Fig. 16.4 do not become zero for small E, because the number of points in the largest component will be a finite fraction of the finite number of points in the square. A check on this effect was obtained by computing results for larger and smaller networks with 2.5 and 0.4 times the number of points in the standard network. The results agreed well with those for the standard network for E greater than 4, but for E less than 2 they diverged from those for the standard network in the way that would be expected from previous argument, as shown by the dashed lines in Fig. 16.4. Because of this effect, the estimates of $P(\infty)$ are so large for small E that it is difficult to estimate E_c accurately. If the true $P(\infty)$ versus E curve hits the E axis steeply (as for the upper limit curve obtained from construction B^*, corresponding to a true branching process), then Fig. 16.4 would suggest a value of E_c somewhere near 3.2. In any event, the value of E_c suggested by Fig. 16.4 is much more accurate than any of the limits obtained by analytical reasoning.

[3] *Ibid.*

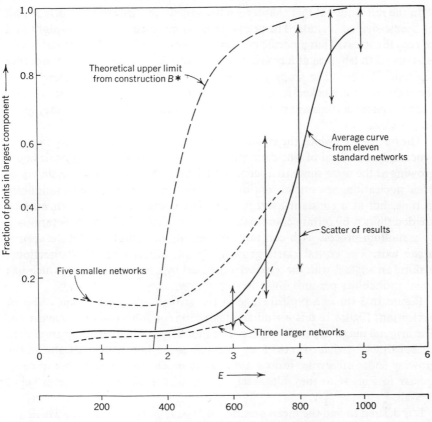

Fig. 16.4 Estimates of $P(\infty)$. The number of points in the larger (smaller) networks are 2.5 (0.25) of those in the standard network.

16.4 Surface Films of Needle-Shaped Crystals[4]

Mathematics Used: Simple probability and ordinary differential equations.

Comment: In the remainder of this chapter, approximate solutions are given for certain models representing crystal growth. These solutions are compared with random number simulations of the problem on a computer.

[4] This is based on an article submitted by E. N. Gilbert, Bell Telephone Laboratories, Murray Hill, N.J.: Surface Films of Needle-Shaped Crystals, A treatment of three-dimensional crystals is given in E. N. Gilbert, Random Subdivision of Space into Crystals, *Ann. Math. Statist.*, **33**, 958–972 (1962), where references to previous work can be found.

In the remainder of this chapter we investigate the growth of a surface film of needle-shaped crystals. The needle crystals are assumed to be straight and of zero thickness. Thus a needle crystal is represented by a line segment which is assumed to lengthen at a constant rate v until its end point touches another segment. The end then stops growing and its end point remains attached to the segment that blocked it. Crystals grow from nuclei or seeds that remain fixed in space; crystals are not allowed to push each other apart as they grow into contact.

The nuclei from which the crystals grow are determined by a simple random process. In one kind of nucleation process (*cell nucleation*), all crystals begin growing at the same time. In a second nucleation process, known as *Johnson-Mehl* nucleation, new nuclei continue to appear as time progresses, randomly in time, but at a constant average rate. The coordinates of the ith nucleus are determined by certain coordinates x_i and y_i, each of which are determined by a random process with constant probability per unit length of the appropriate axis. The crystal starts growing in two directly opposed directions, making an angle θ_i with the x axis determined by a random process which has equal probability per unit angle in $0 \leq \theta \leq \pi$.

Figure 16.5 shows a typical stage in the growth of a surface film with cell nucleation. Figure 16.6 is a similar illustration for Johnson-Mehl nucleation. The original nuclei appear as circles. The numbers in Fig. 16.6 are approximate arrival times. At later times, Fig. 16.5 has some longer crystals and fewer growing ends; otherwise, it does not change much. New arrivals continue to appear in Fig. 16.6; they ultimately fill in all the blank spaces with small crystals.

It is desired to find the mean number of crystal ends per unit area which are growing (that is, are unblocked) at time t. No method is known for finding this number exactly. However, lower bounds can be determined by exact

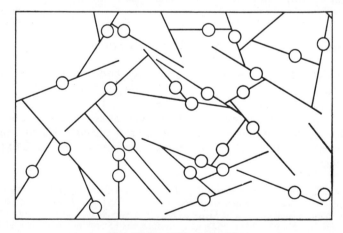

Fig. 16.5   Cell nucleation.

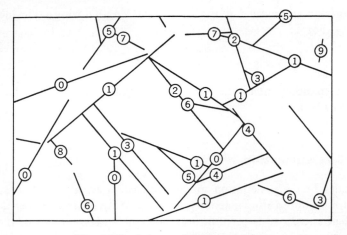

Fig. 16.6   Johnson-Mehl nucleation.

analysis of new crystallization models which use a mathematically convenient, but purely artificial, rule for blocking crystal ends. These new models
will be called *penetration models*. In a penetration model, each end E (Fig.
16.7) grows only until it reaches a point P, which would have been reached
sooner by another crystal C if C were allowed to grow without interference.
In particular, C blocks E at point P even though another crystal C' may have
blocked C from actually reaching P. Thus, for the purpose of determining
the point P at which end E becomes blocked, all other crystals are imagined
to grow unblocked and to penetrate one another when they meet. In the
penetration model, each end becomes blocked at least as soon as in the model
without penetration. Hence the density of growing ends is less in the penetration model than in the real model.

Let $G(t)$ denote the mean number of crystal ends per unit area that
are growing (unblocked) at time t, and $L(t)$ denote the mean total length
of crystals contained in a unit area at time t. Since each growing end

Fig. 16.7   Penetration model.

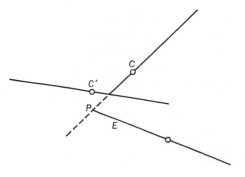

contributes an amount $v \, dt$ to the total crystal length during a time interval dt, it follows that

$$\frac{dL(t)}{dt} = vG(t). \tag{16.7}$$

The corresponding quantities for the penetration model will be starred, $G^*(t)$ and $L^*(t)$.

16.5   Cell Nucleation

Consider first a penetration model with cell nucleation; that is, all the nuclei are produced simultaneously, with a density of ρ nuclei per unit area. Then there are 2ρ ends per unit area, and the fraction $F^*(t)$ of these ends growing at time t is given by

$$F^*(t) = \frac{G^*(t)}{2\rho}.$$

We now introduce the idea of an (x, y, θ) three-dimensional probability space. The mean number of nuclei in the region x to $x + \Delta x$, y to $y + \Delta y$, is given by $\rho \Delta x \, \Delta y$. The mean number of needles in this region that make angles with the x axis between θ and $\theta + \Delta\theta$ $(0 \le \theta < \pi)$ is given by

$$\rho \Delta x \, \Delta y \, \frac{\Delta\theta}{\pi}.$$

We now regard x, y, and θ as coordinates in a three-dimensional space. Suppose x and y vary over some region in the xy plane, and that for any given value of x and y the angle θ varies over a certain range which may depend on x and y. Then x, y, and θ vary within a certain volume V in the x, y, θ space. The mean number of needles with x, y, and θ in the volume V is given by

$$\frac{\rho}{\pi} \iiint_V dx \, dy \, d\theta = \frac{\rho V}{\pi}. \tag{16.8}$$

To calculate this volume we need not, of course, stick to the x, y, θ coordinates. We can use any convenient set of coordinates, and we proceed to exploit this idea to evaluate $F^*(t)$.

Consider a typical end E which, without loss of generality, we can consider to belong to a needle which started at the origin in the xy plane and is growing along the x axis (Fig. 16.8).

To block E before time t, another needle with nucleus at (x, y) and making an angle θ with the x axis must lie within a certain volume of the x, y, θ space. For this needle to block the end E during the time interval T to $T + dT$, the distance r from (x, y) to E must satisfy $r < vT$. Also the orientation angle θ of

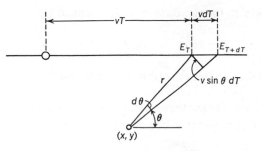

Fig. 16.8 Typical growing end E at times T and $T + dT$.

this needle must lie in an angular range of width $v \sin \theta \, dT/r$. Thus the volume of points (x, y, θ) that can block E during the time element dT is

$$2 \int_0^\pi \int_0^{vT} \frac{v \sin \theta \, dT}{r} \, r \, dr \, d\theta = 4v^2 T \, dT, \tag{16.9}$$

where the factor 2 before the integral sign is included because in the above argument θ goes from 0 to π, but this will include only needles that start from below the x axis, and an equal number will start from above. Since a needle can block the original needle (growing along the x axis) at most once, the elementary regions (of volume $4v^2 T \, dT$) belonging to independent time elements dT are themselves independent, and we have

$$V = \int_0^t 4v^2 T \, dT = 2v^2 t^2. \tag{16.10}$$

The mean number of ends in this volume is given, from (16.8), by

$$\frac{2\rho v^2 t^2}{\pi}. \tag{16.11}$$

The stopping of ends is governed by the Poisson distribution—if N ends on the average can stop growth in a given time interval t, the probability that growth is not stopped is the probability that no ends stop the growth, that is, $\exp(-N)$. In our case N is given by (16.11). Also $F^*(t)$, the fraction of ends growing at time t, is precisely the probability that growth has not stopped at time t. Hence

$$F^*(t) = e^{-2\rho v^2 t^2/\pi} = \frac{G^*(t)}{2\rho}. \tag{16.12}$$

Equation (16.7) holds with L, G replaced by L^*, G^*, and this gives the length $L^*(t)$ per unit area in the penetration model,

$$L^*(t) = \pi \left(\frac{\rho}{2}\right)^{1/2} \text{erf} \left[\left(\frac{2\rho}{\pi}\right)^{1/2} vt\right], \tag{16.13}$$

where "erf" refers to the standard function defined by

$$\operatorname{erf} x = \frac{2}{\pi^{1/2}} \int_0^x e^{-u^2} \, du.$$

The numerical value of this function can be found from tables (see Section 10.1).

To prepare the way for another estimate for $G(t)$ and $L(t)$, we derive (16.12) in another way. Equation (16.12) is equivalent to the differential equation

$$\frac{dF^*}{dt} = -\left(\frac{4\rho v^2 t}{\pi}\right) F^*; \tag{16.14}$$

that is, it is the limit as t tends to zero of

$$F^*(t) - F^*(t + \Delta t) = F^*(t)\left[\frac{2}{\pi}(2\rho vt)(v \, \Delta t)\right]. \tag{16.15}$$

The following heuristic argument suggests this equation directly. The left side of (16.15) is the probability that a crystal end grows unblocked for a time t and then becomes blocked in the next interval of time Δt. Thus it remains to prove that the bracketed term on the right is the conditional probability that an end is blocked at time $t + \Delta t$ given that it is unblocked at time t. The argument uses a Buffon needle experiment. We recall that if a needle of length a is dropped on a plane containing lines of mean total length L per unit area, the expected number of points at which the needle crosses lines is $(2/\pi)La$. (The common form of the Buffon needle problem is that a smooth table is ruled with equidistant parallel lines a distance D apart. A needle of length $d < D$ is dropped on the table. Show that the probability that it will cross one of the lines is $2d/\pi D$.) In the present case the needle is the line element representing the possible growth of the crystal end during the time interval t to $t + \Delta t$, so $a = v \, \Delta t$. The lines in the plane represent all the places at which ends may be blocked at time t. There are ρ lines per unit area and each line has length $2vt$, so $L = 2\rho vt$. Finally, since a is infinitesimal, the expected number of crossings $(2/\pi)La$ is the probability of a crossing plus higher-order terms. But

$$\frac{2}{\pi} La = \frac{2}{\pi}(2\rho vt)(v \, \Delta t)$$

is precisely the bracketed term in (16.15), and this bracketed term is therefore indeed the probability of a block during the time Δt.

In a Buffon needle experiment the needle must drop in a way that is statistically unrelated to the pattern of lines in the plane. The needle in the above argument does have a special relation to the pattern of lines; it is connected to a crystal end of length vt which is known to be unblocked. In this case the relation between pattern and needle seems to make no difference; one obtains the correct result by treating the needle and pattern as though they were unrelated.

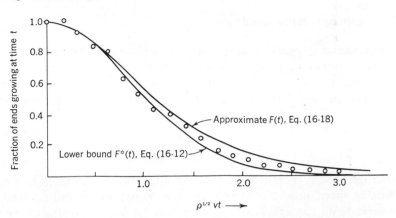

Fig. 16.9   Cell nucleation. The circles are experimental points.

This success tempts one to repeat the Buffon needle argument for the model without penetration. The mean blocking length per unit area is then $L = L(t)$. Instead of (16.15) we have, approximately,

$$F(t) - F(t + \Delta t) = F(t)\left[\frac{2}{\pi} L(t)(v\,\Delta t)\right] \tag{16.16}$$

If we let Δt tend to zero, we find the following differential equation instead of (16.14) $(G = 2\rho F)$:

$$\frac{dG}{dt} = -\left[\frac{2L(t)v}{\pi}\right] G(t). \tag{16.17}$$

Equations (16.17) and (16.16) are a pair of simultaneous differential equations for L and G which are to be solved with initial conditions $G(0) = 2\rho$, $L(0) = 0$. The solutions are

$$2\rho F(t) = G(t) = \frac{2\rho}{\cosh^2\left[vt(2\rho/\pi)^{1/2}\right]}, \tag{16.18}$$

$$L(t) = (2\pi\rho)^{1/2} \tanh\left[vt\left(\frac{2\rho}{\pi}\right)^{1/2}\right]. \tag{16.19}$$

It must be remembered that there is no exact derivation for these results. The Buffon needle argument may not be valid, owing to interference effects. Equations (16.18) and (16.19) represent approximate solutions for the actual problem. In contrast, (16.12) and (16.13) represent exact solutions for a model which only approximates to the exact model.

The solutions (16.12) and (16.18) are plotted in Fig. 16.9, from which it is seen that (16.12) falls below (16.18), as it must. The experimental points in Fig. 16.9 come from a random number simulation of 53 crystals with cell nucleation. The value of $L(t)$ as given by (16.19) is close to $L^*(t)$ given in (16.13). At $t = \infty$ we find that

$$L^*(\infty) = \pi(\tfrac{1}{2}\rho)^{1/2} = 2.22\rho^{1/2}, \qquad L(\infty) = (2\pi\rho)^{1/2} = 2.50\rho^{1/2}. \tag{16.20}$$

16.6   Johnson-Mehl Nucleation

In this case nuclei continue to appear as time progresses, randomly in time, but at a constant average rate which we denote by α per unit time per unit area in the xy plane. Again let $F^*(t)$ be the fraction of ends growing at time t in the penetration model. There are $2\alpha t$ ends per unit area at time t, and $G^*(t)$ growing ends per unit area, where

$$F^*(t) = \frac{G^*(t)}{2\alpha t}. \tag{16.21}$$

Since the process is random in time, we must now work in an (x, y, θ, t) probability space, instead of simply an (x, y, θ) space as in cell nucleation, Section 16.5. We can again use Fig. 16.8, but the needle growing along the x axis is assumed to arrive at time τ, and the needle growing from the point (x, y) is assumed to arrive at time s. Instead of the inequality $r < vT$ we must now have $r < v(T - s)$. In addition to the integrals in (16.9) there must be a third integration over s, the limits on s being 0 to $T - r/v$. Thus the part of the volume V in (x, y, θ, t) space contributed by crystals that block E during dT is

$$2\, dT \int_0^{vT} r\, dr \int_0^{T-r/v} ds \int_0^\pi \frac{v \sin \theta}{r}\, d\theta = 2v^2 T^2\, dT.$$

These contributions must be summed from $T = \tau$ to $T = t$ to get V:

$$V = \int_\tau^t 2v^2 T^2\, dt = \tfrac{2}{3}v^2(t^3 - \tau^3).$$

The number of needles with x, y, θ, and t in the volume V is given by $\alpha V/\pi$ [compare (16.8)], and the probability that end E is unblocked at time t is

$$e^{-\alpha V/\pi} = e^{-(2\alpha v^2/3\pi)(t^3 - \tau^3)}.$$

At time t a needle crystal picked at random has probability $d\tau/t$ of having arrival time between τ and $\tau + d\tau$, $0 \leq \tau \leq t$. Hence

$$F^*(t) = \frac{1}{t} e^{-2\alpha v^2 t^3/3\pi} \int_0^t e^{2\alpha v^2 \tau^3/3\pi}\, d\tau. \tag{16.22}$$

It is convenient to introduce the dimensionless time variable

$$z = \left(\frac{2\alpha v^2}{\pi}\right)^{1/3} t,$$

and, in terms of z,

$$F^*(t) = \frac{1}{z} e^{-z^3/3} \int_0^z e^{w^3/3}\, dw. \tag{16.23}$$

As in the case of cell nucleation, a Buffon needle argument gives the correct result for $F^*(t) = G^*(t)/2\alpha t$. To obtain the differential equation corresponding to (16.14), we argue as follows, working in terms of G^* instead of F^*: The mean blocking area per unit length is now

$$b(t) = \int_0^t 2v(t - \tau)\alpha \, d\tau = \alpha v t^2.$$

As for (15.15), $(2/\pi)G^*(t)b(t)v \, \Delta t$ represents the density of ends that have become blocked during the interval t to $t + \Delta t$. Since the nucleation process also creates new ends with density $2\alpha \, \Delta t$ during the interval, we find

$$\frac{dG^*(t)}{dt} = 2\alpha - \frac{2}{\pi} vb(t)G^*(t). \tag{16.24}$$

The solution of this equation with $G^*(0) = 0$ gives precisely (16.22) for $F^*(t)$.

For the model without penetration, we repeat the Buffon needle experiment with $L(t)$ replacing $b(t)$. The system of differential equations is now [compare (16.7) and (16.17)]

$$\frac{dL}{dt} = vG, \qquad \frac{dG}{dt} = 2\alpha - \frac{2}{\pi} vLG. \tag{16.25}$$

From these equations we see that

$$\frac{dG}{dt} = 2\alpha - \frac{2}{\pi} L \frac{dL}{dt}.$$

Integration, using $G(0) = L(0) = 0$ gives

$$G = 2\alpha t - \frac{L^2}{\pi}. \tag{16.26}$$

If this expression for G is substituted in the first equation in (16.25) we obtain a Ricatti equation for L,

$$\frac{dL}{dt} = 2\alpha vt - \frac{v}{\pi} L^2.$$

The substitution $L = u'/u$ converts this into a linear equation which can be solved in terms of Bessel functions. The final result for $F(t)$ is

$$F(t) = \frac{G(t)}{2\alpha t} \approx 1 - \left[\frac{I_{2/3}(2w/3)}{I_{-1/3}(2w/3)} \right]^2, \tag{16.27}$$

where $w = (2\alpha v^2/\pi)^{1/2} t^{3/2}$ and I_r denotes the usual modified Bessel function of the first kind. The "approximately equal to" sign is used because there is no guarantee that this answer is exact. The derivation depended on treating certain events as statistically independent which are probably not completely independent.

Figure 16.10 shows that the lower bound $F^*(t)$ and the approximate $F(t)$ are close, although the asymptotic behavior for large t are different. The experimental points again come from a random number simulation. A total

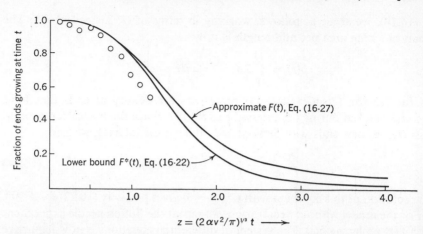

Fig. 16.10 Johnson-Mehl nucleation. The circles are experimental points.

of 91 crystals arrived during the time covered by the simulation. The experimental points lie below the lower bound; some are 15% too low, which is presumably due to the fact that too small a sample was used in the computer simulation. To get a good experimental estimate of $G(t)$ a much larger sample appears to be needed.

In the penetration model, the new crystals which continually arrive become blocked more and more prematurely as time passes. As a result, $L^*(t)$ grows much more slowly than $L(t)$ as t increases. In fact, $L^*(t)$ tends to $4.49(\alpha/v)^{1/3}$ as t tends to infinity, whereas $L(t)$ becomes asymptotic to $(2\pi\alpha t)^{1/2}$. The derivation of these results is left to the reader.

The two examples considered in this chapter are interesting illustrations of the way in which problems that are not amenable to exact theoretical analysis can be tackled by a combination of ingenuity, elementary mathematics, and numerical experimentation.

Name Index

Name Index

(Names marked with an asterisk are associated with submitted articles used in text.)

*Ames, W. F., 245, 248
Amundson, N. R., 122, 127
*Aris, R., ii, xi, 29, 31, 122, 127, 239, 243
Army Map Service, 225

Bacon, D., xi
Balsley, J. R., 158
Barsov, A. S., 31
Beckenbach, F. E., 286
Beek, J., 243
Bell Telephone Laboratories, 79, 135, 270, 271, 282, 329, 337
Bellman, R., 28, 31, 120
*Beurling, A., 87
*Billingsley, Col., 93
Bindschedler, A. E., 15, 26
Biot, M. A., 167
Boas, R., xi
*Bollay, W., 70
Bowman, E. H., 314
Box, G. E. P., 10, 34, 38, 50, 58, 63, 64

*Brady, P. T., 270
Brigham, G., 314
Brouwer, W., 40
Brown, G. W., 286
Brown, W. B., xi
Buck, R. C., ii, x, 34, 66, 153

*California Institute of Technology, 275
*California, University of (Berkeley), 273
*California, University of Southern (Los Angeles), 284
*Cambridge University, 75
*Carnegie Institute of Technology, 100
Carslaw, H. S., 173, 183
*Case Institute of Technology, 213
*Cashman, J. H., 286
Chambré, P. L., 184
Clement, P. R., ii, xi
Commission on Engineering Education, iii, v, vii, 1, 2

349

Subject Index

Subject Index